INTERNATIONAL HUMANITARIAN ASSISTANCE

SCIENTIFIC COLLECTION OF THE HENRY DUNANT INSTITUTE

Frits Kalshoven, BELLIGERENT REPRISALS

Jiri Toman, INDEX OF THE GENEVA CONVENTIONS FOR THE PROTECTION OF WAR VICTIMS OF 12 AUGUST 1949

Michel Veuthey, GUERILLA ET DROIT HUMANITAIRE

Pierre Boissier, HISTOIRE DU COMITE INTERNATIONAL DE LA CROIX-ROUGE, Tome I – De Solférino à Tsoushima

André Durand, HISTOIRE DU COMITE INTERNATIONAL DE LA CROIX-ROUGE, Tome II – De Sarajevo à Hiroshima

Richard Perruchoud, LES RESOLUTIONS DES CONFERENCES INTERNATIONALES DE LA CROIX-ROUGE

INTERNATIONAL RESPONSIBILITIES OF NATIONAL RED CROSS AND RED CRESCENT SOCIETIES

Esbjörn Rosenblad, INTERNATIONAL HUMANITARIAN LAW OF ARMED CONFLICT

Jean Pictet, LES PRINCIPES FONDAMENTAUX DE LA CROIX-ROUGE, Commentaire

THE FUNDAMENTAL PRINCIPLES OF THE RED CROSS – Commentary

LOS PRINCIPIOS FUNDAMENTALES DE LA CRUZ ROJA, Commentario

Jean-Luc Hiebel, ASSISTANCE SPIRITUELLE DANS LES CONFLITS ARMES – DROIT HUMAIN

Gradimir Djurovic, L'AGENCE CENTRALE DE RECHERCHES DU COMITE INTERNATIONAL DE LA CROIX-ROUGE

Jacques Meurant, LE SERVICE VOLONTAIRE DE LA CROIX-ROUGE DANS LA SOCIETE D'AUJOURD'HUI

Dietrich Schindler-Jiri Toman, THE LAWS OF ARMED CONFLICTS (3rd completely revised edition)

1985 **HENRY DUNANT INSTITUTE** – GENEVA

INTERNATIONAL HUMANITARIAN ASSISTANCE

Disaster Relief Actions in International Law and Organization

by

PETER MACALISTER-SMITH

SPRINGER-SCIENCE+BUSINESS MEDIA, B.V. 1985

Library of Congress Cataloging in Publication Data

Macalister-Smith, Peter.
International humanitarian assistance.

1. War victims--Legal status, laws, etc.
2. Disaster relief--Law and legislation. 3. International relief. I. Title.
JX5136.M32 1985 341.7'66 84-1136
ISBN 978-94-017-6882-5

ISBN 978-94-017-6882-5 ISBN 978-94-017-6974-7 (eBook)
DOI 10.1007/978-94-017-6974-7

Originally published by Martinus Nijhoff Publishers, Dordrecht in 1985
Softcover reprint of the hardcover 1st edition 1985

Table of Contents

Foreword

Despite considerable progress in recent decades in the humanitarian field, especially through the United Nations and other international bodies, existing legal instruments and their implementation reveal certain gaps and imperfections. A pressing task facing the international community is to meet the growing challenge presented by colossal humanitarian problems which are either left without a solution or inadequately dealt with under existing law and practice.

While invoking a moral imperative as a guide, Dr. Macalister-Smith has succeeded in producing a book which is comprehensive, creative as well as objective. It combines a rare mix of theory and practice, focusing on the rights and relief of disaster victims.

It is an established fact that in recent decades the number of natural and man-made disasters has been increasing in all parts of the world. There is, consequently, a greater need now than ever before to resolve a variety of international humanitarian issues which emerge from complex and interrelated emergency conditions. The author is concerned both with the traditional areas of humanitarian law and practice, ranging from the role of the International Red Cross to the United Nations System as well as with the increasingly significant role of regional bodies and non-governmental organizations.

What is unique today as compared with past times is the level of international co-operation required in order to carry out disaster relief. More and more, the question of prevention and mitigation of potential disaster situations must be considered. In this respect, the book is most helpful for assessing the potential in international politics and law for meeting the new reality.

Dr. Macalister-Smith rightly stresses that too little attention has been paid to the role of the already existing national and international law in world-wide relief policies. Implementation is the issue, not law. The political and moral will of governments is the key factor. Certainly, the international disaster relief systems must be improved, but what will ultimately be acceptable to governments is not yet clear. In fact the institutional and juridical factors already exist and can be the instruments for the advancement of humanitarian achievements. A comprehensive view is required, and Dr. Macalister-Smith's work is an important contribution toward the construction of such a view.

Another theme, usually considered too delicate to discuss objectively, is handled exceedingly well by the author. This is the question of the disparity between the "symbol and the reality of sovereignty". The author perceives that this disparity is at its greatest height today, yet the need for international cooperation is also at an all time high. Of course, a truly workable international humanitarian order requires free consent and voluntary cooperation, which in turn presupposes an active and spontaneous sense of responsibility. Compulsion, then, can never be a response to such requirements: it is not only undesirable but also impractical.

In the end, however, even when the sense of responsibility is present, the ultimate question is: "who will be entitled to humanitarian assistance". The fact is that disaster relief is needed most in the South by the poorest of the poor. Famine and starvation are only the most obvious of these emergencies. Each contemporary disaster has been a reminder that traditional relief activity, though necessary, is not sufficient to alleviate, even less to eliminate the extreme human suffering it brings in its wake.

The author convincingly argues that root causes must be addressed in disaster relief, and that "material contributions to assistance programmes must be matched by efforts to eradicate the causes of many humanitarian problems".

Finally, Dr. Macalister-Smith stresses the necessity for greater participation in the formation of disaster relief programmes by governments in the South. Only then will the benefits outweigh the costs of disaster relief for the victims and their societies.

Many of the issues addressed by Dr. Macalister-Smith are central to the work of the Independent Commission on International Humanitarian Issues which I have the privilege to co-chair with Crown Prince Hassan of Jordan. Having been closely associated for more than two decades with humanitarian work both within and outside the United Nations System, I have no doubt that all those concerned with alleviation of suffering and welfare of our fellow human beings around the world will find the work of Dr. Macalister-Smith most helpful.

This book is a welcome addition to the growing body of analytical literature on humanitarian issues, one that not only will make a useful contribution to the development and restructuring of humanitarian relief policy, but also represents a growing trend in the thinking of experts in the humanitarian field: that the principle of humanity must prevail upon and condition military necessity, state security and political considerations.

Prince Sadruddin Aga Khan

Preface

We are surrounded by human suffering. Disasters affect more and more people, while the need for urgent relief assistance continues to grow. Our experience of relief operations is greater today than ever before, yet the suffering remains. The acute as well as chronic humanitarian problems in many countries are becoming a world humanitarian emergency. Can it be tackled effectively, and what is the significance of international cooperation in humanitarian matters?

Disaster situations in which relief assistance is required often occur as a result of factors associated with human activity, including environmental degradation, population growth, exploitation of resources and increased vulnerability caused by poverty. As pointed out in a recent report prepared for the Swedish Red Cross, many disasters could be prevented by refraining from creating them (see G. Hagman, Prevention Better than Cure). On the other hand, enormous relief needs exist now. Regardless of any new and much needed emphasis on prevention, even larger relief operations may be necessary soon.

The objective of relief work is to bring people's lives back to normal, but the everyday condition for many is already a serious plight. While it may be supplied with good intentions, relief which only perpetuates a state of marginal survival for the recipients is at best a purely short term measure, and such assistance may even contribute to worse disasters in the future. The realities in humanitarian matters can be stark indeed.

The humanitarian element in international relations seems at times to be enduring and inextinguishable; at other times, the misery of so many people threatens to swamp our capacity and will to offer solutions. Yet the humanitarian retains something of an eternal quality, matching the theme of suffering which accompanies existence. A positive humanitarian force shines through, reflected however faintly or imperfectly in human motivation and action, and even in our institutions. All the same, it would be wrong to insist that there are ready solutions to present humanitarian problems, let alone to future ones however foreseeable.

In seeking progress in the humanitarian field, it has become clear that we must aim not only to improve humanitarian relief operations but also to change the humanitarian order, or the context in which humanitarian problems and responses are set. This book is concerned with the contribution of international law and organization in attaining these goals, and the study concentrates in particular on the role of international law and organization in enabling and facilitating humanitarian assistance. At the same time, it is certain that increased international cooperation is required in many other fields, notably in safeguarding world peace and formulating sustainable and ecologically sound development policies for countries at all levels of development. Faced with competing priorities and urgent practical needs, we must start by taking a realistic approach to operational activities. Relief must above all be effective, and better implementation depends on better planning, law and organization.

Although law is often conservative and may lag behind social requirements, it also serves as a leading instrument for bringing about necessary change. Nevertheless, doubts about the reforming role of law persist. Relief workers specializing in field operations are apt to ask what practical good can be achieved by more law, and in particular by international law. On the other hand, the experience and contribution of such practitioners are essential in developing new solutions, especially at the international level in devising both workable policies and the appropriate legal provisions to support them.

A doubt of a different order is expressed by an eminent historian who writes that, as a rule, "the demand for codification reaches its climax in the penultimate age before a social catastrophe . . . when the legislators of the day are irretrievably on the run in a losing battle with ungovernable forces of destruction" (A.J. Toynbee, A Study of History, Vol. VII, 1954, p. 279). Here is a statement which, if anything can help, should urge us to face the basic causes of our problems. Yet, after all, it is not easy to see into the future. Indeed perhaps it is at least a potential advantage, so far largely unappreciated and unexplored, that we live and act in the present only, albeit conscious that what we do and fail to do now will bring ultimate consequences. Hence the importance in humanitarian matters as in others of preserving a sense of direction and a sense of proportion.

The present study has various origins, including a number of journeys and stays made by the author in places outside the obviously Western world, mainly between 1974 and 1976. Let me therefore first acknowledge with gratitude the unforgotten but as yet unrecorded assistance and hospitality provided then by friends in many countries, adding that I owe a special debt to Caroline Warrior for her contribution throughout that period and afterwards. I am fortunate indeed to have always had the support of my Mother and Father as well as Edward and Anneliese. To name others who have encouraged or inspired me in their own way would make a long list, and brief thanks would not do justice to my gratitude. Those without whom things could not have been the same, for whom my special esteem is reserved, already know.

In the context of international law and organization, my interest in humanitarian assistance was stimulated by the lecture series entitled "Practice, Norms and Reform of International Humanitarian Rescue Operations", delivered by Bradford Morse, Administrator of the United Nations Development Programme, at the Hague Academy of International Law in 1977. I am extremely grateful to Mr. Morse for the initial encouragement and assistance which he most kindly provided. I am also indebted to Lynn Stephens for supplying the first bibliographical material and other useful references.

The research for the study was started in the Bodleian Law Library and in the United Nations Depositary Library, Oxford, and the manuscript for this book was completed at the Max Planck Institute for Comparative Public Law and International Law, Heidelberg. In between, research was carried out at the Institute of Advanced Legal Studies, London, in the Peace Palace Library, The Hague, and in the archives of the League of Nations, in the United Nations Library and in the Henry Dunant Institute, Geneva. Thanks are due to the librarians and staff of all these institutions who provided assistance.

I received considerable help in the form of materials from the organizations concerned with international humanitarian assistance; I should mention in particular the Office of the United Nations Disaster Relief Co-ordinator, the Office of the United Nations High Commissioner for Refugees, the United Nations Relief and Works Agency for Palestine Refugees in the Near East, the United Nations Children's Fund, the United Nations Development Programme, the Food and Agriculture Organization of the United Nations, the World Food Council, the World Health Organization, the League of Red Cross and Red Crescent Societies, the International Committee of the Red Cross, the Sovereign Order of Malta and the World Council of Churches. Other bodies which provided assistance include the International Council of Voluntary Agencies, the International Disaster Institute and the Independent Commission on International Humanitarian Issues. Many officials and members of these institutions were also kind enough to discuss aspects of their work with me and, although not named here, they may be assured that I am grateful for their help.

Several publicists and scholars have kindly shared their views and writings with me; in addition to those who are mentioned elsewhere here, I would like to thank particularly Dr. Thomas Bruha, Dr. S.K. Chatterjee, Dr. Frances D'Souza, Dr. Rainer Hofmann, Mr. Michael A. Meyer, Professor J.W. Samuels, Mr. Ian Reid and Dr. Michel Veuthey. I remain indebted to my ex-supervisor and mentor, Dr. Frank Wooldridge, then Senior Lecturer in the Faculty of Law of the University of Birmingham and Senior Research Fellow at the Institute of Advanced Legal Studies, London, whose most considerate help and guidance enabled me to begin this study in the best possible way.

In 1980 the original version of the present work was accepted for the degree of Doctor of Philosophy at the University of Birmingham. In 1981 I moved to Geneva where I was employed at the secretariat of the League of Red Cross Societies in the Statutory and Juridical Affairs Department and later as a consultant on the League's study project entitled "Disaster Relief and International Law". This project brought me into closer contact with people and organizations active in the area of humanitarian assistance and I learned much from Henrik Beer, then Secretary General of the League, and from Jovica Patrnogic, President of the International Institute of Humanitarian Law, San Remo, under whose direction I worked. In 1982 I joined the Editorial Committee of the Encyclopedia of Public International Law published under the auspices of the Max Planck Institute for Comparative Public Law and International Law under the direction of Professor Dr. Rudolf Bernhardt, since when I have had the opportunity to revise the original study with the objective of publication. It is a pleasure to record my gratitude to Professor Bernhardt for his unfailing scholarly kindness and understanding at all times. The uniquely rich and congenial atmosphere created by the directors, fellows, staff and guests of the Max Planck Institute provided a most agreeable setting during the final stage of my work.

I would like to thank those who contributed by kindly reading and commenting on parts of the manuscript of the present work, in particular Robert E. Hollweg, Jonathan Ignarski, Ann Rustemeyer and Frank Wooldridge, although I cannot claim to have incorporated all their most helpful criticisms. I also owe a special tribute to Professor Atle Grahl-Madsen for his timely interest and counsel beyond the ordinary. In the last rush to prepare the manuscript Margot Lintaller provided her usual exemplary and invaluable secretarial services for which I am extremely grateful. I am also most grateful to Anneliese Neureither for expert and meticulous assistance with the proofs.

My warm thanks and appreciation are extended to Dr. Jiri Toman, Director of Research and Assistant Director, the Henry Dunant Institute, both for extending to me his generous personal hospitality and the facilities of the Institute, and also for his scholarly encouragement and help at all stages of the preparation of this book. I also wish to thank Mr. Zia Rizvi, Secretary-General of the Independent Commission on International Humanitarian Issues, for the time and effort which he most kindly devoted to assisting me.

Profound thanks are addressed to Prince Sadruddin Aga Khan for honouring my work by agreeing to contribute the Foreword, emphasizing the urgency of the subject and the importance of seeking new and better approaches which will give priority to the principle of humanity. My book owes much to the inspiration provided by his work both within and beyond the United Nations.

It is a final pleasure to express my special appreciation to the friends on whom I so often relied during visits to Geneva, and thanks to whom my stays there were made not only possible but also so enjoyable. I am thinking particularly of Chris and Nicole, Brian and Mavis, János, Tú, Al, Louis and Barbara, and, last but by no means least, Anne.

It remains only to add that while acknowledging the contribution of all who helped directly or indirectly to make this book possible, the responsibility for everything here said and left unsaid rests with me alone.

Heidelberg, November 1984 Peter Macalister-Smith

Introduction

> . . . si un peuple est désolé par la famine, tous ceux qui ont des vivres de reste doivent l'assister dans son besoin, sans toutefois s'exposer eux-mêmes à la disette. . . L'assistance, dans cette dure extrémité, est si essentiellement conforme à l'humanité, qu'on ne voit guères de Nation un peu civilisée y manquer absolument. . . De quelque Calamité qu' un peuple soit affligé, la même assistance lui est dûe.
>
> . . . if a nation is visited with famine, all those who have provisions enough and to spare should come to its assistance, though not to the extent of self-impoverishment. . . Help in such an extremity is so much in accord with the dictates of humanity that no civilized nation could altogether fail to respond. . . Whatever the nature of the disaster that overtakes a nation, the same help is due to it.
>
> E. de Vattel, Le Droit des Gens (The Law of Nations), II, I, 5 (1758).

Aims

World problems give rise to complex legal and institutional responses, not least in the humanitarian field. Sometimes the response even becomes part of the problem. The relationship between humanitarian assistance and international law and organization deserves careful consideration, the more so because of the serious nature of present humanitarian problems. Attempts to identify and apply factors which can contribute to improving humanitarian actions and the international humanitarian order are therefore now especially timely, if not overdue.[1]

Although principles of humanitarian assistance have received legal, moral and functional expression at the international level throughout the 20th century, the measures adopted in specific circumstances have often been inadequate as a response to the enormous needs which have had to be met. The relief system today functions with the participation of a wide variety of international actors, including many organizations charged with responsibilities for humanitarian assistance tasks. Provisions relating to humanitarian assistance applicable in armed conflicts have been incorporated in legal instruments which are almost universally accepted. Efforts have also been made to develop and codify principles and to adopt instruments relating to assistance in so-called "natural" disasters. While the results achieved in practice by these approaches do not leave room for undue optimism, the almost predictable recurrence of major humanitarian problems requiring relief actions suggests that further research in the area of international humanitarian assistance must give increased attention to the role of institutional and juridical factors.

The concern of this study with the institutional and juridical aspects of international humanitarian assistance is focused onto an examination of the principal international components of the global disaster relief system. The study aims in particular to assess the existing, developing and potential role of law in the organization and facilitation of international relief actions, especially those conducted for the benefit of the victims of "natural" disasters. More broadly, it seeks to help locate the role of humanitarian assistance within the framework of fundamental international goals pursued within the ambit of general international law and organization.

The study begins with a brief historical survey of humanitarian principles, instruments and action. It then proceeds to consider the international basis for relief actions in armed conflict and for refugees; assistance in such cases falls within the traditional areas of humanitarian law. From this comparative starting point, the basis for the consolidation of a wide-ranging body of international relief law is considered, taking into account the relevance of fundamental general principles of international law, the Charter of the United Nations and human rights instruments. Developments in the principal sectors of the international disaster relief system are examined, including the relief role of the Red Cross, the competences of the most important specialized and related agencies of the United Nations involved in humanitarian assistance, and the role of the UN Disaster Relief Co-ordinator. Attention is also given to the work of relevant non-governmental organizations and to regional developments relating to relief actions. Finally, some necessary measures which have been proposed as well as appropriate legal forms for further progress in the future are discussed.

Notion

The Concept of Disaster

The usual method of classifying disasters follows an etiological approach according to which the most basic division is that between man-made and natural disasters. Man-made disasters may in turn be divided into those which could be said to arise either accidentally or from negligence, and those resulting from deliberate actions; the former include industrial and technological disasters and increasingly may include disasters possessing an ecological or environmental component, while the latter include armed conflict situations in particular. A further category of man-made disaster resulting from the pursuit of ultra-hazardous activities in which great risks are inherent, such as nuclear and space activities, has also been proposed. According to the traditional view, natural disasters are those resulting from the effects of natural phenomena; for the purposes of scientific study they may be further divided according to meteorological, topological, telluric or tectonic causes.[2]

Not all events which could be described as disasters fall within the scope of this study. Problems of definition and delimitation are best resolved by emphasizing the element of humanitarian assistance provided by the international community to the countries or people affected. Briefly, disasters are viewed here as emergency situations in which there is an urgent need for international assistance to relieve human suffering. In such situations normal patterns of social and economic interaction may be disrupted, or the impact of a specific event may simply exceed the local capacity for response within the limits of available resources. This view of disaster encompasses a wide range of empirical situations and suggests that the common urgency of human needs in all such events should be seen as the decisive criterion for their identification.

Disasters and the resulting needs for assistance may occur slowly or suddenly. Sudden disasters may occur from the effects of a variety of natural phenomena having in common speed and relative unpredictability of impact. Famine and humanitarian emergencies arising from the consequences of conflict or political instability provide illustrations of slow disasters which may offer a greater degree of warning, or have effects which endure for longer periods of time. In addition, chronic persistence of emergency needs arising from a variety of causes is now a global problem which raises the question of the relationship between the international disaster relief system and the development process.

In practice, humanitarian emergencies may result from a mixture of causes: they may be partly natural and partly man-made; they may have several independent causes; and they may occur as a series of linked events. It is also apparent that a disaster caused by purely natural phenomena is no longer simply a "natural" disaster when the authorities of the stricken country decline to acknowledge the problem or when the international community fails to respond with the relief that is required. It has therefore rightly been stated that "the multiple causes often associated with disasters make the 'natural' – 'man-made' distinction . . . difficult to uphold in any rigorous way".[3] So-called "natural" disasters are mis-named essentially because they include a component which reflects mankind's relationship with the environment. This is increasingly demonstrated as more people become vulnerable to the effects of natural phenomena.

International Humanitarian Assistance

Disasters may be national or international in character, but for the purposes of this study only those with an international component are considered. Most nations are involved in the operation of the international relief system, whether through participation in the activities of the relevant international organizations or as potential donors and recipients of relief assistance.

The term humanitarian assistance is employed here as equivalent to disaster relief, or relief assistance. The needs for such assistance vary according to the effects of a particular disaster, but relief falls into three basic categories: assistance in kind, financial contributions and the services of trained personnel.[4] Assistance in kind refers to the commodities and materials required in the course of a relief operation: depending on the nature of a given disaster it is likely to include food, clothing, medicines, bedding, temporary shelters or hospital equipment; it may also include vehicles and other means of transport or other heavy equipment for use in search and rescue. Financial contributions may be intended to meet cash expenses in a relief operation, or to be converted into the required commodities. Personnel may be those with operational skills or those providing administrative or coordinating support. All categories of assistance are considered to be restricted to meeting the immediate needs of the victims, and not to serve commercial or other, wider purposes. Humanitarian assistance is distinguished from foreign aid in the general sense by its emergency character and by its use for the relief of victims of disaster.

Relief-related tasks include not only the provision of assistance to those afflicted, but also preparedness measures designed to enable effective action to be taken in future disaster situations which cannot be prevented. The importance of the prior planning of measures intended to be put into effect in emergencies results from the forseeable probability of the recurrence of phenomena which may cause disasters. Such measures, supplementing purely preventive measures, may contribute to the saving of life, the more effective organization of humanitarian rescue operations as well as the reduction of economic damage in disasters.[5]

Exclusively organizational problems of relief management will not be discussed here, nor will legal problems created by disasters which are not directly relevant to the subject of international humanitarian assistance.[6]

International Law and Organization

From the viewpoint of international law and organization, the international community at the world level is characterized at present by several notable features, including a greatly increased number of States, the extension of legal personality to a variety of international organizations created for functional purposes, and an absence of any central legislative or judicial authority apart from that which, to a certain extent, is provided by the United Nations and the International Court of Justice. In addition, the division of the world on territorial lines among formally equal political entities has resulted in much emphasis being placed on State sovereignty in international law doctrine. At the same time, however, international law and international organizations are concerned with an increasingly wide range of matters, some of which were once exclusively within the domestic jurisdiction of States.[7]

Many of the international problems now confronting international law and organization reflect the interdependence of the interests of States. Such problems include those of world population, finite resources, availability of food and energy, and the environment. The scope and competence of international law and organizations have been extended to economic, social and humanitarian problems related to the well-being not only of nations but also of individuals. The increasingly wide concerns of this international system are linked to conditions and needs in many of the poorest and more recently independent States. The nature of these concerns together with the progress of legal attempts to restrain and prohibit the use of armed force in international relations has influenced the orientation of all international law and has given rise to the new concept of an international law of cooperation. Despite the controversial status of this concept and the fact that war has not been abolished as a reality, the legal significance of these trends has been underlined by a number of distinguished authors; their implications for the development of a general humanitarian law must therefore be given due consideration.[8]

The primary emphasis in international law continues to be on the interests of nation States rather than on individual human values. Nevertheless, the ultimate realism in seeking to develop international concern for the well-being of the individual is that such an aim and the tasks which accompany it have a universal character. Although the principal members of the international community are States and State sovereignty remains the corner-stone of international law, the individual may also find a place in the international order. One of the essential functions of the law of nations is thus "to give effect, through appropriate limitation and international supervision of the internal sovereignty of states, to the principle that the protection of human personality and of its fundamental rights is the ultimate purpose of all Law, national and international".[9] If the desire to maintain security and develop peaceful relations is the primary motivation of international law and world organization, the instrumentalities of cooperation serve to link the realization of this ideal with measures designed to promote the interests of individual people.

Scope

Although the concept of international cooperation in humanitarian assistance is not new, it has acquired new significance and urgency at the present time. Less than ten years ago, the global relief system was rightly described as merely a series of *ad hoc* reactions.[10] Despite the considerable element of international cooperation now existing in the planning, organization and coordination of emergency assistance, the international response to humanitarian emergencies continues to be of a fragmentary nature. It is not yet clear what further solutions are required or are likely to be acceptable to States, but it is apparent to many observers as well as to those concerned with the operation of the relief system that increased international cooperation is necessary in order to improve the effectiveness of humanitarian action.[11]

Disasters affecting human beings will probably occur with greater frequency and severity in the future, and new types of disaster may be expected. Some areas of the world are so vulnerable that they are in a virtually permanent state of emergency.[12] The term "mega-disaster" has already appeared.[13] The emergence of these concepts reveals the breadth of response that is demanded of the international relief system, while attesting to the urgency of efforts needed not only to identify the inadequacies of international law and organization relating to humanitarian assistance but also to develop new legal and institutional solutions on which more effective humanitarian action can be based.

Legal questions associated with international relief operations appear to arise at several levels. One important level concerns technical arrangements to expedite relief; the particular concern here is with measures which facilitate the efficient delivery of relief consignments, the movement and functioning of relief personnel and arrangements in connection with communications. A further level of legal interest relates to the principles of humanitarian assistance, analysis of which should help to establish the potential extent of the role of law within global relief policy. Here, it will be necessary to take into account the general principles of international law, customary rules, conventions and other international instruments such as declarations and resolutions which concern relief actions in disaster situations, as well as the practice of States and international organizations. Although the impact of measures remains insufficient to meet the great needs which continue to arise, international humanitarian assistance activities are undertaken by States bilaterally, by governmental organizations and by other international actors, including international non-governmental organizations and private agencies. Developments in all these areas contribute to establishing standards of responsibility for the international community towards disaster victims and in disaster situations, and they provide norms for the conduct and evaluation of relief operations. At the same time, study may demonstrate the need to develop new principles and instrumentalities relating to humanitarian assistance.

The existing principles of humanitarian assistance are neither universally nor uniformly recognized, and newly-developed principles can be expected to suffer from the same defect. The background to this study is therefore the question whether global humanitarian problems may be perceived as uniting the world community rather than dividing it. It remains axiomatic that State consent is necessary for the conduct of relief operations. Nevertheless, respect for the principle of national sovereignty must be balanced by attention to the general principles of international cooperation and solidarity. A further task is therefore to relate analysis of legal and institutional approaches in the field of humanitarian assistance to contemporary understanding of the role and purposes of international law and organization, and thereby to indicate the scope for the further development of humanitarian relief law and relief actions.

The adjective "humanitarian" in ordinary usage can be defined as "having regard to the interests of humanity or mankind at large". The breadth of such a definition corresponds with a wide view of the aim of the system of humanitarian law, the foundation of which is concern for the well-being and development of the individual. More particularly, humanitarian law has the purpose of providing for the avoidance and relief of human suffering. Traditional humanitarian law, which originated within the system of classical international law as a part of the law of war, was concerned mostly with restrictions and prohibitions of States' actions in conflict situations. It was usually a realistic expression of necessity blended with the complementary themes of humanitarian protection and assistance. However, while in principle the ambit of humanitarian law extends to all situations of human suffering, the elaboration of provisions applicable in peacetime, and in natural disaster situations in particular, remains to be undertaken: there is at present no binding global international legal instrument devoted exclusively to humanitarian assistance in peacetime.

The question of the establishment of foundations for a broad field of humanitarian law relevant to the victims of all disasters has not been thoroughly discussed by many publicists, although it is not in doubt that the field of international relief lies within the ambit of international humanitarian law. Juridical problems of international disaster relief actions have been under consideration since 1970 by the International Law Association. The International Institute of Humanitarian Law, at San Remo in Italy, has set up a commission to study the protection of victims of natural disasters. The Henry Dunant Institute, the research facility of the Red Cross, is undertaking an examination of the existing legal instruments which form the framework within which new legal solutions to international relief problems could be developed. In 1982 the United Nations Institute for Training and Research published a detailed study concerning model rules applicable to disaster relief operations. Far-reaching proposals for a new international humanitarian order are currently before the United Nations General Assembly. In 1984 a proposed draft convention on expediting the delivery of emergency relief was annexed to the Secretary-General's report on the Office of the United Nations Disaster Relief Co-ordinator. The substance and implications of these recent developments relevant to future legal progress in the field of humanitarian assistance must be thoroughly examined.[14]

The present study is motivated by the conviction not only that greater humanitarian achievements are attainable but also that a necessary and important contribution to this goal will be supplied by international organization and international law. It is to be hoped that the study will stimulate further research into the obstacles to and the scope for improvement of international humanitarian action. The study may also contribute to the current debate, from which fresh conclusions will no doubt emerge in due course, on the desirability and feasibility of adopting a new international legal instrument devoted to relief actions. Greater understanding of the role of international organization and international law in this field should in turn contribute to the search for ways and means towards more comprehensive and successful programmes of humanitarian assistance.

1. Historical Perspectives on Humanitarian Assistance

1.1 Custom and Law in Armed Conflict Situations

General Background

Efforts to limit the use of force and to mitigate its destructive consequences are probably as old as the history of armed conflict. However, the profound occupation with the prevention of warfare and with the reduction of suffering resulting from it was not for many centuries reflected in a legal recognition of humanitarian principles. The rights of belligerents to adopt any degree or kind of force to defeat the opponent and of conquerors to treat prisoners and occupied territories as was deemed fit were widely accepted. Indeed, in some cases, ancient practice justified the total destruction of the enemy.[1]

The history of civilizations nevertheless includes the development of customs of a humanitarian nature applicable to armed conflict situations. Ancient civilizations possessed codes regulating warfare, and surviving texts include provisions with humanitarian effects. There are records of early examples of impartial relief to the wounded in battle, in both Europe and Asia.

The growth of Christianity provided a qualified stimulus for humanitarian action, although the institutionalized religion soon abandoned the principles of non-violence, accepting with a thin veil of censure the shedding of blood in public wars. In Europe, medieval standards of chivalry required a certain degree of fair conduct and mutual respect between opponents. Elements of restraint in the conduct of warfare are also found in ancient and medieval Indian law and Islamic law.[2]

As to prisoners of war, early custom relating to slavery and ransom may have been the first factor mitigating a brutal approach to captives. The concept of concern for the welfare of prisoners developed so that such usages might not be frustrated by the death of the hostages. Although the institution of ransom was more commercial than humanitarian in intention, its effects included the sparing of life, the avoidance of mutilation and a reasonable standard of maintenance in captivity. Increasing assumption of responsibilities by States led to a more generalized improvement in the condition of prisoners of war in Europe. By the later part of the 18th century, provisions reflecting humanitarian concerns for prisoners began to appear in bilateral agreements and treaties.[3]

An important development relating to humanitarian assistance, within the framework of Christianity, involved the establishment of charitable orders, several of which were organized on an international non-governmental basis. The Order of the Knights of St. John of Jerusalem was concerned from the 12th century onwards with the impartial care of the wounded and sick. During the Crusades Muslim leaders also supported the principle of impartial relief. Early practice thus provides examples of the work carried out in modern times by Red Cross and Red Crescent Societies.

The advance of humanitarian sentiments was generally slow, and cannot be broadly attributed to the religious or secular spheres alone. Restraints on brutal practices of warfare were also derived from enlightened military strategy. The realization that all violence does not contribute to the defeat of the enemy and that the purpose of conflict is not necessarily frustrated by showing consideration to the wounded, to prisoners and to civilians provided one basis for the growth of principles of respect for the human person in armed conflict. Natural law theorists of the 17th century recognized a distinction between combatants and non-combatants and emphasized some moderation in war and the advisability of humane behaviour. New ideas were not put about until the 18th century and the time of E. de Vattel and J.-J. Rousseau, to which period the rise of the secular humanitarianism of the 19th century can be traced.[4] That movement in turn provided the new impetus towards the codification and development of humanitarian principles witnessed during the later part of the same century.

The origins of the Red Cross and of the Geneva Conventions are found in this period, in the efforts of Henry Dunant, a Swiss citizen and civilian witness to the effects of the Battle of Solférino (1859) in Italy, to bring relief and assistance to the wounded. Henry Dunant subsequently advocated rules for the protection of victims of international war as well as the establishment of voluntary relief organizations.[5] The former proposal led directly to the adoption of the Geneva Conventions, the first of which was concluded in 1864, and the latter to the creation of the world-wide Red Cross movement.

Henry Dunant's devotion to the cause of the codification of humanitarian law and to the development of international humanitarian action resulted in the conferring on him of the first Nobel Peace Prize in 1901. More immediately, the formation in Geneva in 1863 of the Standing Committee for Aid to Wounded Soldiers led to the convening in the same year of an international congress which founded the Red Cross. In 1880 the Standing Committee became the International Committee of the Red Cross. Together with the Swiss federal government, the Committee promoted the Diplomatic Conference which adopted the first Geneva Convention of 1864, which in turn gave legal protection to field ambulances, military hospitals and their personnel, and introduced the use of the distinctive red cross emblem. National Red Cross Societies were formed in many countries. The adoption in some States of the appellation Red Crescent Society, together with the corresponding emblem, did not seriously affect the cohesion of the movement, which made rapid progress towards universality.

The 1864 Geneva Convention for the Amelioration of the Conditions of the Wounded in Armies in the Field[6] was the first multilateral convention with the purpose of affirming an international humanitarian law of armed conflict. The Convention was signed by 16 States. It was open to accession by non-signatories and quickly gained world-wide acceptance.

The 1864 Convention is notable for incorporating moral humanitarian ideas into the sphere of inter-State relations. Art. VI of the Convention aimed to extend the protection of international law to humanitarian activity on the battlefield by providing that "wounded or sick combatants, to whatever nation they may belong, shall be collected and cared for". The Convention accorded neutrality to ambulances and their personnel, and protected the humanitarian actions of civilian inhabitants assisting the wounded. Art. VII recognized the distinctive emblem of the red cross on a white ground. The Convention was revised in 1906 and 1929[7] and formed the basis of the First Geneva Convention of 1949.

Early assistance actions of the Red Cross in battle included operations in the Franco-Prussian War (1870), the Boer War (1899 to 1902) and the Russian-Japanese War (1904). Assistance included not only medical care but also the distribution of relief goods, requiring the establishment of supply warehouses and the negotiation of transport and import concessions. During World War I, extensive Red Cross relief activities were carried out on behalf of both military and civilian victims. Between the world wars, humanitarian work was also undertaken by the Red Cross in Ethiopia, Spain and China.

The legal rules designed to ensure humane treatment of non-combatants in conflict situations were progressively extended after 1864 from application solely in favour of military casualties to prisoners of war and to civilians. Regarding prisoners of war, early legal instruments referred only to the applicability of the general rules of international law in their favour, although it was established that prisoners must be humanely treated. A second Geneva Convention of 1929,[8] which in turn subsequently formed the basis of the Third Geneva Convention of 1949, included sections on conditions of captivity, as well as the first provisions conferring the right of prisoners to receive correspondence and relief parcels.

Relief for Civilians: the CRB and UNRRA

Early conventions applicable in armed conflict included only isolated provisions relating to civilians. In theory, civilians were not involved in direct hostilities, a general principle of the law of war being that military operations were confined to armed forces. Specific safeguards for the civilian population were therefore usually thought to be superfluous.

The first large scale international operation of humanitarian assistance was undertaken during World War I on behalf of the civilian populations of occupied Belgium and northern France, in response to the threat of famine in that region. The problem of starvation followed the German occupation of Belgium in August 1914 and resulted from the cessation of industry, the disruption of agricultural production, widespread requisitioning, the flood of destitute refugees from the war, but primarily from the Allied blockade of the North Sea ports. Emergency requirements were such that the relief operation had to face a task of provisioning a population of nine million persons, without means of income, cut off from their sources of supply, concentrated in a territory of 20,000 square miles under enemy control.

Local relief committees emerged in order to care for the destitute, and they attempted to buy food and to obtain a relaxation of the blockade for relief shipments. One such delegation approached Herbert Hoover in London in September 1914 with a request to arrange for the shipment of grain to Brussels. Hoover was able to obtain preliminary agreements from the United States, the German governor-general of occupied Belgium and the British authorities. On October 12, 1914, Hoover announced the formation of the American Committee for the Relief of Belgium, which was soon re-named the Commission for Relief in Belgium (CRB).[9] The Commission enjoyed the patronage of the American, Dutch and Spanish diplomatic representatives in London, Brussels, Paris, The Hague and Berlin.

Hoover succeeded in convincing each side in the war that the relief of Belgium was in their interests. The British and French governments were willing to consider a relief programme and to transfer responsibilities to the CRB, on condition that more detailed undertakings were obtained from the Germans about the conduct of the operations. The German government in Berlin agreed initially to guarantee that relief shipments for the benefit of the civilian population would not be requisitioned. This guarantee was subsequently expanded to include complete freedom of movement for the Commission's staff within Belgium, and was accepted by the Allies.

The CRB was thus accountable to the Western Allies for the fulfilment of German guarantees regarding the protection and equitable use of supplies; and it was accountable to the German government for the conduct of a strictly humanitarian relief operation for the benefit of Belgian and French civilians. It was also more generally accountable to donor States and individuals for the efficient use of its resources. The CRB retained a neutral status between the belligerents, while receiving support from both sides. The agreements with the belligerents were the relief organization's working constitutional texts.

Between 1914 and 1919 the CRB procured, shipped and supervised the distribution of relief supplies sufficient to maintain the entire population at subsistence level. In addition, it supported welfare services and undertook the revival of certain sectors of the economy. In four and a half years of operations it handled over two thousand commodity cargoes, totalling more than 5 million tonnes, with a 1918 value of over $800 million.

The CRB was an organization without precedent in international relations. It appeared to be an *ad hoc* private international organization on a temporary basis, but in the performance of its functions the Commission possessed many of the attributes of State institutions. It negotiated and concluded agreements at the highest level, and enjoyed important immunities granted by the belligerents. Its representatives in military occupied regions operated with wide powers and privileges, and it flew its own flag and issued its own passports. The CRB operated a large fleet of ocean vessels and canal boats, and by its existence and in the actual discharge of its relief functions it assumed the fundamental responsibility of providing for the basic needs of a whole population.

The CRB set important and lasting precedents for the conception and organization of subsequent large scale humanitarian assistance operations, although it operated in an international environment very different from that surrounding the relief problems immediately after World War II or present international humanitarian problems. In particular, the Commission's political neutrality and operational independence, and its director's capacity to negotiate directly and impartially with all sides involved, indicate minimum requirements for any relief operation or relief organization. The level of international cooperation developed by the CRB in its global network of procurement offices and supporting charitable organizations was also a valuable precedent for the conduct of future relief programmes.

After World War I, in accordance with resolutions of the 1921 International Conference of the Red Cross, the International Committee of the Red Cross prepared a preliminary draft convention for the protection of civilians which set out principles relating to deportee, evacuee and refugee civilians and included rights to relief supplies and correspondence. A final draft of this instrument was approved at the 1934 International Conference of the Red Cross in Tokyo, but its submission before a diplomatic conference was prevented by the outbreak of World War II.[10] When the revision of the Geneva Conventions was undertaken after the war, the Tokyo draft was revived and formed the basis of the Fourth Convention of 1949.

During World War II the Allied Governments denied repeated requests to lift the blockade of the continent to allow the passage of relief shipments. The justification for this refusal was based on the existence of a plan for a vast peacetime relief operation which was to commence upon the defeat of the enemy. Although the first proposals did not envisage the creation of an international organization for this purpose, the committees formed in London and Washington to study the needs of the occupied territories and to formulate plans for relief later provided a nucleus of staff and planning for the relief operation. However, the need for the widest possible international coordination led to the drafting of an agreement for the United Nations Relief and Rehabilitation Administration (UNRRA) which was presented to an international conference and signed by the representatives of over 40 governments on November 9, 1943.[11]

The preamble to the Agreement explicitly recognized the humanitarian nature of the purposes for which UNRRA was created. UNRRA had three main tasks: relief, rehabilitation and resettlement of certain groups of displaced persons. Although all UNRRA's duties were not set out exactly, the nature of the relief task was precisely defined in Art. 1 of the Agreement, as follows:

> to plan, co-ordinate, administer or arrange for the administration of measures for the relief of victims of war in any area under the control of any of the United Nations through the provision of food, fuel, clothing, shelter and other basic necessities, medical and other essential services; and to facilitate in such areas, so far as necessary to the adequate provision

> of relief, the production and transportation of these articles and the furnishing of these services ....

UNRRA was created as both an organization for charitable relief and an instrument of international cooperation, as the same article made clear in defining additional functions of the Administration. Those functions extended to the formulation and recommendation of measures for individual or joint action by any or all of the member governments concerning the conduct of the relief operation.

The policy making body of UNRRA was the General Council, consisting of representatives of all member States. Other bodies were established to guide the Administration in its tasks, the procedures of which were characterized by a flexibility reflecting the emergency nature of the organization. Executive authority was vested in the person of the Director General, and, at field level, in the chiefs of country missions.

The first session of the Council was held immediately after the signing of the Agreement, and the financial arrangements and operating principles and policies of UNRRA were established in a series of resolutions.[12] The categories of supplies and services with which UNRRA would be concerned were identified and defined, together with procedures for estimating needs and for creating reserve stocks, and conditions for the distribution of relief were stipulated. Regarding financial arrangements, the Council decided that governments in a position to pay for UNRRA relief should do so, but that no applicant government should be required to assume the burden of an enduring foreign exchange debt. Additional resolutions provided for the facilitation of UNRRA operations by member governments. In particular, measures were agreed upon to protect the independence of UNRRA representatives, to ensure immunity and priority in transit of UNRRA supplies, and to minimize administrative expenses.

The formal establishment of missions in receiving countries was preceded by the conclusion of a detailed agreement between the government concerned and UNRRA. These agreements confirmed the consent of the controlling authorities to UNRRA operations; more importantly, they ensured that the principles and policies established in the resolutions of the General Council were accepted as binding and would be implemented.[13]

The achievement of UNRRA's relief operations was remarkable. The Administration existed from November 9, 1943 to September 30, 1948. Its programmes at their peak in early 1946 required a headquarters staff of 1800, a European Regional Office in London with a staff of 1600, 24 country missions with staff ranging from 1300 in China to 10 in the Ukraine, and an additional 17 regional shipping and procurement offices, numerous short term diplomatic missions, as well as a separate displaced persons operation employing a staff of 5000. The total volume of UNRRA's relief shipments was $2900 million, of which $1230 million represented food supplies, in quantity over 9 million tons.[14]

The nature of UNRRA's constitution and functioning was far removed from that of its only predecessor, the Commission for Relief in Belgium. The size and scope of the relief operation, the structural complexities of the organization and its legal foundations in a multilateral agreement, supplemented by a system of operating agreements with receiving countries, are immediately noticeable differences. Nevertheless, many of the principles upon which UNRRA based its operations were closely related to those adopted by the CRB. Moreover, it was the very precedent created by the existence of the Commission which made it difficult for appeals for similar assistance during World War II to be refused.

UNRRA's enormous relief programme was in practice executed on a selective basis. Assistance was limited to a relatively small group of liberated countries, and resources were restricted to specific types of goods and services. The work of UNRRA did not make unnecessary the additional provision of assistance to many countries; indeed, it was always accepted that even the huge sums made available through the Administration were too small in relation to needs. However, UNRRA's closing period revealed clearly the limits to the commitment to continuing international cooperation assumed by participating States. At the same time, patterns were set for the diversity of subsequent post-war humanitarian efforts.

In assessing UNRRA's performance several aspects of its existence may be distinguished, the primary one being the effective delivery of relief supplies. Judged in terms of the provision of sufficient food to prevent starvation and deterioration of health conditions, clothing for protection and medical supplies to prevent the spread of infectious disease, UNRRA was successful as an operating organization and in the use of the resources placed at its disposal. However, an equally important aspect of UNRRA was the concept itself, namely that a large group of nations should pool their resources and distribute them to meet the immediate needs of their populations. The premise was one of sharing, involving in its practical application the mobilization of resources on the basis of availability and their distribution in accordance with needs.

In 1947, when UNRRA was terminated, many of the tasks started by the Administration remained uncompleted. UNRRA was not disbanded because its work had become unnecessary; rather, a division of functions was made and particular aspects of its work were continued by separate organizations. The limitations of the basic commitment and concept were revealed as the States members of the United Nations found themselves increasingly unable or unwilling to maintain their cooperative approach to humanitarian problems at such a high level.

UNRRA's most direct successor was the United Nations Children's Fund, to which residual assets of over $34 million were transferred. UNRRA's projects in the field of agriculture and health became the responsibilities respectively of the Food and Agriculture Organization and the World Health Organization, which also received financial grants.[15] More broadly, the concept of achieving international cooperation in the solution of international humanitarian problems found a place in the statement of fundamental purposes of the United Nations, in Art. 1 of the Charter. The form and circumstances of humanitarian assistance operations remained to be determined in the practice of the new world organization.

1.2 International Relief for Refugees

Although the history of refugees before the 20th century reveals the existence of groups of entirely destitute persons, there was little early provision of material assistance on an international basis.[16] By the beginning of the present century a number of national and voluntary organizations existed with the purpose of assisting refugees in other countries. International recognition of the need for coordinated action on behalf of refugees arose principally from the problems created by World War I. These problems were increased on an unprecedented scale by more than one million Russian refugees who entered western Europe as a result of the 1917 revolution, and by additional persons fleeing the 1921 famine in Russia.

Following the creation of the League of Nations in 1919, refugees became the object of collective measures beyond the immediate interests of the States of origin and refuge. International concern in this field was expressed both by concluding instruments relating to the status of refugees, and in the creation of agencies for the protection of refugees and for the administration of material assistance. The first organized action for the benefit of refugees consisted of relief measures, confined to specific groups of refugees as they arose. However, neither the Covenant of the League of Nations nor general practice at the time established any permanent obligation for the assumption of responsibilities.[17]

The Council of the League of Nations was from the earliest period of its existence receptive to appeals to its position as a symbol of international unity, not least in humanitarian matters. The outstanding figure in the work of international assistance to refugees throughout the 1920s was Dr. Fridtjof Nansen, who laid the foundations for the subsequent development of protection and assistance efforts at the international level. His initial concern was to mobilize international relief on an emergency basis for displaced persons in the aftermath of World War I. He was appointed to the post of High Commissioner for Russian Refugees in 1921. His mandate was extended in 1924 to cover Armenians and, in 1928, Assyrians, Assyro-Chaldeans and Turks.

The League's interest in the welfare of refugees was necessary because individual governments found it impossible to deal independently with the problems facing them. Cooperation became imperative. However, member States of the League of Nations were not prepared to assume heavy or continuous financial responsibilities on behalf of refugees, although the intervention of Dr. Nansen on various occasions led to urgent appeals for funds by the Council and Assembly. The high personal standing of the High Commissioner also resulted in sums being placed at his disposal by governmental and private sources. Cooperation with private and voluntary agencies was always very close. National Red Cross Societies and the International Committee of the Red Cross were already engaged in important field work for refugees and their activities, together with those of other relief agencies, continued on a basis of cooperation with the new governmental system, including the expending of funds mobilized through the League of Nations.[18]

In 1922 the Assembly of the League of Nations adopted a resolution authorizing the High Commissioner to utilize the Russian refugee organization to assist with the relief of refugees from the Near East, and an appeal for governmental contributions was made. Within three months relief measures were being carried out in Eastern Thrace and in Asia Minor with the support of some eleven States. In the same period, the American Relief Administration (ARA), a private relief organization founded by Herbert Hoover, was undertaking a feeding programme for refugees in Constantinople, in collaboration with the High Commissioner.

Between 1924 and 1929 the task of material assistance for refugees was entrusted to the International Labour Organisation, and protection functions became the main responsibility of the High Commissioner. In 1929 both tasks were reunited in the Office of the High Commissioner. On the death of Dr. Nansen in 1930, the Nansen International Office for Refugees was created by a resolution of the Assembly of the League of Nations, as an autonomous body responsible for the exercise of functions of humanitarian assistance.[19]

The provision of material assistance by the League to certain groups of refugees was achieved within an institutional framework without specific legal formulations relating to relief activities. It was not considered necessary to lay down legal provisions governing the operations undertaken, partly through private efforts, and it would not have been realistic to attempt to establish general obligations relating to relief. The early legal instruments which were adopted took the form of agreements relating to each new group of refugees and their provisions covered only certain basic elements of status. These agreements were ratified by only a few States, in some cases with reservations.[20]

The work of the Nansen International Office was directed towards a termination of the refugee problem as it existed in the early 1930s. Governments were concerned at the continuing expense, at the time of the world depression when they felt obliged to accord priority to their own citizens. In spite of difficulties a ten year plan was agreed, but it proved unrealistic in view of the political circumstances of the period and its implementation was frustrated by the flow of refugees from Germany and Spain. In 1933 a new High Commissioner for Refugees Coming from Germany was appointed under a mandate excluding any role of assistance, which was stated to be in the province of the private organizations.

Despite the work of the Nansen Office and the High Commissioner, well over 500,000 refugees in Europe were in urgent need by 1938. In that year a reorganization took place of the institutions concerned with the protection and assistance of refugees. The Nansen Office and the Office of the High Commissioner were closed and a new High Commissioner for Refugees under the Protection of the League of Nations was appointed, whose competence relating to relief was restricted to facilitating the coordination of humanitarian assistance provided by other organizations.[21] The Evian Conference of 1938, convened to deal with political and economic questions arising from the exodus of refugees from Germany and Austria, set up the Inter-Governmental Committee on Refugees, headed by the High Commissioner. However, World War II interrupted the activity of the new system and created additional problems which formed the background to the establishment of the Office of the United Nations High Commissioner for Refugees.

1.3 Relief in Natural Disasters

Early Development of Relief Actions

The ideal of humanitarian service in peacetime has been expressed since antiquity in the form of samaritan work, usually organized in response to local needs. Bilateral assistance between States in disasters was not unknown in the past. Following the earthquake which destroyed Lisbon in 1755, King George II of England requested Parliament to send "such speedy and effectual relief as may be suitable to so afflicting and pressing an exigency", referring in his statement to religious and humanitarian considerations which should motivate such action. The great 18th century publicist of the law of nations, de Vattel, referred to this case as an example of natural international solidarity.[22]

The first large scale international relief work in cases of natural disaster, organized on a basis of permanent readiness, was undertaken by the Red Cross movement at the end of the 19th century. Although the Red Cross was founded with the intention of bringing aid to the wounded its humanitarian role has never in practice been limited to situations of armed conflict. Resolutions of the first Geneva International Conference of 1863 demonstrate clearly that the founders of the Red Cross envisaged a parallel development of peacetime relief activities. Henry Dunant himself advocated this role from the start.[23]

Various resolutions of the International Conferences of the Red Cross before the close of the 19th century reiterated a mandate for peacetime relief work by National Societies. Resolutions in the first decade of the 20th century were more cautious, as material resources and volunteer staff were limited. Nevertheless, programmes were adopted by most National Societies for the systematic organization of emergency relief. The earliest efforts consisted of the forwarding of supplies and contributions by donor National Societies to the Red Cross Society in the affected country. This type of action was taken particularly in Europe following floods and earthquakes. In the immediate post-World-War-I period the main preoccupation was with Russian refugees. A notable international operation at that time involved the Red Cross in combatting the typhus epidemics in central and eastern Europe which followed in the wake of war-time devastation.

The disastrous famine in Russia in 1921 resulted in the establishment of various international relief organizations and commissions. The operations of the American Relief Administration to bring relief to the needy, especially children, were conducted on the basis of an unusual agreement with the Soviet authorities containing 27 articles permitting the entry and establishment of the ARA, and according its personnel "full liberty to come and go and move about Russia".[24] The ARA expanded its activities during the worst period of the famine, and remained in existence until July 20, 1923. The Red Cross bodies also negotiated directly with the Soviet authorities regarding the relief operations which they carried out.

At the end of World War I the President of the War Committee of the American National Red Cross had proposed to various National Societies that part of the considerable financial resources they still possessed as a result of war time collections should be devoted to international public health work and to organizing international relief in cases of disaster. In 1919 the National Red Cross and Red Crescent Societies created their federal organization, the League of Red Cross Societies, a few weeks before the signing of the Covenant of the League of Nations. Art. 25 of the Covenant, concerning the establishment of Red Cross Societies, stated:

> The Members of the League agree to encourage and promote the establishment and co-operation of duly authorized voluntary national Red Cross organizations having as purposes the improvement of health, the prevention of disease and the mitigation of suffering throughout the world.

This provision underlined the central purpose of the new federation and demonstrated the wide international support at the governmental level behind the moves of National Red Cross and Red Crescent Societies to extend their activities on a constitutional basis to the relief of suffering in disasters in peacetime.

During the 1920s the Red Cross turned its attention to promoting a convention to establish an international relief union. The first Relief Section was created in the secretariat of the League of Red Cross Societies, inaugurating its role of coordination of Red Cross humanitarian assistance. Subsequently, the International Conferences of the Red Cross began to deal in detail with practical questions concerning international relief. A number of important resolutions were adopted setting out principles for action within the Red Cross.[25]

The foundation of the League of Red Cross Societies was thus associated with the possibility of far-reaching developments in the field of international humanitarian assistance. The League of Nations, as the first governmental institution of the universal type, offered a new opportunity for the evolution of humanitarian principles and action at the international level through the cooperative and coordinated responses of States to relief needs. At the same time, international law began to embrace an increasing range of concerns relating to human welfare, including humanitarian questions and disaster relief.

The International Relief Union

In 1921 an Italian senator and President of the Italian Red Cross, named Ciraolo, proposed the creation of an organization which would ensure international solidarity and assistance to the victims of natural disasters. The plan, conceived in the earthquake-ruined city of Messina in 1908, was presented to the 1921 International Conference of the Red Cross in the form of a report entitled "The Necessity for an International Organization for the Immediate Relief of Populations Afflicted by Sudden Calamity". The Conference recommended to States parties of the 1864 Geneva Convention the conclusion of a new convention recognizing the peacetime role of the Red Cross and providing for relief for the victims of natural disasters.

In 1922 the project was taken up by the League of Nations, and discussed at length in committees of the Assembly between 1923 and 1925. Following consultations with governments, the Conference for the Creation of an International Relief Union (IRU) was convened in Geneva, attended by representatives of 43 States. On July 12, 1927 the Conference adopted the Convention and Statute of the IRU.[26] The Convention entered into force on December 27, 1932 upon fulfilment of certain financial conditions and deposit of the necessary ratifications; it was eventually adhered to by a total of 30 States. The Convention laid down the basic principles, aims and structure of the IRU while the Statute provided in greater detail for the organization and functions of the Union.

The Preamble of the Convention recalled the League's purpose of the promotion of international cooperation through just relations between nations. It stated that the IRU was created through the desire of nations "to render aid to each other in disasters, to encourage international relief by a methodical co-ordination of available resources, and to further the progress of international law in this field".

Art. 2 of the Convention set out the IRU's objectives, which were primarily "in the event of any disaster due to *force majeure*, the exceptional gravity of which exceeds the limits of the powers and resources of the stricken people, to furnish to the suffering population first aid and to assemble for this purpose, funds, resources and assistance of all kinds". The same article also laid down three further objectives: to coordinate the efforts of other relief organizations in the event of any disaster; to encourage the study of preventive measures against disasters; and to seek "to induce all peoples to render mutual international assistance". Art. 2 thus envisaged that in some disasters the Union would actively provide relief, and in others it would simply coordinate relief operations.

Relief actions in armed conflict were not explicitly authorized in the Convention, nor were they excluded. Emphasis was thus placed on the meaning of the term *force majeure*, employed in both the French and English texts. In practice, the imprecision of this term enabled some States members of the IRU to express reservations regarding proposed actions of the Union, in the form of legal objections to its competence.

Art. 3 of the Convention provided that the IRU was to operate for the benefit of all stricken people, irrespective of nationality or any other distinctions, while also limiting the Union's actions to disasters occurring in the territory of the parties. Art. 4 of the Convention provided that the IRU's operations were to be undertaken only with the consent of the State concerned. These two articles of the Convention embodied the two main principles of the IRU, namely, respect for the territorial sovereignty of parties and non-discrimination in assistance. Although operations were restricted to the territories of the parties, the hope was that this limitation would be self-correcting and would encourage progress towards the Union's universality.

A General Council composed of delegates of all members of the IRU was created to provide policy directives and to supervise their implementation by the Executive Committee, which it appointed. The Statute detailed the functions of the Executive Committee which included collecting, administering and utilizing funds and therefore extended to the control and organization of relief operations. Arts. 8 and 10 of the

Convention established the legal personality of the IRU and provided for certain immunities, facilities and exemptions for its establishments and personnel and for similar privileges during relief operations.

Both the Convention and Statute attempted to stimulate and to centralize the efforts of private charity. Art. 5 of the Convention envisaged free cooperation with the Red Cross and with all other organizations in a position to undertake humanitarian activities. Under Art. 15 of the Statute, relief work was to be effected on behalf of the IRU by such organizations, under the overall direction of the Executive Committee. The privileges and immunities accorded under Art. 10 of the Convention also extended to all organizations acting on behalf of the IRU. This provision is a notable early example of an inter-governmental organization granting facilities to non-governmental organizations.

The real intention behind these terms was for the International Committee of the Red Cross and the League of Red Cross Societies to supply the permanent central services of the IRU. However, although the Red Cross was accorded a central place in the structure and functioning of the Union, and was represented in the Executive Committee, its activities were to be conducted under the direction of that body. In attempting to place a governmental mantle over the Red Cross it would seem that the IRU was ill-conceived.

The Convention did not provide for termination of the IRU, although provision was made for notification by members of their intention to withdraw. The Convention could not enter into force until at least two thirds of an Initial Fund had been subscribed. Thereafter, the IRU's financial resources, in addition to the Initial Fund, were to consist of voluntary donations from governments and private sources.

The first meeting of the IRU General Council was held in 1933. It was attended by delegates of 24 States as well as delegates of the Red Cross, the Sovereign Order of Malta, the International Institute of Agriculture and the International Labour Organisation. Senator Ciraolo became the first President of the Executive Committee and remained the mainspring of the Union.

From the outset, the meagreness of the funding system of the IRU was apparent. Initial contributions amounted to slightly over Swiss Francs 452,000 and this sum was practically the sole resource ever possessed by the Union. Lacking financial means, it was prevented from giving immediate relief upon the first occurrence of disasters and its means of action were more symbolical than real. Its work was in practice confined to scientific studies. By World War II the IRU had outlived its useful existence.

The internal legal texts of the IRU, in the form of its Statutes, the rules of procedure of the Executive Committee and an agreement with the Red Cross, brought numerous States and interests into an association for the practice of international humanitarian assistance. The 1927 Convention, on the other hand, did not expressly formulate the right of relief. States in effect reserved their freedom of action and the terms of the Convention and Statute provided ample grounds for hesitation, inaction or veto. The spirit of mutual assistance motivating the conclusion of the Convention was inadequately reflected both in the provisions adopted and in the financial resources made available for the IRU's operational activities. Nevertheless, the creation of an organization intended to bring relief to the victims of natural disasters had become a matter of inter-governmental concern.

The 1927 Diplomatic Conference and the creation of the IRU took place in an atmosphere of excitement based on the belief that a major step was being taken towards the realization of the humanitarian objectives of Arts. 23 and 25 of the Covenant of the League of Nations. International solidarity, based on collaboration and mutual assistance in all fields, was a key word of the times. The aim of promoting friendly international relations was pursued with enthusiastic optimism. However, the hopes raised by the Convention were excessive. When the Convention entered into force, over five years after its signature, the general economic depression foreshadowing a retreat into isolationism, nationalism, rearmament and war would seem to have doomed the original intentions of the Union's promoters.

After five years of very circumscribed activity the relationship between the IRU and the Red Cross had still not been settled and the Covenant of the League of Nations was itself all but dead.

The Convention Establishing an International Relief Union was an anticipatory legal expression of international humanitarian concerns; the IRU itself was a premature institutionalization of the desire to take action for the benefit of the victims of disasters. Perhaps the IRU's principal weakness was to have pretended too soon to universality. Thus, the IRU's activities are of significance not for their achievements in the field, but rather as evidence of the early recognition by States of the need for collaboration in matters of humanitarian assistance through international organization, on the foundations of international law.

2. Relief Actions in Armed Conflict: The Red Cross

2.1 The Geneva Conventions and the Red Cross

The original relief activities of the Red Cross were conceived and developed in armed conflict situations. In such situations the Red Cross possesses a legally defined status and traditional functions established both by legal instruments and by practice. Apart from the role of National Red Cross and Red Crescent Societies alongside the medical services of armed forces, the best known relief work of the movement in conflict situations is that performed by the International Committee of the Red Cross (ICRC) in the distribution of material supplies for prisoners of war and for civilian victims. Much of this work is carried out under the terms of the Geneva Conventions and Additional Protocols.

The 1949 Geneva Conventions deal with protection and assistance for victims of conflict, including members of armed forces (Conventions I and II); prisoners of war (Convention III); and Civilians (Convention IV).[1] The achievement of the Diplomatic Conference which brought into being the four Geneva Conventions was based largely on the experience of World War II. The earlier Geneva Conventions were expanded and strengthened and many new provisions were added.

The 1977 Diplomatic Conference on the Reaffirmation and Development of International Humanitarian Law Applicable in Armed Conflicts brought into being two Protocols, Additional to the Geneva Conventions of 1949.[2] Protocol I relates to the protection of victims of international armed conflict, and Protocol II to non-international conflicts. The provisions of the Additional Protocols supplement but do not replace those of the Conventions.

Art. 45 of the First Geneva Convention of 1949 refers to the principles of the Convention as a basis for its implementation, stating: "Each Party to the conflict... shall ensure the detailed execution of the preceding Articles, and provide for unforeseen cases, in conformity with the general principles of the present Convention". It is usually agreed that the general principle underlying all the Geneva Conventions is that persons *hors de combat* and those not participating directly in hostilities shall be respected, protected and treated humanely. "Protection" in the broad sense means defending and supporting the persons concerned under each of the four Conventions;

it takes on a specific meaning according to the beneficiaries or victims involved in a particular situation.

The 1949 Conventions contain a number of articles common to each of the four instruments. Common Art. 2 defines the main field of application of the Conventions, extending to all cases of armed conflict between two or more parties. The Conventions also apply in cases of partial or total occupation of the territory of a party, even if there is no armed resistance. The purposes, intensity or duration of a conflict do not constitute criteria for determining the applicability of the Conventions. However, in Additional Protocol I the concept of international armed conflict was widened to include the struggles of peoples against colonial domination, alien occupation and racist régimes in the exercise of their right of self-determination.

Certain basic or minimum provisions applicable in non-international conflicts are incorporated in Common Art. 3; the extent and limitations of these provisions are examined separately below.

Other common provisions relate to the non-renunciation of rights contained in the Conventions, and to sanctions for certain grave breaches. Moreover, Common Art. 9-9-9-10 states that the provisions of the Conventions constitute no obstacle to the humanitarian activities of the ICRC or any other impartial humanitarian organization. The conduct of operations under this article requires the consent of the parties concerned. The value of this provision lies in the fact that an additional channel is left open for the attainment of the humanitarian objectives of the Conventions. In view of the more complete provisions for protection of and assistance to the wounded in battle, the potential of this article as a basis for humanitarian activities is found particularly under the fields of the Third and Fourth Conventions, with respect to prisoners of war and civilians respectively.

The Geneva Conventions and Additional Protocol I also contain a common provision known as the Martens' Clause, which is found in a variety of forms in a number of other humanitarian instruments as well as in the preamble to the 1969 Vienna Convention on the Law of Treaties. As adopted in Art. 1(2) of Protocol I, the Martens' Clause states:

> In cases not covered by this Protocol or by other international agreements, civilians and combatants remain under the protection and authority of the principles of international law derived from established custom, from the principles of humanity and from the dictates of public conscience.

This formula stresses the importance and binding force of the general principles of international law in the humanitarian sphere, and it prevents the assumption that what is not forbidden by the instrument in question must be allowed. The Martens' Clause was first employed in the second Hague Convention of 1899 dealing with the laws and customs of land warfare, where the intention was that it should be applied until a more complete humanitarian code had been drawn up. The frequent reiteration of the Clause suggests that it must be taken into account when considering the sources of international law, despite uncertainty whether its significance extends beyond the law of armed conflict.[3]

The 1949 Conventions contain comprehensive references to the status and role of both the International Committee of the Red Cross and National Societies. The protective emblem of the Geneva Conventions is the red cross or red crescent on a white background. These signs are also the distinctive and indicatory emblems of the Red Cross movement and their use is regulated by Arts. 38 to 44 of the First Convention of 1949. In their use by the movement the emblems are intended to be international, neutral and without any religious significance. Their adoption as the protective signs of the Conventions is a natural confirmation of the role of the movement in assisting and protecting the wounded.

The provisions of the Geneva Conventions and Additional Protocols relating to assistance are examined in detail below, but those which concern most directly the rights and responsibilities of the Red Cross may be conveniently summarized at this point. The most basic provision, contained in Art. 26 of the First Convention, links the personnel of National Red Cross or Red Crescent Societies with recognized medical teams, enabling them to assist the wounded. This was always the fundamental task of the movement. Other duly recognized and authorized voluntary aid societies are also given the same status.

The International Committee of the Red Cross is competent to undertake international assistance through the provision of relief supplies under the conditions and circumstances set out in the Conventions. In the Third Convention a legal basis for the shipment and distribution of relief supplies to prisoners of war is laid down, and the International Committee is given the necessary representational and organizational responsibilities to carry out its activities. In the Fourth Convention similar provisions are repeated in favour of civilian internees. The provisions concerning relief for civilian populations in general, under the Fourth Convention, were very weak. This weakness is now redressed to some extent by the terms of Additional Protocol I, which define the needs of the population on a basis similar to that for the population of occupied territories. Additional Protocol II has also underlined the role of National Red Cross Societies in non-international conflicts.

The traditional relief activities of the ICRC for the benefit of war victims are provided for out of the institution's ordinary operational budget, which amounts to well over Swiss francs 20 million annually. Much larger sums are available for specially financed operations. About half of the ratifying States of the Geneva Conventions and Protocols contribute financially to the ordinary account and a smaller number contribute to the special accounts on a regular or occasional basis. Additional receipts are derived from National Red Cross and Red Crescent Societies and private donations.[4]

The accumulated experience of the ICRC enables its traditional functions to be taken up quickly in time of need. The reports of the ICRC's activities on behalf of war victims in the International Review of the Red Cross and its Annual Reports demonstrate the world-wide scope of these activities and the apparently permanent necessity for them.

2.2 Assistance for Members of Armed Forces

Wounded, Sick and Shipwrecked

The provisions concerning protection of and assistance to the members of armed forces who are victims of conflict form the core of the Geneva Conventions and Additional Protocols.

The First Convention of 1949 incorporates provisions applicable to the wounded and sick members of armed forces in the field. The Second Convention extends the same provisions to the wounded, sick and shipwrecked members of armed forces at sea. As the wounded and sick are considered together in the Conventions, the references throughout this section to "the wounded" can be understood to include all the above categories.

Art. 12 of the First Convention provides the basis for humanitarian assistance in favour of the wounded, stating:

> Members of the armed forces and other persons mentioned in the following Article, who are wounded or sick, shall be respected and protected in all circumstances.
>
> They shall be treated humanely and cared for by the Party to the conflict in whose power they may be, without any adverse distinction founded on sex, race, nationality, religion, political opinions, or any other similar criteria.

The wide scope of Art. 12 is demonstrated by the use of the expression "in all circumstances". The Geneva Conventions do not define the term "wounded and sick" and even the condition of laying down arms is left implicit.[5] The general spirit of the Conventions was intended to prevail over the letter of any particular provision. However, Art. 8 of Additional Protocol I does provide new definitions, including the condition of refraining from any hostile act.

The detailed rules of protection which support the general principle of humanitarian assistance are found, *inter alia*, in Arts. 19, 24, 33 and 35 of the First Convention. These articles accord protection to fixed and mobile medical units, medical personnel, and their materials and transports. Art. 26 places the staff of National Red Cross Societies and of other duly recognized and authorized aid societies on the same footing as the medical personnel protected under Art. 24. The general terminology employed is "respect and protection".

Art. 18 gives further substance to the principle of assistance by providing that the military authorities may appeal to the charity of the inhabitants voluntarily to care for the wounded and sick. Under this paragraph, assistance is optional and remains under the control of the authorities, although with guarantees of protection and facilities. These guarantees, however, cannot be of the same order as those conferring protection on recognized medical establishments, personnel and materials. National relief societies may be included under the category of inhabitants.

The second paragraph of Art. 18 gives a clear right to the population and relief societies to provide humanitarian assistance, stating that:

> The military authorities shall permit the inhabitants and relief societies, even in invaded or occupied areas, spontaneously to collect and care for wounded or sick of whatever nationality.

This formula makes no direct reference to military supervision. In addition, the penultimate paragraph of Art. 18 prohibits penalties against those offering assistance, and the final paragraph makes it clear that the occupying power has a duty of care to the wounded which is not discharged by the spontaneous relief activities of the population alone.

In Additional Protocol I, Section I of Part II lays down general provisions of protection for the wounded, sick and shipwrecked. Art. 17 requires the civilian population to respect the wounded, even those of the adverse party, and enables the population and aid societies to collect and care for victims in need. It provides that no prosecution or punishment can attach to such humanitarian acts, and refers specifically to the role of National Red Cross Societies.

Non-international conflicts are dealt with only in Common Art. 3 of the Geneva Conventions, in which a number of minimum general provisions are laid down. The first part of Art. 3 extends to persons taking no active part in hostilities, and establishes the rule of humane treatment in all circumstances, without discrimination. This broad group of protected persons includes members of armed forces *hors de combat*, as well as innocent civilians. It was intended that the basic obligation of humane treatment be imposed in an absolute formula, independent of reciprocity of application between the parties.

A further paragraph in Art. 3 states that the wounded and sick shall be cared for, illustrating the greater emphasis throughout the Conventions on the situation of members of armed forces. The full expression "respected and protected" is not employed, reflecting the difficulty States found in reaching any agreement at all concerning non-international conflicts. No elaborations are made on behalf of any other group of victims, and Art. 3 does not expressly extend protection to medical or relief personnel or material.

Art. 3 contains no reference to supervision, but it does provide that an impartial humanitarian body may offer its services to the parties to a conflict. Thus, a legal basis was provided for at least the function of initiative of the Red Cross. In addition, the penultimate paragraph of Art. 3 states that the parties to a conflict should endeavour to bring into force, by means of special agreements, all or part of the other provisions of the Conventions.

Although Art. 3 is often rightly described as highly inadequate, it was considered to be a "bold step forward for human rights",[6] simply because it attempted for the first time to formulate minimum humanitarian rules applicable in internal struggles.

Additional Protocol II treats only a few especially important aspects of the protection of the wounded, sick and shipwrecked in non-international conflicts, although it attempts for the first time to define such conflicts and lays down the requirement of control of a part of a territory by dissident forces as a decisive criterion. In the Preamble and in Art. 1 the continuing importance of Common Art. 3 is confirmed.

In Part III of Protocol II the formula "respected and protected" is introduced. Art. 7 states:

> 1. All the wounded, sick and shipwrecked, whether or not they have taken part in the armed conflict, shall be respected and protected.
>
> 2. In all circumstances they shall be treated humanely....

Arts. 9 to 12 also extend protection to medical personnel, units and transports, as well as religious personnel.

Prisoners of War

Assistance to prisoners of war falls under the Third Convention of 1949. In Part II of the Convention, dealing with general protection, Art. 15 formulates the duty of detaining powers to provide maintenance and medical attention for prisoners. In Part III the conditions of captivity are comprehensively dealt with: separate articles cover quarters, food rations, clothing and medical care, constituting a detailed elaboration of the basic rule in Art. 15.

Section V of Part III, which concerns relations of prisoners of war with the exterior, contains two articles on relief shipments. Art. 72 formulates the right to receive relief supplies including individual parcels or collective shipments. Such shipments alone do not free the detaining power from the obligations imposed on it by the Convention. Without delaying relief supplies, the powers may make special arrangements on the conditions governing the sending of relief. Art. 73 provides that if no agreements are made the regulations in Annex III, containing nine articles on collective relief, shall apply. The same article also preserves the rights of the ICRC and other organizations giving assistance to prisoners under such special agreements.

Art. 125 of the Third Convention establishes a legal basis for the provision of relief supplies and the conduct of relief activities, and grants the necessary facilities to organizations involved in assistance. Part of Art. 125 states:

> Subject to the measures which the Detaining Powers may consider essential to ensure their security or to meet any other reasonable need, the representatives of ... relief societies ... shall receive from the said Powers, for themselves and their duly accredited agents, all necessary facilities for visiting the prisoners, distributing relief supplies and material from any source intended for religious, educational or recreative purposes...
>
> The special position of the International Committee of the Red Cross in this field shall be recognized and respected at all times.

Art. 126 goes on to lay down the right of the International Committee to visit places of detention and to interview prisoners, thereby giving the Red Cross a central role in the supervision of the Convention. The detailed and forceful terms of all the above provisions indicate that realistic account may be taken of both humane and military considerations. Relief for prisoners of war is thus a particularly distinct area within the ambit of international humanitarian law, and the subject is well documented by leading authors.[7]

2.3 Assistance for Civilians

The evolution of rules concerning protection of and assistance to civilians within the humanitarian law of armed conflict illustrates many of the problems faced by attempts to develop international relief law. The civilian population is frequently exposed in modern armed conflict to as much danger as combatants, if not more. Until 1949, civilians were not provided with effective protection from the consequences of war by legal instruments.[8] Nevertheless, international relief operations conducted on behalf of civilians during conflict or in its immediate aftermath, often on a large scale, were undertaken either without any specific legal basis or on the basis of particular agreements concluded at the time of need. In addition, many resolutions of the International Conferences of the Red Cross include references to the protection of civilian populations and to relief activities in conflicts. The provisions of some of these resolutions have been reaffirmed by resolutions of the United Nations General Assembly.[9]

As in the previous categories of assistance, the question of relief for civilians under the 1949 Geneva Conventions and the Additional Protocols of 1977 divides sharply between relief in international and relief in non-international armed conflict situations.

International Conflicts

The Fourth Convention of 1949 adopts two approaches to the protection of civilians in international conflicts, in its Parts II and III respectively. Part II is complete in itself and applies, by Art. 13, to the whole of the populations of the countries in conflict. In Part II, entitled "General Protection of Populations against Certain Consequences of War", military considerations are clearly evident in the provisions, which do not extend beyond what could be expected from the title. No general right of assistance is conferred in Part II, although Art. 14 makes reference to the good offices of the ICRC with respect to hospital and safety zones. However, Art. 23 allows for the free passage of two types of relief consignments: medical and hospital stores and religious objects for civilians; and essential food and clothing for maternity cases and for children under 15 years of age. Although Art. 23 makes some provision for relief, it is also a reminder of the legitimacy of the blockade as a method of warfare. The party allowing free passage of relief consignments under Art. 23 is entitled to be satisfied that the supplies may not be diverted from their intended destination, that controls are effective and that no definite military advantage may accrue to the enemy from the provision of relief.

The principal rules of the Fourth Convention are found in Part III which deals with the status and treatment of protected persons, as defined in Art. 4. The terms of Art. 4 create a narrower field of application than that laid down under Art. 13, as they extend to:

> ... those who, at a given moment and in any manner whatsoever, find themselves, in case of a conflict or occupation, in the hands of a Party to the conflict or an Occupying Power of which they are not nationals.

This definition, being phrased in the negative, also includes persons without nationality, although nationals of a neutral State in the territory of a belligerent and nationals of a co-belligerent State are expressly excluded.

In Part III of the Fourth Convention, Art. 27 provides that:

> Protected persons are entitled, in all circumstances, to respect for their persons, their honour, their family rights, their religious convictions and practices, and their manners and customs. They shall at all times be humanely treated....

Art. 30 goes on to confer on protected persons the right of application to the ICRC or National Red Cross Societies. This is basically a right of communication, but taken together with Art. 142 which describes the status and functions of relief organizations it assumes greater significance without, however, being supported by any enforcement mechanism.

Part III, Section II of the Fourth Convention relates to aliens in the territory of a party to the conflict. Art. 38(1) states that: "They shall be enabled to receive the individual or collective relief that may be sent to them." No mention is made of humanitarian organizations, but in practice relief under this clause would be channelled through a neutral agent. The reference to relief is to relief in kind, for Art. 39 goes on to provide that protected persons may receive allowances from their home country or from relief societies. Apart from the duty to allow the passage of certain relief which these articles demand of a party to the conflict, the terms of Art. 39 provide that the party shall ensure the support of protected persons, especially when they are prevented from taking employment.

Part III, Section III, relates to the population of occupied territory. The obligation of the occupying power with respect to supplies for the population is dealt with first. Part of Art. 55 provides that:

> To the fullest extent of the means available to it, the Occupying Power has the duty of ensuring the food and medical supplies of the population; it should, in particular, bring in the necessary foodstuffs, medical stores and other articles if the resources of the occupied territory are inadequate.

Art. 56 then goes on to provide for the maintenance of medical and public health services by the occupying power.

Arts. 59 to 63 in Part III, Section III relate specifically to relief actions. Art. 59 begins with the duty of the occupying power regarding relief, stating:

> If the whole or part of the population of an occupied territory is inadequately supplied the Occupying Power shall agree to relief schemes on behalf of the said population, and shall facilitate them by all the means at its disposal.

This article specifies more clearly the duty of the occupying power to bring in the necessary supplies, the method of which had been left open in Art. 55. The duty to agree to relief operations is laid down in unconditional terms, and the occupying power also undertakes to facilitate them.

Art. 59 continues:

> Such schemes, which may be undertaken either by States or by impartial humanitarian organizations such as the International Committee of the Red Cross, shall consist, in particular, of the provision of consignments of foodstuffs, medical supplies and clothing.

This paragraph mentions the nature of the relief and lays down the necessary qualifications of organizations undertaking relief work, without making any stipulations concerning the donors of the supplies. The ICRC is placed in the same position as States in the conduct of relief schemes. Contracting parties are obliged to permit the free passage of these consignments and to guarantee their protection.

The other articles in this group refer to the carriage and distribution of relief supplies, the role and protection of relief societies, including the Red Cross, and the right to receive individual relief consignments. Art. 60 recalls the duties of the occupying power under Arts. 55, 56 and 59 and provides that relief consignments from the exterior shall not relieve the occupying power of its responsibilities.

Part III, Section IV, comprises regulations for the treatment of civilian internees and contains a group of articles dealing with relief shipments. These articles follow the same pattern as those relating to relief supplies for prisoners of war. Part IV of the Fourth Convention also includes an article delineating the role of relief societies, the terms of which are almost identical to those employed in the Third Convention. Again, the special position of the ICRC is expressly recognized.

Although Part II of the Fourth Convention has a broader field of application than the detailed rules in Part III which have just been considered, its substantive provisions relating to relief for civilians, in particular those of Art. 23, are weak. This fact was recognized by the conferences which led up to the adoption of the Additional Protocols.

The principal developments introduced by Additional Protocol I are found in Section II of Part IV, which contains several articles dealing with relief in favour of the civilian population. Art. 69 of Protocol I widens the duties of the occupying power under Art. 55 of the Fourth Convention by including the provision of clothing, bedding and shelter and other supplies essential to the survival of the civilian population in occupied territories. The duty of relief is imposed on the occupying power "to the fullest extent of the means available to it and without any adverse distinction".

Art. 70 of Protocol I deals with territory under the control of a party to the conflict, other than occupied territory. It provides that impartial and humanitarian relief operations may be undertaken, with the consent of the parties concerned. However, once agreement is reached on assistance to be provided under Section II of Protocol I contracting parties are obliged to allow the free passage of relief consignments. Art. 71 provides that relief personnel participating with the approval of the parties in assistance activities shall be respected and protected. Contracting parties in receipt of relief consignments are to assist relief personnel in carrying out their mission, subject to the requirements of "imperative military necessity".

Non-international Conflicts

Common Art. 3 of the 1949 Geneva Conventions gives the ICRC the right of initiative. Although this right has provided scope for action in conflicts to which the other provisions of the Conventions do not apply, it is severely limited by the necessity for consent of the parties concerned: there is no express provision for relief actions. These defects were not fully rectified by the Additional Protocols.

Additional Protocol II begins with a short preamble which recalls the importance of Common Art. 3. Art. 1 goes on to confirm the continuing validity of Common Art. 3 in all non-international conflicts, including those covered by Protocol II. The function of initiative of the ICRC in offering its services to the parties to the conflict therefore also remains, even though not expressly confirmed.

Comprehensive draft articles prepared by the ICRC on relief for civilians in non-international conflicts were replaced at the Diplomatic Conferences by much simplified rules formulated in Part IV of Protocol II. Art. 13 deals with general protection of the civilian population and it provides that the civilian population shall not be the object of attacks. Art. 14 establishes without reservation the prohibition of starvation as a method of warfare, and its terms assume particular importance in the light of weaknesses in the remaining provisions concerning relief.

At the Diplomatic Conferences States strongly opposed any references to offers of relief, even emanating from neutral third parties, which might constitute an interference in their internal affairs. Only meagre provisions on relief are included in Art. 18(2), which states:

> If the civilian population is suffering undue hardship owing to a lack of supplies essential for its survival, such as foodstuffs and medical supplies, relief actions for the civilian population which are of an exclusively humanitarian and impartial nature and which are conducted without any adverse distinction shall be undertaken subject to the consent of the High Contracting Party concerned.

The reference to consent in Art. 18(2) is restrictive. However, failure to provide relief may constitute a violation of the prohibition of starvation of civilians laid down in Art. 14.

Notwithstanding mitigating features, a Red Cross commentator has stated that "this drastic formula is regrettable and it is hoped that it will never give rise to restrictive interpretations which would limit relief actions for the benefit of innocent victims".[10] It is clear that the terms of Additional Protocol II fell short of some expectations, but the adoption of any instrument of humanitarian law dealing exclusively with non-international conflicts must be seen in context with the importance of the field and its relatively unregulated state.

The Red Cross has borne much of the practical difficulty of ensuring the application of humanitarian principles and the provision of relief in non-international conflicts and in internal disorders. Some of its first assistance activities were conducted during insurrections, and the International Committee was active in this area long before the incorporation of Common Art. 3 in the 1949 Conventions. The Red Cross is extremely experienced in operating, often on a large scale, without specific legal authority. Since World War II many relief actions in this category have been undertaken with the agreement of the parties. In some situations the Red Cross has not been able to act, when the necessary consent of the parties concerned has been unforthcoming.

The sufferings and dislocation caused by war extend far beyond the cessation of hostilities. The Red Cross has become increasingly involved with the wider effects of conflict, including with refugee situations. The recent period is marked by the phase of adjustment to the recurrence of non-international conflict situations of various types and there is a trend towards larger and more frequent relief operations.

The special relief operations mounted by the ICRC rely on contributions in cash, kind or services from all possible sources. The ICRC may act as a coordinator and intermediary between donors and beneficiaries, or it may conduct its own field operations. The most important relief needs are usually medical equipment and personnel. Special operations may also involve the provision of emergency food aid, for example from the European Economic Community or the Swiss government. Emergency appeals launched by the ICRC can bring in several times its ordinary annual revenue. However, successful operations in the aftermath of large scale conflicts usually require financial support at a governmental level, as well as a high degree of international cooperation.

2.4 Evaluation

The Geneva Conventions and Additional Protocols constitute a highly evolved body of law relevant to humanitarian assistance, the original core of which was designed to operate in favour of members of armed forces in action. Developments which have taken place since 1864 have extended the provisions relating to assistance to a variety of situations and categories of victims, now including the sick and wounded in war, prisoners of war and civilians in occupied territories. Although important provisions have continued to be added to the law, the politicization of the humanitarian movement to reaffirm and develop the law of armed conflict was reflected in the substantive content of the Additional Protocols and it seems likely to continue in the period of acceptance and application of the new instruments. Nevertheless, and despite its complexity, Protocol I at least is generally conceded to have obtained a degree of success in extending the humanitarian element within the legal rules relating to armed conflict.

The regulation of armed conflict by law effects a balance between military necessity and humanitarian considerations. This has been seen as the dilemma of the laws of war: how an inhumane activity may be regulated by humanitarian principles. It has been stated that the Geneva Conventions may suffer from the inherent weakness of being "trampled underfoot on the pretext that necessity knows no law".[11] There is no denying that a major defect in the humanitarian law of armed conflict lies in the weakness of the monitoring system devised for its implementation. However, the positive factor for the observance of international humanitarian law, as the outcome of the interests of the contracting parties, is the enlightened self-interest of those parties, founded on the desire both for constructive reciprocal treatment and for the avoidance of destructive reciprocity. Military and political considerations which point in the opposite direction are based on fears, particularly concerning the prolongation of conflict by conferring any measure of help on the opponent.

An important obstacle to effective humanitarian assistance in all situations is not a matter of legal terminological interpretation alone, but rather is the reluctance of States to give effect to broad humanitarian principles to which they have subscribed. It remains the case that, with the main exception of long-standing and well-defined categories of assistance to the wounded and prisoners of war, the consent of the parties is a prerequisite for humanitarian action.

In this regard the practical experience of the Red Cross is of central importance. However, even the International Committee of the Red Cross cannot be assured of success in cases at the periphery of the Geneva Conventions and Additional Protocols, or outside their terms. Although the efforts of the ICRC to bring non-international armed conflict under the ambit of international humanitarian law have been continuous, and since 1949 the Committee's presence in such situations has been a common phenomenon, this role is not easy to maintain in guerilla, counter-insurgency and national liberation struggles. In particular, one or both parties are likely to perceive serious military or political objections to humanitarian assistance. Thus, it seems probable that the environment within which such relief operations are carried out will not improve in the near future.

Problems caused by revolutionary movements and by the adoption of guerilla tactics in conflict are not exclusive to the 20th century. However, formidable obstacles persist in the extension of even minimum humanitarian provisions to situations which many States regard as falling wholly within their domestic jurisdiction.

The developments introduced by Additional Protocol II resulted in little notable progress in the area of humanitarian assistance. States are extremely reluctant to bind themselves in regard to humanitarian matters in conflict situations, particularly *vis à vis* an unspecified adversary within their own territory. Despite the modifications to Additional Protocol II before its signature that instrument clearly may not receive such wide ratification as Protocol I. In turn, non-universal or non-uniform ratification patterns may have more general detrimental effects. The integrity of the law and the standard of protection to individual war victims suffer when relatively short-term political objectives are pursued in the humanitarian sphere.

Although the Geneva Conventions and Additional Protocols continue to retain their practical importance, the protection accorded to civilians in armed conflict diverges greatly from that accorded to military personnel and prisoners of war. This imbalance is accentuated by the great increase in the proportion of civilian victims of conflict. The practice of aerial bombardment raised an early threat to the effectiveness of humanitarian law, and the regulation of this area of warfare has remained an unsolved problem. The indiscriminate nature of the many modern weapons of mass destruction raises questions of the relevance of any humanitarian provisions. However, although legal instruments alone cannot create certainty that humanitarian principles and practices will be observed, the realization that the avoidance of useless suffering and destruction is not contrary to the interests of the parties has provided a powerful motivation for the adoption and continuing adaptation of a body of detailed humanitarian and legal rules applicable in armed conflict situations.

Questions of humanitarian assistance in armed conflict situations fall within a division of traditional international law. Many situations arise where there is a need for humanitarian action, and where humanitarian action is undertaken, outside the scope of legal instruments providing for assistance, and outside the context of armed conflict. The frequently expressed opinion that every disaster is unique may give rise to doubts concerning the attempt to develop standard solutions for problems of all relief operations in war and peace; but although it warns that stereotyped responses may not be appropriate it does not imply that there can be no common approach in the search for improved principles of action.

Post-impact problems of relief management such as evacuation, emergency feeding, temporary shelter and disease control exist in a similar manner in both armed conflict and other disaster situations. One writer concluded from the experience of a "mixed" disaster situation that "implementation of relief operations during conflict may not differ significantly from that during peacetime".[12] Thus, it seems necessary and possible to adopt a more closely comparative approach to legal problems raised by humanitarian relief operations in conflict and peace. One authority on the humanitarian law of armed conflict found that important problems to be faced by the Diplomatic Conferences on the Reaffirmation and Development of Humanitarian Law included preparatory measures for relief actions; arrangements for contributions; the right to initiate or undertake relief actions; the obligation to accept relief actions; the obligation to grant free passage of relief consignments; and the status of institutions and personnel carrying out relief tasks.[13] All these problems also arise in connection with international relief in cases of natural disaster or other humanitarian emergencies. Such an analysis therefore gives support to an examination of the scope for the development and consolidation of international relief law in all cases where humanitarian assistance is required.

3. Relief for Refugees: The United Nations

3.1 The Immediate Post-World-War-II Period

Various bodies were created in different parts of the world by the Western Allies in order to deal with the refugee problems which, by the end of World War II, included at least an estimated 21 million displaced persons in Europe alone. Many of these persons could not or did not wish to return to their original homes. It was obvious that the extent of the immediate requirements was such that only concerted international efforts could be successful in achieving the necessary solutions.

Plans to establish an international organization with responsibility to carry out social, economic and humanitarian functions on behalf of those in greatest need led to the creation of the United Nations Relief and Rehabilitation Administration (UNRRA) by 44 nations on November 9, 1943. UNRRA, as described in chapter 1,[1] was established as a specialized agency, but before the adoption of the United Nations Charter and the creation of the UN itself. UNRRA was the first major operating agency for refugees and displaced persons in liberated Europe, exercising responsibility for the provision of material assistance to refugees and displaced persons both in Europe and in its other areas of operation, with the participation of over 60 voluntary organizations. In addition, two bodies surviving from the pre-war period also continued to possess limited responsibilities in the early post-war period. The Inter-Governmental Committee on Refugees carried out some relief functions, and the League of Nations High Commissioner undertook certain protection services.

When the League of Nations was dissolved in 1946 the Inter-Governmental Committee assumed independent responsibilities for a period of six months. The imminent closure of UNRRA lent urgency to the creation of a new organization to deal exclusively with refugees.[2] The solution took the form of the International Refugee Organization (IRO), which was established by a UN General Assembly resolution as a non-permanent body charged with responsibility for all aspects of the problems concerning the uprooted people.[3] The Preparatory Committee of the IRO began operations on July 1, 1947, and performed its functions until August 20, 1948 when the conditions for the entry into force of the IRO's Constitution were fulfilled.

The IRO was supported by about a third of the total UN membership of some

50 States. The preamble to its Constitution recognized that the problems of refugees and displaced persons were urgent and international in character. The IRO's mandate was cast very broadly, refugees being defined as those outside their former country of residence, whether or not they retained their nationality. Displaced persons were also included within the mandate and were defined separately. This created at the time a wide and narrow conception of displaced persons, the former taken in a general sense as all those outside their native country, the latter those supported by the IRO. In addition, an innovation in the definition of refugees was the introduction of the notion of well-founded fear of persecution, which brought to the determination of refugee status a partly subjective element.

The main objective of the IRO was the voluntary repatriation or resettlement of refugees and displaced persons, but it was clearly recognized, both in the Constitution's preamble and in Art. 2(1) (a), that maintenance and assistance would also be necessary. The IRO was given full powers for its tasks of material relief. The IRO was thus distinct from other specialized agencies, being charged with a definite operational task. Initially, expenses for immediate maintenance comprised over half the total budget and they remained a substantial proportion of the financial burden on member States, amounting to over $147 million or over 35 per cent of total operational costs.

At the first session of the UN General Assembly more discussion was devoted to the refugee question than to any other issue except international security. The main problem was seen as that of resettlement. In such a climate it was recognized that the burden of care for residual refugees and new refugees would have to be carried by the country of first asylum. It was generally agreed that the primary function of a successor organization to the IRO should be only to provide international protection. Nevertheless, the question of responsibility for material assistance was debated during 1949 and 1950 at the insistence of potential countries of first refuge. The main issue in the debates was simply whether a new High Commissioner should be given any authority whatsoever to handle funds for purposes of assistance, and only extremely limited provisions were eventually adopted.

Drafts of the Statute of the Office of the UN High Commissioner for Refugees were debated in the early sessions of the General Assembly and Economic and Social Council, as were drafts of a new Convention relating to the status of refugees. The decision to establish UNHCR on January 1, 1951 was taken by the Assembly in December 1949, and the proposals show that the life of the new body was not expected to extend beyond the end of 1953. The IRO's operations ceased on March 1, 1952. The winding up period was clearly unsatisfactory and left behind several hundred thousand members of core or residual groups, an unwelcome burden to UN member States. These persons were transferred to the responsibility of the countries of residence and local bodies.

3.2 The UNHCR Statute and the 1951 Convention

The Statute of the Office of the UN High Commissioner for Refugees and the 1951 Convention Relating to the Status of Refugees, with its Protocol, are the principal global international instruments relating to refugees.[4] The Statute is annexed to General Assembly Res. 428(V) of 1950, which is the constitutive instrument of the Office and also called upon governments to cooperate with the High Commissioner in the exercise of his functions. The Office is a subsidiary UN organ established under Art. 22 of the Charter. The High Commissioner is responsible to the General Assembly, through the Economic and Social Council. The continuation of the Office is maintained by quinquennial General Assembly resolutions.

The Statute created a general and universally applicable definition of a refugee and declared that UNHCR's work is humanitarian, social and of an entirely non-political character. The 1951 Convention lays down basic minimum standards for the treatment of refugees, without prejudice to the granting by States of more favourable measures; reservations were not permitted to certain of the most important provisions, including the definition of refugees in Art. 1 and the prohibition of *refoulement*. Art. 35 of the Convention provides for States to cooperate with the Office of the High Commissioner, complementing Para. 8(a) of the Statute, which gives the High Commissioner the role of supervising the application of international conventions for the protection of refugees. Para. 8 of the Statute also charged the High Commissioner with the task of promoting international instruments for the protection of refugees.

After the emergence of new refugee problems had demonstrated the need to extend the provisions of the 1951 Convention, the Protocol Relating to the Status of Refugees was drawn up, and was signed in 1967 by the President of the UN General Assembly and the Secretary-General and transmitted to governments to enable them to accede. The Protocol stands as an independent instrument for States not parties to the Convention. Apart from these instruments, there are other instruments of international refugee law relating to specific categories of refugees or specific matters, such as refugee seamen, which are not directly relevant to questions of international humanitarian assistance.

Under the Statute, UNHCR's competence extends to three categories of persons. The first comprises those who were considered refugees under arrangements and conventions of the League of Nations or the Constitution of the IRO. The second category consists of those who became refugees as a result of events occurring before January 1, 1951 and, except for the date limitation, is defined in terms almost identical to those establishing the third category, which comprises, in the words of Para. 6 B:

> Any other person who is outside the country of his nationality, or if he has no nationality, the country of his former habitual residence, because he has or had well-founded fear of persecution by reason of his race, religion, nationality or political opinion and is unable or, because of such fear, is unwilling to avail himself of the protection of the government of the country of his nationality, or, if he has no nationality, to return to the country of his former habitual residence.

The principal element of the definition is "well-founded fear of persecution", containing both an objective and a subjective component. Two further important elements are the requirements to be outside the country of nationality or former habitual residence and to be unable or unwilling to return.

The definition in the Statute preceded the definition in the 1951 Convention by some seven months. The Convention definition was essentially the same as that quoted above, but subject to two limitations: it covered only those who were refugees as a result of events occurring before January 1, 1951; and governments had discretion to apply it to those who were refugees owing to events in Europe, or owing to events in Europe or elsewhere. Initially, therefore, the definition of refugees in the Statute was the most inclusive, extending the competence of the High Commissioner to future refugees. It provided the widest and most universal definition of a refugee in international law. However, the 1967 Protocol removed the dateline in the Convention, although States' declarations on the geographical limitation were left unaltered.

In contrast to the detailed provisions of the Convention, the Statute contains no explicit reference to the protection of refugees as individuals. Indeed, Para. 2 of the Statute states that UNHCR's work "shall relate as a rule, to groups and categories of refugees". Practice shows that this does not amount to a restriction of actions in favour of any particular refugee. Both in considering the eligibility of refugees and in carrying out functions of protection, UNHCR is bound to become involved in individual considerations and in the provision of services to individuals. This clause reflected the belief that it would be easier to extend a mandate to groups. However, it also demonstrates that UNHCR was not intended to become another organization directly responsible for the individual needs of refugees.

3.3 Office of the UN High Commissioner for Refugees

Basis of Assistance Activities

The General Assembly resolution which undertook to establish UNHCR made it clear that international protection would be the main function of the High Commissioner after the closure of the IRO.[5] Para. 1 of the Statute states that the functions of the High Commissioner are to provide international protection to refugees within his competence and to seek permanent solutions to the problem of refugees, and Para. 8 sets out the High Commissioner's responsibilities in greater detail. The ultimate objective of protection is the acquisition of nationality. The function of seeking permanent solutions was delimited to the areas of repatriation and assimilation in new national communities. UNHCR was charged to ensure that repatriation is voluntary and to facilitate it in conjunction with governments and private organizations. Assimilation comprises local integration in the country of first reception or resettlement elsewhere.

No explicit enabling provisions for UNHCR's material assistance functions can be found in Para. 8 of the Statute or in the 1951 Convention; neither has the question of humanitarian assistance been covered by subsequent conventions dealing with refugees. The failure to grant to UNHCR responsibilities such as were provided for under the IRO Constitution reflected both States' weariness with the vast scale of the relief tasks of the predecessor organizations and the fervent hope that the need for exceptional, urgent or temporary relief measures was past.

The first UN High Commissioner stated that "UN members were led to believe that what the IRO left unfinished was mainly a problem of 'protection'... This was a tragic mistake".[6] The previous organizations had been constituted to work largely in the field, but in UNHCR's Statute the General Assembly avoided conferring any such role and severely restricted the scope of the High Commissioner to provide financial assistance.

Although it was widely understood that UNHCR's task was not to be operational, certain indications concerning functions of material assistance may be found, by interpretation, in the Statute. The achievement of the general objective of finding permanent solutions, expressed in Para. 1, can been to involve at least an element or phase of relief assistance. Assimilation or repatriation are often likely to require the provision of basic maintenance. The Statute recognized that permanent solutions could only be achieved through the coordinated efforts of nations, which could include international relief. In Para. 8 the specific task of coordinating the efforts of private organizations in the field of welfare, subsumed within UNHCR's protection functions, is mentioned along with the general task of establishing and maintaining international contacts. These tasks may assume a particular significance relating to relief in slowly developing or prolonged refugee situations where meeting the basic needs of refugees requires joint action by several organizations.

The preamble to the Convention also noted that the grant of asylum may place undue burdens on particular countries. By reiterating the international character of the problems, it recognized that international cooperation formed part of the solution. The preamble also acknowledges the humanitarian nature of the problem of refugees, leaving room for a potential link between internationally conducted assistance operations and the basic needs of refugees.

Concerning financial provisions, Para. 20 of the Statute stated that only administrative expenditure of the Office would be borne on the UN budget; all other expenditure was limited to financing by voluntary contributions. Para. 10 of the Statute authorized the High Commissioner to administer funds which he might receive from public or private sources, but specified that he could make neither appeals to governments nor general appeals. Para. 9 of the Statute enabled UNHCR to engage in any additional activities determined by the General Assembly. The effect of these paragraphs initially was to make it difficult for UNHCR to raise funds, but possible to disburse any sums received. Taken together with the other limitations of competence they left room for only minimal activities of assistance. Further developments thus depended largely on the response of States within the General Assembly.

Early Development of Assistance

An estimated 2 million refugees came under the competence of UNHCR in 1951, including 100,000 in camps in Europe and several hundred thousand elsewhere who were in urgent need of material assistance. In addition, there was a continuing flow of new destitute refugees from East Europe. From the beginning, the question of humanitarian assistance was an immediate problem for UNHCR, even though legal protection was the primary intended function of the Office.

As a matter of urgency the High Commissioner put forward proposals for long term solutions which incorporated the basic aim of securing funds for emergency humanitarian relief to meet the needs then arising throughout the world. Initially he asked only for approval to launch an appeal for voluntary contributions, which was granted by the General Assembly in February 1952 in a resolution which referred to the purpose of "enabling emergency aid to be given to the most needy groups among refugees within his mandate".[7]

In 1954 a new UN Refugee Emergency Fund (UNREF) was created by a resolution of the General Assembly which recognized that certain countries were facing particularly heavy burdens as an accidental result of their geographical situation and stated that "some complementary aid" had been shown to be necessary to accelerate the implementation of a programme of permanent solutions.[8]

Programme activities under UNREF, later known simply as the UN Refugee Fund, began in June 1955; they included a provision permitting emergency assistance for those in greatest need. A division of responsibilities for planning and implementation between UNHCR and voluntary agencies, respectively, was maintained initially. The UNREF programme was to be financed by an appeal to governments and in practice was beset by constant financial uncertainties.

Soon after the creation of UNHCR an Advisory Committee had been set up to assist the High Commissioner. In 1955 the Advisory Committee was replaced by the UNREF Executive Committee which in turn was replaced by the Executive Committee of the Programme of UNHCR. The Executive Committee, appointed by the Economic and Social Council, remains the guiding body of the Office. An important element in these changes in the control of UNHCR's operations was the creation in 1957 of an Emergency Fund not to exceed $500,000, to be employed according to the directives of the Executive Committee.[9] Its creation opened a new field of activity to the High Commissioner, enabling operations to be conducted in favour of non-mandate refugees as well as mandate refugees, where the latter are not specifically referred to.[10]

These structural changes paved the way for deeper and more comprehensive extensions of UNHCR's competence for material assistance functions. Developments during the late 1950s initiated a series of extensions of competence *ratione personae* which has continued until present times. The dual approach in the progressive widening of UNHCR's mandate, in the form of greater capacity for humanitarian assistance and expanded categories of persons eligible for protection, emerged from the fundamental responsibility to seek solutions to the refugee problem. Considered below in broadly chronological order, these developments reflect UNHCR's efforts to respond to new field situations and to overcome initial statutory limitations.

'Good Offices' and Assistance

The use of the "good offices" concept in a series of General Assembly resolutions provided an important means enabling UNHCR to expand its assistance activities. These resolutions authorized the High Commissioner to use his good offices to work out programmes of assistance to refugees, both for those within his mandate and for those whose mandate status was undetermined. In addition, the High Commissioner was enabled to accept and administer contributions for assistance to refugees benefitting from his good offices and to appeal for funds to assist them.

In the situation involving refugees from Hungary in 1956 the General Assembly requested the Secretary-General to call on the High Commissioner "to consult with other appropriate international agencies and interested governments with a view to making speedy and effective arrangements for emergency assistance".[11] Later resolutions requested the continuation of such work in that particular event.

In 1957 another extension was made in the case of Chinese refugees in Hong Kong, when the High Commissioner was authorized to use his good offices to encourage arrangements for contributions.[12]

The opening of a more general extension appeared in 1958 to 1959 during UNHCR's first activities in Africa. Previously, refugees could only be considered as such outside their country of origin: UNHCR activities on their behalf within that original country were precluded. Algerian refugees in Morocco and Tunisia were already benefiting from asylum and a relief programme with the object of their repatriation and rehabiliation was established on the basis of General Assembly resolutions which authorized the High Commissioner to use his good offices.[13] Later resolutions mentioned expressly "refugees who do not come within the competence of the United Nations", for whom the High Commissioner was enabled to use his good offices to transmit contributions.[14] In 1961 this extension was consolidated when UNHCR was requested to consider assisting with the resettlement of the refugees in their homeland.[15]

A generalized recognition of UNHCR's responsibilities occurred when the High Commissioner was requested by General Assembly Res. 1673(XVI) 1961 to continue "to pursue his activities on behalf of the refugees within his mandate, or those for whom he extends his good offices". The effect of these provisions was to authorize the High Commissioner to use his good offices on behalf of any person considered to be a refugee who was not a mandate refugee or within the competence of any other UN organ, i.e. especially the UN Relief and Works Agency for Palestine Refugees in the Near East.

The definition of refugee in this sense appears to have a very wide scope. The purpose of the last-mentioned resolution was to extend the good offices procedure to refugees who in fact constituted a problem of material assistance rather than legal protection. This was the case in practice with the majority of the new groups of refugees with whom UNHCR was being called upon to deal. The achievement of the good offices resolutions was described by a past High Commissioner essentially as enabling effective large scale operations to be conducted, centered entirely on the provision of material assistance.[16]

In the 1960s, growing refugee problems in Africa, where UNHCR's tasks related to an increasingly wide range of uprooted people, highlighted the need for a corresponding increase in field activities. The new problems also led to changes in the attitude of various States towards the material contributions which UNHCR might provide. In Sudan, alongside the problem of repatriation of refugees in neighbouring countries, there was the additional question of those who had fled to the interior of the country and were equally in need of assistance in returning to their homes; approval was given by the General Assembly for relief measures on behalf of both refugees and other displaced persons.[17]

A subsequent affirmation of the humanitarian character of the High Commissioner's activities for the benefit of both refugees and displaced persons appeared to generalize this extension. A series of resolutions established a new authority for UNHCR in respect of displaced persons, and reinforced the established practice of the Office in assistance activities.[18] These authorizations of the General Assembly expanded the functions of UNHCR and enabled the services of the High Commissioner's Office to be extended to persons originally excluded by the Statute as well as to displaced persons whose situation is analogous to that of refugees. The concept of good offices provided the original foundation for these developments and, although more specific terminology has since been employed, it may still be regarded as "a useful institution for contingencies on the fringe of the normal activities of the High Commissioner".[19]

With the extension of relief to displaced persons, assistance activities underwent a further expansion. Large scale operations were carried out, particularly in Africa and in South Asia. General Assembly resolutions in connection with decolonization have also included reference to material assistance to refugees and to assistance for repatriation following independence. In these situations UNHCR has responded with programmes beyond the normal annual budget of the Office, through the establishment of special funds.

In 1972 provision was made to maintain the reserves of the Emergency Fund, established in 1957, by replenishment from the UN Working Capital Fund. Up to $1 million annually was authorized for allocation in emergency situations. In 1974 this sum was increased up to $2 million, with a limit of $500,000 for any one emergency. The present limits are $10 million and $4 million respectively.[20] The Fund enables the High Commissioner to respond to urgent new situations arising between the annual sessions of the Executive Committee. All assistance operations undertaken within the High Commissioner's annual programme continue to depend on review and approval by the Executive Committee, which was enlarged again in 1978 and now comprises 41 members.

More recent General Assembly resolutions have requested the High Commissioner to continue his activities to alleviate the sufferings of all those of concern to his Office.

The competence of the Office to deal with "problems of refugees and displaced persons wherever they occur" has been confirmed so far as assistance is concerned.[21] The term "displaced person" in this sense would appear also to include persons displaced within their own country.

Coordination of Assistance

The foundations both for cooperation between UNHCR and governments and for the coordination by UNHCR of the efforts of private organizations were laid down in Para. 8 of the Statute. The non-operational function of budgetary coordination and overall financial planning was an important early step in the development of UNHCR's assistance capability. Subsequent practice reveals an expanded role of coordination in regard to relief operations, including as a focal point for United Nations activities in disasters. This role which demonstrates UNHCR's extended competence *ratione functionis* deserves further study, especially in view of the problems of coordination which arise in disaster relief operations generally.

The first substantial delegation to UNHCR of coordinating responsibility was conferred in very loose terms by a resolution of the General Assembly Emergency Session which considered the question of Hungary in 1956.[22] In that situation UNHCR acted to coordinate the overall operations in Austria resulting from the decisions of the United Nations, in cooperation with the Austrian government. The League of Red Cross Societies coordinated the immediate relief tasks. Later, in the situation involving Algerian refugees, UNHCR and the League conducted full joint operations.

The conflict which preceded the creation of the State of Bángladesh, in the aftermath of the severe cyclone and tidal wave in November 1970, led to a disaster of unprecedented scale. International assistance was urgently needed both for the relief of the disaster victims in East Pakistan and for the refugees in India, but the channels for its mobilization and distribution were not apparent. Since relief requirements for the refugees were far beyond the resources of the High Commissioner alone, the United Nations Secretary-General decided in April 1971 to designate UNHCR as the focal point for all UN assistance in favour of refugees from East Pakistan in India. A representative in Dacca was also appointed to ensure the effectiveness of relief for the population of East Pakistan. Both these initiatives were undertaken by the Secretary-General on an emergency basis, without the authority of specific UN resolutions; they created two organizationally separate relief operations.[23]

An estimated ten million people were destitute in camps in West Bengal. The functions of UNHCR as "focal point" included the securing of international support, the procurement and delivery of funds and relief supplies, and liaison with the authorities and agencies involved. Funds were made available by the focal point either directly to the government of India or through UN programmes and specialized agencies.

UNHCR's role of coordination, together with the manner of its designation, was endorsed by the UN after the operation had begun. In 1972 a new resolution established this role by implication on a more general basis by requesting the High Commissioner "to continue to participate, at the invitation of the Secretary-General, in those humanitarian endeavours of the United Nations for which his Office has particular expertise and experience".[24] Under this resolution the Secretary-General subsequently entrusted UNHCR with the repatriation of the refugees, a task accomplished in 1973 and 1974 by airlifts in cooperation with the governments involved and the International Committee of the Red Cross.

In 1972 the Sudanese government made a request to the Secretary-General for international assistance for the South Sudan Region, and UNHCR was called upon to coordinate a programme of immediate relief for one year from July 1972.[25] The resulting relief activities included an airlift of essential supplies, measures in connection with health and agriculture, as well as civil engineering work.

UNHCR was also nominated by the Secretary-General in 1974 as coordinator of UN humanitarian assistance in Cyprus. A large relief programme was undertaken for the benefit of over 200,000 persons. Broad recognition of the role of coordination also led on to other developments in Asia, including special programmes in South East Asia, where joint emergency relief actions have been undertaken with UNICEF, the Red Cross and non governmental organizations.[26]

Present Scope of Assistance Activities

UNHCR assistance activities are divided broadly into General and Special Programmes. The former category comprises activities financed through the annual programme as well as the Emergency Fund, within overall budgets approved by the Executive Committee. Assistance within these groups is normally provided in the traditional areas of the High Commissioner's competence, to refugees outside their country of origin. Relief is provided to destitute refugees in their first country of asylum in the form of food, clothing, shelter and medical care. Special Programmes, on the other hand, comprise activities which are financed from trust funds constituted with particular purposes and conditions. These activities may benefit both refugees and displaced persons, including those displaced within, or returning to, their country of origin. Trust fund operations of a continuing nature for refugees within UNHCR's traditional competence are generally transferred as soon as possible to the General Programme.

Assistance activities are also classified by type according to their aims. The main categories cover local integration, resettlement, and voluntary repatriation. Within these categories there is provision for special groups such as the handicapped and for immediate relief in the form of subsistence or longer term maintenance as well as medical care. A wide range of other assistance measures may also be taken with a view to achieving permanent solutions. Supplementary aid is also available to cover food, clothing, accommodation and travel of destitute arrivals of refugees in transit on a temporary basis. Many millions of refugees and displaced persons benefit directly from UNHCR assistance. The emergency unit established in UNHCR in 1980 is responsible in particular for preparedness measures, while the geographical bureaux are concerned with the management of emergency operations. The recent official reports on UNHCR assistance activities illustrate the magnitude, complexity and constantly changing nature of refugee problems throughout the world.[27]

The continuing emergence of new refugee problems has required the High Commissioner to make international appeals for additional funds to carry out the tasks of the Office. For a number of years UNHCR's annual budget for assistance has stood at over $400 million. In many situations, priority has to be given to meeting the immediate needs of refugees and displaced persons. Relief assistance, particularly under Special Programmes, now represents a major component of overall assistance programmes and absorbs a large percentage of funds. Relief for refugees in conditions of temporary asylum, in particular when no durable solutions are in sight, is one of the most costly aspects of international assistance.

Although relief assistance is phased out as soon as durable solutions can be found, in cases where such solutions are not possible relief may have to be provided for many years. In instances where refugee influxes are so large that the entire caseload cannot be absorbed by traditional measures, large numbers of people may be left dependent on subsistence rations in camps. The conclusions of the Expert Group on Temporary Refuge in Situations of Large-Scale Influx which met in Geneva on April 21 to 24, 1981 laid down basic minimum conditions of treatment of assylum-seekers after admission, including that they should be provided with the essential necessities of life, especially food, shelter and sanitary and health facilities.[28]

A further related issue concerns the boundary between emergency humanitarian relief and development assistance, a borderline which is sometimes difficult to discern. Measures that could be considered as development assistance are often necessary in the early stages of a relief operation. Assistance provided during the emergency phase may include, for example, the creation or improvement of water supplies or other practical steps which may benefit the local population. In addition, promoting the self-sufficiency of refugees is often a desirable step on the way to achieving durable solutions, for which special assistance of a developmental character may be necessary. Special forms of inter-agency cooperation and sharing of responsibilities, including between governmental and non-governmental organizations, may thus be required in order to ensure appropriate and effective material and financial assistance in the emergency phase.[29]

3.4 UN Relief and Works Agency for Palestine Refugees

The refugees from Palestine who were left in urgent need of humanitarian assistance upon the establishment of Israel as a State, on May 14/15, 1948, continue with their descendants to receive international assistance under the aegis of the United Nations through the work of the United Nations Relief and Works Agency for Palestine Refugees in the Near East (UNRWA). The mandate of the international relief programme, laid down by the UN General Assembly late in 1948 with the hope of a speedy termination, has been repeatedly renewed up to the present time, when almost two million refugees are registered with UNRWA. The Agency still relies for its income and resources on voluntary contributions from governments, other UN bodies and other international and national organizations.

The relief requirements of the Palestine refugees were brought to the attention of the General Assembly by the UN Mediator on Palestine during 1948.[30] A temporary relief project under the control of a UN Director of Disaster Relief was able to provide valuable humanitarian services. The General Assembly authorized an advance of $5 million towards the creation of a voluntary fund to be used to provide immediate relief to 500,000 refugees over a nine-month period up to August 31, 1949. The position of the Director of United Nations Relief for Palestine Refugees (UNRPR), with responsibility for administering the fund, was created by General Assembly Res. 212 (III) 1948. Contributions were requested from all States, the UN specialized agencies, the Red Cross and non-governmental organizations.

It was soon recognized that continuing relief actions were necessary to prevent starvation and to further conditions of peace and stability in the region. UNRWA was created by General Assembly Res. 302 (IV) of December 8, 1949, to replace UNRPR, to carry out a direct relief and works programme and to prepare for the time when international assistance would no longer be available. Some $33 million were required for the programme, of which about two-thirds were to be allocated for direct relief during 1950.

The Director of UNRWA, responsible to the General Assembly, was appointed by the UN Secretary-General in consultation with the Advisory Commission of State representatives established by the Assembly. As of March 23, 1962 the title of Director was changed to Commissioner-General.

No express powers or authority were conferred upon the Agency at its creation. UNRWA's legal capacities derive from the UN Charter, as a subsidiary organ under Art. 22; from the 1946 Convention on the Privileges and Immunities of the United Nations; and from particular agreements concluded between the Agency and governments concerned. UNRWA negotiated agreements with several governments in the region, in order to facilitate its operations, including the free movement of personnel, supplies and vehicles.

UNRWA's mandate requires its headquarters to be located within its area of operations. Since 1978, following evacuation from Beirut because of the security problems there, the headquarters have been divided between Vienna and Aman. The UN General Assembly has decided that the headquarters should be relocated in Beirut as soon as the security situation so permits.

Palestine refugees within the concern of UNRWA for operational purposes were defined as persons whose normal residence was Palestine for a minimum of two years preceding the Arab-Israeli war of 1948 and who, as a result of that conflict, lost both their homes and means of livelihood. To be eligible for assistance from the Agency, refugees, and their descendants born after May 14, 1948, were to be registered with UNRWA, be living in the area of its operations and be in need. This working definition was intended to be interpreted flexibly. Following the 1967 Arab-Israeli war, assistance was provided to non-eligible persons displaced as a result of the conflict, in accordance with a decision of the Commissioner-General which was subsequently approved by General Assembly Res. 2252 (ES-V) of July 4, 1967. In the conflicts during the early 1980s it was again considered to be unjustifiable to confine UNRWA's relief services to registered refugees only. Humanitarian assistance is therefore provided on an emergency basis to other persons in need in the area.

Refugees registered with UNRWA and receiving its assistance are excluded both from the competence of the United Nations High Commissioner for Refugees, by Para. 7(c) of the Statute, and from the terms of the 1951 Convention Relating to the Status of Refugees, by Art. 1(D). However, it has been suggested that UNRWA and UNHCR should consult on ways of guaranteeing the safety and legal and human rights of the Palestine refugees, even though the High Commissioner is not responsible for them.

Within a few years after the creation of UNRWA the number of refugees registered with the Agency had doubled to over one million, of whom about half were children under the age of 15. UNRWA's functions were primarily to supply food rations on a vast scale, to administer the camps, to prevent serious epidemics and to provide education and training. A short period when emphasis was placed on projects of a developmental nature such as public works and rehabilitation, without prejudice to claims to eventual repatriation, proved more costly than direct relief. This vicious circle, coupled with the political factors involved, as well as the natural increase in the numbers of refugees, contributed to the failure of attempts to reduce expenditure.

Since its creation UNRWA has faced continuous budgetary deficits while also experiencing serious difficulties resulting from the armed conflicts in the region. A number of States regularly vote for the continuation of the Agency but make little or no financial contribution to its work. Some States call first for a start to the implementation of UN resolutions on repatriation or compensation, while others maintain that so long as a need for humanitarian assistance exists UN members hold joint responsibility for providing UNRWA with the support required.

UNRWA's activities reflect a continuing shift in priorities from the provision of emergency relief to education and health programmes. At present some 700,000 persons, or 35 per cent of the total registered population, live in camps administered by the Agency. Basic rations were issued until September 1982, when over 830,000 persons, or 43 per cent, were receiving them. Contributors have since been encouraged to make their donations not in kind but in cash, which can be used for the higher priority programmes. The area of UNRWA operations includes Jordan (749,000 registered refugees), Lebanon (239,000), Syria (221,000), as well as the Israeli-occupied territories (Gaza Strip, 377,000; West Bank, 341,000). For various reasons the actual number of registered persons present in the area of UNRWA operations is presumed by the Agency to be less than the registered population.

UNRWA's annual budget is close to $200 million, of which, in 1982, $178 million was provided by governments. As with UNHCR, the largest single contributor is the United States, with $67 million in 1982. Other principal contributors, but with much smaller amounts, are Canada, the Federal Republic of Germany, Japan, Saudi Arabia, Sweden, the United Kingdom and the Commission of the European Communities.[31]

Although UNRWA's purposes and activities are humanitarian, the Agency is itself inevitably a factor in the region's politics. A curtailment of UNRWA's services would have serious repercussions because of the nature of the Agency's operations both for the refugees and their host countries. UNRWA serves the Palestine refugees on behalf of the United Nations, pending a more permanent solution to the region's wider problems which the Agency itself is not called upon to resolve. UNRWA's welfare and education programme has not eroded the essentially political character of the situation in which the refugees are involved, or the consequent need for a wider political solution.

3.5 Evaluation

The provision of assistance to refugees is a humanitarian and non-political matter which should not be hindered by political considerations, despite the fact that refugee situations themselves are inherently political in character. The fields of competence and activities of the various international bodies established for the benefit of refugees and displaced persons illustrate that material assistance and legal protection functions are complementary. The idea of refugee protection formed the basis for creating UNHCR's statutory responsibilities, and a substantial core of the legal instruments devoted to refugees relate to this aspect. However, a major function of the Office of the High Commissioner is the implementation of assistance programmes, with the involvement of many other international governmental and non-governmental organizations. An important element of assistance programmes involves the provision of emergency relief, as well as basic support and maintenance.

The States which support UNHCR now recognize that until durable solutions are possible the Office has to provide refugees with material assistance to meet their immediate needs. Humanitarian assistance may be viewed as an adjunct to legal protection inasmuch as the status of refugees established by international instruments includes a number of rights which require appropriate material measures in order to be effective. On the other hand, to the extent that the very survival of refugees may be at stake, emergency or other relief measures are a fundamental prerequisite in the overall scheme of protection.

The inter-complementarity between protection and assistance is particularly evident when material assistance programmes, especially those of an emergency character, are implemented in States which have not contracted any conventional obligations relating to refugees. In such cases UNHCR may give some measure of protection to refugees, *de facto* more than *de jure*, to those falling under its assistance programme. Thus, assistance activities conducted under the High Commissioner's mandate may in practice serve as a vehicle for protection functions for those in need, whatever their legal position with regard to the definition of refugee.

The creation of the various international agencies charged with responsibilities for refugees demonstrates a new approach at the international level to protection of the interests of individuals, especially to achieving minimum standards of treatment.[32]

However, the basic international refugee instruments in force at the present time are defective in that they do not deal adequately with the standards of treatment and material conditions to be accorded to refugees, or yet to asylum seekers pending a determination of their status.

In the attempts to deal with the refugee problems between the two world wars, humanitarian motives were probably as strong as those of self-interest and expediency. Solutions were found through cooperation and collaboration between governments, international organizations and voluntary agencies. Such cooperation was a notable feature of UNRRA operations and was continued during the period of the IRO. Although wide operational responsibilities of a constitutional nature were entirely absent in the original conception of UNHCR, the various assistance functions of the High Commissioner are now carried out on a wide geographical basis, and they bring a degree of mitigation to the consequences of wars and other conflicts, changes of régimes and boundaries, decolonization and other national and international problems.

In adopting the test of fear of persecution, the principal international refugee instruments excluded persons fleeing solely the effects of destructive natural forces. Fugitives from natural disasters are excluded from UNHCR's statutory competence unless a fear of persecution can be demonstrated. It has been rightly commented that, in determining eligibility for asylum, for example, the compassionate claims of fugitives from armed conflicts and natural disasters, where no fear of persecution can be shown, may be as great as those of persons fleeing persecution.[33] An extension of obligations to the former cases would require a broader test in which the decisive ingredient would be that of force alone. This conception would maintain the distinction from such groups as ordinary aliens, migrants and fugitives from justice.

UNHCR's services in connection with natural disasters could be most valuable in migration situations such as those caused by famine. However, with regard to a general assumption of responsibilities in this area, the Office discounts the potential for its involvement beyond its current terms of reference. Broad functions relating to natural disasters have been entrusted to the Office of the UN Disaster Relief Co-ordinator (UNDRO). The responsibilities of UNHCR and UNDRO have been clarified by the conclusion of a Memorandum of Understanding signed in 1978, the terms of which emphasize UNDRO's responsibility for the coordination of assistance to those compelled to leave their homes as a result of natural disasters or as a precautionary measure against their effects. UNHCR's competence is reaffirmed in man-made disasters.

The developments have been examined whereby a basis for material assistance functions has been established and extended, now permitting the provision of international relief to refugees and large numbers of persons whose situation is analogous. UNHCR, unlike the limited institutional structures of previous periods, has been enabled to respond progressively to new situations. The competence of the Office of the High Commissioner has been enlarged and consolidated to allow a more comprehensive discharge of humanitarian responsibilities. By encompassing the needs of greater numbers of people the UN has made the High Commissioner's Office a principal instrument of its humanitarian policies.

The widening of the concept of persons entitled to international protection has made it possible to respond to changing and increasing humanitarian needs arising in different areas of the world. The majority of refugees are in developing countries, often the least developed, and the first receiving countries are usually unable to take care of them adequately without substantial material assistance from the international community. New mechanisms are being sought to ensure that such assistance is appropriately adapted to local development requirements, taking into account the opportunities for refugees to achieve self-sufficiency. The objective should be to formulate assistance programmes so as to provide refugees with the means to reduce their dependence on relief.

At the same time, the international community is faced with the need to recognize and adapt to the fact that many refugee problems are of a continuing nature and, in addition, that mass exoduses are likely to continue to occur despite efforts to reduce their scale and frequency. Large scale influxes may include many persons who may not qualify for durable solutions as refugees but who for various reasons cannot return to their country of origin and require the assistance of the international community. Such persons are frequently liable to be classified and dealt with as illegal immigrants, and so far only relatively crude measures have been applied to avert such influxes and their consequences.[34] Although action to avert new flows of refugees is clearly required, the more immediate future challenge in refugee protection and assistance is likely to be to ensure that adequate and effective measures continue to be taken on behalf of the genuine refugees in the traditional sense, while also making basic provision for the problems resulting from mass migrations motivated by economic and other, wider factors.

These complex and comparatively recent developments focus attention increasingly onto the causes of refugee and migration problems, which in turn has led some to call for a revision of asylum practice and refugee law. However, it is important that any new measures adopted should not adversely affect the humanitarian principles and concepts evolved in international law and organization since the appointment of the first League of Nations High Commissioner some 60 years ago. As a minimum, it is clearly necessary to ensure that asylum seekers receive treatment in accordance with basic humanitarian standards.[35]

The activities of the High Commissioner are carried out under the directives of the UN General Assembly and Economic and Social Council. Nevertheless, in reality the High Commissioner's work "amounts to skillful use of persuasion and the creation of confidence on which its effectiveness depends".[36] In addition, the assistance programmes depend on the continuation of voluntary support by participating governments. In particular, they are subject to the annual scrutiny, review and approval of the States members of the Executive Committee. In the functions of audit, review and authorization possessed by this body repose important indicators of international acceptance of UNHCR's programmes.

The frequent evaluation of the refugee problem as a temporary one has been just as frequently disproved because in the last analysis the only real solution is true world peace.[37] Beyond the world wide humanitarian assistance activities conducted by the High Commissioner, the very existence of many of the refugee problems which UNHCR is charged to deal with fundamentally belies the achievement of the parent UN organs. Against this background, the practice of the High Commissioner's Office over more than 30 years has established patterns and also expectations of humanitarian action which were neither anticipated nor provided for at its inception.

UNHCR's assistance functions have been provided for in both specific and general terms by resolutions of the UN political assemblies. In the field of refugee relief, UNHCR and the General Assembly have thus demonstrated that it is possible to achieve a certain degree of reconciliation in the conflict between legal constitutional competence and the requirements of circumstantial considerations. However, as with other aspects of global humanitarian problems, in the field of refugee relief it is apparent that various national and international factors beyond the immediate humanitarian issues now raise a serious challenge to both the traditional institutional structures and the customary forms of response. Refugee relief must therefore be viewed in context with the wider questions of humanitarian assistance at the international level.

4. An International Basis for Humanitarian Assistance

4.1 Introduction: Sources of a Legal Framework

The new levels of international humanitarian activity witnessed during this century are related to the general expansion of the fields of interest of international law and organization in the same period. The fields in which the nation-State alone cannot ensure the protection of the individual, and where eventually only international planning and action can suffice, now include many problems arising from the interrelationship of world population, resources and environmental factors.[1] Problems of drought, famine, disaster damage and poverty are particularly relevant here. International concern with the donation, acceptance and coordination of humanitarian assistance is an aspect of these problems. The international juridical factors which play their role in the search for the necessary legal elements of a workable and effective relief policy must thus be closely examined, and the very diffuse contribution of these factors must be resolved in order to offer a useful framework for further progress.

In considering what international rules, if any, are applicable to humanitarian assistance, disaster victims or disaster situations, recourse should first be had to the recognized sources of international law. Art. 38(1) of the Statute of the International Court of Justice provides a formal enumeration of these sources, which are principally custom and treaties, along with the general principles of law, and the subsidiary sources mentioned in Art. 38(1) (d). In addition, while some legal publicists have questioned the conventional doctrines and terminology found in this domain, others have looked to new sources of international law, such as consensus.[2]

With regard to treaty law, referred to as "international conventions" in Art. 38(1) (a) of the Statute, there is at present no international body of law relating specifically and exclusively to humanitarian assistance beyond the context of armed conflict. Those existing international instruments relevant to humanitarian assistance are considered below and in the next four chapters. Nevertheless, it should also be kept in mind that a multilateral convention dealing with disaster relief and setting out certain principles of action was concluded during the League of Nations period in the form of the 1927 Convention Establishing an International Relief Union, which was considered in detail in chapter 1 above. Various recent proposals for developing a new international legal instrument relating to disaster relief will be surveyed in chapter 9 below.

Customary law, or, as it is termed in Art. 38(1) (b) of the Statute, "international custom, as evidence of a general practice accepted as law", is the subject of much scholarly discussion. Customary law has been described as the repositary of the common law of nations and as one of the most important manifestations of the interaction between practice and law.[3] The usual view is that the creation of a customary rule requires both the existence of a general practice of States and a second constitutive element which is the *opinio juris*, or the acceptance by States of the practice as law.

The practice of States comprises not only their individual but also their collective acts. Their activities through international organizations can be a factor in the development of international law. Even the UN specialized agencies can thus be seen as an appropriate forum for the generation of customary rules of international law. Resolutions of the United Nations organs which concern disaster relief will be considered in chapters 6 and 8 below. The claim of such resolutions to embody general or particular international law should be briefly referred to, without making an unwarranted diversion into a separate field which has been thoroughly treated by leading authors, especially since the view has been taken that General Assembly resolutions may give rise to new international law by consensus.[4] Whatever role is accorded to consensus, it is apparent that a statement of principles or rules by the General Assembly suitable for application to a given field may give rise to a practice outside the UN which may develop into customary law. In such a case, the role of a resolution is to tend to corroborate other evidence of the existence of a rule of customary international law.

The rules of customary international law in the period before World War II were derived essentially from the practice of the Western nations. The role of customary law today is regarded by some as declining, partly because of the increasing rate of change in international society. Although custom remains an important source of international law, its growth and development in harmony with the needs of the world community presents difficulties. In addition to the requirement of clear and continuous practice, which may be hard to demonstrate, the condition that States accept, by implication or expressly, that their conduct possesses a legal character, means that assertions regarding the existence of particular rules of customary international law are liable to be controversial. It is frequently difficult to determine the precise nature and content of a practice and the imprecision of customary international law is thus in certain cases best remedied by expressing obligations in treaty form. For all the above reasons, the simple practice of international humanitarian assistance is not certain to lead to the creation of unwritten relief law.

The common interests of humanity are of a different order from the particular interests of States, which tend to conflict. Such common interests are expressed ultimately in concern for the needs of individuals. The importance of the first Geneva Convention of 1864 is that a legal principle was created incorporating the moral principle of respect for the human person. Because the aim of humanitarian legislation, which is to assure protection to the individual, is a universal one, rules of general international law created for a humanitarian purpose may even take on the character of *jus cogens*, or an absolute character. This concept has received wide recognition, although some publicists put forward doubts regarding its existence or, if they admit its existence, regarding its content. A judgment of the International Court of Justice has referred to certain international obligations which are "based on general and well-recognized principles, namely: elementary considerations of humanity, even more exacting in peace than in war".[5] In humanitarian conventions, created in the interests of people as individuals, the contracting States demonstrate a high common interest.

In developing humanitarian law to cover a wider range of situations of human suffering in peace as well as war, its role must be to serve and promote international cooperation. For the victims of both armed conflicts and natural catastrophes, humanitarian assistance is a field for action which not only commands the support of a number of States but which also demonstrates a commitment to the purposes and tasks of international organization itself, in the practice of the United Nations and other institutions.[6] A progressively developed relief law may thus eventually make a contribution to general international law as a force for cooperative change in the face of global needs.

In their actions, States may demonstrate that the nature of a particular practice makes its acceptance desirable as in accordance with law, *de lege ferenda*. Whether this is the case in regard to developing practice in the international disaster relief system is a question for consideration throughout the following chapters which deal with the principal actors and actions involved. The greatly increased level of international activity relating to emergency humanitarian assistance, and especially its channelling and coordination through multi-lateral programmes and its institutionalization under the fields of competence of a number of UN specialized agencies may eventually make it possible to derive principles of a growing legal character from established practices. Nevertheless, it should be apparent that the individual nature of at least some disaster situations, the uncertainty as to the general character of humanitarian practices and, above all, the influence of political factors in relief, work firmly against the crystallization of particular customary international rules in this area.

Some are of the opinion that international humanitarian assistance, rather than possessing any legal characteristics, is essentially a matter of comity or international good neighbourliness. In public international law the notion of comity embraces acts, practices and rules of goodwill and courteous treatment habitually observed by States without the conviction that any legal obligation is involved.[7] By definition the rules of comity lack a legal nature, although a broad conception of comity extends so far as to include basic notions of international solidarity and cooperation. Thus, legal writers in various periods of history mention emergency relief actions in disasters as an example, since assistance between States in such cases is frequently accompanied by the expression of sentiments of humanitarian obligation, albeit of a non-binding nature. Nevertheless, although not part of the sources of international law as understood in the formulation adopted in the Statute of the International Court of Justice, it is apparent that comity may still be regarded as a factor influencing the growth of international law.

Art. 38(1) (c) of the Statute of the International Court of Justice refers to the general principles of law as a source of international law. Conflicting positions have been taken by States over the definition and application of the general principles. Some writers have stressed a narrow meaning of the concept, while others have referred much more broadly to the minimum standards of international law as reflections of the general principles. In addition, the notions of "new principles of international law" or "fundamental principles of international law" have developed since World War II.[8] Some of these principles are based on custom that could be described as universal or well-established, but States have often taken the view that references in treaties to general principles could give rise to problems of interpretation. In the Diplomatic Conference on the Reaffirmation and Development of International Humanitarian Law, when considering the adoption of the draft preamble to Additional Protocol I of 1977, States declined to include a reference to the generally accepted principles of international law but preferred instead to invoke the terms of the UN Charter. Thus, it has become usual to speak of the "principles of the Charter", and to assign special attributes to these.

Fundamental humanitarian considerations may nevertheless be recognized as legal principles in international law. In 1951 the International Court of Justice held that the principles underlying the Genocide Convention approved by General Assembly Res. 260 A (III) of December 9, 1948 are recognized as binding upon States irrespective of whether States have accepted the treaty obligations. An authoritative publicist has concluded that "the view can be maintained that nowadays respect for and protection of the rights of individuals directly connected with their existence, dignity and human development, is an obligation of States under international law, also with respect to their own nationals, and is no longer restricted to aliens".[9] International law recognizes obligations which a State holds towards the whole international community, including the prohibition of aggression, genocide, slavery and racial discrimination. All States may be said to have a legal interest in ensuring the observance of such obligations.

In the absence of particular legal rules applicable in disaster situations, the question of the relationship between certain important principles of international law and the achievement of solutions to humanitarian problems of relief assumes particular relevance. However, conceptual and terminological uncertainties hinder definite analysis in this area. Many would regard the sovereign equality of States and the duty of international cooperation as general principles of international law. Whatever their status, these concepts seem to provide both important foundations for, and constraints on, international relief actions; they should therefore be given further consideration.

4.2 Sovereign Equality and International Cooperation

The doctrines of sovereignty and the reserved domain of domestic jurisdiction express the essential interest of States in the protection of their freedom of action. Respect for State sovereignty is thus a central principle applicable to relief actions. A government may request international assistance or it may choose to deal with a disaster in its own way. Likewise, international law imposes no obligation on States to respond to requests for assistance or to make offers of contributions for relief operations in other countries. A government concerned may also set conditions for the use of contributions or the conduct of relief operations.

The doctrine of State sovereignty seems to imply the right of a State to treat its own people as it pleases. However, the adoption of the UN Charter marked a significant development in the relationship between international law and sovereignty, expressed in the terms of Art. 2(1). Sovereignty signifies not unbridled freedom, but rather is an attribute of equality between States and it is subject to the duty to comply faithfully with international obligations. The principle of sovereignty should thus be regarded not as a legal barrier which inhibits international humanitarian assistance, but rather as a necessary pre-condition for the exercise of meaningful cooperation within the community of States.

The question of State sovereignty is related to that of the lack of status of individuals in international law. For traditional international law the individual did not exist, and it can still not be said that the individual is generally a subject of international law. Sovereignty has maintained its position as the cornerstone of international law. However, a distinction exists between the individual as a subject of enforceable claims in international law, and as the beneficiary of a system of international law that emphasizes more strongly than before the rights of the person. The treatment of the individual is increasingly a matter for international concern and the foundation of this development is that people are the ultimate members of the international community and the ultimate objects of international law.[10]

The structure of organized international cooperation in the period after World War II seems to reveal a widening of concern for the economic and social well-being of the individual. The accession of many poor States to UN membership has been accompanied by increasing international attention to questions of development and aid and to the solution of global problems of poverty. This functional development is paralleled by the incorporation in international law of principles of respect for human rights. The fundamental basis for human rights is no longer to be sought in natural law concepts alone, but is formally established in the UN Charter and in specific human rights instruments.

This broad pattern of developments, characterized by the expression "international law of cooperation", represents a significant evolution for the principles and structure of international law. The duty of States to achieve international cooperation in solving international problems, including those of a humanitarian nature, is laid down in Art. 1(3) of the UN Charter, and it was reiterated in the Declaration on Friendly Relations adopted by the General Assembly as Res. 2625 (XXV) on October 24, 1970. The obligation of cooperation has the character of a general principle of international law, and it should therefore take an important place as a basic factor in the establishment of global relief policy.

In this connection, one distinguished jurist has referred to the "incipient recognition of an inchoate duty of samaritanism in international relations", as a manifestation of the principle of cooperation.[11] Another publicist has stated that disaster relief actions provide evidence of international solidarity and both reaffirm and give substance to the principle of cooperation.[12]

The validity of the principles of international cooperation is demonstrated essentially in progress towards their application and implementation. Only practical measures of cooperation can translate formulations of principle into action to meet the challenges of international society, which are fundamentally those of human survival and welfare. An international law of cooperation is therefore universal in the scope of its interests. Such a functional approach to legal rules and their development correlates the evolution of international law and organization with the non-juridical forces of international life, and accepts a multitude of legal and institutional patterns. The gradual adoption by States of a tentative framework for the attainment of mutual benefits, superseding the traditional concept of coexistence, can provide room for a greater variety of approaches to cooperative action in the humanitarian sphere. However, greater appreciation of the potential implications of these changes and tendencies is required more urgently than ever before.

4.3 Foundations of UN Humanitarian Activities

The UN Charter and Humanitarian Objectives

The primary objective of States in adopting the Charter of the United Nations, which was signed on June 26, 1945 in San Francisco and entered into force on October 24, 1945, was to provide for the maintenance of international peace and security; to that end, the importance of economic and social objectives was also recognized. The Preamble and Art. 1 of the Charter deal with the UN's purposes, which are to maintain international peace, to develop friendly relations among nations, to achieve international cooperation in solving international problems, and to be a centre for harmonizing the actions of nations in the attainment of those goals. Art. 1(3) mentions particular problems towards which cooperation should be directed, including "international problems of an economic, social, cultural, or humanitarian character", as well as the promotion of human rights and fundamental freedoms.

Art. 55 of the Charter, in Chapter IX dealing with economic and social cooperation, states that the United Nations shall promote higher standards of living; solutions of international economic, social, health and related problems; and universal respect for, and observance of, human rights and fundamental freedoms. Again, the link between conditions of stability and well-being on the one hand and peaceful relations among nations on the other hand is made plain. However, it may be noted that no field referred to in Art. 55 corresponds explicitly to the humanitarian problems which are included in Art. 1(3). Only the expression "and related problems" in Art. 55(b) could be said to extend into that area.

Under Art. 2 of the Charter, the United Nations and its members shall act in pursuit of the purposes stated in Art. 1, and in accordance with the principles stated in Art. 2.

The second principle referred to in Art. 2 is the obligation to fulfil all obligations. To this, one commentator has stated: "it presupposes as self-evident which are the obligations of Members. The Charter, however, makes it difficult to answer this question."[13] Art. 56 appears to impose an obligation on UN members, through the pledge with which it opens, to act and cooperate to achieve the aims set out in Art. 55. However, commensurate with the extent of the obligation under Art. 56, a clash arises with the provisions of Art. 2(7) in so far as these aims are matters within the domestic jurisdiction of States.

Art. 2(7) provides in part: "Nothing contained in the present Charter shall authorize the United Nations to intervene in matters which are essentially within the domestic jurisdiction of any state". This provision expresses the general idea that State sovereignty should be protected against the acts of international organizations. However, the concept of domestic jurisdiction enunciated here is not defined, and there is no general agreement on its meaning. It seems difficult to draw a line between matters governed by international law and those within the reserved domain.

Realistic interpretation presents Art. 55 as a general declaration of intentions providing a wide foundation for activities directed towards international cooperation. In regard to humanitarian matters, the terms of Art. 2(7) provide a major limitation on the collective actions of UN members through the organization, and thus fundamentally influence an assessment of the UN's competence. However, a reasonable conclusion is that the Charter's interdiction of intervention should be balanced against the duty under Art. 1(3) to achieve international cooperation in solving international problems of a humanitarian character.

The outcome of the agreement at San Francisco was a Charter committing its signatories to act in pursuance of purposes and in conformity with principles that were understood in various ways. The question of interpretation was left to be solved in the practice of the organization. In the course of adaptation to new situations the UN organs have considered the compliance of particular actions with Art. 1, and resolutions have at times urged States to be guided by its provisions. However, Art. 1(3) has not been very frequently referred to in connection with particular measures to be taken and the question arises whether the paragraph contains sufficiently precise standards to be invoked.

Another aspect of the applicability of Art. 1(3), especially with regard to human rights and human welfare, arises from a view that the UN's paramount purpose is the maintenance of international peace and security. Discussing the UN's role in humanitarian assistance, one commentator has stated: "Experience has shown that the UN will only do something about a situation when it is likely to affect the maintenance of peace and security".[14] Nevertheless, in the General Assembly the purpose of solving humanitarian problems has been referred to on a few occasions as a basis for recommending action and initiating operations in the area of humanitarian assistance. In an early resolution dealing with the winding up of UNRRA and the establishment of a Special Technical Committee to study the immediate relief needs of certain countries after World War II, a connection was drawn between the proposed measures and two of the purposes expressed in Art. 1 of the Charter; the preamble to this resolution referred to the objective of international cooperation in solving international problems of a humanitarian character, and the operative paragraphs urged governments to furnish relief supplies accordingly.[15] When the refugee problem was considered by the Preparatory Commission of the UN in 1945, at a period characterized by widespread relief needs, governments considered that the problem came within the UN's competence, under Art. 1(3). In one resolution of the General Assembly on the situation in Hungary in 1956 it was stated that "humanitarian duties can be fulfilled most effectively through the international co-operation stipulated in Art. 1(3)".[16]

In the immediate post-World-War-II period various specific relief operations were undertaken despite the reluctance of States to become involved in generalized assistance activities. Such operations as those in favour of the refugees in the Near East, the civilian population of Korea, and the victims of some natural disasters, were perceived as special post-war problems or as special economic and social questions, and there was almost no reference to their particular humanitarian basis. Nevertheless, all types of measures in the humanitarian field undoubtedly fall within the scope of Art. 55, and they should be regarded as forming a distinct category of activities.

Structural and Functional Framework

The United Nations acts within the framework of the Charter, and of the decisions of its members: it is a political organization. The General Assembly's role as a deliberative organ concerned with any matter within the scope of the Charter is laid down in Art. 10. In addition, Art. 60 confers responsibility for economic and social cooperation on the General Assembly, and, under the authority of the Assembly, on the Economic and Social Council.

The early plans for the Economic and Social Council drew on the late movement in the League of Nations to expand its own economic and social activities. When UNRRA recommended the establishment of successor agencies or organizations to continue the tasks of relief and rehabilitation upon its own termination, the areas of greatest need were those of food distribution as well as health and the provision of other essentials of life.[17] Functionalist reasoning, framed in the context of the objective of an expanding world economy, envisaged a network of international agencies with specific operational tasks and held that international cooperation in economic and social matters would contribute to the removal of political and ideological differences.[18] Economic and social progress was emphasized by the less developed countries. The contribution of the League of Nations, the International Labour Organisation and especially UNRRA was an established pattern of operational activities designed by headquarters secretariats and frequently implemented through regional or country field machinery.

The constitutional arrangements of the UN's founding period established a highly decentralized system for promoting international economic and social cooperation, and specialized bodies were created in the most essential functional areas. It was considered that successful international action within each separate field required participation at the national level, and that only a decentralized system could cope with the size and number of tasks facing the United Nations. The subsequent increase in UN membership, by predominantly poor nations possessing a determination to maximize the possibilities for development assistance, also resulted in a great widening of the scope of international economic and social activities, particularly in the growth of operational programmes and field activities financed mainly by voluntary contributions.

Specialized bodies created in furtherance of the objectives outlined in Arts. 1(3) and 55 included a number with responsibilities extending into the field of humanitarian assistance. Art. 22 of the Charter empowers the General Assembly to establish such subsidiary organs as it deems necessary for the performance of its functions. The method of establishment by a resolution of the Assembly was employed in the creation of the Office of the UN High Commissioner for Refugees, the UN Children's Fund, the more specific operational agencies such as the UN Relief and Works Agency for Palestine Refugees in the Near East and the UN Korean Reconstruction Agency, as well as the Office of the UN Disaster Relief Co-ordinator.

Provision is also made for the creation of specialized agencies under the chapter of the Charter relating to economic and social cooperation, in Art. 59, by negotiations among interested States. The World Health Organization and the International Refugee Organization were created in this manner, at the instigation of the Economic and Social Council. An international conference convened by the President of the United States two years before the creation of the UN also laid the foundations of the Food and Agriculture Organization.

All the bodies competent to carry out relief-related activities have widely varying and distinctive features as regards organizational structure, functions, powers and finance. Several of the important specialized agencies and subsidiary organs involved in humanitarian assistance have undergone considerable constitutional change over the course of time. This has tended to come about through interpretation and usage rather than through formal amendments, and the most important developments in the individual agencies are considered separately in chapter 6 below.

Coordination, Good Offices and the Secretary-General

Almost every activity contemplated by the United Nations requires cooperation with the specialized and subsidiary bodies. Procedures of coordination, designed both to avoid duplication, waste and competition and to further concerted action by several organizations, have become a means to secure the maximum impact of separate programmes in the solution of a common problem. The legal basis for procedures of coordination is found in the Charter, in the basic instruments of the specialized agencies, in the agreements between the agencies and the UN and in the agreements between the agencies themselves.

In the Charter the UN was envisaged as a central coordinating body for its agencies, although in fact the latter presently operate with considerable autonomy. Art. 58 provides for the UN to make recommendations for coordination of both the policies and activities of the specialized agencies. Art. 63(2) gave particular responsibility for coordination to the Economic and Social Council. Acknowledging the autonomy of the specialized agencies, the basis for coordination is found in consultation and recommendation and is essentially a process of voluntary cooperation. The Council's major responsibility for coordination was to be discharged through the Co-ordinating Committee, with the assistance of the Administrative Committee on Co-ordination (ACC), established in 1946 as a standing inter-agency committee, with the UN Secretary-General as chairman. The Council and the General Assembly have expanded the ACC's mandate and have adopted various resolutions concerning the nature and scope of cooperation with the specialized agencies, some of which have emphasized implementation of the UN strategy for international development.[19] However, solutions within the UN system represent only a part of the problem of bringing greater coherence to international activities in general, taking into account the involvement of non-UN organizations and the role of bilateral arrangements. The specialized agencies themselves, therefore, are enabled to make arrangements with both governmental and non-governmental organizations when necessary.

In the aftermath of disaster events in the early 1960s the Co-ordination Committee reviewed the problems connected with the coordination of emergency action by UN organizations and considered a number of matters relating to the provision of disaster relief.[20] At the same time, hope was expressed that procedures would be adopted enabling assistance from both the UN and Red Cross systems to be rendered in an effective and well-coordinated manner. The subsequent developments are considered below in chapter 8, in connection with the Office of the UN Disaster Relief Co-ordinator.

The role of the Secretary-General in coordinating the activities of the UN and specialized agencies is not referred to explicitly in the Charter, although he is directly concerned in carrying out the provisions of Art. 58, which have already been referred to. The Secretary-General has, however, played an important part in the implementation of recommendations of the General Assembly and Economic and Social Council and he has on various occasions been called upon to take steps in the field of humanitarian assistance. Under Art. 98 of the Charter the Secretary-General is enabled to perform any functions that may be entrusted to him by the political organs. Beyond his competence under the provisions of Arts. 98 and 99, which deals with his role in bringing to the attention of the Security Council matters which may threaten the maintenance of international peace, the members of the Security Council have endorsed a statement under which the Secretary-General is entitled to bring to the notice of the Council "basic issues confronting the Organization and disturbing developments in ... any parts of the world".[21] This statement was invoked by the Secretary-General in his early humanitarian initiatives in the situation in East Pakistan in 1970.

Art. 7 of the UN Charter establishes the Secretariat as one of the principal organs of the United Nations. In addition to the functions which are expressly entrusted to the Secretary-General, he is deemed to be authorized to exercise the implied powers of the office and those which may be required for the discharge of his responsibilities, on his own initiative. He is entitled to act in cases where the UN Charter expressly or by implication confers functions upon the United Nations without specifying the organ called upon to fulfil them. The doctrine of implied or inherent competence supplies a firm basis for the exercise of good offices, and it has been invoked on many occasions of humanitarian need.[22]

In the field of humanitarian assistance the Secretary-General was early given a limited role of making information available to UN members so as to facilitate the coordination of their respective post-war relief efforts.[23] With the expansion of international relief activities the coordinating role of the Secretary-General assumed increasing importance. Following a general review in 1963 of the UN's economic, social and human rights programmes, the Secretary-General took initiatives to establish new arrangements for emergency UN assistance and the need for coordination under his leadership continued to be reiterated by the General Assembly and the Economic and Social Council.[24]

In addition, the Secretary-General both assumed and received from the political organs other executive responsibilities involving the exercise of considerable powers of discretion. The expansion of development aid programmes and technical assistance stemmed from the authorization of the Secretary-General to continue the advisory functions of UNRRA in the field of social welfare.[25] Specific functions relating to humanitarian assistance were increasingly entrusted to the Secretary-General and his right of initiative, exercised in a number of large scale disaster situations, received endorsement by the political organs. In the case of the relief operation undertaken by the UN in East Pakistan and Bangladesh from 1970 to 1972 the General Assembly referred to his functions relating to natural disasters.[26] A subsequent resolution of the Assembly endorsed the appointment of UNHCR as a focal point for relief efforts, a designation which had been made by the Secretary-General, as well as his "initiative in establishing the UN E. Pakistan Relief Operation."[27] At the same time, the question of principle was raised: whether a large scale humanitarian programme could be undertaken by the Secretariat in the absence of a decision by the relevant UN organs. At a meeting of government representatives convened to discuss the question of humanitarian assistance to East Pakistan the Secretary-General stated that he had no doubt about his competence to launch such operations.

More recently, the Secretary-General has played an important role in convening special meetings at the governmental and non-governmental levels, as well as international pledging conferences in connection with very large scale humanitarian problems, such as those of refugees, and other emergency relief needs.[28] His initiative in such cases has also been recognized by the General Assembly. Under mandates given to him by the General Assembly, the Secretary-General has continued to implement various programmes of humanitarian assistance funded by voluntary contributions.

When the Secretary-General considers the use of his competences he must of course take into account specific Charter limitations on UN action, particularly Art. 2(7). In those disaster situations where a conflict arises between the restriction on intervention by the UN contained in Art. 2(7) and the general principle, within the framework of economic and social cooperation at the international level, of furthering solutions to humanitarian problems, the Secretary-General's office may prove to be of pivotal importance. However, in tackling humanitarian problems the Secretary-General has no means of enforcement at his disposal. He must rely on the prestige of the office and on his individual persuasiveness. The Secretary-General's initiatives and good offices are inevitably often conducted in private, but a necessary condition for their success and the maintenance of confidence in his role is strict impartiality.

4.4 Human Rights and Relief Actions

Basic Human Rights Instruments

One basis for inquiry into the relevance of human rights to relief actions is the fact that most humanitarian emergencies have a significant man-made component. From recognition of the role of the human agency in disaster situations, with the ready power to prevent or alleviate suffering, arises the question of responsibility for the plight of the victims. The use of the term responsibility is not intended to be understood in the sense of an individual apportionment of liability for suffering. The area of responsibility which must be considered more closely is that of States in the fulfilment of standards and obligations expressed in human rights instruments.

The UN Charter included the promotion of respect for human rights as one of the principal objectives of the UN organization, expressed in the Preamble as a determination "to reaffirm faith in fundamental human rights, in the dignity and worth of the human person". Although the Charter does not list any human rights, the Universal Declaration of Human Rights and the International Covenants articulated these rights in detail, but were accompanied by prolonged disagreement on precise commitments. The Charter itself imposed no strict obligation on members to grant any particular rights or freedoms to individuals, and the collective role of the UN in the protection of human rights is circumscribed by the original and subsequently developed meaning of Art. 2(7). The exact relationship between the human rights provisions of the Charter and this article has given rise to considerable legal and political controversy.

The Universal Declaration of Human Rights[29] itself imposed on UN members no legal obligation to respect the rights which it proclaimed, a fact emphasized by States as strongly as they emphasized the importance of the document. However, the Declaration has been frequently and widely invoked since its adoption and the continuing reaffirmation of its principles, particularly in international conventions and national constitutions, has been regarded as sufficient to clothe it with the character of customary law.

The Universal Declaration attempted to take account of different religious traditions and political philosophies as well as legal, economic, social and cultural systems. However, the definition of specific rights of the individual in instruments that would be binding on a diversity of ratifying States proved more difficult. The Covenant on Economic, Social and Cultural Rights and the Covenant on Civil and Political Rights, which were approved by the General Assembly in 1966 and entered into force on January 3, 1976 and March 23, 1976 respectively,[30] have been described as laying down provisions which are not enforceable obligations but rather goals towards which contracting parties are required to strive. Countries ratifying the Covenant on Civil and Political Rights undertake to protect their people by law against cruel, inhuman or degrading treatment and they recognize the right of every human being to life, liberty and security and other fundamental freedoms. The countries ratifying the Covenant on Economic, Social and Cultural Rights acknowledge their responsibility to promote better living conditions for their people and they recognize everyone's right to work and fair conditions of employment, and adequate standards of living, health and education. The conception and definition of contents of human rights are thus matters fully within the sphere of UN activity, but the question of implementation still remains largely within the domain of the domestic jurisdiction of States.

Among the provisions of human rights instruments which take on special significance in the context of relief actions are the rights to life, health, food and shelter, and to special care for children and the sick. The Universal Declaration of Human Rights opens by recognizing the inherent dignity and inalienable rights of all human beings. The Declaration proclaimed itself to be "a common standard of achievement for all peoples and nations", and by Art. 28 its foundation was understood to be a social and international order within which human rights could be realized. Art. 22 of the Declaration reiterated that everyone is entitled to the economic, social and cultural rights which are "indispensable for his dignity and the free development of his personality". Such rights are to be secured both through national efforts and international cooperation. States set the standards and by States are ensured the rights which are laid down. These general provisions of the Universal Declaration would themselves support important principles relevant to humanitarian assistance, including the principle that one State should assist another in emergency; that States should prepare for disasters within their territory and take measures designed to minimize suffering following a disaster; and that States should accept relief after the occurrence of a disaster if their own resources are inadequate.

The most basic of all human rights is the right to life. Art. 3 of the Universal Declaration states simply: "Everyone has the right to life, liberty and security of person." Art. 6(1) of the International Covenant on Civil and Political Rights states more specifically: "Every human being has the inherent right to life. This right shall be protected by law." UN bodies have endeavoured to promote the realization of the right to life, for example in the context of the abolition of capital punishment and by formulating measures against terrorism and the taking of hostages. However, the fact that the most basic human right is threatened by the consequences of disasters has received insufficient attention.[31]

The relevance of basic human rights to humanitarian assistance is made more clear when rights to the minimum necessities of life are considered. These rights are set out in Art. 25 of the Universal Declaration as follows:

> 1. Everyone has the right to a standard of living adequate for the health and well-being of himself and of his family, including food, clothing, housing and medical care and necessary social services, and the right to security in the event of ... lack of livelihood in circumstances beyond his control.

2. Motherhood and childhood are entitled to special care and assistance.

The specific needs of food, clothing and shelter are also asserted in Art. 11 of the Covenant on Economic, Social and Cultural Rights, the first paragraph of which refers to "the right of everyone to an adequate standard of living for himself and his family, including adequate food, clothing and housing". The terms of this article lend additional support to the case for the relevance of provisions of human rights instruments to disaster situations. Art. 11 goes on to require States to take individually and through international cooperation the measures needed to effectuate "the fundamental right of everyone to be free from hunger".

Recognizing the right to be free from hunger, Art. 11(2) of the same Covenant then provides that individual and international measures including specific programmes shall be undertaken by States parties. Paragraph 2(b) of Art. 11 also states significantly that the distribution of food in the world shall be made in relation to need, and it incorporates the undertaking to implement measures and specific programmes in order to ensure equitable distribution. However, the positive value of this paragraph is limited by the addition of the condition "taking into account the problems of both food-importing and food-exporting countries". Thus, while the question of starvation has become essentially an international and humanitarian concern, not only as a result of human rights provisions but also as evidenced by the inclusion of the prohibition of starvation as a means of warfare in Additional Protocol I of 1977, the aspects of inequity and inefficiency in food distribution remain largely matters within domestic jurisdiction.

The existence of a basic right to food is also recognized in other international instruments. The 1959 Declaration of the Rights of the Child includes the right to adequate nutrition.[32] The Universal Declaration on the Eradication of Hunger and Malnutrition and other resolutions adopted at the World Food Conference of 1974 were also endorsed by the United Nations.[33] The 1959 Declaration of the Rights of the Child itself has wider relevance to relief, for it goes on to assert that children shall be among the first to receive protection and assistance when necessary.

Within international organizations, notwithstanding the above developments, functional progress relating to humanitarian assistance has not generally supposed an explicit association between relief actions and human rights. UN resolutions in connection with the activities of the Office of the Disaster Relief Co-ordinator do not refer to the relevance of human rights instruments, although in the debates on the creation of the Office it was pointed out that effective and coordinated relief was essential in protecting human rights.[34] International human rights law does provide a foundation upon which to base legal principles relevant to relief, but governments are likely to continue to claim that the manner in which they treat their people is of concern to them alone, although some are of the opinion that it is a losing claim with little hope of prevailing in politics if not in law.[35] The view that implementation constitutes the touchstone of the UN human rights programme therefore lends support to the statement that "The development of international human rights law may ultimately have an impact on the world response to natural disasters."[36] Humanitarian assistance deserves the particular attention of the international community because of the concrete application of fundamental human rights involved. Not all of the ethical, cultural and social values which are at the heart of human rights norms are universally recognized, but humanitarian principles applicable in disaster situations represent one area for development in which ideological and political differences at the global level could be most likely to be reconciled.

Disasters and the Right to Development

Most disasters in which a need arises for international humanitarian assistance occur in the developing countries. International relief emphasizes the inequitable distribution of resources among nations. Natural disasters have been referred to as the neglected variable in international development planning, and the link between disasters and development strategy is now recognized in literature and by operating agencies. This recognition forms the basis for international cooperation and action in disaster preparedness, for example in work of the UN Development Programme, and it has also contributed to the creation of a basis for international relief in situations which could be described as economic emergencies. In its resolution on the international development strategy for the Third United Nations Development Decade, the General Assembly recognized the detrimental effects of disasters and stated that "the international community will take measures to improve and strengthen arrangements to provide developing countries with adequate and timely assistance in matters of disaster relief, prevention and preparedness".[37]

In formulating international development policy, the focus on economic and social rights highlights the fundamental issue of the needs of many people for basic diet, clothing and shelter, and access to medical and educational facilities. The urgency of the conditions facing many of the developing countries makes it difficult for them to realize all the rights of the Universal Declaration. The need to guarantee subsistence to their populations has served to justify for the governments of some developing countries the application of relatively permanent restrictions on civil rights and liberties. However, while in such countries many human rights have given way in the face of efforts to combat famine and disease, some new emphasis has been given to the question of the fulfilment of the most basic needs of people.

The view has been expressed that action to promote development is a legal obligation of the international community, and in particular of the industrialized countries. Opinion has founded the right to development on the UN Charter, on the Universal Declaration of Human Rights and the Human Rights Covenants, on the principle of self-determination, or on the right to life itself. Thus, a right to development could be viewed as a synthesis of a large number of human rights, even as a totality of the means available to make specific economic and social rights effective for the people who are deprived of them.[38]

Whatever the status of the right to development, it is clear that the idea of need as a basis for entitlement is one of its central features. Pursuit of the 'basic needs' approach to development is reflected within the UN framework in the content of resolutions and decisions of a number of world conferences on issues such as environment, food, population, and employment. A range of basic needs strategies have been endorsed both within and outside the UN system, but States have not yet accepted legal commitments to programmes of action embodying the concept. Nevertheless, despite some adverse criticism by commentators, the basic needs approach could contribute to realization in practice of the right to development. At the least, its concern with the well-being of the individual should be regarded as a significant advance over previous development strategies concerned primarily with aggregate levels of economic growth.

Issues of development, human rights and humanitarian relief approach most closely to each other in the context of international efforts relating to world food security. The margin between the growth of world food production and that of population is shrinking, focusing attention both on the problems of production and on the question of the distribution of food according to need rather than demand. The fact that presently available world food supplies are sufficient to provide everyone with an adequate diet thus raises a fundamental aspect of the meaning of cooperation in international relations.

A variety of natural phenomena including droughts, floods and storms may cause crop failures and a consequent need for emergency food relief for populations already living at a level of marginal survival. Developing States not unreasonably view their vulnerability to disasters as an integral part of their underdevelopment. In many countries, food problems are increasingly perceived as an issue transcending national boundaries, and this perception should encourage new forms of international cooperation. Modern international law has developed its concern with matters of individual welfare to the point where the inacceptability of hunger, disease and ignorance as the inevitable lot of a large proportion of mankind may come to be the subject of increasingly detailed legal formulations. The role of disasters and disaster relief within this scheme is gaining acceptance. Going beyond the exclusively humanitarian approach, the recognition of the link between poverty and disasters provides a basis for expanded activities of relief and reform. A coordinated system of humanitarian assistance should thus be viewed as a concomitant of an international ecologically sound development strategy.

Some Restricted Principles of Rescue

Although not usually considered within the field of human rights law, it should be briefly noted that the principle of emergency humanitarian rescue has been established as a legal obligation by a number of national and international legal enactments in the special areas of maritime and astronautical safety. The degree of assistance that is imposed does not extend beyond the saving of immediately endangered life, but the provisions in question illustrate the adoption of a moral humanitarian obligation of assistance into legal form through State practice and codification.

The duty to assist persons and vessels in distress at sea, long emphasized in the municipal case law of some maritime States, found a place in the first conventions by which international safety measures were developed. Two conventions adopted by the Brussels Conference of 1910 aimed at the harmonization of rules of law relating to collisions, assistance and salvage at sea. Art. 11 of the Second Brussels Convention,[39] which contained an elaboration of provisions in the First Convention relating to the duty of ships' masters to rescue endangered persons found at sea, stated: "Every master is bound, so far as he can do so without serious danger to his vessel, her crew and passengers, to render assistance to everybody, even though an enemy, found at sea in danger of being lost".

Contracting States undertook to give effect to this principle of assistance by adopting appropriate national legislation. The first International Convention on the Safety of Life at Sea was signed in 1914, and it has since been revised several times. The Regulations on Safety of Navigation included in it in 1948 contained a provision dealing with obligations and procedures in assisting persons in distress.[40]

The same principles of rescue included in these instruments were embodied in Art. 12 of the 1958 Geneva Convention on the High Seas, and in Art. 98 of the 1982 United Nations Convention on the Law of the Sea.[41] The terms of Art. 12 and Art. 98 extend the duty of rescue to include an obligation to divert course upon receiving distress signals. Furthermore, the duty of assistance is imposed not only on the masters of ships but also on all signatory coastal States, who are required to promote search and rescue services. Although designed to operate in favour of individuals or small groups of shipwrecked persons, these principles are also applicable in cases where, for example, large numbers of refugees take to the high seas as a means of flight. Thus, in connection with asylum-seekers at sea in South-East Asia, appeals were made by humanitarian organizations to governments to respect the terms of the applicable instruments.[42]

Concerning astronauts, the duty of States to render all possible assistance in the event of distress, accident or emergency landing has been established in various international treaties, agreements and declarations. The duty of mutual assistance among astronauts themselves has also been formulated. The first relevant instrument, contained in a General Assembly resolution of 1963, took the form of a declaration of legal principles governing activities in outer space, part of which stipulates that "States shall regard astronauts as envoys of mankind, and shall render to them all possible assistance in the event of accident, distress, or emergency landing on the territory of a foreign State or on the high seas".[43] The terms of this Declaration, although regarded by many member States as only recommendatory and not intended to be legally binding, nevertheless expressed principles to which States were prepared to give support. Only four years later, the provision just quoted was incorporated into the 1967 Space Treaty, in which an obligation on astronauts themselves to render mutual assistance in space was also adopted.[44] The 1968 Agreement on the rescue of astronauts reiterated these obligations, referring to their basis in the promptings of sentiments of humanity.[45] The provisions of the Agreement, which were originally annexed to a General Assembly resolution and then independently signed by States involved in space activities as an international treaty, entered into force at the end of 1968.

In conclusion, it is apparent that even in the era before the development of international organization as known today, States found it to be in their best interests to cooperate with regard to potential and predictable emergencies involving a risk to human life in areas outside their territorial jurisdiction, in particular involving ships on the high seas. In this branch of law at least, the development of legal responsibility relating to protection and assistance for the human person has occurred as a response to a common form of disaster which may affect relatively small numbers of people. The importance of the complementary factors of necessity and reciprocity in motivating the development of this law should not be overlooked. The greater humanitarian problems of the present time may also provide a field for international agreement and action which should not only command the support of many States, but could also serve as a signpost towards the possibility of wider forms of international cooperation. There are clearly sufficient humanitarian needs to justify the attempt to work out and adopt the legal formulas which could contribute to the further development of this idea and of international humanitarian assistance actions.

4.5 The Doctrine of Humanitarian Intervention

The most extreme form of humanitarianism (although it is open to grave doubts whether that term can rightly be used in the present sense) is intervention by force in the name of humanity against a State in order to protect the fundamental human rights of the citizens of that State, the latter being unwilling or unable to do so itself. Humanitarian intervention thus presumes an ultimate limit to both a State's sovereign independence and freedom to deal with its citizens as it sees fit. None of the concepts in this short definition of humanitarian intervention may be easily defined in turn without arousing controversy, but there is no great dispute over the meaning of intervention, which is restricted here to the sense of dictatorial, armed or violent interference. Outside the area of forcible coercion the central legal problems raised by the doctrine are avoided.

A large number of situations may reasonably be included within such a definition, but it excludes other forms of pressure, intercession and self-help. Furthermore, the doctrine of humanitarian intervention must not be confused with that of the protection of nationals abroad which, although sometimes treated as a related concern in State practice, is a separate matter in international law.

The purpose of this section is to briefly examine the attempts which have been made to re-formulate the so-called classical doctrine of humanitarian intervention in a manner relevant to present circumstances. More generally, it may also be considered whether any lessons are to be learned from historical practice and scholarship in this area. Although its status was always at best precarious, the doctrine of humanitarian intervention in its classical form was invoked by a number of Western European States during the 19th century and it has been documented by various writers.[46] The injustices against which interventions took effect involved situations resulting from revolutions, persecutions and massacres, and the cases of intervention were usually confined to the protection of Christian minorities. As to the effectiveness of such operations, it is not widely suggested that a genuinely humanitarian outcome usually followed. Nevertheless, it cannot be denied that a number of authoritative publicists maintained the legality of humanitarian intervention, although the doctrine was never developed beyond a vague general formulation and some writers rejected it altogether.[47] In all cases, it appears that strong political interests of the intervening States coincided with their alleged humanitarian obligations.

During the League of Nations period a new version of the doctrine was propounded, based on a view of the expanded opportunities for concerted action by the organization. It was even envisaged that the doctrine could be applied in the broad fields of social and welfare activity with which the League was increasingly concerned.[48] In practice, however, the period witnessed the rapid abandonment of the principle of non-intervention, and with it any remaining pretence to higher international standards.

The main publicists of the doctrine recognized that the prohibition of non-interference in the affairs of another State was a generally accepted principle of international law. The basic question was therefore to establish the existence of the higher "laws of humanity" which would permit intervention in certain cases of humanitarian necessity. The only positive support that could be adduced was the Martens' Clause, first formulated in 1899.[49] Statements of the doctrine thus amounted in some cases to assertions of morality only. Reliance was also placed on natural law theorists, and one basis for humanitarian intervention was found to be a certain "humanitarian solidarity" or the "enlightened public opinion" in each country.

In more recent times, the doctrine has been wishfully resurrected by a few writers, in particular following various situations of great human suffering in Asia and Africa.[50] These writers again envisage an extensive concept of permissible intervention in a wide range of humanitarian emergency situations, while attempting to formulate appropriate safeguards against abuses. The basic position of those who argue the modern case for humanitarian intervention is that there exists a limited collective and individual right of States to take minimum enforcement measures to protect fundamental human rights. Thus, in situations of gross or persistent violations of human rights the UN Charter should be read as permitting humanitarian intervention, and if the UN does not act then groups of States or individual States are not precluded from taking forcible remedial measures. Consequently, it is argued, it is desirable to formulate precise criteria by which such exceptional and humanitarian intervention could be judged.

The modern case for humanitarian intervention relies on a view that the UN Charter provides little guidance as to the implementation of human rights, yet depends also on a major-purposes construction according equal weight to the protection of human rights and to the maintenance of peace and security. With regard to intervention by the United Nations, it is argued that gross or consistent violations of human rights may be a threat to international peace and are not a matter essentially within the domestic jurisdiction of States, and that therefore the principle of non-intervention expressed in Art. 2(7) of the Charter is not applicable. With regard to unilateral intervention, the argument is that the prohibition in Art. 2(4) is only on the use of force for specified unlawful ends, and that there is room for intervention for purposes not inconsistent with the basic purposes of the United Nations. The broad case is thus that the needs and dangers in cases of extreme human rights violations outweigh the risk of the abuse, in its use as an exceptional measure, of humanitarian intervention.

Various criteria have been proposed to enable the legitimacy of such action to be evaluated. It has been suggested that there must be an immediate and extensive threat to fundamental human rights; that the use of force must be no more than proportional to the original threat; that no greater destruction must result than would otherwise have been the case; and that prompt disengagement and immediate reporting to the Security Council must follow. Other criteria that have been stressed by adherents to the doctrine are the lack or exhaustion of other means of recourse, and the relative disinterestedness of the State taking coercive remedial action.[51]

The concept of humanitarian intervention cannot be divorced totally from its context, which is formed by the principles relating to intervention generally. However, a close examination of the term "intervention" is unnecessary in view of the element of force which is admitted to persist in humanitarian interventions of the type under consideration. Some efforts have been made to assert that it is in the nature of such intervention to be "non-authority oriented". Nevertheless, it should be recalled that the explicit purpose of humanitarian intervention is the unilateral or collective enforcement of corrective measures. The conclusion cannot be avoided that humanitarian intervention takes its effect against the authority of the State on whose territory it is practiced. The central issue remains whether a clear exception to the rules of non-intervention can be formulated in this case.

The terminology employed in Art. 2(4) of the UN Charter prohibits "the threat or use of force against the territorial integrity or political independence of any state", and many publicists have concluded that no qualifying or restrictive interpretation to this provision can be allowed. In accordance with this view, no use of force by a State is consistent with the purposes of the UN Charter except in case of self-defence.[52] With regard to collective enforcement action, in the case of a threat to the peace arising from a violation of human rights the Security Council is competent to take action under Chapter VII of the Charter, in particular Art. 39. The proponents of humanitarian intervention in present circumstances must therefore admit that emphasis should not be placed on that case. However, the statement that the United Nations may take such action should not be seen as providing a basis for a role of collective adjudication or settlement of the human rights issues at stake: the purpose of collective action under Chapter VII is to maintain or restore peace. If the Security Council were to decide to take measures following human rights violations within a State, such measures would be taken on the basis of a threat to or breach of international peace with the object of maintaining or restoring international peace and security, and not on the basis of human rights or humanitarian principles with the purpose of attaining human rights or humanitarian objectives.

Although many questions of interpretation of Arts. 2(4) and 2(7) have arisen in practice, the concept of humanitarian intervention has not figured in any prominent way in considerations of the use of force. Indeed, new instruments have been adopted to underline the inadmissibility of the use of force.[53] It is reasonable to conclude that the assertion of a right of forcible humanitarian intervention carries a heavy burden of proof. At no period has it been easy to justify humanitarian intervention under positive international law. Instead, the argument is advanced that respect for the human person imposes a limitation on the excesses of absolute sovereignty. The suggestion is that humanitarian intervention can actually uphold the foundations of law. However, a right to humanitarian intervention cannot be deduced simply from a view that the toleration of atrocities out of alleged respect for State sovereignty has reached dimensions threatening the whole legal order itself. On the contrary, it seems rather that wider solutions should be sought to the fundamental problems raised by the concept of the domain of domestic jurisdiction, which is one of the last vestiges of the doctrine of absolute sovereignty.

The doctrine of humanitarian intervention has never obtained full recognition in positive international law, but its existence can be seen as providing an indication of the importance of upholding certain higher principles concerning respect for the human person. The suggestion is that the implementation of at least the most fundamental human rights must be seen as the first precondition for the foundations of stable and enduring international organization and law.[54] Within this scheme, however, international efforts to alleviate human suffering should be seen as having the characteristic of humanitarian action rather than humanitarian intervention. Although the doctrine of humanitarian intervention may continue to be invoked by individual States pursuing their own regular political interests, a convincing application of the doctrine requires a high standard of non-intervention to be maintained in ordinary international intercourse, including in some cases of pressing need. At the same time, however, a more firm basis for humanitarian action remains to be attained.

4.6 Politics and Relief

Political factors have a prominent role in the global issues of international conflict, cooperation and development which form the setting for international humanitarian programmes. The humanitarian responses of States, bilaterally and through international organizations, are themselves considerably influenced by political considerations. It has been also commented that, increasingly, humanitarian values compete with realpolitik.[55] In fact, all humanitarian action has a political content because it takes place within a political context. Politics is therefore part of the framework not only for relief activities but also for the improvement of the international relief system.

Like other emergencies, disaster situations bring into question a government's competence and authority as it formulates a response. Strong political reasons exist for not publicizing the fact that a country is disaster-prone or has suffered a disaster, especially where there may be allegations of inefficiency in relief efforts. However, even though a government's commitment to relief organization and planning may have a direct effect on the internal political situation, the fact that international efforts are required to urge the implementation of prevention and preparedness measures at the national level indicates that deep obstacles persist to the recognition by many governments of the necessity of taking action against future humanitarian emergencies.

Political factors in relief operations are particularly evident when victims are denied effective assistance because of the deliberate policies of any of the authorities involved. For example, there may be delays in acknowledging the occurrence of a disaster, or the full extent of a disaster. The acknowledgement problem when relief is obstructed or withheld for political reasons has occurred in a variety of slow-developing natural disaster situations, and those involving civil wars. In one form, the problem consists in the reluctance of national authorities to permit international relief operations or to facilitate them. However, similar problems also arise within international relief agencies and donor States. Relief agencies may possess information on impending disaster situations or on the severity of disasters which have already occurred, but they may give priority to factors other than the immediate interests of the victims. Governments which are potential donors of international relief may consider certain regions to be of low priority in their overseas assistance policy. Disaster victims may consequently suffer an absolute or relative lack of assistance.

Another type of inequality in treatment resulting from political factors arises when the distribution of relief is made on a basis other than of need. The conduct of relief operations may be influenced by such considerations as internal security, regional development policy or commercial interests. Humanitarian assistance may be perceived as a political weapon of great value, especially by parties who are in conflict. The problem of impartiality or equity which arises in relief management raises the need for monitoring and assessment functions. The acknowledgement problem raises also the need for measures to ensure the initiation of relief operations, both in cases where governments are reluctant and where they are unable to act. In all situations it is evident that pre-disaster planning forms an important basis for effective action.

Since humanitarian programmes and policies, carried out bilaterally or through international organizations, cannot be approached as an entirely a-political matter, an increasing convergence between the political interests of States and humanitarian interests is necessary before more effective measures can be developed. Humanitarian actions are not always carried out for purely humanitarian reasons, being often motivated by, for example, economic and developmental considerations. There may, however, be compensations in this situation for the advancement of humanitarian aims.

Relief is not a static process. Indeed, disasters even provide certain opportunities for internal reform. The question of relief versus reform introduces a further political aspect into international assistance, since humanitarian action carries with it an opportunity to reshape the future. Political factors are also present in the area of humanitarian assistance in a more profound sense, for it is not people in general but rather the victims and suffering among mankind who are the objects of concern. The expression of such concern is itself a political act and involves a form of political commitment. Those engaged in humanitarian activity are thus engaged in politics, in the broad sense, in the struggle to achieve the implementation of particular principles or policy. From this point of view it is difficult to reject the potential of action within the political sphere for the advancement of humanitarian objectives. At the same time, these objectives may in turn provide routes for the convergence of political interests which today appear as obstacles in the way of an improved international humanitarian order.

5. Red Cross and Humanitarian Assistance

5.1 Introduction: the Red Cross Today

Structure

The Red Cross movement in its present form has a complex organizational structure, and it possesses various focal points and channels for its humanitarian activities. In general, Red Cross relief actions involve the National Societies as donors or beneficiaries and the two Red Cross institutions at the international level, the International Committee of the Red Cross and the League of Red Cross and Red Crescent Societies. A full consideration of Red Cross humanitarian assistance must take account of this framework before examining more closely its relevant functional and legal aspects.

The International Red Cross (IRC), as defined by its Statutes,[1] comprises National Red Cross and Red Crescent Societies, the International Committee of the Red Cross and the League of Red Cross Societies. The IRC's supreme deliberative body is the International Conference of the Red Cross which is composed of delegations of National Red Cross and Red Crescent Societies, the International Committee of the Red Cross, the League of Red Cross Societies and States parties to the Geneva Conventions. The Conference is convened normally every four years on a rotational basis among national member Societies. Certain functions of the International Conference are continued in the interval by the Standing Commission which is composed of nine members, five being elected *ad personam* by the Conference, two being representatives of the International Committee and two representatives of the League.

The Statutes of the IRC, adopted in 1928 and revised in 1952, form the ultimate constitutional point of reference for all parts of the movement. The Statutes provide that the International Conference may take decisions, make recommendations and express wishes, and assign mandates to the International Committee and to the League.

Conference resolutions may be executed either by the League or the Committee, according to the fields of competence established by their respective Constitution and Statutes and by a relationship agreement signed in 1951 and revised in 1969. The International Conference is not empowered to change the constitutional instruments of the League or the Committee; but they in turn cannot take decisions contrary to the Statutes of the IRC or to the resolutions of the International Conference.

States themselves are not members of the IRC, but they take part in the deliberations and decisions of the Conference. Resolutions of the Conferences supply a basis for the activities of the Red Cross, but they may not be regarded as State decisions and there is no commitment of powers by governments. Nevertheless, resolutions are "kept within feasible limits and compatible with the requirements of governments".[2] The Conferences thus offer a unique centre for cooperation towards national and international humanitarian goals.

The International Committee of the Red Cross (ICRC), as the founding body of the Red Cross movement, may be regarded as the guardian of Red Cross doctrine, and is the supremely neutral Red Cross institution exercising its functions primarily in situations of international and civil conflict. The ICRC is a private and independent association of not more than 25 Swiss citizens, and it enjoys legal personality under municipal law in Switzerland. At the same time, the autonomous international personality of the ICRC is recognized in public international law. Since 1947 the ICRC has enjoyed consultative status with the United Nations Economic and Social Council, despite the absence of an explicit provision for granting such status in the case of a private organization in a non-member State.[3] The ICRC's income derives from the Swiss government, National Red Cross and Red Crescent Societies, voluntary contributions from governments and from the proceeds of public collections. The ICRC acts on its own initiative without the authority of any State, but it appeals to governments, negotiates with them and concludes agreements with them.

The present Statutes of the ICRC were adopted in 1952 by the XVIIIth International Conference of the Red Cross. Under the Statutes the particular role of the ICRC is to maintain the fundamental principles of the Red Cross, to recognize any newly established National Red Cross or Red Crescent Society, to fulfil its tasks under the Geneva Conventions and to work for the improvement of international humanitarian law. Under Art. 4 of the Statutes a general role was also laid down in the following terms: "The ICRC may also take any humanitarian initiative which comes within its role as a specifically neutral and independent institution and consider any questions requiring examination by such an institution."

The Members of the ICRC are chosen and appointed by a process of co-optation, renewable every three years. An executive body follows current events and problems, while administrative duties and the implementation of decisions are the responsibility of the directorates. One of the most important responsibilities is the direction of the ICRC delegates in the field. In this task the long term continuity of policy is ensured by reference to the principles of the Red Cross and of humanitarian law, while responding to the exigencies of a specific operational situation.

The first National Societies were established soon after the founding of the movement by Henry Dunant, and at present there are some 130 Red Cross or Red Crescent Societies in existence. Originally constituted in almost all countries for the purpose of supporting the medical services of armed forces in time of war, their sphere of action has since been greatly widened to include many different welfare activities. The structure and activities of member Societies vary considerably from one country to another but remain within limits defined by the International Conference.

National Red Cross and Red Crescent Societies are private organizations governed by the laws of their respective countries but, like the ICRC, are the beneficiaries of the provisions of instruments of international humanitarian law to which they themselves are not parties. Their actions in conflict and the use of the emblems in peacetime are recognized and regulated by the Geneva Conventions and Additional Protocols. The Red Cross aim of the organization of auxiliary medical services for the armed forces necessarily gave rise to close collaboration between governments and National Societies, although the latter seek to maintain their independence in accordance with the fundamental principles of the movement. However, full independence of National Societies from governmental control is difficult to attain.

The role of the Red Cross at the national level in peacetime disaster relief varies from country to country. Several National Societies are the leading assistance organizations in their countries, and others are likely to become so in the future. In certain countries the National Society has become the official governmental agency for disaster relief; in others it reinforces government actions. Relief provided by the Red Cross is based upon needs and is given free of charge. The peacetime role of the Red Cross has been mentioned in resolutions of the United Nations, and the General Assembly and Economic and Social Council have recommended to members to promote the establishment of duly constituted National Societies.[4]

The League of Red Cross Societies (LRCS) was founded in 1919 as the international federation of the 26 National Societies then existing. The League is governed by its own Constitution and financed by member Societies. The League was created specifically to deal with natural disasters and to promote the development of National Societies so that the whole Red Cross movement would be better prepared for relief contingencies of all types.[5]

Constitutional provisions relating to the role of the League in humanitarian assistance are considered separately below. The League's general functions are laid down in the IRC Statutes. The League's Constitution, adopted in 1976, establishes its structure, reflecting its federal character and the range of humanitarian activities of National Societies, and provides in detail for its aims, purposes and functioning. The League's General Assembly, which consists of representatives of all National Societies, is the supreme decision-making body and its decisions have an obligatory character. The functions of the Assembly are continued in the interval by the Executive Council.

The Secretariat implements the League's policy. It is divided into bureaux representing the most important Red Cross activities, organized on a regional geographic basis. Officers responsible for relief operations assess the needs for assistance in stricken areas, launch appeals, coordinate the receipt of contributions and evaluate the relief operations. They also have a certain supervisory role regarding the observance of the Declaration of Principles for International Humanitarian Relief and, especially, the Principles and Rules for Red Cross disaster relief, which are discussed below. Other officers are responsible for relief supplies and disaster preparedness.

Principles

Although the Red Cross has always pursued comprehensive humanitarian aims it has taken the movement about a hundred years to define its fundamental principles. The early period, while not unmarked by notable debates on the movement's role and on the extension of its activities, was essentially one where growth and evolution took place in practice in the field. The immediate almost universal acceptance which the Red Cross gained, its unique constitutional structure and the entrenchment of the legal status of a part of its activities contributed to the development of mutual assistance between peoples and nations, based on the humanitarian actions actually carried out by the members.

In more recent times the principles of the Red Cross have been the subject of much discussion within the movement.[6] During the 1950s an authoritative formulation of seven fundamental principles was made, and subsequently adopted as Res. VIII of the XXth International Conference of 1965. The IRC Statutes refer to the fundamental principles, first among which is that of humanity: that the Red Cross endeavours to prevent and alleviate human suffering wherever it may be found. The other principles are those of impartiality, neutrality, independence, voluntary service, unity and universality.

The humanitarian principles which underlie Red Cross activity confer a special type of independence on the movement and its various organizations. From the principles derives the confidence which the movement inspires, enabling it to act as it does. As a result, most countries recognize and support the Red Cross. States have also recognized the fundamental principles of the Red Cross as basic determinants of Red Cross assistance actions for the benefit of victims of conflict by including mention of them in the Geneva Conventions and Additional Protocols. At the same time, it cannot be denied that these principles deserve to be better known and more widely applied.

5.2 Basis of Relief Activities

Division of Responsibilities

It has been noted that, broadly, the ICRC has responsibility for international assistance during armed conflict while the League is concerned with peacetime relief. The principal Red Cross constitutional texts call for regular liaison between the Committee and the League and require the coordination and harmonization of their activities as far as possible. However, the ICRC Statutes and the League's Constitution contain areas of overlap of functions; those relating to relief actions are referred to in greater detail in the next section below. For example, the ICRC can assume an important role in peacetime relief operations by acting in its capacity as a neutral institution. On the other hand, under Art. 5(1) (i) of its Constitution the League also may bring assistance to victims of armed conflicts, "within the framework of the agreed functions of the League as a member of the International Red Cross, in accordance with the agreements concluded with the International Committee of the Red Cross". In addition, the International Conference may allot joint tasks to both organizations.

Relations between the ICRC and the League are the subject of various mutual agreements: that of 1951 which contained provisions on the coordination of civilian relief was revised in 1969. The 1969 Agreement[7] recognizes that when the intervention of a neutral body is required the ICRC shall become involved. In cases where the League, as the federation of National Societies, is requested to undertake relief in conflict situations the mode of operations is to be determined on an *ad hoc* basis in accordance with agreed procedures. When intervention by a neutral intermediary is not or is no longer necessary, the ICRC is required to reach agreement with the League with a view to associating it with the relief action or even handing over to it the entire responsibility. The Agreement also covers situations where a natural disaster occurs during an armed conflict or where a conflict arises during a peacetime relief operation. The purpose of these provisions is to maintain cooperation between the ICRC, the League and National Societies when necessary, on a case by case basis.

Recent operations undertaken in common by the ICRC and the League, and the long history of such joint operations, serve to underline the unity of the Red Cross in action. However, special problems, especially of coordination, arise during such operations, which thus are only initiated in exceptional circumstances. After World War II the Red Cross was involved in the wider effects of the conflict, including the refugee problems. Joint relief work by the ICRC, the League and the American Friends Service Committee was undertaken for the United Nations in Palestine from 1948 to 1950. This set the pattern for a series of operations where Red Cross and Red Crescent Societies served the United Nations in humanitarian assistance. In the case of Hungary in 1956, the ICRC cooperated with the UN High Commissioner for Refugees and the political authorities involved to bring in supplies, coordinated by the League, while the Austrian Red Cross provided a base for the relief operation. At the ceasefire in Vietnam in 1973 the ICRC and the League created a joint operational entity for the Indo-China region and a special agreement was concluded providing for a cooperative assistance policy in that case. In Cambodia in 1979 a joint relief programme was launched designed to reach some two million people. More recently, the ICRC and the League have again been jointly involved in providing humanitarian assistance, for example to the needy in Poland.[8]

Internal Red Cross Law

The internal law of the Red Cross defining the rights and responsibilities of the various parts of the movement concerning humanitarian assistance may be divided into that contained in the basic constituent instruments, especially of the League and the ICRC, and that deriving from the decisions and resolutions of the governing bodies, particularly the International Conference.

With regard to National Red Cross and Red Crescent Societies, the fundamental principles of the Red Cross are the main determinants of action within their resources.

Aside from their traditional role in conflict, they are ready to undertake assistance on behalf of victims of many types of disaster, accident and misfortune. Some Societies have particular expertise in certain fields. In their work, the National Societies may rely on the active help and encouragement of the League. In this regard, Art. 7(2) of the IRC Statutes provides that:

> The object of the League is, within the framework of the present Statutes...to encourage and facilitate at all times the humanitarian action of the National Societies and to assume the responsibilities incumbent upon it as the federation of those Societies.

The League Constitution is more specific on the question of assistance. Art. 4 provides for the League's general objectives in similar terms to those just quoted. Art. 5 then sets out the League's functions in detail, providing for it to act as a permanent organ of coordination between the National Societies and to give them any assistance they may request. Art. 5 goes on to lay down the relief obligations of the League, as follows:

> c) to bring relief by all available means to all disaster victims;
>
> d) to assist National Societies in their disaster relief preparedness, in the organization of their relief actions and in the relief operations themselves:
>
> e) to organize, coordinate and direct international relief actions in accordance with the Principles and Rules adopted by the International Conference of the Red Cross; ...
>
> i) to bring help to victims of armed conflicts within the framework of the agreed functions of the League as a member of the International Red Cross, in accordance with the agreements concluded with the International Committee of the Red Cross (ICRC).

These provisions consolidate the relief practice of the League established over several decades in cases of natural disaster and armed conflict.

The emphasis of the ICRC's tasks is made clear in the general provision in Art. 6(5) of the IRC Statutes, which states that:

> As a neutral institution whose humanitarian work is carried out particularly in time of war, civil war, or internal strife, it endeavours at all times to ensure the protection of and assistance to military and civilian victims of such conflicts and of their direct results.

The substance of this provision is repeated in Art. 4(d) of the ICRC Statutes, with the addition of the phrase "and to serve, in humanitarian matters, as an intermediary between the parties".

Various resolutions of the International Conference and of the League's governing bodies are also important in regulating the relief activities of the Red Cross. Developments before World War II were considered in chapter 1 above. In the post-war period these resolutions, based on the assent of all the members of the IRC as well as of the States parties to the Geneva Conventions, have come to form a comprehensive system of rules covering questions of relief concerning National Societies, the general organization of relief at the international level and relations of the Red Cross with governments and with other relief organizations. They also deal with technical problems of relief operations. In addition to assuming a central place with regard to the preoccupations of the Red Cross, a number of these resolutions possess a significance extending beyond the movement and its own particular activities. They confront issues faced by all present day actors in disaster relief and some offer a consistent approach to common problems worthy of the attention of those seeking further improvements in the international relief system.[9]

The League's role in facilitating the relief efforts of National Societies, reiterated by Conference resolutions, remained the principal concern of the growing body of Red Cross law relating to international assistance. At the same time, the autonomy of National Societies in their relief actions was reaffirmed in the immediate post-war period. Resolutions were adopted stating, for example, that relief supplies should be forwarded between National Societies, and that the League should only launch appeals upon the express request of the Society of the disaster-stricken country. A resolution of the League's governing body, foreseeing the necessity for greater preparedness, recommended that National Societies should conclude bilateral or regional agreements covering mutual assistance in disasters.[10]

Other resolutions dealt with certain technical questions in relief operations, including exemptions from the usual formalities for the movement of personnel, supplies and funds. National Societies were requested to urge governments to adopt a standard policy in this regard and to accord such facilities as would increase the effectiveness of international Red Cross relief. Facilities were also requested from international organizations in the field of transport and communications. As a result the members of the International Air Transport Association agreed to offer free or reduced rates for the conveyance of relief supplies. Under the heading of "Measures to expedite international relief", a number of these technical questions were debated at the XXIIIrd Red Cross Conference in 1977 and formed the subject of an important resolution which was then endorsed and recited by the United Nations. The question of financial arrangements between National Societies and the international Red Cross institutions relating to the handling and forwarding of relief supplies was also considered in this period, along with the desirability of establishing a central emergency fund to be spent at the discretion of the League.[11]

Two important resolutions adopted in 1969 by the XXIst International Conference at Istanbul, substituted for the previous piecemeal approach to the regulation of Red Cross assistance a comprehensive strategy for international disaster relief by the movement. The first resolution takes the form of a short declaration, entitled Principles for International Humanitarian Relief to the Civilian Population in Disaster Situations.[12] The second resolution approved a set of Principles and Rules for Red Cross disaster relief and is considered separately in the next section below.

The 1969 Declaration opens by referring to the connection between disaster situations and basic human rights, demonstrated by the concern of the international community in disasters for the protection and welfare of the victims. The Declaration goes on to state that relief by impartial international organizations in natural or other disaster situations, for civilian populations, should as far as possible be treated as a humanitarian and non-political matter. It should be provided without discrimination and the offer of relief ought not to be regarded as an unfriendly act. Further paragraphs request all States to facilitate the transit, admission and distribution of relief supplies and to facilitate the disaster relief activities of impartial humanitarian international organizations. The activities of such organizations should be coordinated in order to ensure prompt action and effective allocation of resources.

The 1969 Declaration of Principles was adopted unanimously by the International Conference of the Red Cross, having been proposed by government delegations. It should therefore be regarded as an important statement in the formulation of a general body of principles applicable in global relief activities. The various paragraphs of the Declaration include provisions relating to peacetime relief activities which are comparable to the contents of those articles of the Geneva Conventions which establish relief law applicable in armed conflict. The Declaration is notable in that it concerns equally relief actions in both armed conflict and natural disaster situations. This recognition of the unity of humanitarian problems in all disaster situations is remarkable in an international instrument. However, the force of the Declaration must be regarded as moral or exhortatory only.

The 'Principles and Rules'

The Principles and Rules for Red Cross disaster relief were adopted unanimously by the XXIst International Conference of the Red Cross at Istanbul in 1969 and their provisions have been amended or supplemented by every subsequent Conference.[13] The approximately 30 paragraphs of this instrument provide a detailed basis for regulating the relief actions of National Red Cross and Red Crescent Societies in disaster situations. A reference to the Principles and Rules as the determinants of Red Cross relief actions is included in Art. 5(1) (e) of the Constitution of the League. After describing the provisions of the Principles and Rules, their contribution in the planning, coordination and operation of Red Cross policy and programmes relating to disaster relief will be assessed.

The Principles and Rules deal with the disaster relief and preparedness tasks of National Red Cross and Red Crescent Societies; with relations between National Societies and governments regarding these matters; with relations between the League and participating (donor) and operating (recipient) Societies in relief and preparedness actions; as well as with Red Cross relations with other national and international organizations involved in disaster situations.

Disasters are widely defined in Para. 1 as "situations resulting from natural or other calamities". Various general provisions are then set out, including the principle expressed in Para. 2 that the Red Cross considers it a fundamental duty to bring relief to all disaster victims. From this basic principle devolves the duty of National Societies to prepare themselves to give assistance in disasters. This duty is expressed in Para. 3 which also lays down an obligation of mutual assistance between National Societies in the following terms: "In view of the solidarity binding them together they shall help one another when faced with a situation exceeding their resources ... respecting the independence of each of them and the sovereignty of the stricken country".

Para. 4 continues by stating that disaster prevention, assistance and reconstruction are primarily the responsibilities of the public authorities. Red Cross relief is therefore in principle of an auxiliary or complementary nature, and is provided as an emergency measure; longer-term assistance programmes may also be undertaken if sufficient resources are available. In accordance with Para. 5, Red Cross assistance is provided free of charge and without discrimination on the basis of the relative importance of individual needs and in the order of their emergency. The initial general section of the Principles and Rules concludes with a reference to coordination of assistance, at both the national and international levels. Recognizing that relief operations require coordination, the substance of Para. 6 is that Red Cross programmes should endeavour to take into account assistance provided by other national and international organizations.

The Principles and Rules continue with two sections concerned with rights and duties of National Societies and the League, at the national level and in international assistance. Paras. 7 to 13 have regard to the national level; the main provisions which deserve to be mentioned relate to measures of preparedness for relief actions. Para. 7 states that every country should have a national plan outlining an effective system for the organization of relief. Where such plans do not exist National Societies should promote them and must establish their own plan of action in any case. Under Para. 11 the role of the League is to support National Societies by offering technical services and by facilitating the exchange of information. Paras. 12 and 13 urge National Societies to conclude agreements on mutual disaster assistance, and to seek facilities, privileges and exemptions from governments.

Regarding assistance at the international level, a number of important provisions are set out in Paras. 14 to 27. Para. 14 urges National Societies to inform the League about all large-scale disasters occurring within their country. Para. 15 sets out the procedures for the request and offer of relief. A request by a National Society for international assistance must be addressed to the League, which may then launch an appeal to other National Societies. No appeal will be launched by the League without a request; at the same time, the League has the right to take the initiative to offer assistance. The National Society concerned is bound under Para. 15 to "consider such offers with urgency and goodwill, bearing in mind the spirit in which they are made". In addition, provision is made in Paras. 22 and 23 for National Societies to entrust the local direction of relief operations to the League.

When a National Society is in receipt of international assistance the League will assign delegates or a liaison officer to assist with the relief operations in accordance with Para. 19. Such staff have the task of assisting the National Society and not of taking over its basic responsibilities. Under Paras. 19 and 20 the National Society concerned should grant all the facilities necessary to enable the chief delegate to communicate relevant information to the League, and must permit the liaison officer delegated by the League to view on the spot the use made of relief supplies. Provisions are laid down regarding the assignment and responsibilities of delegates, and these are supplemented by guidelines and instructions for use in the field.

The Principles and Rules are notable for the attention given to exchange of information regarding disaster occurrences, relief needs, commitments of goods and services and their utilization. The League is the information and coordination centre in the event of disaster. In the case of a disaster resulting in an appeal by the League to National Societies for assistance, Para. 16 requires the National Society of the stricken country to keep the League informed of all relevant developments in the situation; Para. 17 requires all National Societies providing assistance to a stricken country, whether as a result of an appeal, or on the basis of a bilateral arrangement or in other circumstances, to inform the League fully regarding the nature of its contributions. Under Para. 24 the spontaneous donation of relief, with the agreement of the National Society of the stricken country when there has been no appeal by the League, and with the agreement of both the recipient National Society and the League when an international appeal has been launched, shall also be reported to the League. National Societies are also required to inform the League of any agreements on mutual assistance which they may conclude.

The remaining paragraphs regulate a number of miscellaneous matters, including collections abroad, the donation of supplies while receiving assistance, the channels for the transmission of relief, the termination of relief operations and budgetary and accounting procedures. Finally, Para. 28 provides that every disaster relief operation carried out in a country where there is war, civil war or internal disorders shall be regulated by the provisions of the 1969 Agreement between the ICRC and the League.

Evaluation of the Principles and Rules should begin by noting that the instrument is based on previous Red Cross practice, which was sufficiently continuous to permit of codification. The Principles and Rules are founded on the fundamental principles of the Red Cross; they also draw on the practical experiences of the members of the Red Cross in humanitarian assistance in disaster situations and follow in the tradition of the large body of resolutions, extending back to 1863, regulating Red Cross relief activities. At the same time, the Principles and Rules are clearly a new step in the growth of Red Cross relief law. Evolving from the early period when emphasis was placed on the sole responsibilities of National Societies, through the period of expansion and consolidation of national activities within the federal framework of the League, the Principles and Rules now associate governments and all parts of the International Red Cross in an attempt to improve the effectiveness of relief operations. As one authoritative commentator stated, analysing the achievement of the 1969 International Conference in adopting the Principles and Rules, the provisions demonstrate a balance between the rights and responsibilities of participating and operating Societies.[14] They reinforce and clarify the powers of the League and help to distinguish the respective functions of the League and the International Committee. The fact that the Principles and Rules contain a number of indications regarding the role of governments in furthering solutions to problems of humanitarian assistance should not be overlooked.

The objective in adopting the Principles and Rules was to establish a set of guiding principles for the Red Cross in disaster relief. This objective gives a special character to the instrument and its contents. States who participated in the adoption of the Principles and Rules may also be regarded as associated with the commitments contained in its provisions. States have accepted the role of National Red Cross and Red Crescent Societies within the national disaster relief system, especially in connection with the adoption of measures of disaster preparedness; they have recognized that Red Cross assistance may only be provided in accordance with the fundamental principles of the Red Cross and with the provisions of the Principles and Rules; and they have accepted implicitly that the success of international disaster relief operations requires the granting of certain exceptions and facilities, and involves the entry of Red Cross delegates or a liaison officer of the League.

The view has therefore been offered that the Principles and Rules constitute a sort of Red Cross convention which should be respected and applied not only by the members of the Red Cross but also by governments.[15] However, it is clear that the nature of the undertakings contained in the Principles and Rules varies considerably from paragraph to paragraph. In a number of instances the involvement of governments in the implementation of provisions of the Principles and Rules only arises following a request for assistance by a National Society. On the other hand it will be recalled that the Principles and Rules enable the League to launch an appeal for relief assistance upon receiving a request from a National Society alone.[16]

The best general conclusion would appear to be that the Principles and Rules should be regarded as binding on the parties to whom they are addressed, namely, on the Red Cross and Red Crescent Societies. The Principles and Rules serve as a valuable point of reference in the field of international disaster relief, by virtue of their aims and content. The instrument is both reflective of general humanitarian principles and also incorporates specific practical solutions to relief problems. Certain of these problems may be encountered by other actors in international disaster relief operations. The Principles and Rules therefore have a potential significance which extends beyond purely internal Red Cross application. The contents and purposes of the instrument reaffirm that Red Cross activity is capable of contributing to the establishment and adaptation at the general international level of principles, rules and procedures relating to international disaster relief. The Principles and Rules are without doubt likely to undergo further progressive development in response to the continuing need for improved relief action within the Red Cross, and they provide sound guidelines for the adoption of more widely acceptable solutions to problems of humanitarian assistance.

5.3 Relief Role and Special Questions

Red Cross relief activities may be divided into three phases: assessment, procurement and distribution. Assessment comprises the surveying of the extent of destruction, the calculation of relief requirements and the ranking of needs in order of priority. Procurement refers to the tasks of fund raising, mobilization and forwarding of relief supplies and the assignment of personnel. The final phase is the conduct of the relief operation itself, both within the affected country and at the international level, including coordination. National Societies and the League are involved in each of these phases, as well as in post-disaster evaluation.

Relief supplies may be provided from a variety of sources, including stocks held by National Societies, local purchase, purchases made in other countries, and emergency reserves kept in a number of warehouses throughout the world. Some National Societies may have stocks of relief supplies sufficient to enable them to meet the most immediate requirements of a disaster. However, many Societies in disaster-prone countries are not in a position to establish and maintain large reserves and they need help from the League and sister Societies upon the occurrence of a disaster. This help may take the form of gifts of merchandise or money. When all parts of a country are not generally affected by a disaster national stocks can frequently be supplemented by local purchase at the time of need. National Societies should have reserve funds available for this purpose and the League may act as a purchasing agent on their behalf. The League also maintains a number of depots of vital basic supplies for use in emergency. When relief is provided from outside the Red Cross movement, the League acts as a clearing house.

Statistics of the volume of relief deliveries cannot alone provide a full picture of Red Cross assistance activities. Other important factors such as speed and efficiency of response and questions of organization should also be taken into account in assessing the impact and success of relief operations. The intangible characteristics of Red Cross assistance should thus be emphasized. One notable feature is that relief services may be adapted to a range of organizational forms for the conduct of particular operations. Another factor is the ability of the movement to act quickly and flexibly through government channels. Bilateral Red Cross assistance may often be supported or complemented by services provided by the government or armed forces of donor or recipient countries, for example the loan of transport aircraft.

An important review of Red Cross activities was undertaken by the Joint Committee for the Reappraisal of the Red Cross, and completed in 1976. The Committee presented its work in five background papers in addition to a final report, known as the Tansley Report, which embodied a series of recommendations.[17] The Tansley Report urged the need for binding guidelines and a basic policy regarding humanitarian assistance, especially in the emergency phase. When the Report was debated at the International Conference in 1977 some considered that there could be difficulties in establishing fixed rules for a far more complex reality in disaster than may be generally imagined. However, the International Conference emphasized that much depends on the role of National Societies within the national framework of disaster planning. Two approaches to the role of the Red Cross in assistance were illustrated at the Conference: on the one hand, some delegates insisted that their Societies' main activity should be general medical and social work with an emergency assistance role only in exceptional cases of need; on the other hand, there were many proponents of an active and broader commitment by the Red Cross to an international humanitarian role.

Despite strong support for the view that Red Cross disaster relief activities should be confined to the emergency phase, difficulties persist in defining objectively the end of the emergency. One proposed alternative to such a definitional approach concentrating on the nature of the emergency phase would require a closer delimitation of the specific types of assistance services which the Red Cross can provide.[18] This problem has often arisen in famine situations. Usually, but not always, the emergency phase for the Red Cross ends with the arrival of governmental assistance, either bilateral or through inter-governmental agencies.

The Red Cross is motivated and organized essentially for short term relief assistance in acute situations, but it may also be placed under pressure to undertake lengthy and large scale relief actions involving major feeding and supplementary nutrition programmes. It has been argued that the capacity of the Red Cross for relatively fast decision-making and implementation imposes a moral duty to accept tasks outside the movement's traditional field, as long as other solutions are lacking. In general, the policy of the League itself continues to stress the initial, emergency and temporary character of Red Cross assistance, although longer term operations are also mounted in particular cases and these operations may include joint actions with other organizations. The role of the League in the initial phase of disaster relief has also been acknowledged by the United Nations.[19]

In practice over the last two decades, Red Cross involvement in famine situations, at least at the acute stage, has been regarded as a natural function of the movement; to consider it as a notable extension of the Red Cross mission would be rather artificial. However, the definition of Red Cross responsibilities and the formulation of practical measures in regard to famine situations continue to receive special attention from the League and from many National Societies. The resolution of the XXIIIrd International Conference concerning famine recognized that the fundamental principle of humanity demanded Red Cross intervention in the many situations of famine and malnutrition in the world; and the League of Red Cross Societies has since started to give more attention, in addition to its emergency role and active field work, to the question of ultimate prevention.[20] The existence of many large scale semi-permanent emergency situations due to a variety of causes, including problems of extreme poverty, indicates the need for adjustment by the Red Cross to a non-traditional role. These problems, intimately associated with medium and long term development prospects in numerous disaster-prone countries, also confront other actors in the international disaster relief system.

Red Cross humanitarian assistance activities extend to beneficiaries other than victimes of natural disasters, especially to aliens, refugees and children. Since the time of the League of Nations and the creation of the post of High Commissioner for Russian Refugees with the support of the movement, Red Cross relief activities for refugees have expanded and they have in some cases been able to remedy deficiencies in assistance from more competent organizations.[21] In view of the early restrictions placed on the Office of the UN High Commissioner for Refugees, the ICRC made a statement in 1951 considering the refugee problem in strictly humanitarian terms and opening a great field of potential involvement for the movement.

Despite the expanded competence of the UN High Commissioner for material assistance the Red Cross has developed and maintained an active role of its own in refugee relief, particularly at the level of the National Societies. A statement in 1964 by the Secretary General of the League on refugee problems emphasized the wide meaning of the humanitarianism that underlies Red Cross assistance activities, making it clear that the concept of emergency is impaired if it is given a meaning taking more account of 'duration' than 'need'. Thus, when it is a question of resettling refugees the emergency may continue until those refugees become self supporting. The League has acted as the operational partner of UNHCR in some major refugee assistance operations, for example in the programme of assistance to returnees in Ethiopia. Responsibilities in such cases may be divided between the ICRC and the League. The legal basis for the activities of the Red Cross in favour of refugees may be deduced from provisions in all the primary constitutional texts of the Red Cross. A further basis is to be found in the articles of the Geneva Conventions and Additional Protocol I which grant certain competences of the ICRC, the League and National Societies. Concerning relief actions for refugees victims of armed conflicts, Art. 10 of the Fourth Convention of 1949 and Art. 81 of Protocol I of 1977 are particularly relevant.

The Tansley Report also recommended that the Red Cross should move to more assured methods of financing for its disaster relief activities. The League has expanded a system of guarantees established in 1973 by National Societies to cover immediate expenses in the initial stages of relief operations. Its reserve of funds backed by various Societies enables the League to make some immediate commitments upon the occurrence of sudden disasters.

Concerning prevention and preparedness measures, the Tansley Report concluded that Red Cross pre-disaster planning should be conceived and applied broadly: to cover both natural disaster and conflict situations, and donor and recipient National Societies, and to involve both the League and the ICRC. At the national level, one element of disaster preparedness measures includes the necessary legislative support. A national disaster relief plan is likely to have its foundation in municipal law or in a government decree or other administrative order. Such an instrument should include a definition of emergency and should set out the responsibilities and authority of the various bodies concerned with disaster relief actions. National Red Cross and Red Crescent Societies, supported by the ICRC and the League, have the duty to press for the adoption of legislation applicable in disasters. States themselves, in the Principles and Rules for Red Cross disaster relief, accepted that where a national relief plan does not exist the National Society should work for the establishment of one.[22]

The traditional humanitarian activities of the Red Cross fall within a framework of concern for world peace, a mission which the Red Cross regards itself as entitled to pursue. The original approach of Henry Dunant was not only to respond to human suffering and to mitigate the evils of warfare, but to put an end to war. The realization, expressed in the Charter of the United Nations, that there can be no true peace when human rights are violated and when inequality, injustice and discrimination prevail, reinforces the view that the discharge of the Red Cross duties of protection, assistance and community service are a contribution to peace. Impartial humanitarian activities and the application of the fundamental Red Cross principles form the basis of this contribution.

The League owes its foundation to hopes for an end to war and to the motivation of developing relief activities in a setting of peace. The fundamental principle of humanity inserted in the preamble of the League's Constitution stresses Red Cross responsibility for promoting mutual understanding, friendship, cooperation and lasting peace amongst all peoples. The statement of the general object of the League in Art. 4 of the Constitution refers to the purpose of preventing and alleviating human suffering, continuing: "and thereby contributing to the maintenance and the promotion of peace in the world". This clause suitably expresses the sense of the motto adopted by the League in 1961, *Per humanitatem ad pacem.*

5.4 Evaluation

The Red Cross is a world-wide movement in which humanitarian independence is pursued to the greatest possible extent in separation from politics. It has thus been described as "a network of humanitarian agencies potentially available for global action".[23] The universal presence and character of the Red Cross supplies its potential for action, based on its status deriving from its fundamental principles. At the international level, the Red Cross appears as a permanent and unique organization structured so as to combine private, non-governmental and governmental interests.

Disaster relief activities are the quintessential function of the Red Cross; their hallmarks are the constant readiness of the movement and the norms which underlie the conduct of its operations. The scope and scale of Red Cross actions in disasters provide an indication of its influence, and the resources it commands in terms of membership place it among the most important international organizations in the field of humanitarian assistance. In this sense, the Red Cross has an international status which may be best described as an international strength.

The Red Cross works on a long term basis for humanitarian ends and it thus seeks to be universally acceptable to all types of governments. Its mission has been characterized as "neutral humanitarianism".[24] The strict humanitarian stand which the Red Cross maintains has even provided grounds for criticism to the effect that its actions do not touch the roots of suffering: in short, that the Red Cross serves charity rather than justice.[25] Indeed, the Red Cross rarely concerns itself with legal proceedings and does not seek to be associated with the judicial investigation of allegations of illegal treatment. Nevertheless, the exclusion of legal and open political involvement from its functions does not reflect a disregard for practical problems. On the contrary, the continuing survival and achievements of the Red Cross suggest a remarkable expertise in apprehending and responding to the realities of international problems and relations.

In particular, the capacity of the Red Cross for extensive humanitarian actions in areas without clear authority in a specific body of law indicates the extent of the fund of respect and goodwill which it has built up internationally and nationally, maintained by intimate and confidential links of diplomacy. The Red Cross is not a static organization but its established mission and traditions provide stability and a constant source of reference in realizing new efforts in the face of relatively unchanging problems. By remaining outside the political sphere and pronouncing no judgments the Red Cross has acquired a status beyond its formal legal status which may enable it to intervene in humanitarian situations, even between a government and the people, more effectively than any other permanent international organization. In situations where the Red Cross works alongside other organizations, and on an equal footing with them, it retains a special position. All parts of the Red Cross benefit from this status.

Although the Red Cross is independent of governments, one component of its supreme deliberative process is governmental. This partnership undoubtedly accounts for part of the strength of the movement. However, the predominantly non-governmental character of the Red Cross as a whole and of its central operational institutions at the international level renders only tentative any evaluation of the juridical nature and status of the system. Several aspects of the structure and functioning of the Red Cross possess an obvious *de facto* existence but an uncertain *de jure* standing. It is probably for this reason that a past President of the ICRC wrote: "if there is a branch of law in which it is impossible to plunge directly *in medias res* into the analysis of legal rules, it is undoubtedly the law of the International Red Cross".[26] Other writers have agreed that Red Cross law is complex and difficult to characterize on a comparative basis; it should thus be regarded as a system *sui generis*. The influence of the Red Cross in fact depends not only on its formal status, but also on its practical aims, work and achievements.

At the national level of the movement, referring to potential donors and recipients of assistance, member Societies command the necessary public confidence to attract support and contributions, and are constituted so as to discharge their relief responsibilities in an efficient manner, normally in close conjunction with municipal authorities. At the international level, an effective system for the mobilization and coordination of relief is provided by the ICRC and the League within their respective fields of competence.

The ICRC's international status is established by the Geneva Conventions as well as by the decisions of the International Conferences of the Red Cross and by the acceptance of its practice by States. In its operations even within the Geneva Conventions and Additional Protocols, the ICRC may have no choice but to take "the approach of a friendly legal adviser rather than a policeman",[27] and the conclusion must be that its *locus standi* is a subsidiary issue to its actual presence in a humanitarian role. Its record shows a capacity to respond in practice, and the numerous circumstances not within the Geneva Conventions or Protocols when humanitarian principles need urgently to be applied have accustomed the ICRC to intervening by informal and unofficial means. In many situations, it performs a useful service to the parties as a guarantor of good intentions or as a reliable intermediary, and in filling the need for such a service it attempts also to secure objective humanitarian gains.

The League's logistical and technical abilities enable it to respond to all types of disaster situations in peacetime. Red Cross assistance includes a large bilateral component but, although relief is coordinated rather than directed by the League and concern for sovereignty on the part of National Societies is highly respected, increasing responsibilities have been conferred on the League. This trend is particularly evident in the Principles and Rules, where the duties of the League and National Societies in regard to international assistance are formulated in detail and in terms which are clearly intended to be binding within the movement.

Particularly since the International Conferences of 1965 and 1969 the Red Cross has produced a number of resolutions, which have been unanimously adopted, revealing several approaches to the current problems of disaster relief: they attempt to establish general humanitarian principles applicable in natural disasters; they lay down principles governing the actions of the Red Cross in natural disasters; and they provide recommendations for specific measures to improve the efficiency of international relief operations. Some provisions of these resolutions have been recognized and reiterated by the UN General Assembly, which has also noted the competence of the Red Cross in providing emergency humanitarian assistance.

All parts of the Red Cross have responsibility for the task of working for the dissemination and application of international humanitarian law, and for its further development. Red Cross activity at the national and international level is contributing in a number of specific areas to a growing movement towards concrete legal progress relating to international relief operations in humanitarian emergencies. The content and thrust of the Principles and Rules give particular support to this contention, as do the various steps taken under the heading of measures to expedite international relief. In addition, serious consideration has been given in recent years to the feasibility and desirability of proposing the adoption by States of a new instrument of international law dealing with protection and assistance for victims of natural disasters. These developments are extremely relevant to future legal progress in the field of international disaster relief, and they indicate that solutions to current problems of international humanitarian law and action are being sought on various levels. Based on increasing awareness of problems, obstacles and needs in relief, and stimulated by the concern of the humanitarian law of armed conflict with aspects of the control of relief supplies, during the preparatory conferences leading to the adoption of the Additional Protocols of 1977, a growing momentum is revealed for legal change in regard to international relief operations in peacetime.

More broadly, the proposal in the Tansley Report that the Red Cross should take a wider view of the possibilities open to it with regard to assistance should be noted.[28] One of the most important possibilities open to the movement is to be a spokesman or advocate for those in need. There is also room to develop the potential of the Red Cross as a network of humanitarian organizations to recall to governments the extent and significance of the commitments which have been undertaken already in developing Red Cross relief law.

The present period of evolution is of great importance for the Red Cross. The humanitarian law of armed conflict has flourished during the 20th century, but its central principle of respect for the human person is threatened by the existence of weapons of mass destruction. The problem of mass suffering arising from injustices and inequalities in the world may also prove to be a severe test for the Red Cross. However, the movement possesses considerable untapped resources. In particular, the

League of Red Cross and Red Crescent Societies retains a great potential as a humanitarian organization enjoying a special character and having a unique role: this potential derives especially from the membership, the activities and the scope for development of the world wide network of National Red Cross and Red Crescent Societies. Although it may be said that the law is less important than the opportunities and motivation available to the movement, the struggle to maintain and further extend the basis for humanitarian action in future situations of great need is likely to remain among the principal concerns of the Red Cross.

6. United Nations and Humanitarian Assistance

6.1 Early Developments in the Political Organs

The first United Nations resolutions on humanitarian assistance related to the immediate post-war situation and dealt with such matters as establishing a basis for relief for refugees, and with relief needs generally following the termination of UNRRA. In one resolution in 1946 the General Assembly directed the Secretary-General to consider ways and means of collecting contributions from persons, organizations and peoples all over the world for the purpose of helping to meet relief needs during 1947. The same resolution reaffirmed two important principles applicable to relief efforts, stating that "at no time should relief supplies be used as a political weapon, and ... no discrimination should be made in the distribution of relief supplies".[1] These early developments reflected some recognition by the United Nations of its humanitarian role in relief actions.

Other resolutions enabled relief programmes to be initiated and carried out for the benefit of Palestine refugees, and for relief and rehabilitation in Korea.[2] A further chain of developments began within the framework of the food planning functions of the Food and Agriculture Organization when an early General Assembly resolution expressed concern at the widespread existence of hunger in the world and recognized that the situation was exacerbated by many types of natural "accidents".[3] This resolution also urged governments to facilitate the emergency transport of food to famine areas, and it started consideration of the feasibility of establishing a world food reserve through the efforts of the United Nations. Developments in this area are considered below in the sections on the Food and Agriculture Organization and the World Food Programme.

Although few resolutions of a general nature relating to humanitarian assistance were adopted during the 1950s, both the Economic and Social Council and the General Assembly gave attention to relief in cases of natural disaster upon the occurrence of specific events calling for emergency action. In some instances relief actions were implemented through the United Nations. In the case of an earthquake in Ecuador in 1949 the Economic and Social Council invited the World Health Organization and the UN Children's Fund to give their attention to the problems arising which fell within their competence. In 1951 the General Assembly also considered the need for international relief for flood victims in Italy. Usually in such cases, resolutions took the form of a request for assistance addressed to the specialized agencies combined with an expression of hope that governments would take into account the special needs of the afflicted countries. Later, more specific requests were incorporated into resolutions, for example urging the increase of assistance and contributions from the specialized agencies, and inviting the participation of non-governmental organizations in relief efforts.[4] Concern was also shown regarding emergency situations arising from political events, and some UN programmes of assistance, including rehabilitation, were undertaken in the aftermath of armed conflicts.[5]

In 1963, following the earthquake which destroyed the Yugoslavian city of Skopje, the General Assembly urgently requested the heads of the relevant specialized agencies to bear in mind the immediate needs of that country when allocating their funds. A few days later this request was repeated on behalf of victims of a severe hurricane which had struck the Caribbean.[6] In the case of Skopje, in addition to immediate relief efforts, a special UN project was initiated to assist with reconstruction.

An increase during the 1960s in the direct provision of disaster relief by the United Nations was reflected in the frequency and content of resolutions of the General Assembly and Economic and Social Council. Voluntary contributions also began to be channelled through emergency trust funds established by the Secretary-General following specific disasters. In 1963 basic arrangements for inter-agency coordination in disaster relief were set out by the ACC.[7] In the following year the Economic and Social Council, in Res. 1049 (XXXVII) 1964, made the first request to the Secretary-General to study the types of assistance which the UN might be in a position to provide following natural disasters, as well as the magnitude of resources required and possible means of financing. This request marked a turning point in UN disaster relief policy: for the first time member States called on the Organization to examine its role in humanitarian assistance.

The corresponding reports which were submitted to the General Assembly and Economic and Social Council in 1965 described the resources of the UN available in cases of natural disaster, explained the coordination procedures set up by the ACC and expressed the Secretary-General's willingness to act as a coordinator.[8] It was noted that the UN system placed emphasis on rehabilitation and reconstruction rather than immediate assistance upon the first impact of a disaster. The Secretary-General's recommendations, following some suggestions of the Secretary General of the League of Red Cross Societies, stressed the possibility of the provision by the UN of specialized equipment and experts for immediate post-disaster assessment of damage and for supervision of urgent technical work during a relief operation. In addition to involvement in relief operations themselves, the reports gave equal emphasis to the importance of promoting understanding among governments of the necessity for pre-disaster planning, in particular with respect to the designation of a single national responsible authority. It was believed that a useful contribution by the UN could be made along the above lines with quite modest additional resources.

This review of UN programmes and policies relating to assistance in cases of natural disaster was consolidated in General Assembly Res. 2034 (XX) 1965 which noted the readiness of the Secretary-General to assist in coordination, and also to be at the disposal of international non-governmental organizations concerned with relief. The heads of all UN organizations and programmes concerned were invited to intensify their efforts to improve coordination, under the leadership of the Secretary-General. The resolution also recommended to member States the setting up of appropriate national machinery to assess relief requirements and to give unified direction to relief operations, if possible in cooperation with UN resident representatives. It recommended that the channels so established should be followed when external assistance was provided. It explicitly requested member States, when offering emergency services, to inform the Secretary-General of the type of assistance proposed.

This resolution also approved a proposal of the Secretary-General that he be authorized to draw on the UN Working Capital Fund to the amount of $100,000 for emergency assistance in any one year, with a normal ceiling of $20,000 per country per disaster. In the following two years the use of funds under this arrangement was made on eight occasions and the allocation was increased to $150,000 in 1969.[9]

6.2 Attempts to Revive the International Relief Union

During this early period of developments, various efforts were made to revive the International Relief Union, the assistance activities of which had ceased by the time of the outbreak of World War II. After the creation of the UN, the IRU had urged its member States to support a plan to bring it into relationship with the new Organization. At the fourth session of the IRU General Council, held in 1947 and attended by representatives of 17 States, a financial deficit was noted and it was recognized that future activities, if any, would necessarily be confined to scientific studies. However, a survey of the views of the membership revealed little support for continuation of the IRU in its then-existing form. Several proposals for its termination were put forward, as well as for its incorporation into the specialized agencies of the UN.[10]

The formal withdrawal of the Red Cross from the Union took place in accordance with a resolution of the XVIIth International Conference of the Red Cross in 1948.[11] During the early deliberations of the Economic and Social Council concerning its relations with inter-governmental organizations it was decided to defer a recommendation on the position of the IRU in view of a written appeal from the President of the ICRC advocating an attempt at the re-negotiation of the 1927 Convention.[12] The ICRC proposal reviewed the need for inter-governmental cooperation in humanitarian assistance in the past, demonstrated by the establishment of numerous *ad hoc* and temporary organizations, and argued that a simplified and more flexible organization should be supported by members of the UN, under a revised convention.

A report of the UN Secretary-General in 1950 contained brief notes bearing on possible options for the future of the IRU, but put forward no recommendations. However, the report did raise the question of whether the existing international framework for international relief offered a suitable basis for meeting humanitarian needs in disasters, especially where the resources of the stricken people were inadequate. Notwithstanding this report and the efforts of the ICRC, in 1950 the Economic and Social Council recommended to members of the UN also members of the IRU to terminate the Union.[13] However, by 1953 only Burma, India, New Zealand, the United Kingdom and Yugoslavia had notified their withdrawal and when the first UN list of recognized inter-governmental organizations was drawn up in the same year the Economic and Social Council agreed to the inclusion of the IRU under the category of organizations concerned with human rights, social welfare and migration.[14]

In 1966 a resolution was adopted by the Economic and Social Council requesting the Secretary-General to implement the transfer of the IRU's assets and responsibilities to the United Nations.[15] It was agreed that the UN Educational, Scientific and Cultural Organization was the most appropriate body to continue the study of preventive measures against disasters and that it would take over that function. No further mention was made of the IRU's functions of mobilization and coordination of relief. The final transfer of assets was effected during the late 1960s.[16]

At that period, the failure of the IRU was used as an argument by the Secretary-General against proposals for the creation of additional UN disaster funds constituted on a voluntary basis.[17] It was felt that yet another fund relying on voluntary contributions would not be a useful development, and therefore the recommendation was put forward for authorization to draw on the Working Capital Fund. However, in the following years the idea of such a voluntary fund was not entirely forgotten, and it was seriously revived upon the occurrence of various disasters. Following the severe earthquake in Peru in 1970 both the Committee of the Whole of the Economic Commission for Latin America and the Governing Council of the UN Development Programme recommended the establishment of a disaster emergency fund. This proposal was embodied shortly afterwards in a resolution of the Economic and Social Council which set up a general emergency fund, the first task of which was to assist Peru.[18] This fund did not receive substantial continuing support.

6.3 Appointment of the UN Disaster Relief Co-ordinator

In the late 1960s progress under General Assembly Res. 2034 (XX) was reviewed.[19] The most important development was the initiation of consideration to strengthen staff arrangements within the Secretariat for dealing with relief in natural disasters. Proposals included the establishment of a coordinating section, and the Secretary-General was requested to undertake a comprehensive study of UN assistance in cases of natural disasters. A survey of the activities of the relevant UN organizations was completed and in 1970 the Secretary-General submitted an Interim Report, entitled "Assistance in Cases of Natural Disaster", which prepared the way for a new phase of UN involvement in disaster relief.[20]

The allocation of $150,000 from the Working Capital Fund was acknowledged to be only a token gesture. It was openly recognized as inadequate in the first resolution which followed the devastation in East Pakistan as a result of the cyclone and tidal bore of 1970.[21] In the next year the amount which the Secretary-General was authorized to expend was increased to $200,000 per annum by the General Assembly resolution which established the Office of the UN Disaster Relief Co-ordinator.[22] Allocations from this source proved to be of use in the early life of the Co-ordinator's Office, but the new role given to the Secretary-General by his ability to draw on the Working Capital Fund remained largely symbolic and could not greatly alter the established patterns of international assistance.

During the preparation of the comprehensive report on UN disaster assistance the Secretary-General's terms of reference were further elaborated. The Economic and Social Council and the General Assembly recommended that the study should maintain a distinction between assistance during the emergency phase and subsequent reconstruction. The study was to incorporate recommendations on the capabilities of the different parts of the UN to contribute assistance, on the areas and means for increasing assistance, on procedures for immediate assessment of damage and requirements and for better coordination; it was to suggest measures to improve national and international pre-disaster planning; and it was to study the processes of reconstruction.[23] Against the background of the international response to a number of emergency situations which occurred at about the turn of the decade, including the Nigerian civil war, the Peruvian earthquake of May 1970 and the catastrophe in East Pakistan and Bangladesh beginning with the cyclone of November 1970, general agreement on the expansion of the UN role in disaster relief was achieved, despite continuing differences of opinion between States on the nature of that role.

The Comprehensive Report of the Secretary-General, entitled "Assistance in Cases of Natural Disaster", was submitted in 1971.[24] It recommended that countries affected by disasters should be able to count on the help of the international community, provided through governments, the League of Red Cross Societies, and other voluntary agencies, or the United Nations organizations.[25] In accepting the report the General Assembly noted the competence of a number of UN specialized agencies to render assistance in natural disasters and other disaster situations. It was apparent that the informal and *ad hoc* emergency procedures of the UN were insufficient, and the outcome of the report was the establishment of the Office of the UN Disaster Relief Co-ordinator by General Assembly Res. 2816 (XXVI) 1971. The role and evolution of the Office, along with the most recent developments in the political organs concerning relief coordination, are considered in chapter 8 below.

Following the appointment of the Disaster Relief Co-ordinator, resolutions of the UN Economic and Social Council and General Assembly continued to refer to assistance in cases of disaster and continued to mention the role of the Secretary-General in this connection. Better measures were urged for dealing with disasters and for more effective maintenance and utilization of emergency stockpiles within the UN system. Increasing concern was shown for preparedness and prevention, and for the question of immediate needs resulting from economic emergencies.

Concerning pre-disaster planning, General Assembly Res. 2034 (XX) had contained the first statement that the UN could offer advice and assistance upon receiving requests from governments regarding all types of planning measures. Such measures were soon given a place of importance alongside attempts to improve emergency relief. In the Comprehensive Report of 1971 the Secretary-General placed emphasis on the importance of national responsibility for disaster planning. It was pointed out that many national emergency plans were inadequate and that many countries in disaster-prone areas had no plans at all. Therefore, planning and prevention were also important fields for increased international assistance. The Secretary-General was subsequently authorized to use $25,000 in 1973 from the Working Capital Fund for the elaboration of national preparedness measures. Planning and prevention continues to be an important element of the work of the Office of the UN Disaster Relief Coordinator.[26]

With regard to economic emergencies, the connection between disasters and development is to be noted in the 1970 Interim Report of the Secretary-General, which stated that although the primary concern of the UN system with the problem of natural disasters was humanitarian, the economic implications, especially for the developing countries, could not be disregarded.[27] Within the context of international development, and in particular of the establishment of a new international economic order, this connection has been expanded to provide a basis for international emergency assistance. The programme of action established by the General Assembly following its 1974 Declaration on the Establishment of a New International Economic Order included a Special Programme designed to provide emergency relief and development assistance to the most seriously affected developing countries.[28] At the same time, the Secretary-General was requested to launch an emergency operation to maintain essential imports during 1975 in these countries, which were defined as the least developed, the land-locked, and other low income developing countries whose economies had been seriously dislocated as a result of economic crisis, natural disasters and acts of aggression and occupation.

In 1975 the General Assembly's Seventh Special Session on international economic cooperation adopted a resolution which stated: "Special attention should be given by the international community to the phenomena of natural disasters which frequently afflict many parts of the world, with far-reaching devastating economic, social and structural consequences, particularly in the least developed countries".[29] The General Assembly was requested to adopt appropriate measures at its 30th session, and in Res. 3510 (XXX) 1975, entitled "Immediate Needs Resulting from Economic Emergency Situations", called for remedial action against the consequences of such emergencies, particularly on behalf of the most vulnerable people in the poorest countries. The Secretary-General was requested to submit proposals to the Economic and Social Council for identifying and proclaiming economic emergencies, as well as for strengthening UN coordination within the existing financial limitations.

For the purpose of assessing the UN's role, the Secretary-General's report in 1976 grouped the category of "disaster-like economic emergency situations" with other disasters faced by the UN system, which also included the category of "permanent or semi-permanent emergency situations" characterizing the condition of the lowest income groups within developing countries. The report did not make specific proposals for an operational response to such situations, although suggestions were made relating to monitoring and the assessment of data indicating emergencies, as well as coordination generally. These proposals were repeated in a similar report of 1977,[30] in connection with the creation of the Office of the Co-ordinator for Special Economic Assistance Programmes within the UN Secretariat.

The Economic and Social Council continued to deal with the question of immediate needs resulting from economic emergency situations. More recent resolutions of the General Assembly reveal some development of the concept and refer to the provision of assistance to meet immediate requirements within that framework. For example, measures of assistance have been urged from the developed countries in favour of developing island nations, and in favour of other particular countries with immediate food and material needs within the context of their economic independence and development.[31] Questions of special economic and humanitarian assistance continue to appear regularly on the agenda of the Economic and Social Council, reflecting the needs to be met in disasters or other emergency situations. The involvement and activities of the UN and the specialized agencies in such situations continue to increase. The most recent developments which have taken place under the rubric of strengthening the capacity of the United Nations system to respond to natural disasters and other disaster situations are examined in chapter 8 below.

6.4 Principal Agents of UN Humanitarian Assistance

United Nations Children's Fund (UNICEF)

Created in 1946 as the International Children's Emergency Fund, UNICEF was established by the General Assembly with reference to Art. 55 of the UN Charter to work for the immediate relief of children in countries where UNRRA aid was being received.[32] It was initially financed partly by assets transferred upon the closure of UNRRA and by other voluntary contributions. The General Assembly resolution which brought UNICEF into being established an Executive Board consisting of government representatives headed by an Executive Director appointed by the Secretary-General in consultation with the Board. The Director acts in accordance with the policies laid down by the Board, under the general supervision of the Economic and Social Council.

Following the gradual termination of its immediate relief tasks after World War II, UNICEF's assistance programmes were intensified and extended geographically. In 1953 UNICEF was continued on a permanent basis, with the name UN Children's Fund, and three years later the membership of the Executive Board was increased to 30 States.[33]

UNICEF's original function of aiding needy children, as well as nursing and expectant mothers, was fulfilled by the direct provision of food, clothing and medical supplies. UNICEF's potential role in disasters was recognized by the General Assembly when it referred to the necessity for continuing action "to relieve the suffering of children, particularly in under-developed countries that have been subjected to the devastation of war and other calamities"; UNICEF was also commended for its role in humanitarian assistance in cases of emergencies such as floods, earthquakes and droughts.[34] In most disaster-prone developing countries about half the total population is under the age of fifteen; many children suffer from some form of malnutrition and are susceptible to increased incidence of disease, and therefore constitute a specially vulnerable group among disaster victims. Infants and young children have particular needs which should be taken account of in disaster assistance. Separate estimates of relief requirements for the adult population, pregnant and nursing mothers, and children are desirable.

Along with the expansion of UNICEF's activities into fields other than immediate relief, oriented towards general health and welfare goals within the framework of long term development needs, the provision of assistance to the least developed countries was intensified. As a result of increasing requests for emergency relief for children in the late 1960s and early 1970s, an emergency fund was established enabling up to $100,000 per annum to be drawn for immediate relief purposes. The Executive Board also agreed that UNICEF would provide procurement and other services beyond its usual role, in order to contribute to the development of the overall UN system of emergency assistance. During this period UNICEF commitments to purely relief activities amounted to about ten per cent of its total aid programmes and the UN continued to endorse its relief functions "in natural and other disasters".[35] Further developments have taken place. The Executive Board authorizes annual expenditure of an increased emergency reserve for immediate relief. Additionally, local UNICEF representatives are empowered to use funds from regular programmes for emergency assistance, or to divert supplies in hand when more appropriate. The Executive Board also approved the creation of the post of Co-ordinator of Emergency Operations and special relief programmes are authorized to the extent that voluntary contributions are forthcoming. Special appeals for emergency contributions are also regularly made.[36]

UNICEF, which began as an emergency relief agency and then developed long term assistance objectives, retains an active role in disasters. Its objective in disaster relief is to ensure the survival and well-being of children and UNICEF discharges this function particularly in situations where other donors do not respond adequately. UNICEF has developed its own emergency information, coordination, supply and funding systems enabling it to react quickly and effectively in its special field. In many recent cases UNICEF relief actions have been part of wider international operations, but have concentrated on meeting the special needs of children which are not always understood or are neglected in the provision of basic relief. UNICEF continues to be financed entirely by voluntary contributions.

United Nations Development Programme (UNDP)

UNDP came into being in 1965 when the General Assembly combined the Expanded Programme of Technical Assistance and the UN Special Fund which had been established in 1950 and 1959 respectively to provide technical assistance to the less developed countries, using finance from outside the UN regular budget.[37] UNDP is the major coordinating and funding body for UN development assistance, as well as "a potent unifying force in the UN system"[38] in that it carries out the key task of coordinating important operational activities at headquarters and country level. The Programme's work continues to be financed by voluntary contributions from governments of States members of the United Nations and its related agencies.

Development programmes are conducted by UNDP in virtually every country and territory of the world, in which resident representatives are maintained. Being closely involved with many disaster prone areas, UNDP has evolved various roles in connection with emergency humanitarian relief. UNDP is able to provide various types of direct assistance in disasters and also gives particular emphasis to supporting disaster preparedness and prevention projects; its country development programmes may also be adapted to the needs of rehabilitation and reconstruction following disasters.

The members of UNDP's Governing Council, which has responsibility for approving projects, allocating funds and overseeing operations, are elected from among nations at all stages of development. The Programme is directed by the Administrator and his staff in New York, taking into account the advice of an Inter-Agency Consultative Board.

Since 1972 UNDP resident representatives have acted in the field on behalf of the UN Disaster Relief Co-ordinator. This arrangement has been referred to in various resolutions of the General Assembly and Economic and Social Council. Instructions concerning disaster relief issued by the Administrator advise resident representatives on such matters as relationships with national disaster relief authorities, with governmental and non-governmental donor sources and with representatives of other UN organizations. These instructions also deal with procedures for communication with the Office of the Disaster Relief Co-ordinator, with local coordination of UN disaster relief activities, and with other matters including disaster preparedness and prevention.[39] UNDP can thus play an important and even pivotal role in disaster situations and continues to undertake many disaster-related projects.

In 1976 the UN Sahelian Office, set up within the UN Secretariat for coordination and fund management purposes during the early UN response in the Sudano-Sahelian drought disaster, and directed by the present Administrator of UNDP, was transferred from the Secretary-General's Office to the Development Programme.[40] The expertise of the Sahelian Office reinforced the capacity of UNDP in regard to disaster relief. Various projects have been organized in collaboration with the Permanent Inter-State Committee for Drought Control in the Sahel (CILSS).

In 1980 the Governing Council again considered the Programme's response in natural disaster situations. The criteria for UNDP assistance in disasters were further defined in a Council decision and guidelines for expenditure on longer term disaster-related assistance were also provided. Since 1981 new procedures laid down by the General Assembly relating to the responsibilities of the resident representatives have been followed in many emergency situations.[41]

Food and Agriculture Organization (FAO)

FAO was created in accordance with the Final Act of the UN Conference on Food and Agriculture of 1943 and its Constitution, which has since been amended several times, came into effect in 1945.[42] The principal issue which faced the Conference and which led to the creation of FAO was the urgent short term food problem foreseen before the end of World War II, but the humanitarian and moral implications of world-wide inequalities in availability of food supplies were also debated. FAO's purposes as set out in the preamble to the Constitution include raising levels of nutrition and standards of living, securing improvements in the efficiency of the production and distribution of food and agriculture products, and improving the conditions of rural populations. FAO's governing body is the Conference, composed of one representative from each member country and empowered by the Constitution to take the necessary action to implement the purposes of the Organization as set forth in the preamble.

One particular objective of FAO's policies was the relieving of famine and other emergency food shortages. However, FAO was conceived only as an advisory organization; it possessed no operational international functions beyond a limited provision for certain types of technical aid. FAO's early activities are significant for their contribution to the development of concepts of more equitable distribution and availability of food. FAO has also made an important contribution to emergency humanitarian assistance through the World Food Programme, a joint UN-FAO venture established in 1961, which is considered separately below. In addition, developments examined briefly here have included the creation of subsidiary offices as the focal point for concerted UN emergency relief. A further shift in emphasis to field operations has also taken place within FAO itself.

The post-war situation of relatively temporary stringency in Europe was transformed by droughts and the severity of the winter of 1946 to 1947 into a world food crisis, which highlighted the inadequacy of existing machinery for meeting emergency food needs. A new agency, the International Emergency Food Council, to which FAO acted as secretariat, was established and functioned until 1949 to allocate food supplies to claimants such as UNRRA. Further UN efforts relating to emergency food relief were initiated in the Economic and Social Council in 1951, but little progress was made beyond the existing pattern of bilateral assistance arrangements.[43] Against this background, in 1952 the General Assembly expressed interest for the first time in setting up procedures for dealing with future famine emergencies resulting from natural causes, recognizing that "in addition to widespread conditions of hunger, famines are created through plague, drought, flood, volcanic eruption, earthquakes and similar accidents of a natural character".[44] The Secretary-General was requested to report on ways of bringing about concerted action by governments, inter-governmental organizations and voluntary agencies in famine situations, and governments were urged to facilitate the transportation of food to famine areas.

The report which was submitted in 1952 to the Economic and Social Council suggested various sources for increased financial assistance, including advance voluntary pledges by governments, formal budgeted contributions, use of the Secretary-

General's authority to make special disbursements from the Working Capital Fund, and refundable advances from the specialized agencies.[45] FAO also made its own parallel study of the feasibility of an emergency relief fund, but in 1953 the FAO Conference declined to pursue the idea further. Despite all the preparatory work, the political commitments necessary for further progress were not forthcoming.

Separate efforts continued towards the creation of a world food reserve, one of the originally proposed functions of which was to meet any emergency that might arise through failure of crops in any part of the world. However, within the FAO Conference and the UN itself only very slow progress was made in recognizing the need for such a reserve, despite recognition that a favourable interaction would probably exist between food reserves and emergency relief, in particular by reducing delays in delivery of assistance. In the 1960s various resolutions of international bodies were devoted to problems of economic development in poor countries, but no direct mention of emergency situations was made, except upon the creation of the UN-FAO World Food Programme in 1961.[46] By the early 1970s the world was suffering the effects of increasing disruptions in the global food system and the plight of millions already malnourished became a special international concern in the context of the growing food deficits of many developing countries. Non-aligned countries called for an emergency meeting on food shortages, which led in 1974 to the World Food Conference, the adoption of a Declaration on the Eradication of Hunger and Malnutrition, and the creation of the World Food Council.[47] The World Food Council, charged to work for the implementation of the World Food Conference resolutions, has a membership of 36 States nominated by the Economic and Social Council and elected by the General Assembly; it is the highest UN organ dealing exclusively with world food problems, including emergency food aid.

The 1974 Conference resolutions announced a strategy to attack the major aspects of the world food crisis, including food production, food security, food aid, nutrition and food trade. Resolution 17 contained a non-binding undertaking by governments to ensure the availability of adequate world supplies of basic foodstuffs "so as to avoid acute food shortages in the event of widespread crop failures or natural disasters". The World Food Council's Manila Communiqué of June 24, 1977 set out specific objectives for the strategy, urging support for an International Emergency Food Reserve of half a million tons of cereals, which has now been achieved. A system to monitor the world food supply and to identify and assess possible emergency requirements was also set up by the World Food Conference and is operated by FAO.[48]

Within FAO itself, the Office for Sahelian Relief Operations (OSRO), founded in 1973 to act as the focal point for UN emergency relief to the Sahelian zone affected by drought, was renamed in October 1975 as the Office for Special Relief Operations. OSRO's aim was widened to include global emergency operations falling within FAO's fields of competence. The Sahel has continued to be one of OSRO's main preoccupations and multidonor missions under its aegis have been carried out to examine the prospects of local food production and requirements, and to estimate the deficit to be met by external assistance.

In July 1976 the FAO Council approved a new Technical Co-operation Programme emphasizing field operations and providing for assistance in four main categories, one of which comprises emergencies following disasters and the outbreak of pests and diseases. The purpose of the emergency assistance capability is to permit FAO to meet urgent rehabilitation needs after disasters or disturbances which affect a country's food and agriculture situation, and which cannot be covered by the activities of the Office of the UN Disaster Relief Co-ordinator or the World Food Programme.

World Food Programme (WFP)

Since it became operational in 1963, as an experimental three-year joint UN and FAO venture, WFP has become an important source of food aid for development. WFP possesses a significant role in disaster assistance operations through the supply of basic foodstuffs, fulfilling one of its constitutional functions, namely to contribute to "establishing adequate and orderly procedures on a world-wide basis for meeting emergency food needs".[49] WFP is headed by the Executive Director who reports to the UN Secretary-General and the FAO Director-General. The General Regulations and other internal rules, approved by the Economic and Social Council, constitute the basic texts governing the management and activities of the Programme. These instruments set out the acceptable methods of financial and commodity pledging and specify the categories under which food aid may be provided.

Three areas of assistance were envisaged: to meet emergency food needs and emergencies inherent in chronic malnutrition; to assist in pre-school and school feeding; and to use food as an aid to economic development in pilot projects. Emergency needs were interpreted as "food needs arising from sudden and unexpected natural disasters, such as earthquakes, floods, droughts, pests and epidemic diseases ... and man-made emergency situations, including political conditions rendering persons homeless".[50] Twenty five per cent of the Programme's commodity resources were earmarked for use in emergency situations. Cash contributions, for example to pay for food transportation, are also sought on a voluntary basis.

In 1965 WFP was established on a continuing basis, subject to the regular review of its pledging conferences.[51] A programme of studies on multilateral food aid within the context of the first and second Development Decades was followed by a General Assembly resolution which drew attention to WFP's role in multilateral operations and stressed the importance of food aid for humanitarian as well as economic objectives; the reference in the resolution to emergency humanitarian requirements included the problem of chronic nutritional deficiency generally.[52] It was apparent that as a multilateral organization administering food aid WFP was bound to bear responsibilities in cases of natural and man-made disasters and cooperation between the Programme and other UN agencies and the League of Red Cross Societies was strengthened. At the completion of its first decade of operations, 159 emergency operations had been supported by WFP in 76 countries at a cost of $110 million, representing 15 per cent of its total expenditure; drought situations absorbed 44 per cent of total emergency allocations, while other natural disasters and man-made emergencies took 33 and 23 per cent respectively.

Following the conclusion of food aid conventions, more States began to channel contributions through WFP and larger allocations for emergency relief were possible. In 1975 internal reorganization changed WFP's governing body to the Committee on Food Aid Policies and Programmes, with membership increased to thirty countries. An Emergency Services office was established to assess emergency requirements and coordinate assistance; it also provides a service for bilateral relief donors on request. New regulations increased the maximum allocation for emergency assistance. Additional commodity resources also became available to WFP from the International Emergency Food Reserve for "crisis situations in developing countries".[53] Expansion of WFP emergency assistance activities has continued to take place, especially for the benefit of victims of floods and droughts, refugees, and other displaced civilians in conflict situations.

World Health Organization (WHO)

Following the convening of the International Health Conference in New York in 1946, in conformity with Art. 59 of the UN Charter, WHO's Constitution was adopted by 61 governments on July 22, 1946.[54] WHO's central organs are the World Health Assembly, the Executive Board and the Secretariat, under the Director-General. The members of the Assembly meet annually and may exercise legislative regulative powers within defined limits and adopt agreements or conventions within WHO's competence.

According to Art. 1 of the Constitution, WHO's objective is the attainment by all peoples of the highest possible level of health, defined as "a state of complete physical, mental and social well-being and not merely the absence of disease or infirmity". Various functions were laid down appropriate to WHO's role as a directing and coordinating body in international health work, including, in Art. 2(d), provision for WHO "to furnish, in emergencies, necessary aid upon the request or acceptance of governments".

Although WHO has only a limited capacity for direct relief assistance, various initiatives have strengthened its role in relief actions and in response to disasters. In 1954 the Executive Board established a special fund to meet emergencies and unforeseen contingencies. Small field teams were enabled to assist directly with specific relief tasks and both field and headquarters activities are conducted in close cooperation with the League of Red Cross Societies and national health services. More recently, the Executive Board and the Assembly reviewed WHO's role in emergency situations and strengthened the Organization's capacity for meeting the needs of disaster stricken countries. In 1974 the position was created of the Responsible Officer for WHO Emergency Relief Operations, to serve as a link between emergency situations and the office of the Director-General. A special account for disasters was also created, enabling WHO to act as an independent donor.

An internal survey of WHO's emergency operations completed in 1975 suggested that existing resolutions of the Assembly provide a mandate for relief activities and recommended that relief actions should be expanded along with rehabilitation programmes. More recently, higher financial allocations for emergency relief have been approved to enable WHO to undertake a more active operational role.[55] Under an emergency programme emphasizing national responsibility for relief coordination, regional directors have allocated as much responsibility as possible to field representatives. Close cooperation is maintained with other UN agencies and with non-governmental organizations involved in relief.

Other UN Organizations

Many UN specialized agencies, subsidiary organs, and associated bodies are concerned with disaster related matters, including preparedness, finance, reconstruction, technical services, communications and transportation. The principal agencies considered above are all to some extent dependent on the personnel, resources and skills of the constellation of other UN organizations and it is appropriate to note briefly the role of a number of these organizations in the preparation, support and implementation of relief operations.

The United Nations Conference on Trade and Development (UNCTAD) is concerned with permanent or semi-permanent emergency situations. UNCTAD IV recommended special measures in favour of the least developed, developing island and developing land-locked countries and referred in its Resolution 98(IV), paragraphs 98 and 99, to the need for effective and speedy relief by the international community in cases of natural disaster in such countries. The Conference also recommended that these countries should take into account vulnerability to natural disasters in elaborating their economic development programmes, and that bilateral and multilateral assistance should be provided in the establishment of national or regional disaster preparedness plans.[56]

The United Nations Educational, Scientific and Cultural Organization (UNESCO) is concerned with scientific and technical aspects of disaster prevention. UNESCO studies the causes and mechanisms of natural phenomena with the aim of defining vulnerable zones and providing effective forecasting and warning. Special attention has been given to volcanology and to measures to predict earthquakes and to mitigate earthquake damage. UNESCO can also assist in the reconstruction of educational and cultural establishments that have suffered damage from disasters. A project is being developed on the protection of cultural property in natural disasters which may lead to the promotion of an international legal instrument on the subject.[57]

The United Nations Environment Programme (UNEP) has accepted natural disasters as an important programme area. International cooperation in environmental emergencies includes various legal and institutional developments which seek to establish a basis for remedial action.[58]

The International Bank for Reconstruction and Development and its affiliate the International Development Association are able to extend financial support to member countries following disasters, without participating in direct relief. The International Monetary Fund may provide financial assistance to disaster stricken member countries, to meet exchange and balance of payments consequences of disasters, and other financing facilities are designed to provide means of coping with emergencies.[59]

The International Labour Organisation (ILO) has an emergency employment-generating scheme for the aftermath of natural or other disasters. ILO assistance in such cases includes identification of emergency projects and specific tasks such as organizing and constructing refugee camps. ILO may also assist in the rehabilitation, retraining and placement of workers disabled or dislocated by disasters.

The International Atomic Energy Agency (IAEA) is concerned with emergency assistance in the event of radiation accidents, and has made efforts to formulate a general instrument to facilitate such assistance to member States. The Agency publishes periodically information concerning the types of assistance that might be made available. A recent study designed to assess the most appropriate means of responding to the requirements for assistance and for facilitating the necessary international cooperation was followed by the adoption in 1983 of guidelines for mutual emergency assistance arrangements in connection with a nuclear accident or radiological emergency.[60]

A number of international organizations are concerned with planning and coordination of global warning systems for dangerous natural phenomena. The World Meteorological Organization (WMO) has implemented a World Weather Watch programme and is involved in developing countries, in collaboration with the League of Red Cross Societies and the Office of the UN Disaster Relief Co-ordinator, in the strengthening of monitoring and communications counter-measures against the destructive forces of nature. Meteorological satellites and other modern communications technology are used to provide storm warnings and general forecasts. The International Telecommunications Union (ITU) may assist in disaster situations with the establishment of emergency radio communications to stricken areas, and with the restoration of normal telecommunications. Recommendations of the ITU and of the World Administrative Radio Conferences have dealt with technical aspects of radio communications in the event of natural disasters and with the emergency use of frequencies and wavebands by relief organizations such as the Red Cross.[61]

6.5 Evaluation

In the aftermath of World War II large scale relief actions were carried out over several years by operational inter-governmental organizations established principally by the Allied States. The precarious situation of many victims of the war led to relief actions which were based to a considerable extent on the urgent humanitarian needs then existing. The subsequent response of the United Nations in the face of new disasters was at first confined largely to simple invitations to States members to provide relief assistance, but increasing support was also given to the humanitarian programmes of the specialized agencies.

Although extensive operational tasks had not been generally envisaged for the implementation of the UN's wide competence in economic and social matters, the foundations of the specialized agencies were laid sufficiently broadly to allow for the initiation and evolution of a great variety of programmes and field activities. The progressive expansion of humanitarian relief activities through the UN specialized agencies and subsidiary organs has involved the majority of States, as members and as donors or recipients of assistance. Several of the agents of UN humanitarian assistance were conceived during particular situations of extreme urgency and some were created to solve humanitarian problems which initially seemed to be only of a temporary or transitional nature. The ability of the specialized agencies to solicit, receive and disburse funds, together with the discretionary executive authority provided at their establishment, has enabled these bodies to respond to humanitarian needs with notable independence from the UN political organs. Thus, the norms regulating the humanitarian actions of the specialized agencies are in part constitutional and in part are established in practice.

In addition to the regular activities of the specialized agencies, the UN has created a number of operational bodies of limited duration in order to mobilize, administer and coordinate international relief in certain large scale emergencies. New humanitarian problems which have arisen have been met by an extension of internationally organized activity which has required an increasing degree of coordination and cooperation between States. The UN system developed both general and specific roles in marshalling relief and managing the political factors involved.

Within the UN itself, early resolutions relating to humanitarian assistance followed much the same pattern for a number of years: adopted upon the occurrence of specific disaster situations, they expressed sympathy with the afflicted State and they attempted to stimulate relief offers by putting forward an invitation to contribute assistance. The next period was characterized by the realization on the part of various member States and of the Secretariat that the UN, although possessing a fundamental potential role in emergency relief assistance, lacked adequate procedures for response. After gaining experience in a number of international relief operations a re-evaluation of procedures resulted in a gradual movement to place the UN Secretariat at the centre of international humanitarian assistance activities. However, the principal specialized agencies concerned had by then developed their own largely independent responses. In addition, only some member States favoured a stronger role for the UN in disaster relief.

The relief problems following the attempted secession of Biafra from Nigeria, where there was no effective UN response, represented a further turning point into the present period of mass humanitarian emergencies.[62] By the beginning of the 1970s it was apparent that the international mechanism of providing relief should be strengthened; that improved coordination of UN assistance as well as of assistance directed through the UN was necessary; and that improved exchange of information was an important factor in achieving these goals. The Secretary-General's Interim Report of 1970 touched on two issues which had until then been considered particularly sensitive: the equation of international relief in natural disasters with relief in armed conflict situations, and the role of the Secretary-General, especially in relief coordination.

The UN's involvement in providing humanitarian assistance to Bangladesh, a country then recently seceded from a member State and not yet admitted to UN membership itself, demonstrated a recognition of the priority of humanitarian needs in that situation and revealed a new operational approach to international relief actions.[63] The objective to avert further disaster in an already devastated country was pursued through the efforts of bilateral donors, non-governmental agencies and the UN system. The UN itself undertook direct responsibilities in the field, notably in the food, communications and transportation sectors.

On the other hand, although later expanded to considerable proportions, the emergency relief operations in the Sahel were clearly unsatisfactory in the early stages of the drought disaster.[64] Despite the relative absence of local political complications, the question of procedures for ensuring impartial and equitable distribution of supplies, and the question of the acceptance of international monitoring proved as usual to be extremely delicate issues. In a wider context, the slow initial response of the major donors in that situation has been attributed to the minor strategical importance of the region. Data gathered by agencies in the field indicated the growing needs, but the international reporting system was inadequate in signalling the alert before crisis point was reached.

The consistently repeated themes which emerge in resolutions of the General Assembly and Economic and Social Council and in reports submitted to these bodies at this period and thereafter are the problems of coordination, both within and beyond the UN system; of national responsibility for preparedness, which includes a link to international relief; and the importance of comprehensive information-sharing. Attention is now being given to the potential contribution of modern forms of technology, especially in information gathering, monitoring, communications, logistics and planning generally.

Recognition of the increasingly serious consequences of so-called natural and man-made disasters has led to a degree of international agreement and cooperation to prevent and mitigate their effects. These gradually evolving efforts must be viewed in relation to the history of humanitarian action at the level of international organization. History demonstrates that although the pressure of circumstances alone is often found to be the motivating force behind developments and adaptation at the operational level, only comparatively slow change or progress may be expected with regard to the assumption by States of binding or general responsibilities.

The UN General Assembly and Economic and Social Council possess no statutory legislative powers, but although the recommendations and resolutions of the UN do not usually purport to have binding legal consequences such resolutions nevertheless attest significantly to the validity of certain concerns of member States. Even those opposed to the attribution of any legal effect to UN resolutions concede that such instruments are capable of contributing material which influences the growth of law. In matters of humanitarian assistance, the importance of UN action is all the more pronounced because of the inadequacies of international humanitarian law relating to relief operations in so-called natural disasters. There is still no international convention setting out obligations of States concerning the donation or acceptance of humanitarian assistance or regulating the coordination of relief in peacetime.

All the important UN agencies and subsidiary bodies involved in humanitarian assistance have evolved progressively in response to new events. In some cases assistance activities have been mandated, but States have clearly not intended to create binding obligations in this field. Functional activities remain largely matters of policy, and resolutions of the UN in the humanitarian field are to be regarded generally as recommendatory or exhortatory, although they may of course contribute to the growth of humanitarian principles over a period of time.

The view that the UN's concern with development issues and human welfare is also a contribution to the implementation of human rights has gained some acceptance, despite the fact that human rights involve the relationship of individuals with their government. However, the UN's welfare aims still remain to be accomplished. In addition, international problems concerning the sharing of resources, the solution of which is necessary for the achievement of even the most basic standards of life for many people, seem likely to lead to deeper political controversy and conflict at a time when international cooperation for development is more urgently required than ever before.

The transformation of functional humanitarian responsibilities into legal obligations first requires new national commitments to humanitarian action. Such change both depends on and should lead to greater participation of States in relief programmes. Most operating agencies are at present, and have always been, largely reliant on voluntary support; some are dependent on regular review and renewal by States members of their governing bodies. However, the use of independent voluntary trust funds for a range of purposes not necessarily corresponding to established agency priorities has enabled problems of absolute consensus to be overcome and has provided scope for certain extensions of activity demanded by particular circumstances.

The various developments which have been considered reveal a basis and potential for future international action to meet increasingly urgent global humanitarian needs. The provisions of the UN Charter establish aims which shape the framework for the activity of the Organization but the realization and implementation of programmes depend on the degree of commitment supplied by all member States. Governments, through their representatives in the political organs and on the controlling bodies of the specialized agencies, provide the decisions which are the source of authority for operational programmes. State support for relief activities, through the regular budget of the UN and through the additional voluntary contributions on which operations depend, is an indicator of the strength or weakness of the principle of international humanitarian solidarity. The existence and nature of the UN's humanitarian activities thus attest to both the level of interest of States in humanitarian objectives and the extent of international cooperation in the field of humanitarian action, in particular at the global level between governments.

7. Other Actors in International Humanitarian Assistance

7.1 Inter-Governmental Organizations

The European Economic Community (EEC)

The EEC's humanitarian policies and activities make an important contribution to international relief, and are closely associated with the Community's development cooperation programmes which extend to many developing countries and involve various aid instrumentalities. EEC disaster relief is provided in several separate ways, including to States of the African, Caribbean and Pacific (ACP) group, under the emergency assistance provisions of the Lomé Conventions; to any beneficiary, under the provisions for cash payments in the Community budget; and in the form of special food aid. Important contributions are also supplied by the EEC to international governmental and non-governmental organizations involved in relief activities. In addition, the EEC may conclude special agreements providing for humanitarian assistance to associated and non-associated States or other recipient parties. Each of these areas is examined here in turn, with the particular object of assessing the existing and evolving contribution of the EEC in the form of law and action to the global relief system.

Early relations between the EEC and the developing world were established under the Yaoundé Conventions during the 1960s.[1] An important innovation was the creation in 1963 of the European Development Fund (EDF), which was continued into the period of the renewed and enlarged regional commitments contained in the Lomé Conventions of 1975 and 1979, enabling the financing of exceptional aid grants under the conventions. The 1975 Lomé Convention[2] extended to some 54 ACP States with a combined population of over 300 million. Art. 59 of the Convention stated: "Exceptional aid may be accorded to ACP States faced with serious difficulties resulting from natural disasters or comparable extraordinary circumstances." Under this provision 150 million European Units of Account (EUA) were made available for grants as emergency financial assistance during the five year period of the Convention.

The second Lomé Convention, between the EEC and 58 ACP States, entered into force on January 1, 1981.[3] Lomé II consolidates and extends the scope of the previous convention, and a notable evolution occurred in the provisions which regulate disaster assistance. These provisions are found in Title VII, which deals with financial and technical cooperation. Under Art. 92(2) (d) one of the purposes of the EEC's policy and projects in this field is "to enable the ACP States faced with serious economic and social difficulties of an exceptional nature resulting from natural disasters or extraordinary circumstances having comparable effects to benefit from emergency aid".

Two aspects of the terminology adopted here should be noted. First, EEC disaster relief is no longer characterized as exceptional, but rather is categorized as emergency aid. The term "exceptional" is used to describe only the nature of the problems, rather than the nature of the aid: the assistance itself acquired a status of its own. Second, the use of the word "comparable" extends the field of application of the provisions beyond purely natural disasters. The previous Convention referred to natural disasters or comparable extraordinary circumstances, whereas Lomé II refers to natural disasters or extraordinary circumstances with comparable effects. Thus, under Lomé II assistance may be granted in the form of emergency aid to ACP States facing serious and exceptional difficulties. Such difficulties may result from natural disasters or from other extraordinary circumstances. The terminology adopted recognizes that a range of disasters may have comparable effects and it removes any ambiguity as to whether armed conflict situations are included.

Emergency assistance under Lomé II is dealt with in detail in Chapter 9 of Title VII of the Convention. Art. 137(1) repeats the above-quoted formula of Art. 92, providing authorization for such assistance. Subsequent paragraphs of Art. 137 establish budgetary appropriations for the five year period of the Convention, and a special appropriation is constituted for this purpose within the EDF. The total allocation for emergency assistance for the duration of the Convention was fixed at 200 million EUA but provision was made for appropriate measures to be taken in the event of the exhaustion of this sum before the expiry of the Convention. Up to 60 million EUA may be committed for emergencies in each year. Emergency assistance is non-reimbursable, and is allocated on a case by case basis in accordance with special emergency procedures. Art. 137(5) stipulates the means of assistance, including "works, supplies, or the provision of services and cash payments".

Reference to assistance in cases of disaster is also found in other paragraphs of Title VII. The general provisions of Chapter 1 recognize that an objective of financial and technical cooperation is to help the least developed, landlocked and island ACP States overcome specific obstacles which hamper their development efforts. Such obstacles could include disasters which have an appreciable effect on the process of development. Art. 93(6) recognizes the special problems of island ACP States and paragraph (d) of that article provides that the EEC shall give priority to measures aimed at "reducing the adverse effects of the special difficulties of those States which are further handicapped by reason of ... their particular susceptibility to natural disasters."

These provisions relating to emergency assistance constitute only a small part of the 1979 Lomé Convention but their inclusion contributes to demonstrate the cooperative purposes of the instrument. Although change in the relations between industrialized and developing countries is likely to be only a gradual process, Lomé II represents an unmistakable step towards increasing cooperation, including in the field of disaster relief, by providing an entitlement to humanitarian assistance to members of a large group of developing countries.

The EEC also provides limited amounts of financial aid in emergencies to States outside the ACP group, under two separate articles of the EEC regular budget. The non-associated programme began in 1976 as a new aspect of the Community's policy of assistance to developing countries, based on allocations under Art. 930 of the budget. In the 1978 programme an element known as the catastrophes reserve was introduced for needs resulting from exceptional circumstances. This allocation provides for reconstruction in the aftermath of disasters, and for disaster prevention and planning measures. Such projects should be distinguished from immediate emergency assistance, for which another provision exists, under Art. 950 of the budget. Under Art. 950 cash payments for immediate disaster relief, initially limited to 800,000 EUA annually, but increased by special arrangements to much larger sums, have been made in a wide range of catastrophes, including earthquakes, droughts, refugee situations and internal conflicts.

Decisions relating to finance for humanitarian assistance purposes are taken by the Commission, in accordance with the terms of Art. 205 of the EEC Treaty which enables the Commission to implement the budget. The urgent nature of action required in cases of disaster suggests that the Commission, in its role as the permanent executive, is the appropriate organ to implement emergency relief procedures while the Commission's role as an initiator of Community legislation augments its autonomy and powers in connection with expenditure on humanitarian assistance.

Disaster relief is also supplied in kind as a part of EEC food aid operations, under emergency schemes for free distribution to particularly affected or vulnerable sections of population. The range of foodstuffs, which are usually delivered free of charge to a port of entry, includes skimmed milk powder, butteroil, cereals, sugar and egg products from Community surpluses. Although such aid has not been formally based on any article of the EEC Treaty, the Commission has proposed Art. 43, on which the agricultural policy is founded, as the legal basis of Community food aid, while the Parliament has considered that such a basis would confuse the two fields of agricultural policy and food aid which it regards as separate. The opinion was also expressed in the Parliament that a more appropriate basis for Community food aid is to be found in Art. 235 of the Treaty, on which technical and financial aid to non-associated countries has been based. Alternatively, it has been proposed that a mixed legal basis could be adopted.[4]

The question which this discussion addressed was whether Community food aid should be dependent on the internal agricultural policy of the region, or whether it should form part of the EEC's external development aid policy. The proposals made in the Parliament were intended to reduce the potential legal link between disposal of surplus food on the one hand and humanitarian and development assistance on the other. The effect of a reference to Art. 235 would also be to increase the voluntary aspect of food aid policy and the non-automatic nature of its financing, giving Parliament a greater influence in the fixing of these expenditures. The outcome of this debate can thus have important consequences for the nature of EEC food aid, including emergency relief assistance, and its long term continuation. In the short term, however, the most important consideration in review of the basis and procedures for emergency relief is the avoidance of delays in reaching decisions and in implementing specific programmes.

In June 1982 the Commission presented proposals for a special programme to combat world hunger, covering both immediate relief and structural measures. Following evaluation of Community food aid programmes the Commission proposed new food aid policy guidelines in March 1983 according priority to development objectives while also recognizing the importance of emergency food aid for disaster relief and of nutritional aid for refugees.

A large number of agreements on the supply of foodstuffs for humanitarian purposes have been concluded between the EEC and recipient parties. Under these agreements, which usually follow a standard form, the country of destination or other consignee undertakes to make the food products available for consumption by distribution free of charge to those in need. In some cases, particular beneficiaries are specified, for example, refugees, "the needy populations", and "the needy populations, in particular ... children, pregnant women, ill and old people".[5] In these agreements, the recipient parties usually undertake to inform the EEC Commission regarding the number and nature of beneficiaries and the places, rate and method of distribution of the food. In some cases there is provision for the EEC to send observers to the site of operations. Such agreements may relate both to relief provided on an *ad hoc* basis and to longer term assistance programmes.

The EEC's contributions to the relief programmes of other international governmental and non-governmental agencies complement its bilateral disaster assistance programme. Such contributions, both financial and in kind, are supplied to UN agencies, to the various Red Cross organizations and to other non-governmental and voluntary bodies.[6] Regular support is given to a number of UN relief programmes, including UNHCR and UNRWA, where donations have represented an important element in both general and supplementary programmes. EEC emergency food relief is closely coordinated with that of WFP and with the food aid of the United States. Emergency financial aid is also channelled through the FAO, and the EEC has responded to various appeals launched by the UN Disaster Relief Co-ordinator. In addition to food relief supplies, transport and distribution costs are sometimes met by the EEC. As well as providing assistance to the Red Cross, the EEC also supports relief activities of Catholic Relief Services and Oxfam, *inter alia*, and agreements have been concluded with such non-governmental organizations relating to the supply of food commodities. These agreements follow a similar pattern to those concluded with recipient States.

The EEC's response to disasters has focused during the last decade on relief action, especially in developing countries, although emphasis is also being given to disaster prevention and pre-disaster planning. Although considered principally in operational and administrative terms and as a political issue, EEC activity in this field also makes use of law to establish both general foundations for relief assistance and, in particular, enabling agreements concluded with recipient parties.

Some are of the opinion that the Lomé Conventions mark a transition from grants of aid to a system of entitlement. While it may be that this is a change which will characterize the development of international relations in the future, EEC member States are still unable to agree on the size and duration of Community aid commitments. EEC member States do not all give the same priority to emergency assistance, and associated ACP States generally consider the sums available to be insufficient. The re-negotiation of the terms of Lomé II, due to expire in 1985, will also involve a review of the European Economic Community's humanitarian policies and programmes. Thus, while an important contribution to international relief is supplied by the EEC's experience of both the obstacles and scope for improvement of emergency assistance, a full definition of EEC humanitarian assistance is still emerging.

Other Inter-Governmental Organizations

Various developments including some in the legal field have resulted from approaches to disaster relief and pre-disaster planning in a number of regional communities of States and in other inter-governmental organizations. In Western Europe several proposals have been made for inter-governmental action to improve relief to victims of natural disasters which occur in the region. A Council of Europe survey on solidarity in disaster relief in 17 member States, completed in 1969, included an analysis of national relief machinery which revealed that only three countries possessed adequate comprehensive plans for emergency actions in natural disasters. A draft motion prepared for the Assembly of the Council of Europe referred to the frequency and severity of disasters occurring in Europe and urged that the effectiveness of international and national relief organizations be increased.

A report presented to the Council of Europe Assembly in 1971 placed emphasis on the establishment of effective national disaster relief machinery, but also recognized that such national measures should provide for the integration of external assistance at the local level. International assistance was thus intended to be based first and foremost on national preparations, in particular on the provisions of national disaster plans. The expectation was that the eventual harmonization of national instruments and policies concerning disaster relief would create a basis for a European legal initiative in this field. In turn, it was expected that such a development could lead to the European regional disaster relief arrangements being incorporated within a global system planned by the United Nations.

In 1972 the Committee of Ministers of the Council of Europe adopted a resolution on disaster planning and preparedness, but proposals for a European emergency fund and for the conclusion of bilateral and multilateral agreements to facilitate disaster relief were not implemented.[7] Other proposals to assess the role of stand-by relief units, and to examine a possible legal status for them, were also not taken up. The Assembly nevertheless continued to take an interest in disaster-related matters.

In 1978 the Conference of Local and Regional Authorities of Europe adopted a resolution dealing with civil protection and mutual aid in the event of disasters occurring in frontier regions. The resolution recommended that member States should conclude bilateral agreements governing the organization of international relief assistance in cases of natural and other disasters in frontier regions. Local and regional authorities in frontier regions were also to be encouraged to expand transfrontier cooperation with regard to disaster relief by adopting their own agreements. The resolution included models of both types of agreement.[8]

In 1982 the Committee of Ministers adopted a revised text constituting an outline model agreement between local and regional authorities relating to disaster relief in frontier areas.[9] A draft resolution incorporating a recommendation to member States to conclude bilateral inter-governmental agreements on the same subject failed to be adopted by the Committee of Ministers. The model bilateral inter-State agreement concerning civil protection and mutual aid in cases of disaster seeks to regulate this matter within the framework of the development of transfrontier cooperation generally.

Other regional organizations have developed machinery and procedures relating to disaster relief. The North Atlantic Treaty Organization (NATO) established a basic framework for mutual emergency assistance between its member States in 1953. In the early 1970s a revision of NATO's arrangements for disaster relief coordination between member States was prepared by its Committee on the Challenges of Modern Society. NATO possesses technical resources of great potential value in disaster situations, for example in the field of communications, but political and security considerations operate to hinder their incorporation into the international civil relief system. Nevertheless, responsible proposals have been made regarding the placing of NATO's technical facilities relevant to disaster relief at the disposal of international non-political relief organizations, such as the League of Red Cross Societies.[10]

Disaster relief activities are carried on by a number of other regional organizations. The Organization of American States has developed welfare institutions which include provision for disaster assistance between member States; a small relief coordinating office and an Inter-American Emergency Fund have been set up. The Pan American Health Organization also has a role in disasters affecting its member States.[11]

The Organization of African Unity has acted as a forum for discussion and organization for disaster relief. After the prolonged drought in the Sahelian region of Africa during the late 1960s and early 1970s six countries situated on the perimeter of the Sahara established a sub-regional organization in order to coordinate their responses and to mobilize resources to finance drought prevention and relief programmes. Known as the Permanent Inter-State Drought Control Committee for the Sahel (Comite permanent de la lutte contre la secheresse au Sahel, CILSS), this organization was founded on a multilateral agreement concluded after the declaration of disaster proclaimed in 1973 by the governments concerned. At the request of the CILSS member States the question of assistance measures for the benefit of drought victims was included on the UN General Assembly's agenda in late 1973. Formed at a late stage in the crisis, CILSS concentrated on the task of formulating medium and long term development strategies for the region, while FAO served as a focal point for the UN's operational relief efforts.[12]

The Association of South East Asian Nations has also taken various actions in connection with both disaster planning and mitigation of the effects of disasters, as well as adopting a short Declaration on mutual assistance in natural disasters.[13]

Apart from these regional developments, other international organizations of a more specialized nature, particularly in the field of transport and transit of goods and persons, play a role in the disaster relief system. The Customs Co-operation Council (CCC), an inter-governmental organization established in Brussels in 1950, has worldwide activities and influence in customs matters. The Kyoto Convention, promoted by the CCC to simplify and harmonize customs procedures, includes an annex adopted in Brussels in 1976 relating to urgent consignments.[14]

Such consignments include relief materials sent in the event of disasters. Detailed provisions in the form of recommendations on speedy clearance for export, import and transit of relief consignments include the following statement: "Absolute priority shall be granted to relief consignments." War and conflict situations are specifically excluded from the types of disasters for which the arrangements are intended.

7.2 Non-Governmental Organizations

Humanitarian assistance provided through a wide variety of international non-governmental organizations (NGOs) is an important aspect of the global disaster relief system. The absence of an international legal regime governing the status and activities of NGOs creates difficulties in acknowledging fully their role and the significance of their agreements. However, the association of NGOs with the relief activities of governmental agencies, for example in carrying out operational tasks within an affected country, further extends their contribution to humanitarian activities. In fact, greater attention should be given to the wider application and consolidation of experience and principles relating to humanitarian assistance found within this sector of the international relief system.[15]

The first international NGOs were created in the mid-19th century mainly in the humanitarian and religious fields; at present there are many thousands of NGOs active in all fields. The humanitarian and social service functions of such organizations may be unusual in the overall pattern of inter-State relations, but are one of the predominant characteristics of NGOs as a group. In the area of disaster relief NGOs, frequently known as voluntary agencies, act as a medium for the transformation of individual humanitarian concern into direct assistance measures. Such NGOs may both carry out their own field activities and act as pressure groups at the international and national levels. NGOs should be viewed as tending to bridge functionally the separation that exists between the State and the individual in international law doctrine.

NGOs and their personnel do not benefit from any special privileges, facilities or immunities, such as those commonly accorded to inter-governmental organizations, except through their association with an inter-governmental organization or by involvement as a beneficiary in an international convention including provision for such special treatment. In the field of humanitarian assistance the latter exception applies in certain circumstances to the Red Cross. Although the activities of international NGOs on the international plane preceeded and even promoted inter-State organizations, there are no agreements granting NGOs a single legal capacity over the territory of all States in which they have local activities. Many individuals and institutions have envisaged an eventual international treaty status for NGOs, but it is generally conceeded that no instrument granting such a status is likely to be uniformly adopted or implemented.[16] The first claim to recognition of an international status of NGOs remains the pragmatic toleration and acceptance of their *de facto* existence. What is important is not simply how they have been formed, but that they exist and carry out their activities.

Art. 71 of the UN Charter provides a basis for the regulation of NGO participation in the work of the Economic and Social Council, through the establishment of consultative relations. The system of consultation was revised in 1968.[17] Consultative status, which is subject to various conditions, is intended to permit the securing of information and advice from organizations with particular competences and enables their views to be expressed. The grant of consultative status does not amount to a contractual relationship. Consultative arrangements with NGOs have also been laid down by various UN specialized organizations. In the field of humanitarian assistance, UNHCR and UNICEF are examples of organizations which have established close relations with NGOs.

Although cooperation between the United Nations and NGOs in humanitarian matters has been extensively developed, those entities which are not States are still far from being in a position to decisively shape international policy. Nevertheless, the role of NGOs is not negligible in this regard. Indeed, "it has long been evident that NGOs have played a significant part in the promotion of multi-lateral treaties especially in the humanitarian and social fields."[18] In this context, the role of NGOs is particularly to influence governments towards the adoption and ratification of treaties and adherence to their provisions. However, despite the significant extent to which NGOs have been brought into the work of the UN, the limitations of the consultation procedures leave the main NGO contribution, to both general and humanitarian activities, outside the framework of the UN and firmly upon their own plane of activity.

The gradually increasing assumption of international institutionalized responsibility for humanitarian assistance by States has not undermined the value of private action, and has occurred often as a result of private action. For example, after the eastern region of Nigeria declared its secession in May 1967 the Nigeria-Biafra civil war became a test case and a turning point for international humanitarian assistance. The world-wide publicity given by the news media to the plight of the civilian victims, in particular children dying of starvation as a result of the blockade which was established, led to private donations of funds on a huge scale for relief purposes. Various non-governmental organizations came into existence to support the relief efforts:

public concern in this case led not to governmental but to non-governmental initiatives.

The weakness of existing humanitarian law, particularly problems of applicability of Common Art. 3 of the 1949 Geneva Conventions and Art. 23 of the Fourth Convention, became apparent at the outset in this situation.[19] Despite the objections of the Nigerian government, non-governmental relief agencies organized a number of separate airlifts of supplies, of which that run by the group known as Joint Church Aid, supported by American and European Catholics and Protestants, was the most conspicuous. Governments generally did not take any direct relief actions. Joint Church Aid eventually comprised some 30 participating organizations from about the same number of countries and it operated over 5000 relief flights to deliver a total of more than 60,000 tons of supplies. This assistance was meagre in relation to the needs of the people and, in reality, the function of the non-governmental actors was largely to draw attention to the moral issues involved. The ineffectiveness of the international relief system, including most of the established operating agencies, was demonstrated by the fact that only private individuals and groups with few resources were able to find ways and means to express in action in the field the international concern which undoubtedly existed for certain suffering human beings.

NGOs are perhaps always more ready than governments to perceive disasters, and to report on and respond to them. As one commentator has stated: "It is well-known that the NGOs are usually the best-informed group."[20] They may thus function as intermediaries and as international pressure groups by bringing problems to light, by mobilizing contributions and by taking direct action. Their role of providing information and stimulating action by governments and international organizations reflects their independence and the fact that they are less circumscribed by restrictive objectives than official bodies. The financial value of NGO's relief contributions is generally smaller than that provided bilaterally or through inter-governmental organizations, but the immediate impact of NGO action can be much greater than might be suggested by the level of their resources alone. The speed of response and local organization and experience are crucial factors in the emergency phase of disaster relief operations. Voluntary agencies often have personnel on the scene before official action can be taken; they may also be able to help in situations and locations where governmental organizations are unable to act for political or other reasons.

NGOs work in all types of relief operations. Some are able to provide assistance immediately while others must obtain authority from their governing bodies. Some assistance is given unconditionally; in other cases there may be limitations. This diversity of interests enables rapid mobilization of funds from a variety of sources, but also extends a degree of confusion into relief operations. The major NGOs active in disaster relief are therefore increasingly working out among themselves methods of cooperation applicable to the various stages of operations. This is being achieved without creating a "super-organization".

Many of the NGOs of importance in international humanitarian assistance represent Christian religious groups. Their activities, initially in the form of inter-church aid, began before the establishment and growth of most other international relief agencies and are now usually centrally organized from permanent international headquarters. The World Council of Churches (WCC), with headquarters in Geneva, is an international ecumenical organization established in 1948 to promote cooperation between the churches of the Protestant, Anglican and Orthodox confessions. Its membership currently comprises over 280 churches in more than 100 countries. WCC's principal relief activities are conducted through its Commission on Inter-Church Aid, Refugee and World Service, the mandate of which includes the provision of financial and material assistance in natural and other disasters. Responsibility for assessing the requests and needs of peoples and churches in emergencies and for initiating action rests primarily with the Emergencies Officer. In large disasters assessment teams may visit the affected area, and appeals for contributions are sent throughout the WCC network. WCC also receives and administers funds from sources other than its own membership and acts as a national operating agency in the field on behalf of other organizations.

The Lutheran World Federation (LWF) was founded in 1947 as a free association of Lutheran churches and now comprises over 80 members in approximately 50 countries. LWF is listed on the Economic and Social Council's roster of NGOs, along with most of the other Geneva-based NGOs active in disaster relief. Its emergency relief programmes are conducted in Asia, Africa and Latin America. Another organization falling within the same group is Catholic Relief Services (CRS) which is itself associated to other bodies of the Catholic church charged with humanitarian responsibilities, including the Pontifical Council or Cor Unum and Caritas Internationalis. CRS operates in most disaster-prone developing countries as a representative in international charitable work of the Catholic church and to promote relief actions. Caritas Internationalis, established in 1950 with statutes approved in 1951 and revised in 1969, is an international confederation of Catholic organizations engaged in charitable and social action in some 90 countries. One of its aims is to stimulate and coordinate the relief activities of its members in cases of disaster. It is not uncommon for WCC, CRS and LWF, along with other organizations to act as administering agents for relief contributions from governmental sources.

The relief activities of the Society of Friends should also be mentioned since the Quakers pursue a successful policy of unobtrusive international humanitarianism backed by strict principles of neutrality and impartiality. The Society of Friends was one of the first organizations to act as an agent of the United Nations in relief operations, on behalf of Palestine refugees in Gaza, and in numerous other cases has acted as a channel for governmental assistance of a humanitarian nature.

Other international NGOs have a more limited capacity to provide emergency assistance in disasters. At the national level there are also many religious and secular bodies which have the object of representing their membership in relief and rehabilitation assistance activities. Some of them, such as Oxfam, have achieved a form of international status through the widespread international activities which they carry out, and this position is often found to be in part a result of their association with the programmes and policies of international governmental or other non-governmental organizations. Within the scope of this study it is not possible to deal further with the role of this category of organization.

Possibly the clearest indication of the role of international NGOs as a group in humanitarian relief is found in the constancy of their operations. They have frequently been present in situations of need before and after any governmental response. With the national and international news media they carry the burden of arousing and channelling the concern of private individuals throughout the world for disaster victims. The aim of the work of NGOs is to be directly effective at the level of the individual human being. This is expressed, for example, in a statement made in connection with refugee problems: "Our millions of constituents demand that we be concerned about people, not politics: about salvaging lives not placing guilt. Those we represent want an immediate humanitarian response."[21] The implications of this approach have led one author to characterize the activities of some NGOs in humanitarian assistance as "revolutionary humanitarianism",[22] a term intended to refer to the actions of NGOs over and against the political and legal objections of States. Limited revolutionary humanitarianism may be a possible and not entirely ineffective response to a particular event. However, the term cannot be said to accurately reflect the general tendency of the humanitarian actions of NGOs as a group, which are based necessarily on a more considered approach to the preservation of their role over the long term.

Finally, the role of two international organizations active in the field of transport should be briefly mentioned. The airline companies which are members of the International Air Transport Association (IATA) may authorize free or reduced rate fares for personnel or goods sent for disaster relief purposes, in accordance with resolutions of the IATA governing body. This dispensation, the granting of which is discretionary, applies to "any person or supplies to provide relief in case of general epidemic, disaster or other calamitous visitation but not transportation to or from zones of military operation".[23] Many carriers respond favourably to emergency requests and the League of Red Cross Societies, among other relief organizations, is a major beneficiary of this concession.

The International Road Transport Union, founded in 1948 and currently with more than 100 members in five continents, acts as an organization of coordination and cooperation in all aspects of road transport.[24] The Union has created a special disaster fund, renewable annually, which is intended to enable means of transport to be provided to relief organizations during emergency assistance operations. Transport companies concerned have provided their services free of charge or on a non-profit-making basis in numerous disaster situations.

7.3 The Holy See and the Sovereign Order of Malta

The Holy See

The international personality of the Holy See is manifested in a wide variety of activities, including those in the humanitarian field. The Holy See participates in international governmental conferences; it enters into general international agreements, particularly those of a humanitarian nature; its active and passive right of legation is internationally recognized; and its diplomatic representatives enjoy the privileges and immunities of other diplomatic agents. Its personality and status as a subject of international law is not in doubt.

Although the Holy See lacks the conventional elements of a sovereign State, its international status is not extraordinary, especially in view of the gradual recognition of new subjects of international law. The particular significance of its status lies in the fact that international personality is possessed by an entity having objectives different from those inherent in ordinary nation States: "A way is thus opened for direct representation in the sphere of international law of spiritual, economic and other interests lying on a plane different from the political interests of states."[25]

The Holy See pursues its humanitarian activities on both the legal and the charitable levels. Its involvement in general legal activity is not as great as that of many States, but is extensive in matters of humanitarian law. At times, decisive initiatives have been made in this area by the Holy See. At the Diplomatic Conferences which drew up the 1949 Geneva Conventions the delegation of the Holy See was instrumental in achieving the incorporation of certain provisions dealing with relief societies. In the Diplomatic Conferences preceding the adoption of the two Additional Protocols of 1977, the Holy See also successfully advocated the retention of some humanitarian provisions which had been proposed for deletion.[26]

The international charitable activities of the Holy See are pursued through a variety of bodies, the role in humanitarian assistance of a number of which is referred to briefly in the section on non-governmental organizations above. Token financial contributions are made by the Holy See to the humanitarian work of several UN specialized agencies.

The Sovereign Order of Malta

The full title of the Order of Malta is the Sovereign Military Hospitaller Order of St. John of Jerusalem, of Rhodes and of Malta. The Order possesses an uninterrupted history of international charitable work for the sick and the poor dating from the time of the first Crusades in the eleventh century. Today, it remains both a religious order of chaplains and lay brothers and an order of chivalry composed of professed and secular knights and other associates. The Order is governed in accordance with its Constitutional Charter and its own legal Code. It is a unique international body which still pursues an active humanitarian role in some parts of the world. The Order, which was an important naval and military power for a number of centuries, has remained without territory since 1798, although its headquarters in Rome enjoy extraterritorial status. The Order maintains diplomatic relations at ambassadorial level with over 40 States. It issues passports to its officers, and has issued them to refugees, and these documents are more widely recognized than the Order itself.

The international personality of the Order is firmly established, although less broadly than that of the Holy See. Anachronisms, inconsistencies and weaknesses in its structure and functioning may perhaps have hindered the more effective development of its supranational character, but the Order's unique history and role among international humanitarian organizations and its present, albeit restricted, humanitarian activities prevent it from being ignored as purely a curious anomaly on the international scene. Indeed, it seems possible to assert that the present status of the Order of Malta may derive not so much from its erstwhile territorial sovereignty as from recognition in customary international law of its ancient position as an international humanitarian organization.[27]

Art. 2 of the Order's Constitutional Charter sets out the objective of the Order, which is to promote the glory of God by service to the faith and the Holy See and by pursuing its secular traditions of humanitarian assistance. Art. 2(2) enumerates the works of mercy performed by the Order and states that, in particular, "the Order succours those stricken by natural disasters and the casualties of war". Like the Holy See, the Order pursues its humanitarian mission on both the legal and charitable planes. At the legal humanitarian level the Order's activities include participation in the International Conferences of the Red Cross. The Order also maintains a delegation at the Council of Europe and has official consultative status with UNESCO, UNHCR, WHO and other inter-governmental organizations.

The Order of Malta participated in the 1927 conference which established the International Relief Union, and it was accorded recognition as an international relief organization within the terms of the IRU's Statute. The 1929 Geneva Diplomatic Conference, which revised the 1906 Geneva Convention and adopted a new convention relating to the treatment of prisoners of war, considered the status of the Order. The Final Act of the Conference contained a recommendation in the following terms: "In view of a request by the Sovereign and Military Order of ... Malta the Conference considers that the provisions laid down by the Geneva Convention governing the position of Aid Societies with armies in the field are applicable to the national organizations of this Order."[28] The importance of this provision, albeit outside the central legal framework of the 1929 Convention, lay in its extension to the Order of the articles establishing respect and protection for medical units and their materials, transports and personnel.

At the Diplomatic Conference which adopted the Additional Protocols of 1977 the representative of the Order made a statement explaining the international status of the Order and its potential role under the Conventions and Protocols.[29] In connection with the role of relief societies in collecting and caring for the wounded and sick, under Art. 17 of Additional Protocol I, the delegate of the Holy See at the Diplomatic Conference expressed the view that the reference to National Red Cross Societies as examples of relief societies did not imply any limitation on initiatives and action by other duly recognized relief societies; such societies could include those of the Order of Malta.[30]

These provisions, together with the Order's international and humanitarian status, may invite a comparison with the Red Cross. However, the particular denominational foundations and continuing associations of the Order are reflected in the nature of its activities generally and thus constitute a qualification to its international humanitarian role. The Order's principles of impartiality and independence present the same characteristic of universality, but are not backed by the same degree of world-wide application in practice, as those of the Red Cross.

The Order of Malta's present welfare activities include the maintenance of hospitals, the care of the wounded and sick in armed conflicts, and relief for other needy persons. The international humanitarian status of the Order is particularly important in its wartime relief work. The Order has provided ambulance corps in every European war since 1864, when the Red Cross was founded. In World War II the Order enjoyed a position of neutrality and operated ambulance aircraft, relief trains and hospital ships. International relief activities were also conducted by the Order in Hungary, Biafra and Vietnam. In Biafra and Vietnam the French and German Associations respectively operated hospitals and ambulance aircraft under the Order's insignia.

The hospital care of the sick has long been the Order's primary welfare obligation and hospitals, leprosaria, ambulance corps or specialized medical research centres are maintained by the Order in over 60 countries. In peace time the Order's national ambulance corps serve in cases of emergency and assist the victims of major catastrophes; in some cases their work may extend overseas. For example, following the earthquake in the Van region of Turkey in 1976 the West German relief programme was supervised by the directorate of the Federal aid services of the Order of Malta. A centrally administered institution known as Aide Internationale de l'Ordre de Malte, possessing a global mandate against hunger, disease and lack of education, was established to support humanitarian and development activities with financial and material contributions. In long term relief situations project agreements may be concluded between the Order and recipients or other parties concerned. An example of such an agreement is that signed in 1972 between the government of the Philippines, UNICEF and the Order under which the latter assumed responsibilities for distributing medical supplies in connection with a programme of leprosy control. The Order is also associated with the international assistance work of UN organizations such as UNHCR and WHO.

7.4 Bilateral Humanitarian Assistance

The most important contributions to relief operations are frequently made bilaterally. The direct provision of humanitarian assistance by one State to another is a broad area of the international relief system in which many questions of largely national interest are involved. However, it is apparent that the basis of State practice in bilateral relief may include both humanitarian and international factors. Relief assistance is not usually given in the expectation of reciprocal treatment in the future, and it is frequently provided to countries with few resources and great problems of economic and social development. On occasions, such assistance is also given across ideological frontiers. Relief contributions are often accompanied by an expression of sentiments of humanitarian obligation, albeit usually of a non-binding nature.

The existence of established bilateral relations provides a common basis for the extension of relief assistance in time of need. The politics of humanitarian assistance are evident in the bilateral area as well as in the multilateral area. Bilateral assistance may not always accord with the humanitarian and impartial principles that must motivate the efforts of international relief organizations. However, some States whose actions are in accordance with such principles undoubtedly consider that bilateral donation provides the most effective way of delivering their contributions. Assistance provided directly from a donor to a recipient State permits a flexibility of response and may in some cases avoid delays inherent in the procedures of intermediary organizations. Another advantage is that donor States are able to maintain the individual identity of their contributions. However, the potential benefits of bilateral assistance must be offset against the inevitably increased problems of coordination of the overall international response.

The offer through diplomatic channels of a sum of money provides perhaps the simplest method of bilateral assistance, involving no association with the actual tasks of relief. Alternatively, assistance may be supplied in kind and delivered to a port of entry or to the zone of operations. This method permits a response to specific requests or requirements and may channel the expenditure through the home market. Additionally, it is not unusual for equipment or personnel, including members of the armed forces, to be made available on a bilateral basis for emergency tasks in the civil sector.

Special emergency units are maintained by the armed forces of numerous potential donor countries and the provision of military transport services, in particular, can be an important factor in some relief operations.[31] Military discipline and skills as well as the factors of mobility, readiness and logistical self-sufficiency can contribute greatly to relief tasks. However, although the capacity of armed forces for disaster relief may be readily acknowledged, the deployment of military units in the critical early stages of disaster relief operations may not always be possible. Direct military involvement in international relief is not as widespread as it could be. Foreign relief teams must first gain political acceptance before their legal and operational status can be agreed. Thus, disaster assistance involving armed forces is nearly always offered and accepted on a strictly bilateral basis, and is usually improvised at the time of need.

A disaster relief unit was established by Sweden as a part of her stand-by forces for UN service.[32] Norway has also organized a surgical emergency unit and a field hygiene team within her emergency forces which are at the disposal of the UN. A federal constitutional law adopted in Austria provides for the sending of Austrian units for assistance work abroad at the request of international organizations. The provisions of this law also apply expressly to the sending of units on missions in the event of natural disasters, at the request of the League of Red Cross Societies.[33] Switzerland has also considered the question of establishing a volunteer corps for disaster relief in foreign countries, and other proposals have been made regarding bilateral disaster assistance by civil stand-by relief units.[34]

Most developed industrialized countries possess special funds for foreign disaster relief, some of which are established at a percentage linked to the total national budget for general development aid. However, not all donor States have established a formal or precise legal basis for their overseas relief actions. A number of donor countries have set up special disaster bureaux within their ministries responsible for foreign aid, in order to organize and coordinate their relief operations. In some cases, humanitarian assistance may be provided in accordance with the terms of a bilateral agreement concluded with the recipient party. In the case of assistance provided on a government to government basis, such agreements frequently take the form of an exchange of letters at ambassadorial level. A bilateral agreement may provide for relief assistance to be supplied to the national or local public authorities, or also to non-governmental or voluntary agencies.

A further aspect of bilateral activities with legal significance is that national Red Cross and Red Crescent Societies have been urged both to conclude agreements on mutual disaster assistance and to encourage governments to do the same.[35] Although an agreement between Red Cross Societies does not have the same legal status as a treaty between States, Societies concluding such agreements are likely to do so in close association with their national governments. Such agreements are likely to include provisions which are backed by governmental approval and in practice they may have effects similar to those of inter-governmental agreements.

Bilateral assistance may be provided automatically in accordance with enabling provisions at the national level, or on an *ad hoc* basis upon the occurrence of disasters. Alternatively, agreements of a general or specific nature may be concluded in advance in order to establish contingency procedures and to facilitate relief operations. Such arrangements can be briefly illustrated by a few examples.

An early example after World War II is provided by an exchange of notes between the United Kingdom and the United States on the duty-free treatment to be accorded to relief goods imported from the USA.[36] An agreement signed in 1964 between the United Kingdom and India provides for the entry into India free of customs charges of goods donated for purposes of relief and rehabilitation. This agreement applies to goods supplied by British relief agencies approved by the British government and consigned to organizations recognized by the government of India.[37] In addition, many bilateral agreements relating to assistance have been concluded by UN organizations such as UNDP, UNHCR, UNICEF and UNRWA with governments concerned.

Some bilateral agreements between States have laid down provisions in considerable detail governing mutual assistance in cases of disaster. For example, one bilateral agreement dealing with relief activities in frontier areas provides for the crossing of the border between the two countries by not more than 15 kilometres by specified types of relief detachments and physicians, upon request. In the event of flood or other natural disaster the agreement also permits the inhabitants to cross the border at any place or time without formality. Under the agreement, the costs of assistance rendered by relief teams are borne by the requesting party.[38]

Other bilateral agreements have been concluded relating to disasters both in frontier areas and in general.[39] International cooperation in nuclear safety has led to the conclusion of a number of agreements which are relevant to international assistance in cases of disasters or incidents with radiological consequences.[40] Some international agreements concerning environmental emergencies also establish procedures or contain other provisions relating to assistance between States in such cases.[41]

7.5 Relief and Planning at the National Level

Pre-disaster planning and relief assistance are primarily the responsibilities of the public authorities at the national level. The degree of functional responsibility assumed at the national level in disaster situations is frequently underestimated. In addition to the duty of governments to respond with the necessary measures, the sense of solidarity generated by a disaster usually results in material and human contributions by the people of the affected country, on a scale that is often greater than the international assistance which may be provided.

Beyond its role as a major if not the most important donor, the government of an affected country is usually responsible for various functions which foreign agencies, except in the most exceptional cases, may not perform. The local authorities are generally in the best position to assume the task of notification of an impending disaster to the threatened population. Existing local and national infrastructures provide valuable sources of estimates of disaster damage and the relevant government ministries should be able to assess relief needs. The local government is responsible for the overall conduct of a relief operation, including the distribution of relief supplied by international sources, even though the distribution of such relief may in practice be administered by donor agencies. Monitoring and evaluation of relief operations are also likely to be functions within the particular competence of the national government.

The practical management functions in relief operations are of fundamental importance, but they are not conducted in isolation. Legal measures or administrative measures based on legal foundations are often necessary or desirable, for example, to reinforce the effectiveness of a national disaster plan. Many disaster plans are incorporated into national legislation, or have foundations in the national constitution or in a statute, decree or other legal instrument.[42] Comprehensive disaster legislation should strengthen the legal, administrative and financial powers of the responsible authorities, enabling them to better coordinate the resources urgently required after a disaster has occurred.

The role of national legislation in connection with disaster preparedness measures may assume considerable importance. Preparedness, defined as those measures taken in advance to facilitate relief operations in the event of disaster, is a concept applicable both to potential relief donor countries and to recipient or disaster-prone countries. If the international relief system is to work effectively, donors and recipients alike must be in a state of preparedness. In this regard, General Assembly Res. 2816 (XXVI) which established the Office of the UN Disaster Relief Co-ordinator contained a number of sub-paragraphs addressed to potential donors as well as others addressed to potential recipients, including recommendations relating to measures to be taken at the national level.

Notwithstanding the variety of situations which may occur, plans designed to operate in disasters face a number of common legal questions. Above all, such plans must set out clearly the duties which are placed upon governmental or non-governmental agencies and upon individuals. A disaster preparedness plan should also ensure that agencies to which particular tasks are assigned possess the necessary authority to carry out their functions. The disaster plan must be designed to apply uniformly and any jurisdictional conflicts which may arise during its implementation must be dealt with. Provision should be made in national and local legislation for the declaration of a state of disaster emergency. The powers of the executive in the event of an emergency should be clearly set out, with appropriate safeguards and limitations. National disaster preparedness plans should also have an international component, designed to expedite the delivery of international relief. In fact, it is difficult and undesirable to separate entirely the national and international factors in both the organization of relief and the application of legal instruments in this field.

A number of countries possess well established bodies of law relating to disaster prevention, preparedness and relief. Many countries have enacted at least some legal provisions concerning disaster assistance. The range of sources of national relief law includes the constitutions of individual countries, as well as their public statutes, administrative rules, regulations, decrees and other legal texts.

Probably no State would deny that disaster relief can be regarded as a fundamental responsibility or duty of governments. A number of basic constitutional concepts recognized by most countries are relevant in disaster situations. Such concepts as the maintenance of public order, the promotion of the common welfare and the protection of economic and social rights, which are given legal expression in many constitutions, supply foundations for the rights and duties of individuals and governments in disaster situations. In many countries, other forms of legislation are used to facilitate the exercise of the necessary humanitarian functions of governments and individuals in disasters. Further comparative study of national legal provisions concerning humanitarian assistance would clearly be useful.

The task of compilation and comparison of such national legislation would face certain difficulties. The relevant instruments are likely to be scattered throughout the body of the law, and administrative decrees and regulations may be buried or little known. A special problem exists in that some countries may not publish all instructions relating to disaster situations. A further complication would arise where a country has a federal system of government with an overlapping system of laws. In addition, an adequate treatment would involve not only analysis of the formal legal framework but also the question of compliance with the law, requiring the investigation of practice and results in the relief field.

8. Relief Coordination

8.1 Introduction

Relief actions involve potentially a great variety of institutions and other participants, including national civil defence organizations, military units, Red Cross and Red Crescent Societies, international governmental agencies and religious and secular non-governmental organizations. Relief coordination is therefore inevitably a complex matter. Since it is not questioned that the overall effectiveness of relief operations can be increased by coordination designed to take into account the existence of many different organizations and forms of relief administration, an important problem of humanitarian action at the global level is to define and achieve the most appropriate international and national coordination mechanisms.

During the 1960s and early 1970s various writers as well as those involved in the operation and administration of the international relief system emphasized the need to improve the international response to disasters, in particular the coordination of relief. A number of proposals were made envisaging the creation of an international body with responsibilities for pre-disaster planning and relief assistance. Such proposals, although having in common an acute perception of the lack of a permanent international mechanism concerned with humanitarian assistance, usually failed in providing an adequate indication of the ways and means of achieving the creation of the proposed body. The types of organization envisaged ranged from a form of institutionalized international insurance scheme against disasters to the creation of a standing United Nations emergency service possessing considerable autonomy and active operational functions. The need was frequently expressed for a strong centrally organized relief authority which would take charge of the assessment of disaster damage and relief requirements, the management of the flow of relief shipments to the recipient country, monitoring and distribution to the affected people.[1]

Such proposals diverged widely from the response adopted by the General Assembly in the creation of the Office of the UN Disaster Relief Co-ordinator, but similar proposals continued to be made even after the appointment of the first Co-ordinator.[2] The questions concerning the scope of UNDRO's activities and the adequacy of the Co-ordinator's mandate are examined further below. The early development of concern for relief coordination deserves attention first, as a background to the creation of UNDRO.

8.2 Background to UN Relief Coordination

Initial Debates and Decisions

The first request, from the Economic and Social Council, to the UN Secretary-General to study the arrangements for coordinating international disaster relief was made in 1964. The subsequent report drew attention to two difficulties in laying down coordination machinery.[3] First, the potential benefits of additional administrative procedures at the early stages of relief operations were questioned in relation to the disadvantages of duplication of effort resulting from a lack of coordination. Second, the desire of donors to maintain the individual identity of their contributions was emphasized as a factor which could serve as a stimulus to the mobilization of resources. Nevertheless, the report recognized that at least some of the duplication, delays and cases of donations unsuited to local conditions could be avoided, or at least reduced, by coordination. The 1964 report concluded that the coordination of relief operations themselves should remain entirely the responsibility of governments at the national level. Difficulties were envisaged in the assumption of an authoritative or comprehensive role by the United Nations. In general, the UN's main role was to make available expert planning adivce.

In debates in the General Assembly's Third Committee at the same period, UN members emphasized the need for maximum coordination between the UN, the specialized agencies and the League of Red Cross Societies. The members of the Advisory Committee on Administrative and Budgetary Questions (ACABQ) also emphasized the potential importance of a UN relief coordination function. In 1965 the General Assembly adopted a resolution which drew attention to the role of the Secretary-General in several aspects of disaster planning and relief coordination, including coordination functions relating to bilateral assistance, UN assistance and to non-governmental organizations. A subsequent report of the Secretary-General in 1968 mentioned new procedures established to ensure that the specialized agencies and the League of Red Cross Societies were appraised of requests for assistance and proposals for relief action. Strengthened staff arrangements in the secretariat were authorized by the General Assembly in the same year but it was not until 1970 that an Assistant Secretary-General for Inter-Agency Affairs was appointed, providing the initial administrative framework for a permanent UN focal point for disaster relief coordination.[4]

By 1970 it was apparent that governments would continue to look to the UN both to mobilize assistance and to provide assistance following natural disasters. An interim report of the Secretary-General of the same year also referred to other cases where international action is needed "in emergencies due to other causes, including civil conflict", when arrangements designed to meet the impact of natural disasters could be brought into effect if requested by the government concerned.[5] The potential scope of UN action in disasters was only beginning to be explored at this period, but the report concluded that a focal point was lacking from which to initiate action and exercise more effective coordination.

In resolutions of the Economic and Social Council and the General Assembly, the Secretary-General was then invited to give special attention in a comprehensive report to a number of particular questions of coordination in natural disasters, including maintenance of a distinction between coordination of relief operations during the emergency phase and coordination of reconstruction; improvements at a national and international level in coordination of the donation, acceptance and delivery of relief; and consultation with governments, specialized agencies, the League of Red Cross Societies and voluntary agencies. Most important, the Secretary-General was to recommend organizational arrangements for a "permanent office in the UN Secretariat responsible for the co-ordination of action relating to natural disasters, epidemics, famines and similar emergency situations, and the resources required therefor".[6] This was the first time that such an office was envisaged in such definite terms.

The 1971 Comprehensive Report of the Secretary-General, entitled "Assistance in Cases of Natural Disaster" and prepared with the collaboration of the UN and non-governmental organizations directly concerned, reiterated the need for the establishment of a focal point within the UN system to initiate action and to exercise the function of coordination.[7] The proposed UN disaster office was envisaged as especially necessary in four areas: to obtain reliable information about the extent of disaster damage and the needs that cannot be met from within the stricken country; to transmit this information to potential donor governments and organizations; to stimulate and coordinate the provision of assistance from the UN system, in accordance with the resources and constitutional responsibilities of each agency; and to facilitate arrangements for the transport and delivery of relief. The basic intention was to facilitate the actions of governments, without prejudicing their freedom of action. The Report recommended that the expenses of the new office, estimated at about $205,000 per annum, should be met out of the UN regular budget.

The proposals in the 1971 Report formed part of overall recommendations for national measures to strengthen pre-disaster planning and for increased contributions and cooperation by donors. Various disaster situations which occurred at this period demonstrated the need for permanently establishing an effective relief coordination mechanism. Several UN resolutions referred to the necessity for increased general international cooperation in relief activities and advances continued to be made from the Working Capital Fund for emergency assistance.[8] After the failure of international governmental humanitarian action in the Biafra situation, the large relief operation initiated by the Secretary-General in Dacca focused particular attention onto wide problems of relief coordination, covering assistance provided by the UN, bilateral sources and non-governmental organizations.[9] Thus, the 51st session of the Economic and Social Council concluded by calling on the Secretary-General to appoint a disaster relief coordinator to head a small permanent office and to carry out functions listed by the Council.[10] Debates in the General Assembly and its Third Committee revealed the influence of the continuing disaster in Bangladesh on views concerning the need for new solutions to relief coordination. However, some objections were raised with regard to the competences of the proposed coordination office, in particular that the function of mobilizing and directing relief activities fell within the jurisdiction of national governments alone, although the draft resolution which had been prepared already included the phrase "in response to a request for disaster assistance from a stricken State".[11]

General Assembly Res. 2816 (XXVI) 1971

In late 1971 the General Assembly discussed the question of disaster relief and adopted in a slightly elaborated form the action for which the Economic and Social Council had called. General Assembly Res. 2816 (XXVI), entitled "Assistance in cases of natural disaster and other disaster situations", established in Geneva the Office of the UN Disaster Relief Co-ordinator and laid down the Co-ordinator's mandate. The Co-ordinator was nominated on March 1, 1972 by the Secretary-General. He is appointed for a term of five years and reports directly to the Secretary-General.

UNDRO was created to be "the focal point in the United Nations system for disaster relief matters".[12] The Office was established as an entity within the UN secretariat and provision was made for its staff to be augmented when necessary by the secondment of additional personnel during particular emergencies. Res. 2816 (XXVI) authorized the Co-ordinator to carry out specific functions and responsibilities, on behalf of the Secretary-General, designed to meet two basic purposes: the mobilization and coordination of international relief, and the promotion of pre-disaster planning including measures of preparedness and prevention. Other operative paragraphs of the resolution were directed to potential recipient and donor governments. All organizations concerned were invited to cooperate with the new Office. Although UNDRO was enabled to receive and channel donations for relief operations, the Office was not conceived as a relief agency but rather as a central service to governments and organizations engaged in disaster assistance activities.

The preamble to Res. 2816 (XXVI) expressed UN members' recognition of the need to strengthen the collective efforts of the international community, and particularly the UN system, in the field of disaster relief. The economic and social consequences of natural disasters, especially in the developing countries, were referred to and it was acknowledged that relief can contribute to the rehabilitation and development of stricken areas. The preamble also noted the competence of the specialized agencies and other UN bodies to render assistance, as well as the role of the Red Cross and other voluntary agencies.

The detailed responsibilities of the Co-ordinator, set out in Para. 1 of the resolution, embrace a wide range of functions. The Co-ordinator was authorized to establish the closest cooperation with all organizations concerned, including the conclusion of advance arrangements designed to ensure effective relief assistance. Other sub-paragraphs authorized UNDRO to "mobilize, direct and co-ordinate" the relief activities of the various organizations of the UN system in response to a request for disaster assistance from a stricken State; to coordinate UN assistance with that from other sources, and to serve as a clearing house for such assistance; to assist governments to assess their relief needs; and to disseminate information to those concerned. Various functions relating to disaster research and to pre-disaster planning were also laid down and UNDRO was authorized to retain an interest in post-disaster rehabilitation and reconstruction. In the area of pre-disaster planning, particular reference was made in the resolution to cooperation with the League of Red Cross Societies in providing advice to governments.

The provisions addressed to potential recipient governments included the invitation to adopt contingency plans, to establish national emergency stockpiles of supplies and to consider "appropriate legislative or other measures" to facilitate the receipt of assistance. Potential donor governments were invited to respond promptly to appeals by the Secretary-General or the Disaster Relief Co-ordinator, to offer assistance on a wider basis and to inform UNDRO in advance about facilities and services which they could provide immediately. These sub-paragraphs addressed to potential donors and recipients demonstrate that governments which promoted the concept of international relief coordination and the creation of UNDRO recognized the necessity also for continuing cooperation by States in order to ensure the proper working of the new system.

The Secretary-General was also authorized by Res. 2816 (XXVI) to draw on the Working Capital Fund up to $200,000 for emergency assistance in any one year, with a normal ceiling of $20,000 per country per disaster.

8.3 The Office of the UN Disaster Relief Co-ordinator

Early Practice

General Assembly Res. 2816 (XXVI) provided UNDRO's legal framework, but left open the question of the organizational structure to be adopted. UNDRO began its activities slowly and the creation of the Office did not immediately alter the established patterns of international action relating to disaster relief. In the very early period it was not even possible for UNDRO to take up many of its responsibilities because of funding and staffing difficulties, although there were high international expectations with regard to the development of its role.

The first report of the Secretary-General to the Economic and Social Council concerning UNDRO stressed the need for an essential minimum of permanent staff. Later in 1972, the Secretary-General's report to the General Assembly noted that UNDRO's relief coordination policy was to encourage the creation at the national level of coordinating groups with which the UN resident representatives and representatives of relevant UN agencies and non-governmental organizations could enter into liaison. The General Assembly then adopted a short resolution which recognized that the Co-ordinator should be provided with the necessary resources in the area of preparedness.[13]

The 1973 report of the Secretary-General referred to the limitations imposed by lack of staff and stated that "the Office of the Co-ordinator has had some difficulty in discharging its basic functions, not to mention certain activities which it had to postpone or could not pursue as vigorously as desired".[14] A significant expansion in UNDRO's permanent establishment was urged, and a recommendation was made for the inclusion in the regular UN budget of an appropriation for direct relief assistance, to replace the withdrawals from the Working Capital Fund. The resulting Economic and Social Council resolution put emphasis on the development of UNDRO's responsibilities in the area of prediction, prevention and control of disasters and the General Assembly subsequently authorized the use from the Working Capital Fund of increased sums for developing national preparedness measures.[15]

Against the background of the worsening situation in the Sudano-Sahelian region affected by drought and the relief problems arising in Ethiopia and in natural disasters in Bangladesh and elsewhere, which again underlined the importance of relief coordination, UN members continued to give close attention to UNDRO's role and capabilities. The need for a more systematic approach to, and strengthening of, UN operatins before, during and after natural disasters and other disaster situations was expressed by the Economic and Social Council.[16] In 1974 the General Assembly adopted Res. 3243 (XXIX), entitled "Strengthening the Office of the United Nations Disaster Relief Co-ordinator", which reaffirmed UNDRO's mandate for the mobilization and coordination of disaster relief. The resolution referred to UNDRO's position to fulfil these functions on a global level and it called for the strengthening of the capabilities of the Office as a matter of priority and urgency. It was decided that the necessary additional costs should be met by voluntary contributions under a trust fund until 1977, when the financing procedure could be reviewed.

During this period UN members expressed concern that UNDRO should not itself become a major donor of relief. It was realized that the provision of material assistance was likely to remain largely a bilateral matter. At the same time, the Economic and Social Council called on the General Assembly to consider increasing the resources available to UNDRO for direct emergency assistance, as well as augmenting its functions relating to preparedness and prevention. The General Assembly responded to these proposals by expanding UNDRO's trust fund in order to strengthen the capability of the Office "to provide instantly emergency assistance for countries stricken by natural disasters or other disaster situations".[17] A further resolution established two new sub-accounts within the voluntary fund: the first intended to augment resources available for emergency assistance, with a target of $400,000 for the biennium 1976/1977; the second with a target of $600,000 for technical assistance in prevention and pre-disaster planning.[18] The Secretary-General was also authorized to increase the maximum allocation for emergency assistance per country per disaster to $30,000, the amount having remained at a ceiling of $20,000 since 1965. The purpose of the new financial arrangements relating to emergency assistance was not so much to enable UNDRO to move towards becoming a primary source of relief funds, but rather to permit the UN to establish an early presence in a disaster area and to take immediate steps to meet urgent needs prior to the arrival of other donations.

Further suggestions made in debates in 1976 advocated the transfer of UNDRO's administrative costs to the UN regular budget, in view of the limited amounts contributed to the voluntary trust fund. A number of delegates reiterated the importance of an international coordinating mechanism. On the other hand, the Secretary General of the League of Red Cross Societies noted in a statement that the main problem in relief work was not central administrative coordination but rather the need to ensure more effective work in the field. Other delegates advocated increased attention to slowly developing disasters, as well as involvement in man-made disasters.[19]

Financial questions continued to remain prominent. Progressive transfers of the costs of the Office from voluntary to regular funding were made and the life of the trust fund, the sub-accounts of which suffered from both uncertainty and paucity of contributions, was further prolonged.[20] However, UNDRO was not in practice mobilizing, directing or coordinating the UN's relief efforts in a systematic way. Within the UN Secretariat the Office of the Co-ordinator for Special Economic Assistance was also created, in 1977, but governments and organizations continued to pursue their relief activities largely as before. The view of representatives of UN member States was increasingly that UNDRO's mandate should be reduced to a bare role of information sharing.

Memoranda of Understanding

Between 1976 and 1979 UNDRO acted to clarify its working relationships with other UN agencies involved in disaster relief by concluding a series of memoranda of understanding which delimit the responsibilities to be exercised jointly and separately upon a request for UN assistance in cases of disaster. Similar agreements were also concluded with other inter-governmental organizations.

The first memorandum was signed in 1976 by the Disaster Relief Co-ordinator and the Director-General of the Food and Agriculture Organization. Under the agreement FAO recognized the responsibility of UNDRO to coordinate disaster assistance to a stricken State and to mobilize funds for such assistance. In turn, UNDRO recognized FAO's operational responsibility for relief activities in the agricultural sector. A paragraph common to agreements with other agencies provided that any request by a government for disaster relief assistance addressed to UNDRO would be regarded as having been addressed to the UN system in general. The agreement also provided in general terms for cooperation in relief activities in natural disasters and other disaster situations. Financial arrangements were set out under which the direct costs and clearly identifyable administrative costs incurred by FAO in supplying assistance at the request of UNDRO would be met through UNDRO. Other provisions of the agreement dealt with exchange of information, covering prompt reciprocal notification of requests, action being considered or proposed, and knowledge of other contributions. Review, evaluation and updating of all the measures in the agreement was also provided for.

A similar memorandum was concluded at the same period with the World Food

Programme. In 1977 a less formal agreement was signed by the Co-ordinator and the Executive Director of UNICEF. The basic purpose of this agreement was also to lay down guidelines serving to ensure effective consultation, exchange of information and coordination of activities. In an agreement with the International Atomic Energy Agency emphasis was placed on the joint actions to be taken before any disaster involving radiation occurs. In the event of an accident, the agreement provides for the IAEA to assist UNDRO in the relief operation and, in particular, to delegate staff to work in UNDRO's coordination centre during the emergency phase. The memorandum of understanding signed in 1978 between UNDRO and UNHCR gives the former responsibility for coordinating relief assistance in refugee situations, other than those which are man-made or deliberate, where people are compelled to leave their homes by "natural" disasters or as a precautionary measure against their effects.

In total, some 13 memoranda of understanding have been concluded between UNDRO and organizations within the UN system, in addition to a multi-agency agreement with the ILO, UNEP, UNESCO, UNIDO, WFP, WHO and WMO. Rather than defining areas of constitutional responsibility in a legal sense, the multi-agency agreement takes the approach of setting out functional responsibilities in different kinds of activity related to disaster prevention, preparedness and relief.

Memoranda of understanding were also concluded with the Intergovernmental Committee for Migration, the Inter-Governmental Maritime Consultative Organization (now the International Maritime Organization) and the Organization of American States. The latter agreement was concluded following a decision of the Inter-American Emergency Aid Committee with the intention of facilitating the coordination of disaster relief to OAS member States.

Mandate Problems

Although the expression "other disaster situations" occurs in UNDRO's mandate, it was never clearly defined. An important question is whether it should be understood to include disasters resulting from deliberate acts, in particular armed conflict situations. The Comprehensive Report of the Secretary-General stated that no direct reference was intended to emergency situations not resulting from natural disasters, in view of the wording of General Assembly Res. 2717 (XXV) which had delimited the Report's scope. However, it was acknowledged that the effects of wars, civil conflicts and disturbances can give rise to needs comparable to those in natural disaster situations, and that measures designed to cope with the effects of natural disasters can be applied in "other" emergencies.

In discussions prior to the adoption of the draft of Res. 2816 (XXVI) some delegates considered that the text should refer only to "natural disasters" and not also to "other disaster situations". These delegates held that the latter phrase might lead to jurisdictional conflicts with UNHCR or even enable the Co-ordinator to intervene in internal conflicts; inclusion of the phrase "other disaster situations" was referred to as outside the scope of the Secretary-General's Report. It should also be noted that

Economic and Social Council Res. 1612 (LI), which first proposed UNDRO's terms of reference in detail, used the phrase "natural disasters and other emergency situations".

Although an investigation of the preparatory background to Res. 2816 (XXVI) cannot conclusively resolve the issue of definition, the fact remains that the additional phrase "other disaster situations" was adopted. Without discounting the political problems inherent in situations such as civil conflict, it should be recalled that some drafts which contributed to the formulation of UNDRO's mandate indicate that relief coordination procedures were regarded as applicable to both so-called natural and man-made disasters. After the appointment of the Co-ordinator one delegate stated in discussions that his government "attached great importance to the interpretation given to the expression 'other disaster situations'.... It shared the view of the UN Legal Counsel that the Co-ordinator's mandate, and consequently also his responsibilities, covered disaster situations caused by war or civil disturbance, i.e. the so-called man-made disasters."[21]

It should also be noted in this connection that the draft versions of Protocols I and II Additional to the Geneva Conventions of 1949, as considered at the Diplomatic Conference on the Reaffirmation and Development of International Humanitarian Law, envisaged and referred to a potential role for UNDRO in armed conflict situations. In the section dealing with relief actions in each Draft Protocol; a paragraph was proposed to the effect that the parties to a conflict should accept UNDRO and the Red Cross, in cooperation with other impartial international relief organizations, as a relief coordinator. These paragraphs were subsequently withdrawn at the insistence of government representatives.[22]

A distinction between the deliberately and the innocently caused disaster is made in the 1978 Memorandum of Understanding between UNDRO and UNHCR, Para. 2 of which states: "Responsibility for the co-ordination of relief assistance to persons compelled to leave their homes as a result of, or as a precautionary measure against, the effects of natural and other disasters such as earthquakes, volcanic eruptions, droughts, floods, storms and epidemics and also aviation, maritime, industrial or nuclear radiation accidents shall rest with UNDRO."[23] These terms limit UNDRO's mandate in regard to "other disaster situations" to innocent or accidental disasters and the agreement thus provides a useful, but not necessarily exclusive, definition of UNDRO's area of competence. Indeed UNDRO has emphasized its role in prevention, preparedness and relief in cases of other disaster situations resulting from peaceful activities, and under the wide heading of disasters associated with man's impact on the environment the Co-ordinator has specified industrial, maritime, nuclear and aviation accidents as falling within the competence of his Office.

Particular difficulties arise from problems of mixed disaster situations, such as famine occurring during or in the aftermath of civil conflict. Although the 1978 Report of the Secretary-General relating to the Office of the Co-ordinator stated that arrangements were made to deal with relief coordination in war or civil disturbance, in practice UNDRO's activities to mobilize and coordinate relief in situations involving hostilities have been very limited.[24]

Another mandate question concerns UNDRO's role in disaster prevention and preparedness. Although it was generally agreed that relief coordination should be the primary role of the Office, some governments wished more emphasis to be given to functions of pre-disaster planning. Finding a suitable balance between these activities was the subject of considerable debate, especially among those governments which were contributing most to UNDRO's trust fund. Some also considered that UNDRO should become a project-executing agency while others preferred to restrict the role of the Office to that of a catalyst for change by the identification only of needs to which operational agencies would respond. General Assembly Res. 3243 (XXIX) of 1974 supported the view that UNDRO's coordinating role should be developed first, and by 1976 the Office was working to a 60-30-10 per cent ratio in its respective relief coordination, preparedness and prevention functions.

A final issue which should be mentioned concerns the relationship between UNDRO's mandate activities and the processes of development. Under Res. 2816 (XXVI) the Co-ordinator is to phase out post-disaster activities as a stricken country moves into the period of rehabilitation and reconstruction. However, the boundary line between the emergency and recovery periods is not always clear, and once engaged in the initial stages of a relief operation it may prove difficult or counter-productive to withdraw. In some disaster situations the emergency element in the relief assistance provided may assume a continuing or even semi-permanent character. UNDRO's activities in the area of disaster prevention also raise the question of this relationship, as prevention projects are likely to have economic and developmental benefits. However, UNDRO's limited constitutional role beyond the relief phase may hinder the use of the post-disaster period as an opportunity to emphasize the elaboration of certain preparedness and prevention measures which may have been lacking before the disaster occurred.

In some operational situations it has been found that relief and rehabilitation are regarded by the government of a disaster-affected country as inseparable processes. When long term development measures are emphasized the implementation of an international post-disaster assistance programme over a period of several years may be necessary. The report of one multi-agency mission in 1980 therefore posed the question of the possibility of establishing some new form of organizational machinery in order to deal with cases in which immediate humanitarian needs arising from natural and man-made causes coincide with each other and with urgent requirements for development assistance.[25] At the same time, members of the Economic and Social Council and the General Assembly were giving increased attention both to UNDRO's own programme record and to broader issues of responsibility within the UN system for humanitarian assistance.

Strengthening UN Relief Actions

As a result of questions raised concerning the adequacy, efficiency and readiness of the UN system in its involvement in humanitarian emergencies, two important studies, published in 1980 and 1981, were undertaken with a view to strengthening UN relief coordination in both man-made and natural disaster situations. The first study took the form of an evaluation report on UNDRO, prepared by the UN Joint Inspection Unit (JIU).[26] After reviewing UNDRO's management and operations in relation to the origins, purposes and mandate of the Office, the JIU Report concluded that UNDRO had not proved very effective as a focal point or in fulfilling its programme objectives and that its original mandate was too wide. Two major problems arising from UNDRO's mandate were emphasized: the uncertainty over the intended responsibilities of the Office in "other disaster situations"; and UNDRO's responsibility to "mobilize, direct and co-ordinate" UN relief activities, which had in practice been resisted by most UN organizations concerned. The Report consequently recommended that UNDRO's basic role should be confined to sudden natural disasters with information sharing and relief channelling functions set out in a modified mandate. It was also recommended that the trust fund should be eliminated, except to allow UNDRO to receive earmarked voluntary contributions for disaster relief.

The Inspectors also concluded that UNDRO had suffered from the lack of a governing body to give it policy directions and to take appropriate decisions. In this regard, the JIU Report recommended that UNDRO should report to the UNDP Governing Council, while remaining under the general authority of the General Assembly. In addition, the Co-ordinator should report to the Director-General for Development and International Economic Co-operation for routine guidance.

The JIU Report also considered problems of longer term and large scale emergency situations and proposed a possible new approach to UN disaster coordination in this broader context. Under the proposal, with UNDRO continuing to operate with a mandate limited to sudden natural disasters, an inter-agency emergency assistance committee would be created with functions including: the approval of a plan of action for UN assistance; the specifying of the role and contribution of each agency concerned in the relief effort; the possible designation of a lead agency; and the organization of technical cooperation in disaster preparedness and prevention. The Report envisaged that UNDRO would serve as a secretariat for the committee, whose chairman would normally be the Disaster Relief Co-ordinator, and that the committee would report to the Economic and Social Council through the Governing Council of UNDP and the Administrative Committee on Co-ordination.

The second study, entitled "International Efforts to Meet Humanitarian Needs in Emergency Situations",[27] related to the UN role in coordinating and implementing relief assistance in cases other than those caused by natural disasters. Commonly known as the Davidson Report, this study reviewed thoroughly the UN involvement at the agency level in man-made disasters and the developments in inter-agency coordination of emergency humanitarian assistance. The Report concluded that the main progress achieved during the previous ten years consisted in the strengthening of the resources available to the individual agencies rather than in the creation of working coordination procedures. The Davidson Report placed emphasis for further progress not so much on the development of new mechanisms but rather on the general flexibility and adaptability of the organizations and personnel involved in adjusting to new and unforeseen situations.

The UN's review of the emergency relief system, with the intention of suggesting means to strengthen the international capacity to respond to complex emergencies in a more effective and well-coordinated manner, was continued during the second regular session of the Economic and Social Council in 1981, when the JIU and Davidson Reports, as well as other documents, were considered by representatives of member States. Observations prepared by the UN Secretary-General[28] emphasized that attention should be given to improving the implementation of UNDRO's functions as envisaged in General Assembly Res. 2816 (XXVI) rather than modifying the Coordinator's mandate. With regard to UNDRO's trust fund and its sub-accounts, the Secretary-General broadly concurred with the JIU's recommendation to rationalize the fund's components and clarify its purposes. However, on the question of reporting procedures, it was considered that the existing machinery was adequate and effective. Concerning the JIU's case for a new approach to UN relief coordination in emergency situations, it was agreed that a need existed to develop forms of inter-agency action in which UNDRO's contribution could be optimized. According to the Secretary-General's document, consideration could be given to convening an *ad hoc* inter-agency coordinating committee at headquarters level when necessary.

At the same period the Administrative Committee on Co-ordination adopted in its Decision 1981/2 a series of measures designed to strengthen the UN response to exceptional and complex humanitarian emergencies.[29] The ACC decision made provision for consultations to be held in order to determine whether an exceptional situation exists requiring special *ad hoc* arrangements for collaboration between existing UN organizations. When such a situation is found to exist, the Secretary-General may, in consultation with the executive heads of the UN organizations directly concerned, designate a lead entity in the form of either an organization or a special representative. The lead entity is competent to review the scope and duration of relief operations in consultation with participating organizations and potential donors. The ACC decision also dealt with the questions of gathering and sharing of information on emergencies, the role of emergency units and special missions, and the nature of appeals for contributions made to the donor community. The decision referred to consultation with the Red Cross and to support by the UN system of the Red Cross and other organizations when it is necessary for them to assume operational responsibility in an affected country without other UN involvement in the field.

The debate on UNDRO conducted in the Economic and Social Council during 1981 focused on two particular questions: coordination in the field and coordination at headquarters level. Delegates insisted there was no need for new institutional structures, and the outcome of the debate was that UNDRO's position at the centre of the UN disaster relief coordination system was reaffirmed.

At its 36th session later in 1981 the General Assembly adopted RES/36/225 which not only again reaffirmed UNDRO's mandate but also called for the strengthening of the Office and laid down further guidance for international action in emergency situations.[30] The resolution, which made a number of references to "natural disasters and other disaster situations", endorsed the approaches outlined by the Secretary-General in his comments on the JIU Report and reiterated the basic elements of ACC Decision

1981/2. The ACC was invited to examine further the role of the lead entity and participating organizations in complex and exceptionally large disaster situations. With regard to coordination at the field level, the UN resident coordinator was required, with the consent and participation of the governments concerned, to convene the necessary meetings of the relevant organizations in order to plan, monitor and take action to provide assistance. RES/36/225 also called for the creation of emergency units by those UN bodies that had not already done so. Finally, the Secretary-General was requested to submit progress reports on the implementation of the resolution.

A set of guiding principles concerning the role of the lead entity and participating organizations in exceptional or complex disaster situations was subsequently prepared by the ACC, based on the 1981 decision, and was noted by the General Assembly in its RES/37/144 of 1982, which reiterated that "it is essential to strengthen and improve the capacity and effectiveness of the Office of the United Nations Disaster Relief Co-ordinator and the United Nations system as a whole in order to enable the Office to respond to natural disasters and other disaster situations".[31] The resolution also authorized the Secretary-General to respond to requests for relief with grants up to a total of $600,000 per annum, with a normal ceiling of $50,000 per country per disaster.

On the basis of these resolutions and decisions, it would appear that some agreement has been reached on identifying three categories of humanitarian emergency situations with which the United Nations could be involved. Firstly, there are disaster situations which fall clearly within the competence of one UN organization or specialized agency and for which that body holds primary responsibility. Secondly, there are disaster situations in which UNDRO is required to play a coordinating role for the UN system. Thirdly, the General Assembly has recognized that in exceptional circumstances involving complex disasters or emergencies of great magnitude special arrangements can be required to mobilize, coordinate and deliver international relief assistance. In addition, the General Assembly has envisaged and reaffirmed that UNDRO may play a role not only for the UN system but also in the wider international response in certain disasters. For this reason, the Co-ordinator was requested to establish and maintain the closest cooperation with all organizations concerned and to make all feasible advance arrangements with them for the purpose of ensuring effective assistance.

8.4 Other Aspects of Relief Coordination

Governmental Level

The concept of coordination, like that of general preparedness, is relevant to both donor and recipient countries. Important responsibilities for relief coordination are exercised at the national level, and it is only on the development of successful solutions at the national level that an improved international system can be based. In particular, the ultimate results of cooperation and coordination achieved among international relief agencies depend considerably on the scope and effectiveness of national coordinating mechanisms. National relief coordination problems include the general aspect of coordination between the national and international levels of activity in relief matters, and the specific aspect of coordination in the course of a relief operation. Although the national governments concerned should provide the principal coordinating mechanisms, in practice a variety of governmental, Red Cross and private solutions are often to be found coexisting with each other. In countries where insufficient attention is given to pre-disaster planning the necessary coordination functions are likely to be inadequately performed.

National disaster coordinating offices established in many countries contribute to international relief coordination. In some countries the voluntary agencies active in foreign disaster relief have set up their own coordinating mechanisms, often with the involvement of the national Red Cross Society. General Assembly Res. 2816 (XXVI) explicitly invited potential donor governments to inform UNDRO of the facilities and services they would be in a position to provide in the event of a disaster, thereby recognizing that coordination at the international and national levels is a process of complementary interaction.

The failure of coordination in the disaster affected country accounts for much of the confusion which may accompany relief operations in major disaster situations, although to some extent such confusion is by definition inherent in a disaster situation. In disaster prone countries the national plan setting out emergency relief procedures should envisage coordination through a central responsible office. The functions of a national coordinating office established by governments as part of overall disaster preparedness have been given much attention within the Red Cross. A particular responsibility of National Red Cross and Red Crescent Societies under the terms of the Principles and Rules for Red Cross disaster relief is to ensure that such a governmental plan exists and that it includes all the necessary elements relating to coordination.

The UN General Assembly has also repeatedly indicated the importance of potential recipient governments establishing disaster contingency plans which provide for a single national disaster relief coordinator. A particular function of such a coordinator is to facilitate the receipt of international assistance.

Some regional governmental organizations which have taken action on relief coordination within their region were referred to in chapter 7 above. Even in the absence of specific developments relating to disaster relief, the very existence of such regional organizations may provide an additional focal point for the consideration of humanitarian problems requiring international cooperation and coordination.

Developments in the Council of Europe have included the proposal of various measures related to emergency solidarity in disaster relief. Reports prepared for the Assembly placed primary emphasis on the establishment of effective national machinery, and explicitly recognized that national measures should be taken to facilitate the coordination of international relief. The intention was that an improved structure for international assistance should be based first and foremost on preparations made at the national level. Within the EEC, discussions led to the adoption in 1977 of a resolution on the coordination of member States' responses in the donation of emergency humanitarian assistance in natural disaster situations. In the resolution, increased and more effective EEC assistance was proposed in the two categories of immediate relief and post-disaster short term assistance. Existing procedures for decision making may be improved by the appointment of a coordinator to act as a focal point for information supplied by designated national offices and responsible to define guidelines for each relief operation.

The ASEAN Declaration for Mutual Assistance on Natural Disasters adopted in Manila on June 26, 1976 includes a statement of intent concerning the designation in each member country of a national governmental agency to act as the internal coordinating body in connection with natural disaster relief. The Declaration went on to envisage that these agencies would also have primary responsibility for implementing necessary measures of international cooperation in disaster relief. Other governmental organizations such as the OAS and the OAU have acted in a general coordinating capacity with regard to humanitarian questions within their competence. Several proposals also exist relating to relief coordination and organization within Islamic States, including an Islamic relief organization and an international Islamic humanitarian solidarity fund.

Red Cross

The Red Cross is involved in relief coordination at the national, regional and international levels. At the national level Red Cross or Red Crescent Societies are usually a major if not the principal responsible agency for disaster relief; their functions are performed in close collaboration with governmental authorities. The National Society serves also as a focal point for assistance provided from the exterior by other Red Cross or Red Crescent Societies, the League and the ICRC. There also exists the possibility for direct contacts between the National Society and other foreign bilateral donors or international organizations.

At the regional level the question of relief coordination often falls within the general field of Red Cross regional disaster-related cooperation, which includes both relief and disaster preparedness and prevention. In recent years important questions of relief coordination have been discussed in regional settings, including in Asia and the Pacific, Central America, the Caribbean, the Mediterranean, the Maghreb and Southern Africa. Red Cross and Red Crescent Societies in the ASEAN group of States have met periodically to discuss means of implementing the Declaration for Mutual Assistance on Natural Disasters. Regional consultations within the Red Cross in Central America have led to improved coordination procedures at the National Society level and to the preparation of recommendations designed to serve as a guide to other Societies. A model mutual aid agreement has also resulted from this regional activity, setting out an arrangement for coordination within a framework of mutual collaboration in relief matters. A further example of a regional agreement between National Societies is the tripartite agreement between the Red Crescent Societies of Algeria, Morocco and Tunisia which has functioned for a number of years. A guide to the elaboration of such agreements is published in the Red Cross Disaster Relief Handbook.

At the international level Red Cross relief coordination takes effect between the various components of the movement, and at this level Red Cross assistance is also coordinated with that of other organizations in the global relief system. The relief coordination functions of the League, which are designed to facilitate the international relief assistance provided through the National Society network, derive naturally from its federal role. The International Red Cross Statutes refer to the League's general role of coordination between National Societies and the League's Constitution lays down the specific function of coordinating international relief actions. These provisions formally consolidate the established relief practices of the League and National Societies. Numerous resolutions of the International Conferences of the Red Cross and of the League's governing bodies have dealt with the question of coordination. The Principles and Rules for Red Cross disaster relief form a detailed code regulating the planning, coordination and operation of Red Cross assistance policy and programmes. A notable general characteristic in the Red Cross approach to relief coordination is the attempt to achieve the correct balance between the rights and responsibilities of donor and recipient Societies, within the federal framework provided by the League.

The Principles and Rules emphasize international information sharing and give a wide range of coordination functions to relief delegates. Special provision is also made for National Societies to entrust the local direction of relief operations to the League when the national administrative organization is inadequate to meet the demands of the situation.

The Principles and Rules include a general statement on relief coordination beyond the movement itself, at both the national and international levels. Recognizing that relief operations require such coordination, the substance of this provision is that Red Cross programmes should endeavour to take account of assistance provided by other national and international organizations; this provision is comparable to that contained in General Assembly Res. 2816 (XXVI) according to which UNDRO may be brought into contact with not only UN bodies and donor and recipient governments but also non-governmental organizations. Thus, the UN and Red Cross coordinating mechanisms envisage the possibility of establishing their own relationships throughout the international disaster relief system and of interacting with each other.

In practice, the general Red Cross role of international relief coordination includes relationships with numerous other governmental and non-governmental organizations. The League gave support to the efforts to establish UNDRO, in the belief that an intergovernmental organization could perform various functions *vis à vis* donor and recipient governments that are not easily possible for a non-governmental organization. Both the League and UNDRO envisaged a beneficial degree of cooperation with each other and their contacts have generally been close, extending on occasions to both headquarters and field collaboration. At the same time, the League enjoys a close working relationship with the other UN agencies concerned with relief activities.

A system of working cooperation was also developed between the main non-governmental relief organizations based in Geneva. In 1972 the "Licross/Volags" Joint Steering Committee for disasters was formed by Catholic Relief Services, the Lutheran World Federation, the World Council of Churches and Oxfam, together with the

League of Red Cross Societies. In 1980 Caritas Internationalis accepted an invitation to join the Committee as a member. The Secretary of the Steering Committee, appointed jointly by the members, was located at the League. A sub-committee of this body met monthly to enable relief operations officers of each member organization to review current disaster situations. Officers of the principal UN organizations concerned based in Geneva attended these meetings. The International Council of Voluntary Agencies (ICVA), an association of many non-governmental organizations, may also play a role in coordination. Thus, a number of ecumenical, religious and non-sectarian groups, each themselves at the hub of world wide humanitarian assistance activities, have found it beneficial to meet together in a relatively informal and flexible manner for purposes of relief coordination.

8.5 Evaluation

Although major responsibilities for the planning, implementation and coordination of disaster relief rest with national authorities, the concept of international relief coordination is not in question. The need for a coordinating body within the international relief system is generally accepted, but it has proved difficult in practice to define coordination more precisely and to agree on the necessary action. In particular, the great variety of organizations capable of contributing to disaster relief operations, as well as the great potential scale and complexity of relief tasks, demonstrate the need to maintain an appropriate mechanism of international relief coordination. While some are of the opinion that the international disaster relief system will continue to be dominated by bilateral actions, others expect the role of international governmental and non-governmental organizations to continue to increase. Whatever developments do in fact take place, the necessity for maintaining and also improving the relief coordination mechanism will remain.

The collective role of governments within the UN deliberative organs and the role of the UN specialized and related organizations themselves in mobilizing and channelling relief assistance and undertaking relief operations supply the bare bones of a global system of coordination of humanitarian assistance in disasters. However, the UN Charter contains a specific limitation on UN action in the terms of Art. 2(7), which shields from UN intervention those matters which are essentially within the domestic jurisdiction of States. This problem is one which can only be resolved at the broadest political level.

The UN Secretary-General possesses implied functions of initiative, inherent in the nature of his office, which enables him to act upon his own discretion in humanitarian matters which require the exercise of his authority. In practice, the Secretary-General has taken the lead in a variety of cases in establishing arrangements for emergency humanitarian assistance by the UN with a particular view to achieving more effective concerted action. The UN itself has assumed direct responsibilities for relief in a number of the largest disaster situations witnessed during the life of the organization. Specific UN agencies have also played a major role in relief coordination in large scale humanitarian emergencies.

A variety of labels have been attached to the concept of relief coordination – such as focal point, lead agency, one voice and concerted action – but UN practice over the last twenty years reveals a continuing concern for improving the coordination mechanism. The creation of UNDRO in 1971 in accordance with General Assembly Res. 2816 (XXVI) of 1971 was regarded at the time as a significant step towards a coordination system which would function more effectively and smoothly: it represented the first move by the UN to institutionalize its responsibilities in the form of a single permanent coordinating office. The UN had no pre-eminent standing relief organization as such. Coordination was thus regarded as of importance not only for the success of particular disaster relief operations but also for the improvement of the whole structure of international response to global humanitarian assistance problems. For these reasons the Office of the Disaster Relief Co-ordinator was established on a foundation of cooperative practice, common to other UN activities and programmes in the economic, social and humanitarian sphere. UNDRO's role in humanitarian assistance is therefore different in conception from that of the International Committee of the Red Cross or the UN High Commissioner for Refugees, the latter derived from their capacities as agents of international protection.

The creation of UNDRO, some forty years after the ill-fated International Relief Union was brought into being by members of the League of Nations, was based on recognition of the increasingly serious international problems of disaster assistance, and on clear support by UN members, the UN secretariat and non-governmental organizations. Like the IRU, UNDRO was created in a manner which required the continuing wide cooperation of States for the fulfilment of its purposes. Governments which supported the creation of UNDRO clearly recognized the need for such cooperation, demonstrated by the fact that Res. 2816 (XXVI) contains some nine subparagraphs addressed to potential donors and recipients of relief setting out guidelines intended to contribute to the functioning of the new coordination mechanism.

UNDRO was not extensively involved in the major disaster situations which occurred during the early period of its existence, when special *ad hoc* coordinating mechanisms continued to be employed. For several years the Office suffered from a severe lack of resources and had difficulties in performing many of its tasks. However, the continuing momentum for strengthening UNDRO's capabilities, supplied not so much by the established UN agencies but rather by the primary relief donor governments, resulted in the resources of the Office being somewhat augmented. UNDRO is now in a better position than before to carry out its tasks effectively, within the framework of the cooperation of governments.

At the same time, a number of obstacles persist to the success of international relief coordination. The JIU evaluation report noted that the principal UN agencies with responsibilities in disaster situations possess well-defined areas of operations as well as considerable financial resources. UNDRO's potential role is consequently overshadowed by the competences and established practices of these organizations. An important question remains concerning the extent to which the functions of a coordinating body should include the directing of the relief efforts of others, beyond a role of central information gathering and exchange. In practice it seems difficult to make a firm distinction between a role as a catalyst within the established patterns of relief activity, and a more operational or managerial role. In this connection, the increasing use of the institution of inter-agency missions should be noted as a means of attaining greater flexibility.

The political problems inherent in relief situations create special difficulties for all coordinating bodies. Even the simple coordination task of transmitting information and requests raises not only questions of the limits of organizational independence, for example with respect to verification or assessment of needs, but also the possibility of differences with government sources. Such political problems were not discounted by governments which supported the creation and strengthening of the Co-ordinator's Office, and the moves to provide UNDRO with greater resources and clear objectives reflect recognition of the need for improved relief coordination based on continuing cooperation of States.

Under the terms of UNDRO's mandate the Office is brought into contact not only with UN bodies and donor and recipient governments, but also with non-governmental organizations. UNDRO thus has a potential relationship with most elements of the international disaster relief system, of which the UN is only one part. Some writers have looked for a solution to closer coordination between the activities of governmental and non-governmental organizations, particularly between the UN and the Red Cross, while respecting the independence of each group. The position of the League of Red Cross Societies within the non-governmental sector is of particular relevance here. The League possesses long experience of relief coordination through the world wide network of National Red Cross and Red Crescent Societies. The League's position within the Joint Steering Committee for disasters which was established only shortly after UNDRO, created an additional focal point for coordination within the whole international relief system, indicating the potential role of non-governmental relief organizations in the creation of a more effective framework for humanitarian action.

Within the context of coordination activities based on more formal cooperation, both the Red Cross and United Nations systems have considered adopting by legal means certain measures designed to expedite international relief. Although joint League/UNDRO recommendations dealing with a variety of technical matters were endorsed by the International Conference of the Red Cross and by the UN Economic and Social Council and the General Assembly as long ago as 1977, these recommendations have not yet been adopted in a binding form. These approaches, together with others in the same area, are considered in greater detail in chapter 9 below. Such legal moves relating to coordination and relief are necessary steps in the process of the closer definition by States of the parameters within which the donation, acceptance and coordination of humanitarian assistance will be undertaken in the future.

9. Further Development of International Relief Law

9.1 Retrospect: National and International Responsibility

The institutional and legal aspects of international humanitarian activities interact and are mutually complementary. This relationship is illustrated in the approach and provisions of the traditional bodies of humanitarian law: the Geneva Conventions and Additional Protocols, which are closely associated with the Red Cross; and refugee law, including the statutory and non-statutory competences of the Office of the UN High Commissioner for Refugees. Humanitarian law can be adequately assessed only when it is viewed in context with the nature and practice of the institutions most closely involved in its implementation.

The themes of humanitarian assistance and legal humanitarian protection unite when legal instruments incorporate rights and duties relating to relief which are fulfilled in practice only through functional, operational measures. Protection of people in humanitarian emergencies appears to depend first of all on the existence of an effective relief system through which appropriate action can be taken. At the same time, legal measures in the form of both principles and rules can contribute to maintaining and improving that system.

Many governments are concerned to improve the framework for peacetime humanitarian actions at the national and international levels, and most of these have already assumed functional or legal responsibilities in varying degrees for action relating to relief in emergency or disaster situations. At the national level, the aspect of functional responsibility is frequently underestimated even by those accustomed to viewing the relief system as a whole. Many provisions relevant to or directly involving matters of disaster preparedness and relief have already been incorporated into municipal legislation. National law approaches and concepts may supply useful analogies for developments at the international level. However, the feasibility and desirability of adopting a new international legal instrument regulating the donation, receipt and coordination of humanitarian assistance is still a controversial matter.

Bilateral humanitarian assistance remains an important and traditional form of providing disaster relief. In some cases bilateral actions may be carried out in accordance with specific or general types of agreement between States or between other assisting and receiving parties. States have also made relatively extensive commitments to humanitarian action by supporting the work carried out through international organizations, especially in the period after World War II. The UN Charter was framed so as to include a simple provision relating to international humanitarian cooperation. Specialized agencies and other organizations possessing various humanitarian responsibilities were created with a wide range of structural and functional features. New humanitarian problems which have arisen have been met by an extension of internationally organized relief actions including in some cases important regional governmental responses.

Cooperation and coordination between the diverse actors involved has been required to an increasing extent. Coordination is of central importance to the success of international relief operations. For this reason UNDRO was established as an independent entity within the UN Secretariat, on a foundation of cooperative practice common to other UN activities and programmes in the economic and social spheres. However, despite these developments, the expansion of functional humanitarian activity has not been matched by corresponding legal developments at the international level, even though there is a clear need to seek further improvements in relief actions and the relief system by all available means.

Beyond the exclusively governmental sector lies a great range of other actors on the international scene, providing an intricate network of relationships between the governmental and non-governmental areas. There is also a long tradition of involvement of private organizations and individuals in humanitarian matters. The almost universal presence of the Red Cross and Red Crescent Societies supports the potential for international humanitarian action possessed by the ICRC and the League of Red Cross and Red Crescent Societies. Resolutions of the International Conferences of the Red Cross, in addition to a variety of other approaches within the movement, reveal a certain momentum for the development of law in relation to both general principles and specific rules or other measures designed to improve international relief actions and the international relief system. The humanitarian activities of non-governmental organizations as a group reflect the concerns of their individual members and of the contributors to their programmes; they also illustrate the universal nature of humanitarian concerns and play a notable role within the wider framework of international cooperation in humanitarian matters.

International functional responsibility with regard to relief actions is thus based on extensive governmental and non-governmental practice. Such responsibility is expressed essentially in the form of financial and material contributions to relief actions and is frequently exercised through the intermediary of international institutions. It frequently also requires from participating parties a degree of commitment to the humanitarian purposes of the organizations concerned, through their constitution or other basic legal texts.

The formulation of a general and global concept of international governmental responsibility in humanitarian matters goes back to the Covenant of the League of

Nations, in Art. 25 of which the member States agreed to promote the establishment of Red Cross Societies for the purpose of mitigating suffering throughout the world. An important attempt to give this concept a specific legal content and character was made in the 1927 Convention Establishing an International Relief Union, which was the first multilateral legal instrument to be concerned exclusively with relief actions beyond the context of armed conflict. Some observers have foreseen that international law will eventually incorporate fundamental principles and necessary rules relating to international humanitarian assistance in all situations, but this has not yet happened. Nevertheless, the relief actions which are carried out demonstrate that some common principles exist relating to humanitarian assistance, the application of which in practice is usually regarded as desirable. Some of these principles, such as impartiality and independence of relief organizations, are also reflected in existing international legal instruments of a humanitarian nature, especially those relating to protection and assistance for victims in armed conflict situations. Other important principles relevant to relief actions, including those of international cooperation and non-intervention in domestic matters, take the form of general principles of international law.

As the International Court of Justice has stated: "Humanitarian considerations may constitute the inspirational basis for rules of law .... Such considerations do not, however, in themselves amount to rules of law."[1] The effective regulation of relief actions thus depends on specific measures being taken to develop the necessary and appropriate legal solutions. The failure of a previous attempt, now more than 50 years ago, to establish a legal principle of international humanitarian assistance and to regulate international relief actions by legal means should not be regarded as invalidating the basic approach itself. Nevertheless, it is clear that the requisite balance between wide questions of principle and specific questions of practice is difficult to attain in a single instrument. Against this background, various proposals made in recent years for the development of international relief law may now be considered.

9.2 Legal Proposals and Studies

A Legal Status for Disaster Relief Units

The organization and provision of international humanitarian assistance in disaster situations is usually undertaken directly between States on a bilateral basis or through the established international agencies holding the appropriate responsibilities. In some cases special relief units may be deployed. The questions of legal status, jurisdiction and liability which arise whenever relief personnel or relief units undertake activities outside their own country or are made available by international organizations were raised during the 20th session of the UN General Assembly in 1965. Proposals which were made relating to the legal status of disaster relief units covered three situations in which such a relief unit might operate: as an organic unit of the United Nations; as a national unit placed at the disposal of the stricken country, with the United Nations as an intermediary in the arrangements; and as a national unit operating under a bilateral agreement. It was suggested that a long term objective might be to regulate this matter by an international agreement.

Where a specific relief agency is specially created by the United Nations, for example in very large scale operations, such a body possesses the status of a UN subsidiary organ. Alternatively, where a relief unit is established by an authority other than the United Nations, but with UN assistance or cooperation, a contractual or less formal relationship could obtain between the United Nations and the establishing authority. An example of such a unit was the Technical Cadre Unit of the Swedish Stand-by Force for United Nations Service. It was established by the government of Sweden and was made available for service in Peru following an earthquake in 1970, under a tripartite agreement between the United Nations and the governments of Sweden and Peru.[2] The agreement provided for cooperation between the United Nations and the governments.

In whatever form such relief units are made available, the conclusion of an agreement between the United Nations and the receiving country was recommended in the UN Secretary-General's Comprehensive Report of 1971 on assistance in cases of natural disasters.[3] When the unit has an entirely separate legal status from the United Nations, the degree of association of the United Nations with the relief services would determine whether the United Nations should also be a party to an agreement.

The provisions of such agreements should include sections recognizing the international nature and purposes of the unit, the authority responsible for its command and the relationship obtaining between the United Nations and the unit. The Tripartite Agreement in favour of Peru, for example, provided that the Technical Cadre Unit would be made available for up to six months to assist in reconstruction of devastated areas. Under the Agreement, the members of the Unit were responsible for the performance of their functions solely to their commander, who submitted reports on the operations to the UN Secretary-General and the governments of Sweden and Peru. It was further provided that the United Nations would bear no operational responsibility in connection with the Unit.

The Convention on the Privileges and Immunities of the United Nations provides for the grant of privileges and immunities to *inter alia* the United Nations, officials of the United Nations and experts on mission for the United Nations.[4] Where the status of a relief unit is that of a subsidiary organ, the provisions of Arts. I, II and III of the Convention would automatically apply. However, these provisions would not apply to a unit with a legal status separate from the United Nations. Art. I concerns the juridical personality of the United Nations and recognizes its capacity to contract, to acquire and dispose of property, and to institute legal proceedings. Art. II provides relative to the present context for the immunity of the United Nations and its property and assets from legal process, search or other interference and for exemption from currency controls, direct taxes and customs duties. Art. III deals with the privileges and immunities of the United Nations concerning communications facilities.

Other provisions of the Convention would apply to UN personnel working with a relief unit irrespective of its status as a subsidiary organ. Art. V provides for the immunity of officials from legal process in connection with their official acts, and from immigration restrictions and alien registration and also provides for exchange facilities. Art. VII, Sections 24 and 25, provides for the UN laissez-passer to be accepted and for the grant of travel facilities. The provisions of Art. VI would apply to experts on missions for the United Nations, irrespective of whether a relief unit were a subsidiary organ; these provisions extend certain privileges and immunities considered necessary to enable official functions to be exercised independently. In addition, the provisions of Art. VII, Section 26, would apply to members of a unit who, although not holders of a UN laissez-passer, could be said to be travelling on the business of the United Nations; these provisions refer to the grant of travel facilities.

In cases where the Convention is not applicable, for example where a relief unit has an entirely separate legal status, a special agreement could grant privileges and immunities similar to those accorded in the Convention to a unit and its members. An agreement with a receiving country should also provide for coordination, both as between the parties to the agreement and between the relief unit and others engaged in the operations. The Tripartite Agreement mentioned above dealt with these matters in several articles. Art. 1 provided that the work of the Unit would be carried out together with other work being performed, in accordance with the decisions of the competent UN organs and under the general plan of the government of Peru. Art. 2 provided that each party would designate a representative authorized to act for it on all matters covered by the Agreement. The assignments of the Unit were to be determined between the government representatives with the assistance and advice of the Secretary-General's representative. Other articles provided for the submission of reports to the Secretary-General and to the governments, and for the use of the Secretary-General's good offices with regard to any matters arising out of the Agreement, even though no responsibilities were borne by the United Nations.

The preparation of guidelines enumerating the desirable elements of such agreements was given consideration following the 1971 Comprehensive Report of the Secretary-General on assistance. However, despite general consensus on the need to facilitate relief operations, the differing views of potential donor and recipient States as well as widely varying field conditions must be taken into account in assessing the likely scope for wider development and use of such agreements.

The Swedish Technical Unit for assistance to Peru was relatively unusual in that it took the form of a national military relief team brought into operational activity through the intermediary of the United Nations. However, the capability of armed forces for relief in disaster situations may be readily acknowledged. Other countries have organized special relief or other emergency units as an integral part of their armed forces, including those which are at the disposal of the United Nations. In these cases national legislation or administrative decrees may specify the conditions governing such forces and provide for their operations. Provisions are likely to deal in particular with the chain of command during service abroad on behalf of an international organization. Special importance also attaches to provisions concerning the scope of a unit's undertakings, the geographical areas to which a unit is to be assigned and the procedure by which it is to be charged with specific tasks, as well as the question of responsibility for costs.[5]

International Law Association Model Relief Agreement

The International Law Association (ILA), in its committee on International Medical and Humanitarian Law, began to study legal problems of disaster relief operations in the early 1970s. The ILA has concentrated on formulating a draft model agreement intended to regulate some of the technical questions of relief actions, based on agreements which have actually been used in relief situations.

The draft Agreement presented in 1978 proposed two models, with largely similar provisions but for different parties. The parties to the Agreement are intended to be the beneficiary State and either a donor State or a donor organization. In the case of assistance provided by an organization, the ILA proposal foresaw two variants: relief provided by an inter-governmental organization, and relief by a non-governmental organization.

The Agreement, in its somewhat revised form presented in 1980,[6] begins with a section including a number of articles dealing with relief organization. Art. 1 enables the relief requested by the beneficiary State to be specified, together with the places of operation. Several articles then deal with questions of status. By Art. 2, the assisting party undertakes to respect the law of the receiving country, and to maintain a non-political position. Art. 3 provides for the appointment of a relief director to assume overall control of the relief unit and its operations. The use of a distinctive emblem is provided for, to identify the relief personnel, installations and vehicles. Art. 4 grants immunities and privileges to the relief organization. Arts. 5 to 9 provide in greater detail for facilities, including the right to import the necessary goods and equipment, access to telecommunications, freedom of movement and assistance from the responsible authorities. Art. 10 provides for the distribution of relief to be performed either by a relief organization of the receiving State, or by the foreign relief organization, under the supervision of the local authorities. Art. 11 requires liaison to be maintained between the director and the authorities of the receiving State. The organization shall accept specified measures of coordination. Art. 12, the final provision in section I, sets out a scheme for the division of financial responsibility.

A group of three articles in section II deals with the personnel attached to the relief organization, and in particular with the status of those who are not citizens of the receiving State. Under Art. 13 the members of the mission are defined; they are bound to respect national law and to refrain from any act incompatible with the humanitarian nature of their functions. The personnel are exempted from the immigration requirements of the receiving State by Art. 14. Art. 15 requires a distinctive emblem or uniform to be worn. The third Section of the Agreement goes on to deal with compensation for injuries, liability being incurable by either party, and with the settlement of disputes. The final Art. 18 in section IV provides for the duration and termination of the Agreement.

The ILA proposals recognize and make allowance for the wide variety of relief situations which may arise. The Agreement is proposed as a source of new ideas from which parties can draw according to their needs. The Agreement does not presume to cover the whole potential field of international relief law. It is concerned in particular with some technical matters which can be of significance during a relief operation. Such an operation, within the context of the Agreement, is exclusively one which has been requested or accepted by the receiving State.

'Measures to Expedite International Relief'

In Res. 2816 (XXVI) which established UNDRO, the General Assembly invited potential recipient governments to consider adopting appropriate legislative or other measures to facilitate the process of disaster relief.[7] The resolution referred to the problems of overflight and landing rights and necessary privileges and immunities for relief units as issues which should be tackled to further effective operations.

A study of this matter, started jointly by UNDRO and the League of Red Cross Societies, concentrated initially on identifying obstacles to the delivery of emergency relief supplies to consignees within disaster stricken countries. A step in this connection was taken when the Customs Co-operation Council adopted the Convention on customs procedures and its subsequent annex relating to urgent consignments, including detailed recommendations on speedy clearance for export, import and transit of relief shipments. In 1977 UNDRO and the League of Red Cross Societies presented a final report dealing with these technical questions, after consultation with a number of governments and international inter-governmental and non-governmental organizations concerned with relief activities. The proposals in the report took the form of a series of recommendations designed to expedite international relief by facilitating the functioning of relief personnel and the delivery of relief consignments.[8] The recommendations were based on the premise that potential recipient governments would designate a single national relief authority to coordinate all domestic relief activities and to work together with the appropriate government departments and international relief agencies.

The proposals included recommendations directed to potential recipient governments intended to facilitate the importation of relief supplies, including the waiving of usual customs and other documentation requirements. It was also recommended that advance measures be taken by such governments to allow recognized external relief personnel to have access to available communications facilities. It was recommended that governments of transit and recipient countries should issue standing instructions to the customs authorities concerning the processing of relief shipments in their custody. All governments were recommended to waive the usual visa requirements for entry and transit of relief personnel acting in their official capacity as representatives of internationally recognized relief agencies. Attention was drawn to a resolution of the Board of Governors of the League of Red Cross Societies which urged similar treatment. Two other recommendations dealt with the relaxing of air traffic regulations and normal procedures for authorizing overflight and landing rights for disaster relief flights. It was further recommended that national airlines should accord free or reduced rates to relief shipments and personnel in addition to those concessions already being granted. Finally, three recommendations were aimed at donors.

These recommendations were intended to ensure greater suitability of relief contributions, a more rapid response to the most essential needs, and correct notification of impending relief shipments.

In 1977 the Economic and Social Council recommended States to adopt the proposals by appropriate national legislative, administrative or operational measures, and thereby to hasten the delivery of relief. The XXIIIrd International Conference of the Red Cross unanimously endorsed the measures and urged their implementation to the fullest possible extent. The UN General Assembly subsequently reaffirmed the Economic and Social Council resolution.[9] The sponsors of the measures to expedite international relief hoped that the endorsements thus gained would enable the proposals to constitute useful guidance for all governments and organizations concerned.

Although the question of these measures has been debated by the International Conferences of the Red Cross and referred to within the United Nations, the expected progress with regard to the granting of the necessary facilities and exemptions and other relevant action resulting therefrom has not yet taken place. In 1977 the Economic and Social Council requested the Disaster Relief Co-ordinator to continue efforts to identify and remove obstacles impeding the rapid delivery of international relief assistance. In a subsequent annual report on the activities of UNDRO it was stated that "international relief assistance may well continue to be subjected to unnecessary delays if the Co-ordinator cannot advance the project for some kind of international accord on this humanitarian question".[10]

Based on a comparative survey conducted to establish the extent of common ground in legislation and practice in this matter, UNDRO's annual report for 1980 reached the qualified conclusion that "there would appear to be some hope of achieving at least a limited accord on the main points identified in the original investigation and recommendations".[11] Further developments were thus possibly to be expected, especially taking into account the parallel work of the ILA. Initially, the matter was carried forward in a study published by the United Nations Institute for Training and Research.

UNITAR Model Rules for Relief Operations

The proposals made by the UN Institute for Training and Research (UNITAR) entitled "Model Rules for Disaster Relief Operations" were published in 1982. The stated purpose of the Model Rules is "to contribute to closing the lacunae in international humanitarian law regarding assistance to victims of disasters" and "to overcome some of the legal restrictions and bureaucratic impediments which are often major obstacles to the success of a relief operation".[12] A total of 17 model rules for bilateral agreements are formulated in the UNITAR study; relevant rules from this body are then grouped into three sets of rules, each set being applicable to a particular category of potential parties.

The scope of application of the proposed Model Rules extends to natural and man-made disaster situations. The Rules are thus intended to be potentially applicable in armed conflict situations. However, no definition of disaster was considered necessary by the authors of the study, because the Rules are designed to be brought into effect only as a result of an agreement between the parties in particular circumstances. Such an agreement could take the form of an exchange of letters specifying that a relief operation will be conducted in accordance with the appropriate set of rules. An agreement of this nature could be concluded upon the occurrence of a disaster, or in anticipation of one.

The three types of relations envisaged in the proposal are the following: an agreement between an assisting State and the receiving State regulating the provision of assistance; a similar agreement between an assisting organization, whether governmental or non-governmental, and the receiving State; and an agreement between an assisting State or organization or a receiving State on the one hand, and a transit State on the other hand, governing the transit of assistance. The Model Rules are primarily designed for the initial emergency phase of a relief operation, and the period of time for which the chosen instrument is to be brought into force should be specified in an exchange of letters between the parties. The Model Rules do not deal with disaster prevention or post-disaster rehabilitation, although it would be possible to extend their temporal period of application by mutual agreement.

The proposed Model Rules consist largely of practical and technical measures designed to facilitate relief operations. However, the general principle that relief supplies shall be distributed without discrimination is inserted as the second sentence of Rule 3, the first sentence of which provides that the receiving State shall employ assistance exclusively for the purpose for which it is supplied. Rule 1 is also of a more general nature, and is likewise addressed to the recipient of relief; it provides that the receiving State shall designate a national relief authority to coordinate relief activities. Some donor commitments of a general nature are included in Rule 2, in particular that the assisting party shall ensure that relief which is provided is appropriate to the needs of the recipient State and is correctly timed.

The remaining rules, Rules 4 to 17 respectively, deal with such matters as correct packing of relief supplies in accordance with agreed standards; the waiving of normal commercial documentation requirements; exemption from customs duties; relaxation of other import and export requirements, in particular for foodstuffs; air transport facilities on national airlines; waiver of air traffic control restrictions; overflight and landing rights; transport and handling facilities for relief goods, and the right of transit in third countries; communications facilities; exchange facilities; general facilities, privileges and immunities; waiver of visa requirements; freedom of movement within disaster areas; and protection and security of relief personnel, premises and equipment.

As the UNITAR study points out, the Model Rules represent the continuation of previous research efforts aiming in the same direction, in particular the joint efforts of the League of Red Cross Societies and UNDRO. Other sources of the Model Rules include the Principles and Rules for Red Cross disaster relief and the Red Cross Declaration of Principles for Relief to the Civilian Population of 1969, as well as General Assembly Res. 2816 (XXVI) of 1971. The approach of the UNITAR proposals is to emphasize practical rules which are intended to be non-controversial. The Model Rules are thus firmly based on the assumption that relief will be provided only at the request or with the consent of the recipient State, and with cooperation between assisting and recipient parties.

Other Proposals for a New Relief Instrument

A number of other proposals relating to necessary humanitarian measures and suitable instruments in which they could be incorporated have been made in recent years. Some of these proposals and the issues involved deserve to be briefly summarized.

The question of adopting a multilateral relief convention has been the subject of various proposals. Some have emphasized the need for a statement of fundamental principles such as the right of disaster victims to protection and assistance or the obligation of States to provide and accept assistance when necessary, while others have given priority to more detailed, technical and practical provisions addressed to States and organizations actually participating in relief actions.

The scope and details of the proposals of individual authors vary considerably. One author in 1977 emphasized as the fundamental element in a relief convention a statement of principle to the effect that protection and relief must be accorded to the victims of natural disasters.[13] A suggested foundation for such a statement was that the denial of relief is a violation of the basic right to life guaranteed under Art. 3 of the Universal Declaration of Human Rights.

The same proposal for an international convention also gave considerable weight to the institutional instrumentalities of relief, including the granting of the necessary authority to an international organization. It was recommended that an appropriate organization should be given defined responsibilities in regard to fact-finding, supervision of relief operations and protection services in natural disasters. Clearly, even the partial adoption of this proposal would require a far-reaching commitment on the part of donor and recipient States, involving changes in relief practice as well as an extension of the concept of legal protection to natural disaster situations. In effect, a new "Geneva convention" on international disaster relief was envisaged with the International Committee of the Red Cross assuming the necessary role of protector. It was not the first occasion that a new Geneva convention to cover cases of natural disaster had been proposed, but the implications of such an approach have yet to be widely and openly discussed, not least by the Red Cross.[14]

The recommendations of a report of the United Nations Association of the United States in 1977 also focused on the adoption of some form of international instrument and concluded that a relief convention would be useful to establish responsibilities of donor and recipient governments.[15] The purpose of a relief convention was seen as to assert the principle that all governments should ensure relief for disaster victims. Such a standard, it was proposed, could also be set by a declaration of the UN General Assembly. The report envisaged that, on the basis of such a declaration of principle, specific resolutions in cases of disaster could call upon the Secretary-General to ensure the provision of humanitarian assistance for the victims.

Within the Red Cross, the Tansley Report's evaluation of the movement's assistance actions gave some attention to the question of promoting a new international relief convention applicable in natural disaster situations, The Report introduced this matter by referring to the multilateral relief convention adopted during the League of Nations period. The Report then mentioned that the Principles and Rules for Red Cross disaster relief had incorporated provisions designed to solve some of the problems of international relief actions, while also acknowledging that these provisions are not always adhered to in practice. Noting the concern of the Diplomatic Conference which was then considering the draft Additional Protocols with matters relating to relief during armed conflict, the Report went on to state that the "Red Cross might explore whether another useful vehicle might not be a broader convention, outlining the duties of states in natural disasters as well as conflicts".[16]

The possible scope of such a convention was the subject of a submission quoted by the Tansley Report, which rightly opened by stating the premise of the inadequacy of international law relating to the administration of international humanitarian assistance, both governmental and non-governmental. Three principal concerns of importance for any new relief convention were identified, namely, the establishment of criteria for the donation, the acceptance and the coordination of humanitarian assistance. When the Report was considered before the XXIIIrd International Conference of the Red Cross in 1977, speakers emphasized that governments could not be expected to concede that humanitarian offers could be forced on them. A joint statement by the ICRC and the League of Red Cross Societies also raised the question of the extent to which States would accept obligations relating to humanitarian actions in circumstances within the scope of a new convention.[17]

In accordance with a resolution of the 1977 International Conference of the Red Cross which urged the ICRC and the League of Red Cross Societies to set up individually and jointly procedures to identify aspects of the Tansley Report which required further examination, the Secretary General of the League took an initiative which led to the development of a study project entitled "Disaster Relief and International Law – Protection of Human Beings in Natural Disaster Situations".[18] The Study Project, which commenced in 1981 and was carried out in cooperation with the ICRC, was designed to determine the extent of the actual and potential role of law within international relief policy. An important task of the Study was to codify the experience and practice of the Red Cross, and in particular of the League, in disaster relief. The resulting recommendations were intended to contribute to channelling the existing interest in reforms, as well as to provide a basis for action.

In 1981 a proposal concerning the promotion of a new international humanitarian order was brought before the UN General Assembly.[19] The proposal emphasized that humanitarian problems remain relatively neglected issues in international relations between States, and that the codification of international humanitarian law in the context of peace lacks a comprehensive approach. Still in its early stages, the objective of the new international humanitarian order is to adopt the necessary comprehensive approach to humanitarian problems, and to fill the existing gaps in basic humanitarian instruments and mechanisms for remedial action.

The tasks envisaged by the proposal for a new international humanitarian order range from increasing the awareness of the need for such an order, to creating the theoretical, legal and institutional frameworks necessary for strengthening the international response to disasters. One suggestion in the proposal was that a new order might be launched by framing a universal declaration of humanitarian principles, which could in turn support the development of further regimes of humanitarian law beyond the humanitarian law of armed conflict.

In recent years UNDRO has also continued to consider possible legal measures which could contribute to improving the provision of disaster relief. In order to take a further step towards the acceptance of measures designed to expedite relief, following the proposal of such measures in 1977, the Disaster Relief Co-ordinator invited a consultant to report on the history of attempts to expedite the flow of international relief, to examine the principles of international law concerned as well as the present practice and problems, and to propose appropriate solutions. The objective pursued by UNDRO in these developments and the action resulting and expected from them is to expedite international relief in cases of natural disaster and other disaster situations which fall within the competence of UNDRO under the mandate given to the Disaster Relief Co-ordinator by the General Assembly.

The report of UNDRO's consultant, presented in 1983, stated that its purpose was to examine efforts to eliminate obstacles to relief, to identify existing obstacles as disclosed in actual situations, and to propose solutions. The report analysed a wide range of measures relating to the delivery of relief supplies and included a draft convention for expediting emergency relief.[20] During 1983 the report of UNDRO's consultant was considered by an informal group of experts who provided further recommendations with a view to enabling the proposals to expedite the delivery of emergency assistance to gain acceptance by governments. At the 38th session of the General Assembly, the Disaster Relief Co-ordinator in his introductory statement to the discussion on the annual report of UNDRO briefly outlined the kinds of problems which needed to be solved, and reported on the progress which had been made; the subsequent resolution of the General Assembly took note of the Co-ordinator's statement.[21] In the discussion, several delegations commented favourably upon the action which had been taken and the proposals which had emerged.

In 1984 the Secretary-General's report on the Office of the United Nations Disaster Relief Co-ordinator included an addendum containing the text of the proposed draft convention on expediting the delivery of emergency relief. The draft convention was placed before the Economic and Social Council for a decision on a possible further review by a group of governmental experts.[22]

9.3 Prospect

International concern with humanitarian assistance is demonstrated in the relief actions actually carried out at the governmental and non-governmental levels, and seems to be founded on a humanitarian motivation which is common to people everywhere. This functional humanitarian response is also reflected in humanitarian principles which are widely recognized and are incorporated implicitly or explicitly in a variety of existing national and international instruments. Faced with the scale and complexity of present humanitarian problems, attempts should be made to strengthen the principles which are generally accepted as fundamental to humanitarian actions. In addition, several proposals already exist relating to the formulation of technical measures or rules designed to expedite the delivery of relief and the appropriate means should be sought to adopt those measures which are widely acknowledged to be useful and practical.

The range of possible legal instruments in which it could be envisaged to incorporate technical measures and principles relating to relief actions at the international level includes treaties, declarations, resolutions and other less formal instruments or commitments. The undertakings in such instruments could be made at the multilateral level between States, bilaterally, perhaps even unilaterally in some circumstances, or through the intermediary of international organizations.

An advantage of the approach based on a multilateral convention is found in the potentially universal and uniform nature of the results intended to be achieved. On the other hand, it can be feared that in practice the problems resulting from reservations and non-universal acceptance of a multilateral relief convention might even increase the difficulties faced by those involved in humanitarian actions. For this reason among others, a strictly realistic view of the possibilities open for the formulation of principles and rules relevant to relief actions should be urged when considering proposals for a relief convention. In this regard, it may be most productive in the long run to proceed cautiously with initial efforts to codify relief law. A set of technical rules of a relatively detailed and specialized nature which could be adopted and applied without deviating from currently accepted practices could prove to be a useful and realistic way of expediting international relief.

Another question which remains to be explored fully is the possibility of promoting the development of regional instruments and solutions. Regional cooperation has the advantage of being able to take account of special local factors relevant to humanitarian assistance. In addition, some humanitarian problems are inherently of a predominantly regional character. Efforts leading to the development of regional cooperation in humanitarian assistance should therefore be encouraged.

The option of bilateral agreements, on the other hand, is a weak form of compromise in a field requiring closer international coordination. Various examples of bilateral agreements which have been concluded, as well as draft models, already exist. Likewise, an international declaration on humanitarian assistance, the models for which also already exist, should not be expected to contribute greatly to solving the problematic aspects of international relief action. Such a declaration is likely to be simply an expression of aspirations. At the same time, a declaration could perhaps prove useful in emphasizing the principle of respect for sovereignty and non-interference in domestic affairs, the duty of international cooperation and the need to preserve the non-political character of international humanitarian assistance.

As a separate but not unrelated matter, an important further need which can be identified is to improve the legal foundations on which humanitarian principles and rules are based. This is perhaps even a primary need at the present time. The fundamental assumption that the great problems of human suffering require an international response is expressed in one of the purposes of the United Nations, in Art. 1(3) of the UN Charter. However, no field referred to in Chapter IX of the Charter, and in particular in Art. 55, dealing with international economic and social cooperation, corresponds explicitly with the humanitarian problems included in Art. 1(3).

The omission of the reference to humanitarian problems in Art. 55 has not prevented the development of the present capacity of the UN system to respond to such problems. Nevertheless, the omission suggests that new international legal measures designed to further humanitarian assistance actions could start with a basic statement of purpose relating to the achieving of solutions to humanitarian problems. Such a statement should refer to the duty of international cooperation set out in Art. 1 of the UN Charter and in other instruments, which is accepted as being a general principle of international law. A further statement could then complete the link to the question of humanitarian assistance for affected people in disasters or other emergency situations. In this way, a form of humanitarian charter would be constructed to provide a basis and a frame of reference for whatever supplementary instruments could be agreed upon. If it were considered feasible, specific provisions relating to the donation, receipt and coordination of humanitarian assistance could also be included at this stage.

The need for a common willingness to take action is an essential complement to the initial need for a common awareness of problems. As in other areas of policy, an approach to humanitarian problems based on cooperation reinforces mutual respect for the independence of each party concerned, which is a necessary ingredient for achieving durable solutions. Such an approach could help to bridge the gap which exists at present between general approbation of principles and individual acceptance of particular obligations. All those States which are most closely involved in the operation of the international relief system should therefore continue to act to improve the foundations for a comprehensive humanitarian order capable of supporting effective programmes of humanitarian action, drawing on the existing but as yet insufficiently systematic normative texts. Although in many fields the prospect of rapidly changing conditions appears to negate the value of past experience, in the humanitarian field the main requirement will be sensitively to adapt traditional solutions to the new circumstances and needs.

Conclusion

... teilet, Was ihr habet, zusammen,
damit ihr Barmherzigkeit findet!

share what you have, together,
that you may meet with compassion!

Johann Wolfgang von Goethe,
Hermann und Dorothea, V, 203-204.

Humanitarian problems have existed at all periods of history, but there is now a new and urgent need to tackle many questions of international humanitarian assistance which arise in a wide variety of emergency situations. In addition to necessary political and administrative responses to the problems of relief actions, greater attention must be given to the potential role of international law in enabling and facilitating humanitarian solutions. No adequate definition of humanitarian emergency or disaster can be found in international law. However, the diversity of the humanitarian tasks carried out by the many different actors in the field lends support to a wide definition which should be framed to take account of the plight of those people whose situation may be characterized as a permanent state of humanitarian emergency, in particular some of the poorest in the least developed countries.

The elaboration of new legal provisions concerning relief actions will contribute to the evolution of international humanitarian law beyond the context of armed conflict, and possibly to the whole of international law as an instrument of international cooperation. The development of international law and organization is influenced by the requirements of international life; simple necessity is a strong motivating force in humanitarian matters as in other areas of policy. States may perceive both self-interest and mutual interest in cooperation for humanitarian purposes, and such cooperation may have positive effects in other areas of international relations.

Relief will be required in larger quantities and on a wider scale until adequate preventive measures have been formulated, applied and have taken effect. Prevention is of the greatest importance as a solution and unavoidably demands that attention be given to the root causes of humanitarian problems. However, a focus on prevention cannot hide the urgency in the short and medium term of providing the necessary relief.

The history of large scale relief operations conducted with wide international support indicates that when general consensus is reached on objectives, governments will also conclude the specific agreements required to facilitate effective practical measures and will put forward the necessary resources. Although there is no place for undue optimism, experience in the humanitarian field tends to show that international legal instruments can have an effect in reducing the incidence of inhumane practices and alleviating the condition of suffering individuals. Such instruments can lead to progress in a number of ways, for example through the creation, development and activities of humanitarian institutions. In such institutions the complementary themes of humanitarian protection and assistance and the aspects of functional and legal responsibility for humanitarian action may be united. Existing international instruments authorize an active role for international humanitarian organizations of an impartial character, for example the Red Cross and the Office of the United Nations High Commissioner for Refugees. The special experience of the Red Cross demonstrates this blending of humanitarian law and action in a unique way. Governmental organizations which are competent in relief-related matters also illustrate the role which institutions may play in transforming the commitments of States into practical humanitarian measures.

An important body of law relevant to international humanitarian assistance is formed by the Geneva Conventions and Additional Protocols. Although many instances of flagrant breaches can be cited, the convergence of military and humanitarian considerations in the Geneva Conventions and Protocols is a strong factor working in favour of compliance with the law. The extension of such a body of law to the area of humanitarian needs arising in peacetime disasters would require a high degree of international commitment by States, which so far has been forthcoming only to a slight extent. Compared to the humanitarian law of armed conflict, efforts to develop parallel law applicable in time of peace have been inadequate and have yielded disappointing results. Greater efforts should be made to identify the points of convergence between humanitarian interests and the wider political interests of States, with the effect that the required commitments to new humanitarian instruments and actions might be more readily forthcoming.

The response of governments in the past to particular humanitarian problems contributed to the growth of the idea of international responsibility for emergency relief assistance. Early organized and institutionalized relief actions in the 20th century were initiated on an *ad hoc* basis for various groups of refugees, in some natural disaster situations, and as a part of general post-war rehabilitation work. The concept of general international humanitarian responsibility found expression, for example, in Art. 25 of the Covenant of the League of Nations in which the members agreed to promote the establishment of Red Cross Societies for the purpose of mitigating suffering throughout the world. An important attempt to give this concept a specific legal content was made in the 1927 Convention Establishing an International Relief Union, which was the first convention seeking to deal comprehensively with relief actions beyond the context of armed conflict. The International Relief Union was founded on excessive hopes and inadequate experience, but despite its failure the 1927 Convention marked a notable beginning and testified to the awareness of the international community.

In the separate field of maritime law the principle of emergency assistance to save endangered life on the high seas was developed into a legal obligation through State practice and codification. This principle has been extended into the special area of astronautical safety.

The practice of States since World War II has continued to contribute to the development of both relief action and principles applicable to humanitarian assistance. The international response to humanitarian emergencies is reflected in particular in the ever-increasing involvement of international organizations, including some possessing wide membership, in the mobilization, coordination and delivery of relief. The United Nations system is committed to humanitarian assistance in institutional and financial terms. The functioning and activities of the various UN agencies and programmes supply an indication of the extent of international cooperation relating to relief action. Several UN organizations are at present involved with humanitarian emergencies on a larger scale and more intensively than at any previous time in their history. All the important UN organizations with competences for humanitarian assistance activities have evolved considerably in response to new events. However, the humanitarian responsibilities of the specialized agencies and subsidiary organs are still far from being transformed into widely accepted legal obligations. The increase in functional activity within the UN system has not yet been matched by corresponding legal developments.

Many humanitarian situations are also inherently political in character and most involve some political factors. The provision of international assistance both as a general question and in particular situations remains a matter often subject to wider political considerations. Against this background, the organs of the United Nations continue to give close attention to global humanitarian problems and to the improvement of the international relief system and relief actions. Increasing concern is being shown for the questions of the immediate needs and other needs of the poorest developing countries, and for humanitarian needs arising from economic emergencies and in especially complex or large scale disasters. International humanitarian problems are thus set in the context of wider global problems. Humanitarian assistance is a subject linked to the wider aspects of world organization, law and order.

Aside from the United Nations, a number of regional organizations are also concerned with international humanitarian policy and programmes. The European Economic Community's activity in international humanitarian assistance is reflected not only in the relief operations which benefit from supplies provided by the EEC, but also in the disaster relief provisions of the Lomé Conventions concluded with African, Caribbean and Pacific States. The role of law in enabling and facilitating the EEC's response to humanitarian emergencies deserves to be given due attention by those concerned with the improvement of the global relief system.

The many non-governmental organizations active within the international relief system have reinforced the significance of private individual action in the humanitarian field, and some non-governmental organizations have considerably influenced the development of international humanitarian law, in particular the Red Cross. In addition, the role of the Holy See and the Sovereign Order of Malta should be mentioned. These entities are not conventional States or organizations, but they possess a special status under international law. The Holy See and the Sovereign Order of Malta pursue objectives and perform functions which have contributed to the promotion and development of humanitarian law, and they also practice their mission through various field activities.

The tendency of non-governmental organizations and religious and secular private actors on the international scene is to support the formulation of a functionalist international law. Importance lies not in the legal personality of these actors or in the nature of the constitutions of such organizations, but rather in the fact that these entities exist and carry out certain activities. Many of the humanitarian non-governmental organizations enjoy a consultative status with the United Nations. However, the difference between participation and consultation is still a fundamental one.

The development by the Red Cross of the instrument known as the Principles and Rules for Red Cross disaster relief deserves special mention. The Principles and Rules associate all parts of the Red Cross and governments represented at the International Conferences of the Red Cross with the attempt to improve the effectiveness of relief operations. This text enables the League of Red Cross and Red Crescent Societies to take the initiative to offer relief. The instrument is designed and serves to effect a balance between the rights and responsibilities of donor and recipient Societies, while taking account of the need for international coordination in accordance with the League's functions as the federal body of all Red Cross and Red Crescent Societies. The Principles and Rules thus provide a valuable point of reference in regard to the problems and relationship of international relief law and action.

Coordination of humanitarian assistance is inevitably a complex matter, given the great range of international humanitarian actors. The need for coordination is not in doubt and the creation of the Office of the United Nations Disaster Relief Co-ordinator in 1971 was welcomed at the time as an important step forward. UNDRO was created in a form requiring the continuing cooperation of States and organizations concerned in order to fulfil its purposes. The moves to reaffirm and strengthen UNDRO's mandate have helped to meet the clear need to continue to build on and improve UNDRO's competences and capabilities. Further moves to strengthen the system of coordination of humanitarian assistance both within and beyond the United Nations are likely to be necessary, taking into account operational experience.

Although the increased capacity of the international system to provide humanitarian assistance is not reflected to a corresponding degree in legal provisions regulating the donation, receipt and coordination of relief, international humanitarian activities are clearly based on the objective expressed in Art. 1(3) of the United Nations Charter, namely to achieve international cooperation in solving international problems of a humanitarian character. However, the present territorial division of the world among formally equal political States is accompanied by the placing of great emphasis on the concept of sovereignty by governments and in international law doctrine. The question of sovereignty has been seen as an obstacle to improving humanitarian assistance, although some have argued that respeect for humanitarian principles strengthens sovereignty and others have suggested that real sovereignty is strengthened by an increased practical ability to deal with humanitarian emergencies. At the same time, the fact that the world is organized on the basis of exclusive States, upholders of the doctrine of sovereignty, suggests that change and progress in the international humanitarian order is most likely to come about primarily through State actions.

The disparity between the symbol and the reality of sovereignty has perhaps never been greater than at present, and the need for international cooperation is correspondingly urgent. The process of cooperation is based on free consent and independence. A viable humanitarian order presupposes a spontaneous sense of responsibility and obligation. The developing relief law and organization therefore cannot seek compulsion, but must express and facilitate international cooperation in humanitarian matters.

It is true that some disaster situations where relief is denied or unnecessarily delayed focus attention onto the problem of sovereignty in international humanitarian action. However, the question of sovereignty in relation to the donation, acceptance and coordination of relief does not seem likely to be a fundamental issue in responding to global needs for humanitarian assistance in the near future. The real question for resolution is who will be entitled to humanitarian assistance.

Disasters in which the need arises for international humanitarian assistance most frequently occur within the developing countries, although various forms of technology are capable of leading to large scale disasters also in developed countries. In the future, disasters are almost certain to affect many of the poorest people in the least developed countries. Famine, starvation and the consequences of malnutrition threaten a constantly increasing number of people. In many situations traditional relief assistance, although urgently required, is hardly a solution and may even be detrimental to the longer term recovery prospects of the victims. Of course, in some situations the rapid delivery of emergency relief consignments or personnel is still the essential and primary requirement. However, the emergence of chronic, mass, complex and recurrent humanitarian problems is accompanied by deeper questioning of the concept itself of relief. Instead, the so-called root causes of humanitarian problems deserve emphasis in the search for preventive solutions and a more sensitive response, such as that exemplified in aspects of the practice of the United Nations Development Programme and a few other organizations.

The subject of international humanitarian assistance is thus set in the context of rural and wider development issues, which in turn are set in the context of the attempts to resolve the conflicting problem-forces of population, resources, environment and political power. In fact, the human and humanitarian factors relevant to relief actions are central to development policy and are also fundamental to the attempts to change the present world order sufficiently to allow for a viable future for all people.

The organizations responsible for humanitarian actions are not charged to deal with the root causes of humanitarian problems,but governments are fully responsible in this regard. The existence of many humanitarian situations which require the response of international agencies belies the achievements of the governments in particular in the primary political organs of the United Nations, *inter alia* in maintaining international peace and security, developing friendly relations and promoting cooperation between nations. The increasing frequency and severity of humanitarian problems suggests that the greater international humanitarian response which is required in the form of financial and material contributions to assistance programmes must be matched by efforts to eradicate the causes of many humanitarian problems.

A rigid distinction between relief and reform cannot be maintained in many situations of humanitarian need. The purpose of relief actions is not simply to efficiently administer a state of destitution, dependency and misery. The objective of international measures is to enable an advance beyond the present state with all its imperfections.

If humanitarian principles are to have an appropriate effect in a period of greatly increased need for them, they must be carefully adapted to the requirements and expectations of the many recipient countries in the developing parts of the world. One concern of recipients is that humanitarian assistance should become less interventionist, while donors often seek for assurances that assistance will reach those in need. Finding the correct approach to establishing the appropriate principles of entitlement will be a particular concern in developing international humanitarian law and humanitarian action.

Within and beyond the United Nations, humanitarian assistance is no longer considered to be simply an *ad hoc* response, but is perceived as a complex process related to human rights and development issues and requiring a high degree of international coordination. The issues of human rights, development and humanitarian assistance are perhaps most closely associated with each other in the context of international measures relating to world food security. However, although some steps are being taken which contribute towards the construction of a framework for international action and coordination in the humanitarian field, it is not yet clear what solutions will ultimately emerge.

It may seem that governments will be more willing to respond to concrete needs in particular cases by conceding authority to a competent international organization rather than by accepting legal formulations framed to cover hypothetical cases. An increase in operational activities would require relatively informal decisions on the part of States members of the appropriate organizations, as well as the necessary financial commitments. The eventual success of attempts to achieve progress depends greatly on the organizational forms adopted. Effective operations thus require clear responsibilities to be accorded to the various organizations involved and, in particular, to the coordinating mechanism with the agreement of all those concerned in the process of coordination.

It is apparent that major responsibilities for planning, organization, coordination and implementation of relief rest with national and local authorities. However, national and international efforts are complementary. The scale and complexity of relief tasks demonstrate the importance of an appropriate international response being directed to creating the necessary awareness and supporting the necessary action at the national level. The purpose of international action is thus not only to respond effectively to needs at the international level, in particular in the area of coordination, but also to devise more effective responses at the national level in both donor and recipient States.

Apart from financial commitments, functional cooperation and the requirements of coordination, an important need for further progress is to develop both the principles and technical measures applicable to relief actions. There is considerable merit in the approach based on relatively detailed technical rules, because progress depends ultimately on the success of practical measures. At the same time, a comprehensive framework of relevant principles for international humanitarian assistance would usefully supplement the technical measures which have been proposed. More broadly, it is also appropriate to examine how to develop the foundations for international humanitarian cooperation contained in Art. 1(3) of the United Nations Charter. The requirement for firm foundations as well as guiding principles for humanitarian action is more than ever necessary in a period of greatly increased humanitarian needs.

It is possible that regional humanitarian activities could be developed and coordinated to a greater extent than is feasible at the global international level. Regions with particular problems can organize their responses in keeping with their special needs. At the same time, regional procedures and instruments could be integrated with the global relief system. However, one consideration which must be taken into account is that the most disaster-prone regions may not all have the resources necessary to achieve an effective response. Nevertheless, it is clear that efforts leading to the development of regional humanitarian cooperation should be encouraged.

The problem for the development of humanitarian relief law is that it should be based on objective criteria of human need, but must also take account of the practical political requirements of donor and recipient States. Law which is proved inadequate in real situations falls into disrepute. However, it should not be expected that essentially political problems can be solved primarily by legal means. Some problems of international humanitarian assistance require political solutions in the first instance, but those solutions should be based on humanitarian principles. The changeable elements inherent in the political aspects of relief can then give way to more stable features of response based on international regulation, adherence to consistent policy and the wide acceptance of responsibilities for meeting humanitarian needs.

The question of the acceptance of obligations by donor and recipient States should be viewed in a realistic light, while resisting the politicization of humanitarian assistance itself. It is clear that increased international cooperation is necessary to solve humanitarian problems, but greater cooperation is also required in many other fields. International welfare activities conducted by international organizations possessing the appropriate responsibilities constitute a transitional stage in the creation of an improved world order. International law itself is in a process of change, and it has become more difficult to identify rules of law with certainty. The expanding involvement of international organizations in many aspects of international relations, seen as an intermediate phase for the international community, prepares for the more direct acceptance of responsibilities by States and by people. The idea that the cooperative international action which is required to tackle the humanitarian problems of extreme poverty, famine, refugees and other disasters may engender wider beneficial international effects therefore deserves to be recognized and expressed in a general legal formula capable of supporting the international humanitarian order for the forseeable future.

To be widely acceptable, humanitarian actions should conform to several basic conditions. As a minimum, humanitarian actions should be free from partisan political objectives; they should be carried out in accordance with appropriate international instruments; and they should be impartially administered by humanitarian organizations.

In the move towards increasing international responsibility for humanitarian assistance, the requirement for effective relief performance will take priority at the intergovernmental level. The humanitarian and social functions of the United Nations, in particular, serve a dual purpose: they have the objective of meeting real national needs especially in the field, and they must contribute to the wider objective of safeguarding international peace and order by fostering and expressing international goodwill and cooperation. One part of the purpose of the functional and operational programmes is therefore to contribute to the continuing welfare of the UN itself, a fact which can lead to tension between particular and general goals and between short and long term perspectives in any given situation. On success in the field, on efficient and effective activities, depends success in the attainment of the wider objectives. Yet, at the same time, wider political considerations may often play a role in determining the response to apparently purely local problems. This constant interplay between political and humanitarian factors sets the context for the activities of the principal inter-governmental organizations involved in humanitarian action. The separate forces which are at work must be focused and channelled productively by devising and implementing realistic policies at the widest possible international level, requiring a clear formulation of both objectives and acceptable means for attaining them. Herein lies the challenge for those involved with humanitarian law and organization in the future.

Above all, relief actions must be effective. The idealistic aspect of humanitarian law and organization is the life-force of their gradual establishment, but genuine advances depend essentially on a realistic approach to operational activities in the field. Practical measures designed to expedite assistance are therefore the most important need at present, but such measures must be supported on suitable foundations. There is much room for further progress, based on awareness that the development of international humanitarian law, organization and action is a reciprocating and self-reinforcing process which seeks to fulfil the purpose of bringing positive humanitarian benefits to individual people.

ABBREVIATIONS

ACABQ	Advisory Committee on Administrative and Budgetary Questions
ACC	Administrative Committee on Co-ordination
ACP	African, Carbibbean and Pacific
ADIM	*Annales de Droit International Médical*
AFDI	*Annuaire Français de Droit International*
AJIL	*American Journal of International Law*
ARA	American Relief Administration
ASIL	*Proceedings of the American Society of International Law*
BFSP	*British and Foreign State Papers*
BYIL	*Britis h Yearbook of International Law*
CDDH	*Diplomatic Conference on the Reaffirmation and Development of International Humanitarian Law Applicable in Armed Conflicts, Geneva, 1974-77, Documents*
CE	Council of Europe
CECA	Consultative Assembly of the Council of Europe
CEPA	Parliamentary Assembly of the Council of Europe
CILSS	Permanent Inter-State Drought Control Committee for the Sahel
CJTL	*Colombia Journal of Transnational Law*
CMLRev	*Common Market Law Review*
CRB	Commission for Relief in Belgium
CRS	Catholic Relief Services
CTS	*Consolidated Treaty Series*
CYIL	*Canadian Yearbook of International Law*
Doc.	United Nations Document (unless otherwise indicated)
ECTS	*European Communities Treaty Series*
EEC	European Economic Community
EPIL	*Encyclopedia of Public International Law*, R. Bernhardt (ed.)
ESC	Economic and Social Council of the UN
ESCOR	Official Records of the ESC
EUA	European Unit of Account
FAO	Food and Agriculture Organization of the UN
GA	General Assembly of the UN
GAOR	Official Records of the GA
GC	Geneva Convention, 12 August 1949
HILJ	*Harvard International Law Journal*
IAEA	International Atomic Energy Agency
ICEM	Intergovernmental Committee for European Migration
ICIHI	Independent Commission on International Humanitarian Issues
ICJ	International Court of Justice
ICLQ	*International and Comparative Law Quarterly*

ICM	Intergovernmental Committee for Migration
IConfRC	International Conference of the Red Cross
ICRC	International Committee of the Red Cross
ICVA	International Council of Voluntary Agencies
IGCR	Inter-Governmental Committee on Refugees
IJIL	*Indian Journal of International Law*
ILA	*International Law Association, Reports of Conferences*
ILM	*International Legal Materials*
IRC	International Red Cross
IRevRC	*International Review of the Red Cross*
IRO	International Refugee Organization
IRU	International Relief Union
IYHR	*Israel Yearbook on Human Rights*
JAIL	*Japanese Annual of International Law*
JICJ	*Journal of the International Commission of Jurists*
LN	League of Nations
LNTS	*League of Nations Treaty Series*
LRCS	League of Red Cross and Red Crescent Societies
LWF	Lutheran World Federation
MLR	*Modern Law Review*
NGO	Non-Governmental Organization
NYIL	*Netherlands Yearbook of International Law*
NYUJILP	*New York University Journal of International Law and Politics*
OAS	Organization of American States
OAU	Organization of African Unity
OSRO	FAO Office for Special Relief Operations (formerly Office for Sahelian Relief Operations)
ÖZöRV	*Österreichische Zeitschrift für öffentliches Recht und Völkerrecht*
PCIRO	Preparatory Committee of the IRO
RBDI	*Revue Belge de Droit International*
RdC	Académie de Droit International de La Haye, *Recueil des Cours*
RDH	*Revue des Droits de l'Homme (Human Rights Journal)*
RDPMDG	*Revue de Droit Pénal Militaire et de Droit de la Guerre*
RDPSP	*Revue de Droit Public et de la Science Politique en France et à l'Etranger*
RevICR	*Revue Internationale de la Croix-Rouge*
RGDIP	*Revue Générale de Droit International Public*
RICJ	*Review of the International Commission of Jurists*
RIDC	*Revue Internationale de Droit Comparé*
SCOR	Official Records of the UN Security Council
SF	Swiss Francs
TGS	*Transactions of the Grotius Society*
TIAS	*Treaties and Other International Acts Series*
UN	United Nations

UNCIO	UN Conference on International Organization
UNCURK	UN Commission for the Unification and Rehabilitation of Korea
UNDP	UN Development Programme
UNDRO	Office of the UN Disaster Relief Co-ordinator
UNEP	UN Environment Programme
UNEPRO	UN East Pakistan Relief Operation
UNESCO	UN Educational, Scientific and Cultural Organization
UNHCR	Office of the UN High Commissioner for Refugees
UNICEF	UN Children's Fund
UNITAR	UN Institute for Training and Research
UNKRA	UN Korean Reconstruction Agency
UNREF	UN Refugee Fund
UNROB	UN Special Relief Office in Bangladesh
UNROD	UN Relief Operation in Dacca
UNRPR	UN Relief for Palestine Refugees
UNRRA	UN Relief and Rehabilitation Administration
UNRWA	UN Relief and Works Agency for Palestine Refugees in the Near East
UNSO	UN Sahelian Office
UNTS	*UN Treaty Series*
USAID	US Agency for International Development
VJIL	*Virginia Journal of International Law*
VJTL	*Vanderbilt Journal of Transnational Law*
WCC	World Council of Churches
WFC	World Food Council
WFP	World Food Programme
WHO	World Health Organization
WMO	World Meteorological Organization
YILC	*Yearbook of the International Law Commission*
YLJ	*Yale Law Journal*
YUN	*Yearbook of the UN*
ZaöRV	*Zeitschrift für ausländisches öffentliches Recht und Völkerrecht*

Notes

Introduction

1. See the work on which this book is based, Macalister-Smith, P., *International Disaster Relief*, Ph.D. Thesis, Faculty of Law, University of Birmingham, England, 1980. See also Morse, B., 'Practice, Norms and Reform of International Humanitarian Rescue Operations', 157 *RdC* 1977-IV, p. 125; Patrnogic, J., 'Protection de la Personne Humaine au Cours des Catastrophes Naturelles', 27 *ADIM* 1977, p. 16; Samuels, J.W., 'The Relevance of International Law to the Prevention and Mitigation of Natural Disasters', in Green, S. and Stephens, L.H. (eds.), *Disaster Assistance*, 1979, p. 245.

2. For various classifications of disasters, see Western, K.A., *The Epidemiology of Natural and Man-Made Disasters*, dissertation for the Academic Diploma in Tropical Public Health No. 189, London School of Hygiene and Tropical Medicine, University of London, 1972; Ads, O.H., *International Disaster and International Law*, Ph.D. Thesis No. 3592, University of Sheffield, 1974; and Westgate, K.N. and O'Keefe, P., *Some Definitions of Disaster*, Occasional Paper No. 4, Disaster Research Unit, University of Bradford, 1975.

3. Turner, B.A., *Man-Made Disasters*, 1978, p. 14. See also statement of the Secretary-General of LRCS, ESC Policy and Programme Co-ordination Committee, ESC 59th Session, a.i.20, Doc.E/AC.24/SR.574 (1975), p. 179; 'The ICRC, the League and the Tansley Report, Considerations of the International Committee of the Red Cross and of the League of Red Cross Societies on the Final Report of the Reappraisal of the Role of the Red Cross', ICRC – LRCS, 1977, p. 21; Samuels, 1979, p. 246.

4. See e.g. Skeet, M., *Manual for Disaster Relief Work*, 1977; *Red Cross Disaster Relief Handbook*, LRCS, 1976 (updated); UNHCR, *Handbook for Emergencies*, 1982.

5. See e.g. *Prevention Better than Cure, Report on human and environmental disasters in the Third World*, Swedish Red Cross, 1984; the UNDRO series of publications *Disaster Prevention and Mitigation, A Compendium of Current Knowledge*; and see chapter 7, note 42.

6. Cf. Ads; Manning, D.H., *Disaster Technology, An Annotated Bibliography*, 1976; and *Disaster Prevention and Mitigation, A Compendium of Current Knowledge*, Vol. 9, 'Legal Aspects', UNDRO, 1980.

7. See Bernhardt, R. (ed.), *Encyclopedia of Public International Law*: e.g. Jennings, R.Y., 'International Law'; Kimminich, O., 'History of the Law of Nations, Since World War II'; and Steiner, H.J., 'International Law, Doctrine and Schools of Thought in the Twentieth Century'.

8. Fitzmaurice, G., 'The Future of Public International Law and of the International Legal System in the Circumstances of Today', Institut de Droit International, *Livre du Centenaire 1873-1973*, 1973, p. 196; Friedmann, W., *The Changing Structure of International Law*, 1964; Friedmann, W., 'Human Welfare and International Law', in *Transnational Law in a Changing Society*, (ed.), 1972, p. 113; Kimminich, O., *Humanitäres Völkerrecht – Humanitäre Aktion*, 1972.

9. Lauterpacht, E. (ed.), *H. Lauterpacht, International Law: Collected Papers*, Vol. II, 1975, p. 47.

10. Green, S., *International Disaster Relief*, 1977, p. 30.

11. Cf. Morison, R.F., 'International Disaster Action: Advancing Slowly but how Surely?', 4 *The International Journal of Disaster Studies and Practice* 1980, p. 93; UNA – USA, *Acts of Nature, Acts of Man: The Global Response to Natural Disasters*, United Nations Association of the USA, Policy Studies Panel on International Disaster Relief, 1977; 'New international humanitarian order', A/RES/36/136 (1981), and 36 GAOR, Ann., a.i. 138, Doc.A/36/245 (1981).

12. Tansley, D., *Final Report: An Agenda for the Red Cross*, Joint Committee for the Reappraisal of the Red Cross, 1975, p. 58; Green, S., pp. 23-26; Turner, p. 14.

13. Green, S., p. 20.

14. For references to the developments mentioned, see Chapter 9, notes 6 to 22.

Chapter 1

1. E.g. Holy Bible, Joshua, 6:21, 8:22-29, 11:20; Deuteronomy, 20:16-17. Cf. Francisco Suarez, *De Triplici Virtute Theologica, Fide, Spe et Charitate*, 1621, Disp. XIII, 16.

2. See e.g. Nikam, N.A. and McKeon, R. (eds.), *The Edicts of Asoka*, 1966; Chacko, C.J., 'International Law in India', 1 *IJIL* 1960-1, p. 184 and 2 *IJIL* 1962, p. 48; Singh, N., 'International Law in India', 2 *IJIL* 1962, p. 65; Sastry, K.R.R., 'Hinduism and International Law', 117 *RdC* 1966-I, p. 503; Rechid, A., 'L'Islam et le Droit des Gens', 60 *RdC* 1937-II, p. 371; Griffith, S.B., *Sun Tzu, The Art of War*, 1963; Diallo, Y., 'Humanitarian Law and Traditional African Law', *IRevRC* 1976, p. 57, and 'African Tradition and Humanitarian Law', *IRevRC* 1976, p. 387. In Europe, cf. *Las Siete Partidas* of Alfonso X ('El Sabio', 1252-1284); the *Tractatus Represaliarum* (1354) by Bartolus and the *Arbre des Batailles* (c. 1385) by Honoré Bonet marked notable stages in the development of humane standards and of modern international law.

3. Draper, G.I.A.D., 'The Law of Ransom during the Hundred Years War', 7 *RDPMDG* 1968, p. 263; Rosas, A., *The Legal Status of Prisoners of War*, 1976.

4. Hugo Grotius, *De Jure Belli ac Pacis*, Book III, Chapters XI and XII; Jean-Jacques Rousseau, *Contrat Social*, Book I, Chapter IV. See Gurlt, E., *Zur Geschichte des internationalen und freiwilligen Krankenpflege im Krieg*, 1873; Coursier, H., 'L'Evolution du Droit International Humanitaire', 99 *RdC* 1960-I, p. 361; Freidman, L. (ed.), *The Law of War, A Documentary History*, Vol. I, 1972; Schindler, D. and Toman, J. (eds.), *The Law of Armed Conflicts, A Collection of Conventions, Resolutions and Other Documents*, 1973.

5. Dunant, H., *Souvenir de Solférino*, 1862.

6. 129 CTS, p. 361; Friedman, p. 187.

7. Geneva Convention of July 6, 1906, for the Amelioration of the Condition of the Wounded and Sick in Armies in the Field, 202 CTS, p. 144; Geneva Convention of July 27, 1929 for the Amelioration of the Condition of the Wounded and Sick in Armies in the Field, 118 LNTS, p. 303; for the 1949 Conventions see Chapter 2 below, note 1.

8. Geneva Convention of July 27, 1929, relative to the Treatment of Prisoners of War, 118 LNTS, p. 343.

9. See Gay, G.I., *The Commission for Relief in Belgium, Statistical Review of Relief Operations*, 1925; Gay, G.I. and Fisher, H.H., *Public Relations of the Commission for Relief in Belgium, Documents*, 2 vols., 1929; Weissman, B.M., *Herbert Hoover and Famine Relief to Soviet Russia: 1921-23*, 1974.

10. See Pictet, J., *Commentary, The Geneva Conventions of August 12, 1949*, 4 vols., Vol. 4, p. 4.

11. Agreement for the UN Relief and Rehabilitation Administration, Washington, November 9, 1943; text at Woodbridge, G., *UNRRA, The History of the UN Relief and Rehabilitation Administration*, 3 vols., 1950, Vol. 3, p. 23, and British Command Paper, Cmd. 6491(1943).

12. See Woodbridge, Vol. 3, pp. 42f.

13. *Ibid.*, Appendix 6, pp. 210f. and Appendix 7, pp. 238f.

14. *Ibid.*, Appendix 10, pp. 428-429.

15. For agreements made between UNRRA and UN agencies concerning the continuation of welfare functions, see *ibid.*, e.g. pp. 352, 354 and 356; see also UNRRA Council Res. 103.

16. See generally Balogh, E., 'World Peace and the Refugee Problem', 75 *RdC* 1949-II, p. 363; Grahl-Madsen, A., *The Status of Refugees in International Law*, 2 vols., Vol. 1, 1966, pp. 10f.

17. But see League of Nations Covenant, Art. 23; Reut-Nicolussi, E., 'Displaced Persons and International Law', 73 *RdC* 1948-II, p. 1 at p. 34; Grahl-Madsen, A., 'The League of Nations and the Refugees', *AWR Bulletin*, No. 2, 1982, p. 86.

18. See 'Report on the Work of the High Commissioner for Refugees', 4 September 1923, presented by Dr. Nansen to the 4th Assembly, LN Doc. A.30.1923.XII. See also Simpson, J. Hope, *The Refugee Problem*, 1939; Kraus, H., *International Relief in Action, 1914-1943*, 1944.

19. See LN Official Journal 1931, p. 309, and Special Supplement 84, p. 157.

20. See e.g. Weis, P., 'The International Protection of Refugees', 48 *AJIL* 1954, p. 193. For some of these agreements see 13 LNTS, p. 237; 89 LNTS, p. 47; 159 LNTS, p. 201; 192 LNTS, p. 59; 189 UNTS, p. 152.

21. See LN Doc. A.54(1938) XII, 30 September 1938; Reut-Nicolussi, p. 42; Grahl-Madsen, *supra*, note 17.

22. See Hansard, Parliamentary History, Vol. XV, 1753-1765, p. 543; Journal of the House of Commons, reprinted 1803, Vol. XXVII, 1754-1757, 29 Geo II, pp. 320f; E. de Vattel, *Le Droit Des Gens*, Book II, Chapter I, 5.

23. See Henry Dunant, *Un Souvenir de Solférino*, edition of Amsterdam, 1902, p. 68; and see autograph manuscript of the 7th ed., Bibliothèque publique et universitaire, Geneva, f. 64. See also resolutions of the Geneva Conference, 26-29 October 1863, Art. 4; IInd IConfRC 1869, Berlin, Res. III, 20 and 21; Perruchoud, R., *Les Résolutions des Conférences Internationales de la Croix-Rouge*, 1979, p. 222; Coursier, H., *The International Red Cross*, 1961, p. 31.

24. Cit., Weissman, p. 47; see also Fisher, H.H., *The Famine in Soviet Russia, 1919-1923*, 1927; 'Report of the Work of the High Commissioner for Refugess', LN Doc.A.30(1923) XII, 4 September 1923, p. 2.

25. See e.g. General Council of the League, IIIrd Session, Paris, 1924, Res. XXI; Perruchoud, 1979, pp. 224-225.

26. Text of the Convention, LN Official Journal, 8th Year, No. 8, August 1927, p. 997; 135 LNTS, p. 247; *Manuel de l'Union Internationale de Secours*, Geneva, July 1938. See Borgeaud, M.-A., *L'Union Internationale de Secours*, 1932; Ciraolo, G., *L'Unione Internazionale di Soccorso*, 1934; Macalister-Smith, P., 'The International Relief Union', 5 *The International Journal of Disaster Studies and Practice*, 1981, p. 147. See also 'Functions of the Red Cross in the Working of the IRU', XVth IConfRC 1934, Tokyo, a.i.7, Doc. No. 27. The Convention appears to be still in force for 16 States.

Chapter 2

1. For the texts of the Final Act of the Diplomatic Conference and the Conventions of 12 August 1949 see 75 UNTS, p. 1. See also 'Final Record of the Diplomatic Conference of Geneva', 4 vols., 1949. As of March 1983 there were 154 States parties.

2. For the texts, see 72 *AJIL* 1978, p. 457; Doc. A/32/144; 38 *ZaöRV* 1978, p. 86. See also 'Official Records of the Diplomatic Conference on the Reaffirmation and Development of International Humanitarian Law Applicable in Armed Conflicts, Geneva, 1974-1977', 17 vols., 1978. As of March 1984 there were 40 States parties to Protocol I and 34 States parties to Protocol II.

3. See Convention With Respect to the Laws and Customs of War on Land, The Hague, 29 July 1899, preamble, para. 9, in Friedman, p. 221 at p. 222. See also GC I, Art. 63, para. 4; GC II, Art. 62, para. 4; GC III, Art. 142, para. 4; GC IV, Art. 158, para. 4; Münch, F., 'Die Martens'sche Klausel und die Grundlagen des Völkerrechts', 36 *ZaöRV* 1976, p. 347.

4. See ICRC, Annual Reports.

5. See Pictet, *Commentary...*, Vol. 1, p. 136.

6. Burwell, D.G., 'Civilian Protection in Modern Warfare', 14 *VJIL* 1973-4, p. 123. Cf. Wilhelm, R.-J., 'Problèmes relatifs à la protection de la personne humaine par le droit international dans les conflits armés ne présantant pas un caractère international', 137 *RdC* 1972-III, p. 311; Dinstein, Y., 'The International Law of Civil Wars and Human Rights', 6 *IYHR* 1976, p. 62; Kalshoven, F., 'Reaffirmation and Development of International Humanitarian Law Applicable in Armed Conflicts, The Diplomatic Conference, Geneva 1974-1977, 8 *NYIL* 1977, p. 107, 9 *NYIL* 1978, p. 107; Sandoz, Y., 'La Place des Protocoles additionels aux Conventions de Genève du 12 août 1949 dans le droit humanitaire', 12 *RDH* 1979, p. 135; Veuthey, M., *Guérilla et Droit Humanitaire*, 1976, and 1983.

7. See e.g. Rosas, A., *The Legal Status of Prisoners of War*, 1976; Levie, H.S., *Prisoners of War in International Armed Conflict, Documents on Prisoners of War*, 2 vols., 1978-1979; Veuthey.

8. See Bernhardt, R. (ed.), *Encyclopedia of Public International Law*: e.g. Kalshoven, F., 'War, Laws of'; Schlögel, A., 'Geneva Red Cross Conventions and Protocols'; Zayas, A.-M. de, 'Civilian Population, Protection'.

9. E.g. GA Res. 2444 (XXIII) 1968; GA Res. 2675 (XXV) 1970, para. 8.; GA Res. 2676 (XXV) 1970; Declaration on the Protection of Women and Children in Emergency and Armed Conflict, GA Res. 3318 (XXIX) 1974; see also e.g. Doc. A/7720 (1969), p. 7; cf. GA Res. 2675 (XXV) 1970, para. 1.

10. See IRevRC 1977, p. 369.

11. Pictet, '*Commentary...*', Vol. 1, p. 12; cf. Doc.CDDH/SR.49, para. 5, CDDH, Vol. VII, p. 60; and Doc.CDDH/SR.56, para. 77, CDDH, Vol. VII, p. 209. See also Jessup, P.C., 'Political and Humanitarian Approaches to Limitation of Warfare', 51 *AJIL* 1957, p. 757, e.g. at p. 761; Kaplan, M.A. and Katzenbach, N. de B., *The Political Foundations of International Law*, 1961, e.g. at p. 227; Best, G., *Humanity in Warfare*, 1980.

12. Chen, L.C., *Disaster in Bangladesh*, 1973, p. 271.

13. See Bothe, M., 'Rechtsprobleme humanitärer Hilfsaktionen zugunsten der Zivilbevölkerung bei bewaffneten Konflikten', in *Beitrage zur Weiterentwicklung des humanitären Völkerrechts für bewaffnete Konflikte*, 1973, p. 24 at p. 25. Cf. 'Special Economic, Humanitarian and Disaster Relief Assistance', Note by the Secretary-General, Doc.E/1981/16 (19 March 1981), Annex, 'International Efforts to Meet Humanitarian Needs in Emergency Situations', p. 4, para. 4; International Medical and Humanitarian Law, 'Assistance Internationale aux Victimes de Guerre', 60 *ILA* 1982, pp. 467-477. See also Hocké, J.P., 'Action humanitaire: protection et assistance', *RevICR* 1984, pp. 11-17.

Chapter 3

1. See chapter 1, note 11.

2. See e.g. 'International Assistance to Refugees', Report submitted by Sir H. Emerson, 11 March 1946, LN Doc.A.10.1947.XII; ESC Res.3(I) 1946; ESC Res.18(III); GA Res.8(I) 1946.

3. GA Res.62(I) 1946, to which the Constitution was annexed; see also 18 UNTS, p. 3. See Holborn, L.W., *The International Refugee Organization*, 1956.

4. Statute, GA Res.428(V), 14 December 1950. Convention Relating to the Status of Refugees, 28 July 1951, 189 UNTS, p. 150; the Convention entered into force on 22 April 1954 and at 31 March 1983 there were 93 States parties. Protocol Relating to the Status of Refugees, 16 December 1966, see GA Res.2198(XXI) 1966 and 606 UNTS, p. 168; the Protocol entered into force on 4 October 1967 and at 31 March 1983 there were 92 States parties. See e.g. Grahl-Madsen, A., 'International Refugee Law Today and Tomorrow', *Archiv des Völkerrechts*, 1982, p. 411f.

5. GA Res.319(IV) 1949.

6. Heuven Goedhart, G.J. van, 'The Problem of Refugees', 82 *RdC* 1953-I, p. 265 at p. 362.

7. GA Res.538B(VI) 1952, para. 1.

8. GA Res.832(IX) 154.

9. GA Res.1166(XII) 1957, which also requested the ESC to establish the Executive Committee.

10. See GA Res.1166(XII) 1957, paras. 5(c) and (d); GA Res.1673(XVI) 1961; E/RES/1978/36.

11. GA Res.1006(ES-II) 1956, Res. II, para. 1. See also GA Res.1039(XI) 1957, paras. 3, 4 and 7; and GA Res.1129(XV) 1956, para. 1.

12. GA Res.1167(XII) 1957.

13. GA Res.1286(XIII) 1958; GA Res.1389(XIV) 1959; GA Res.1500(XV) 1960.

14. GA Res.1388(XIV) 1959, para. 2; and GA Res.1499(XV) 1960.

15. GA Res.1672(XVI) 1861.

16. See Schnyder, F., 'Les Aspects Juridiques Actuels du Problème des Réfugiés', 114 *RdC* 1965-I, p. 339 at p. 430, para. 76 and p. 434, para. 83.

17. GA Res.2958(XXVII) 1972, para. 2.

18. See GA Res.3454(XXX) 1975, preamble; ESC Res.2011(LXI) 1976; A/RES/31/35 (1976), paras. 2 and 4.

19. Aga Khan, S., 'Legal Problems Relating to Refugees and Displaced Persons', 149 *RdC* 1976-I, p. 290 at p. 342. See also GA Res.3143(XXVIII) 1973.

20. See GA Res.2956B(XXVIII) 1972; GA Res.3271B(XXIX) 1974; A/RES/35/41 B. In 1983 $5,455,000 were allocated from the Emergency Fund.

21. Cf. ESC Res.2011(LXI) 1976; A/RES/34/60 (1979); A/RES/35/41 (1980); A/RES/36/125 (1981); A/RES/37/195 (1982).

22. GA Res.1006(ES-II) 1956.

23. See Reports of the Secretary-General Concerning the Implementation of General Assembly Resolution 2790 (XXVI) and Security Council Resolution 307 (1971), Doc.S/10539/Add.3 (11 August 1972), 27 SCOR Supp.; Doc.S/10853 and Add. 1 (1 January 1973), 28 SCOR Supp.; and Doc.S/10853/Add.3 (26 April 1973), 28 SCOR Supp. See also Holborn, L.W., *Refugees: A Problem of Our Time*, 1975, pp. 754-793; and Oliver, T.W., *The UN in Bangladesh*, 1978.

24. GA Res.2956A(XXVII) 1972. Cf. GA Res.2790(XXVI) 1971; UNHCR Statute, Para. 17.

25. ESC Res.1655(LII) 1972; see also ESC Res.1877(LVII) 1974.

26. See e.g. Doc. S/14490 (1981); Doc. S/14778 (1981); 'Report of the United Nations High Commissioner for Refugees', Doc. E/1982/29; *infra* note 27.

27. See e.g. 'Report on UNHCR assistance activities in 1981-1982 ...', Doc. A/AC.96/606 (1982); 'Report of the United Nations High Commissioner for Refugees', Doc. E/1983/47, and Doc. E/1984/61 (30 May 1984).

28. See also Doc. E/CN.4/1503; and 'Human rights and mass exoduses', A/RES/37/186 (1982). Cf. 'New international humanitarian order', A/RES/36/136 (1981); and 36 GAOR, Ann., a.i. 138, Doc. A/36/245, Annex, para. 6.

29. See e.g. 'Refugee Aid and Development', Doc. A/AC.96/627 (1983); cf. Doc.A/AC.96/631 (1983), pp. 27-29. See also Doc. A/AC.96/645 (1984).

30. E.g. Doc.A/648, 16 December 1948; Doc.A/689/Corr.1/Add.1, 18 October 1948; see also Doc.A/1451 (1949).

31. See Annual Report[s] of the Commissioner-General, GAOR, Supplements; and, generally,

El-Farhan, A.H., *The United Nations Relief and Works Agency for Palestine Refugees in the Near East*, Ph.D. Thesis, New York University, 1979.

32. See e.g. Weis, 1954, p. 195; Aga Khan, 1976, p. 314.

33. Plender, R., 'Admission of Refugees: Draft Convention on Territorial Asylum', 15 *San Diego Law Review* 1977, p. 45 at pp. 54-55 and 61. Cf. IRO Constitution, Annex I, Part I, Sec. C(1) (a) (i); UNHCR Statute, Paras. 6A and B; 1951 Convention, Art. 1A. See also Aga Khan, 1976, p. 296; Grahl-Madsen, A., 'Identifying the World's Refugees', 467 *Annals of the American Academy of Political and Social Science* 1983, p. 11.

34. See e.g. 43 ZaöRV 1983, pp. 358-360.

35. See e.g. GAOR, 36th Session, Supp. 12A, Doc.A/36/12/Add. 1, para. 57(2); A/RES/36/125, 14 December 1981.

36. Aga Khan, 1976, p. 331.

37. See e.g. Heuven Goedhart, p. 359; Plender, R., *International Migration Law*, 1972, p. 216; Weis, 1954, p. 220.

Chapter 4

1. See Fitzmaurice, p. 260.

2. But see e.g. Parry, C., *The Sources and Evidences of International Law*, 1965; Virally, M., 'The Sources of International Law', in Sørensen, M. (ed.), *Manual of Public International Law*, 1968, p. 116; D'Amato, A.A., *The Concept of Custom in International Law*, 1971.

3. See e.g. Visscher, C. de, *Theory and Reality in Public International Law*, 1968, p. 155; see also Thirlway, H.W.A., *Customary International Law and Codification*, 1972, p. 67.

4. See Thirlway, pp. 66f; Bleicher, S.A., 'The Legal Significance of Re-Citation of General Assembly Resolutions', 63 *AJIL* 1969, p. 444; D'Amato, A.A., 'On Consensus', VIII *CYIL* 1970, p. 104.

5. Corfu Channel Case (Merits), Judgment of 9 April 1949, ICJ Reports 1949, p. 4 at p. 22. See also Vienna Convention on the Law of Treaties, 23 May 1969, Arts. 53 and 64; and cf. Art. 60(5). See e.g. Mann, F.A., 'The Doctrine of Jus cogens in International Law', in *Festschrift für Ulrich Scheuner*, 1973, p. 399.

6. Cf. Gottlieb, G.A.G., 'International Assistance to Civilian Populations in Armed Conflicts', 4 *NYUJILP* 1971, p. 4 at p. 419.

7. See Macalister-Smith, P., 'Comity', in Bernhardt, R. (ed.), *Encyclopedia of Public International Law*.

8. See Friedmann, W., 'The Uses of 'General Principles' in the Development of International Law', 57 *AJIL* 1963, p. 279; Virally, pp. 144f; Patrnogic, 1977, pp. 18f.

9. Mosler, H., 'General Principles of Law', Section C(2) (d), in Bernhardt, R. (ed.), *EPIL*, Instal-

ment 7 (1984), pp. 102-103. Cf. Reservations to the Convention on the Prevention and Punishment of the Crime of Genocide, Advisory Opinion of May 28, 1951, ICJ Rep. 1951, p. 15 at p. 23; Case Concerning the Barcelona Traction, Light and Power Company, Limited, Second Phase, Judgment of 5 February 1970, ICJ Rep. 1970, p. 4 at p. 32.

10. Cf. e.g. Lauterpacht, H., *International Law and Human Rights*, 1950, p. 121; Friedmann, W., 'The Relevance of International Law to the Process of Economic and Social Development', 60 *ASIL* 1966, p. 8; Friedmann, W., 'General Course', 127 *RdC* 1969-II, p. 47 at pp. 93f; Kimminich, 1972.

11. Fitzmaurice, p. 324.

12. See Patrnogic, 1977, p. 19; Patrnogic, J., 'Protection from Disasters – A Human Right', UNDRO News, March 1980, p. 5.

13. Kelsen, H., *The Law of the United Nations*, 1950, p. 88.

14. Samuels, 'Commentary', in Paxman, J.M. and Boggs, G.T. (eds.), *The United Nations: A Reassessment. Sanctions, Peacekeeping and Humanitarian Assistance*, 1973, p. 135 at pp. 135 and 140.

15. GA Res.48(I) 1946.

16. GA Res. 1007(ES-II) 1956, preamble.

17. See UNRRA Council, Res.100, entitled 'Future Relief Needs'; Woodbridge, Vol. 3, p. 164.

18. Mitrany, D., 'The Functional Approach to World Organization', XXIV *International Affairs* 1948, p. 350.

19. E.g. ESC Res.1768(LIV) 1973; A/RES/32/197 (1978).

20. E.g. Doc.E/3833 (1963).

21. See SCOR, Meeting 1392, 2 December 1966; Oliver, pp. 35-38.

22. Cf. Oppenheim, *International Law*, Lauterpacht, H. (ed.), 2 vols., Vol. I, 8th ed., 1955, p. 441; 26 GAOR, Supp. 1A, Doc.A/8401/Add.1 (1971), p. 15; Repertory of Practice of UN Organs, Vol. 5, p. 123; Ramcharan, B.G., *Humanitarian Good Offices in International Law*, 1983.

23. See e.g. GA Res. 48(I) 1946.

24. E.g. GA Res.2034(XX) 1965.

25. GA Res.57(I) 1946; GA Res.58(I) 1946; and ESC Res.51(V) 1947.

26. GA Res.2643(XXV) 1970.

27. GA Res.2790(XXVI) 1971, para. 2. See also Ramcharan, 1983, pp. 92-110.

28. E.g. the International Conferences on Assistance to Refugees in Africa, 1981 and 1984, see Doc. A/37/522 (1982); cf. A/RES/37/197 (1983). See also Doc. A/8401/Add.1 (1971); and Doc. A/35/33 (1980), e.g. at pp. 61-62.

29. Text attached to GA Res.217A(III) 1948; see e.g. Lauterpacht, H., 'The Universal Declaration of Human Rights', XXV *BYIL* 1948, p. 356.

30. Texts annexed to GA Res.2200(XXI) 1966.

31. But see Samuels, J.W., 'Organized Responses to Natural Disasters', in MacDonald, R.St.J. *et al.* (eds.), *The International Law and Policy of Human Welfare*, 1978, p. 675 at pp. 684-685; Patrnogic, 1977, pp. 20-21.

32. GA Res.1386(XIV) 1959. Cf. Declaration on the Protection of Women and Children in Emergency and Armed Conflict, GA Res.3318(XXIX), 14 December 1974.

33. GA Res.3348(XXIX) 1974.

34. Cf. GAOR, 26th Session, 3rd Com., Meeting 1890, ai.59, paras. 22 and 31.

35. Henkin, L., 'The UN and Human Rights', 19 *International Organization* 1965, p. 504 at p. 506.

36. Samuels, 1978, p. 684. For reports on implementation of Art. 11 of the International Covenant on Economic, Social and Cultural Rights see e.g. Doc.E/1980/6 and Doc.E/1980/22 (with addenda).

37. A/RES/35/36 (1980), Annex, para. 161; cf. the series *Disaster Prevention and Mitigation*, UNDRO publications. See also Cuny, F.C., *Disasters and Development*, 1983.

38. See e.g. 'The International Dimensions of the Right to Development as a Human Right', Doc. E/CN.4/1334 (1979). See also 'The Third World and International Law, Selected Bibliography – 1955-1982', United Nations Library, Geneva, Publications Series C, No. 5, 1983.

39. Convention for the Unification of Certain Rules of Law With Respect to Assistance and Salvage at Sea, Second Brussels Convention, 23 September 1910. See also Art. 8 of the First Brussels Convention of the same date. The French texts are at 103 BFSP, p. 434.

40. Regulation 10; the text of the 1960 Convention for the Safety of Life at Sea is at 536 UNTS, p. 27.

41. Geneva Convention on the High Seas, 29 April 1958, 450 UNTS, p. 82. United Nations Convention on the Law of the Sea, 10 December 1982, Doc.A/CONF.62/122 (1982). Cf. Convention on the International Maritime Satellite Organization (INMARSAT), 3 September 1976, 15 ILM 1976, p. 1051, Art. 3(1).

42. E.g. see IRevRC 1979, pp. 208-209; Doc.E/1980/79, para. 22; Doc.A/AC.96/586 (1980), p. 10; Doc.A/AC.96/626, p. 5.

43. Declaration of Legal Principles Governing Activities of States in the Exploration and Use of Outer Space, Para. 9, see GA Res.1962(XVIII) 13 December 1963.

44. Treaty of Principles Governing the Activities of States in the Exploration and Use of Outer Space, Including the Moon and other Celestial Bodies, 27 January 1967, Art. 5 (see also Art. 9); 610 UNTS, p. 205, and GA Res.2222(XXI) 19 December 1966.

45. See GA Res.2345(XXII) 19 December 1968, Annex, Agreement on the Rescue of Astro-

nauts, the Return of Astronauts, and the Return of Objects Launched into Outer Space, Arts. 2 and 4; 672 UNTS, p. 119.

46. E.g. Stowell, E.C., *Intervention in International Law* 1921, pp. 86-205; Stowell, E.C., 'Humanitarian Intervention', 33 *AJIL* 1939, p. 733; Ganji, M., *International Protection of Human Rights*, 1962, pp. 22-37; Sohn, L.B. and Buergenthal, T., *International Protection of Human Rights*, 1973, pp. 143-177 and 181-195; Rougier, A., 'La Théorie de l'Intervention d'Humanité', 17 *RGDIP* 1910, p. 468.

47. See Brownlie, I., *International Law and the Use of Force by States*, 1963, p. 338. Cf. Stowell, 1921, p. 58.

48. E.g. Graham, M.W., 'Humanitarian Intervention', XXIII *Michigan Law Review* 1923-4, p. 312 at p. 328.

49. See chapter 2, note 3.

50. See in particular Lillich, R.B., 'Forcible Self-Help by States to Protect Human Rights', 53 *Iowa Law Review* 1967, p. 325; Lillich, R.B., 'Intervention to Protect Human Rights', 15 *McGill Law Journal* 1969, p. 205; Lillich, R.B., 'Humanitarian Intervention: A Reply to Ian Brownlie and a Plea for Constructive Alternatives', in Moore, J.N. (ed.), *Law and Civil War in the Modern World*, 1974, p. 229. Cf. Schutter, B. de, 'De Rol van de Verenigde Naties in Humanitaire Interventies', in *Miscellanea, W.J. Ganshof van der Meersch*, 1972, Vol. 1, p. 435; Franck, T.M. and Rodley, N.S., 'After Bangladesh: The Law of Humanitarian Intervention by Military Force', 67 *AJIL* 1973, p. 275; Gottlieb, 1971, p. 425.

51. Moore, J.N., 'The Control of Foreign Intervention in Internal Conflict', 9 *VJIL* 1969, p. 205 at p. 338; Nanda, V.P., 'The US Action in the 1965 Dominican Crisis', 43 *Denver Law Journal* 1966, p. 439 at p. 475; Lillich, 1967, p. 350; Lillich, 1969, p. 218. Cf. Fairley, H.S., 'State Actors, Humanitarian Intervention and International Law: Reopening Pandora's Box', 10 *Georgia Journal of International and Comparative Law* 1980, p. 29.

52. Cf. Brownlie, 1963, p. 431.

53. E.g. Declaration on the Inadmissibility of Intervention in the Domestic Affairs of States and the Protection of their Independence and Sovereignty, GA Res.2131(XX) 21 December 1965; Declaration on Principles of International Law concerning Friendly Relations and Co-operation among States in accordance with the Charter of the United Nations, GA Res.2625(XXV) 24 October 1970; Charter of the OAS; Charter of the OAU.

54. Cf. Stowell, E.C., 'La Théorie et la Pratique de l'Intervention', 40 *RdC* 1932-II, p. 91 at p. 148; Gottlieb, 1971, p. 403; Falk, R.A., 'The US and the Doctrine of Nonintervention in the Internal Affairs of Independent States', 5 *Howard Law Journal* 1959, p. 163 at pp. 166-167; Lauterpacht, H., 'The Grotian Tradition in International Law', XXIII *BYIL* 1946, p. 1 at p. 46; Visscher, C. de, *Théories et Réalités en Droit International Public*, 1970, p. 154.

55. Forsythe, D.P., *Humanitarian Politics*, 1977, p. 42. See also Wiseberg, L.S., 'Humanitarian Intervention: Lessons from the Nigerian Civil War', 7 *RDH* 1974, p. 61 e.g. at pp. 80-83.

Chapter 5

1. The texts of the Statutes and other constitutional instruments of the IRC, as well as regulations, resolutions and other relevant materials are to be found in the International Red Cross *Handbook*. See Ruegger, P., 'The Juridical Aspects of the Organization of the International Red Cross', 82 *RdC* 1953-I, p. 483; Bindschedler-Robert, D., 'Red Cross', in Bernhardt, R. (ed.), *Encyclopedia of Public International Law*.

2. Coursier, H., *The International Red Cross*, 1961, p. 78; cf. Perruchoud, 1979, p. 386.

3. See ESC Res.57(IV) 1947.

4. E.g. ESC Res.21(III) 1946; GA Res.55(I) 1946; GA Res.2034(XX) 1965; GA Res.2816 (XXVI) 1971.

5. Cf. Art. 5(1) of the 1927 Convention Establishing an International Relief Union, *supra*, Chapter 1, note 26; Art. 81(3) of Additional Protocol I of 1966, *supra* Chapter 2, note 2.

6. See Pictet, J., *Red Cross Principles*, 1956; Pictet, J., 'The Fundamental Principles of the Red Cross', *IRevRC* 1979, pp. 130f; Perruchoud, 1979, p. 133. See also Coursier, 1961, p. 49; Emden, A. van, 'The Special Position of the Red Cross', *IRevRC* 1966, p. 321.

7. 'Agreement between the ICRC and the League of Red Cross Societies for the purpose of specifying certain of their respective functions', 25 April 1969, text in IRC *Handbook* and Red Cross *Disaster Relief Handbook*.

8. See recent issues of the *International Review of the Red Cross*; ICRC Annual Reports; LRCS annual Review of activities.

9. See Perruchoud, 1979, pp. 219f.

10. LRCS Board of Governors, XXIst Session, 1950, Monte Carlo, Res.VI.

11. E.g. XVIIth IConfRC 1948, Stockholm, Res.XXXIX; LRCS Board of Governors, XXIVth Session, 1957, New Delhi, Res.XIII(a); XIXth IConfRC 1957, New Delhi, Res.X; XXth IConfRC 1965, Vienna, Res.XV and XVI.

12. Declaration of Principles for International Humanitarian Relief to the Civilian Population in Disaster Situations, XXIst IConfRC 1969, Istanbul, Res.XXVI; text in Red Cross *Disaster Relief Handbook*.

13. Principles and Rules for Red Cross Disaster Relief, XXIst IConfRC 1969, Istanbul, Res.XXIV. The original text is in *IRevRC* 1969, p. 625; that with revisions and additions is in the Red Cross *Disaster Relief Handbook*.

14. Perruchoud, 1979, p. 227.

15. See Patrnogic, 1977, p. 21.

16. See La Pradelle, P. de G. de, 'L'Organisation des Secours Aériens en Cas de Désastre Naturel', XXXV *Revue Générale de l'Air et de l'Espace* 1972, p. 129 at p. 134.

17. Joint Committee for the Reappraisal of the Red Cross, relevant papers include: Forsythe,

D.P., 'Present Role of the Red Cross in Protection', Background Paper No. 1, 1975; Holdsworth, D., 'The Present Role of the Red Cross in Assistance', No. 3, 1975; Reid, I., 'The Evolution of the Red Cross', No. 2, 1975; Tansley.

18. See 'The ICRC, the League and the Tansley Report, Considerations of the International Committee of the Red Cross and of the League of Red Cross Societies on the Final Report on the Reappraisal of the Role of the Red Cross', 1977, p. 6; Tansley, p. 76.

19. E.g. Doc.E/4994 (1971), p. 30, para. 63; see also comments in *IRevRC* 1978, p. 155.

20. XXIIIrd IConfRC 1977, Bucharest, Res.IV; LRCS, General Assembly, Third Session, 'Contribution of the Red Cross to the Elimination of Famine', Doc.AG/12.3/1 (October 1983).

21. See 'International Red Cross Aid to Refugees', XXIVth IConfRC 1981, Manila, Doc.CPA/7/1 (1981); XXIVth IConfRC 1981, Res.XXI entitled 'International Red Cross aid to refugees' (1981).

22. Principles and Rules, Art. 7; see also 'The ICRC, the League and the Tansley Report', 1977, pp. 40-41 and 46.

23. Forsythe, 1977, p. 25.

24. Gottlieb, 1971, p. 442.

25. Cf. e.g. Forsythe, D.P., 'Political Prisoners: The Law and Politics of Protection', *VJTL* 1976, p. 295 at pp. 315 and 316.

26. Ruegger, p. 525. Cf. Pictet, J., 'La Croix-Rouge et les Conventions de Geneve', 76 *RdC* 1950-I, p. 1 at pp. 22 and 23.

27. Forsythe, D.P., 'Who Guards the Guardians: Third Parties and the Law of Armed Conflict', 70 *AJIL* 1976, p. 41 at p. 59; cf. Knitel, H.G., *Les Délégations du Comité International de la Croix-Rouge*, 1967, e.g. pp. 113-114.

28. Tansley, p. 74; cf. 'The ICRC, the League and the Tansley Report', 1977, p. 9; Perruchoud, 1979, p. 253.

Chapter 6

1. GA Res.48(1) 1946, final preambular paragraph; see also para. 8. See also GA Res.8(I) 1946.

2. UNRWA, see Chapter 3, notes 30 and 31. On Korea, UNCURK and UNKRA, see Security Council Res.S/1657 (31 July 1950); GA Res.376(V) 1950; GA Res.410(V) 1950; Doc. A/2936 (1955); GA Res.1433(XIV) 1959. Cf. Security Council Res. 143 (14 July 1960).

3. GA Res.525(VI) 1952.

4. See e.g. ESC Res.254(IX) 1949; 6 GAOR, 3rd. Committee, Mtg.350, (1951); ESC Res.746 (XXIX) 1960; ESC Res.766(XXX) 1960; GA Res.1753(XVII) 1962.

5. E.g. GA Res.1746(XVI) 1962. See also *supra*, note 2. On relief operations in the Congo, 1960, see e.g. Simmonds, R., *Legal Problems Arising from the United Nations Military Operations in the Congo*, Martinus Nijhoff, 1968, pp. 242-245.

6. Skopje, see GA Res.1882(XVIII) 1963; ESC Res.970(XXXVI) 1963. See also GA Res.1888 (XVIII) 1963; ESC Res.930(XXXV) 1963; ESC Res.1014(XXXVII) 1964.

7. See the 28th and 29th Reports of the ACC, 36 ESCOR, Ann., ai. 4 and 6, Doc.E/3765 (1963); 37 ESCOR, Ann., a.i. 6, Doc.E/3886 (1964).

8. 20 GAOR, Ann., a.i. 53, Doc.A/5845 (1965); 39 ESCOR, Ann., a.i. 4, Doc.4036 (1965).

9. See 45 ESCOR, Res. Sit., Ann., a.i. 1, Doc.E/4544 (1968), e.g. paras. 21 to 24; and GA Res. 2608(XXIV) 1969.

10. See Doc.E/1318 (1949), p. 41, and /Add. 1, p. 13; Doc.E/1574/Add. 1 (1950).

11. XVIIth IConfRC 1948, Stockholm, Res.XLII.

12. See ESC Res.262(IX) 1949, Res.L; Doc.E/1574/Add. 1 (1950), Annex III, Appendix A, p. 6, and /Add. 2, p. 4; Ruegger, p. 530.

13. Doc.E/1574 (1950); ESC Res. 286(X) 1950.

14. See 15 ESCOR, Plenary, Mtg.676 (2 April 1953), p. 21, para. 29. See also Doc.E/2361 (1953), p. 29; Rapport de la Commission d'Etude institutée par décision du Ve Conseil Général de l'Union Internationale de Secours, Geneva, October 1956; Doc.E/4402 (1967), p. 98; La Pradelle, P. de G. de, 'L'Organisation des Secours en Cas de Désastre Naturel', 55 ILA 1972, p. 317.

15. ESC Res.1153(XLI) 1966.

16. See ESC Res.1268(XLIII) 1967; Doc.E/4544 (1968), paras. 13 to 20. See also 41 ESCOR, Ann., a.i. 39, Doc.E/4227 (1966).

17. See 20 GAOR, Ann., a.i. 53, Doc.A/5845 (1965), paras. 23 to 26.

18. ESC Res.1533(XLIX) 1970; see also Doc.E/4883/Rev.1 (1970), p. 16; Doc.E/4884 (1970), Ch. X.

19. See GA Res.2435(XXIII) 1968.

20. Doc.E/4853 (1970).

21. GA Res.2643(XXV) 1970.

22. GA Res.2816(XXVI) 1971, para. 10.

23. See ESC Res.1533(XLIX) 1970; GA Res.2717(XXV) 1970; Doc.E/AC.24/SR 394.

24. Doc.E/4994 (1971).

25. *Ibid.*, para. 100.

26. See GA Res.2816(XXVI) 1971, para. 1(g). See also GA Res.2435(XXIII) 1968, paras. 1 to 3; GA Res.2717(XXV) 1970; Doc.E/4994 (1971), p. 18; GA Res.2959(XXVII) 1972. Cf. *infra*, note 39; and Brown, B.J., *Disaster Preparedness and the United Nations*, 1979.

27. Doc.E/4853 (1970), p. 1; see also GA Res.2717(XXV) 1970.

28. See GA Res.3202(S-VI) 1974. The Declaration was adopted in GA Res.3201(S-VI) 1974.

29. GA Res.3362(S-VII) 1975, II.14.

30. See GA Res.3510(XXX) 1975; Doc.E/5843 (1976); Doc.E/5989 (1977).

31. A/RES/31/156 (1976); A/RES/32/92 to 101 (1977); ESC Res.2101(LXIII) 1977. Cf. A/RES/37/159; A/RES/37/163; A/RES/37/165; A/RES/37/206; and see A/RES/38/203 to 225.

32. GA Res.57(I) 1946.

33. See GA Res.802(VIII) 1953; GA Res.1038(XI) 1956.

34. See GA Res.417(V) 1950.

35. E.g. GA Res.2335(XXII) 1967; GA Res.2855(XXVI) 1971.

36. See e.g. 'Special Economic, Humanitarian and Disaster Relief Assistance', Report of the Secretary-General, Doc.A/38/202: E/1983/94 (1983), p. 8, para. 28 and p. 17, para. 62; Report[s] of the UNICEF Executive Board, ESCOR, Supplements; 'An Overview of UNICEF Policies, Organization and Working Methods', Doc.E/ICEF/670/Rev. 2 (1983).

37. See GA Res.2029(XX) 1965, and ESC Res.1020(XXVII) 1965. See also GA Res.2688(XXV) 1970. The antecedents may be traced back to UNRRA, the advisory functions of which in the field of social welfare were passed on to the Secretary-General, see GA Res.57(I) 1946; GA Res.58(I) 1946; and ESC Res.51(V) 1947.

38. Hill, M., 'Towards Greater Order, Coherence and Co-ordination in the UN System', UNITAR Research Report No. 20, 1974, p. 26.

39. See 'Role of Resident Representatives in respect of Pre-Disaster Planning and Disaster Relief', Doc.UNDP/PROG/73, /FIELD/110, /HQTRS/125 (129). See also e.g. GA Res.2816(XXVI) 1971; A/RES/32/56 (1977); Doc.A/31/88/Add. 2 (1976), p. 3; Doc.A/35/228 (1980), p. 6; A/RES/36/225 (1981), para. 8.

40. See Doc.A/9178 (1973), pp. 6 to 7; Doc.E/5374 (1973); Doc.A/9733 (1974).

41. See Doc.DP/GC/XXVII/CRP.2 (1980); A/RES/36/225 (1981).

42. The original FAO Constitution is at XXIII BYIL 1946, p. 416. See Basic Texts of the Food and Agriculture Organization of the United Nations, 2 vols., 1980.

43. ESC Res.405(III) 1951.

44. GA Res.626(VI) 1952.

45. Doc.E/2220 (1952).

46. GA Res.1714(XVI) 1961; FAO Conferences Res.1/61. Cf. GA Res.827(IX) 1954; GA Res.1025(XI) 1957; GA Res.1496(XV) 1960.

47. WFC, GA Res.3348(XXIX) 17 December 1974. See also e.g. GA Res.3362(S-VII) 1975; Report[s] of the World Food Council, GAOR, Supplements, e.g. Doc.WFC/1982/12, paras. 22, 30, 105, 132.

48. Global Information and Early Warning System in Food and Agriculture, see Doc.E/5989, Annex, p. 6.

49. WFP Constitution, para. 10(a); see GA Res.1714(XVI) 1961. See also 32 ESCOR, Ann., a.i. 8, Doc.E/3509 (1961); ESC Res.878(XXXIII) 1962; and GA Res.1914(XVIII) 1963.

50. See 39 ESCOR, Ann., a.i. 16, Doc.E/4043 (1965), paras. 20 and 21.

51. See GA Res.2095(XX) 1965; ESC Res.1080(XXXIX) 1965; 39 ESCOR, Ann., a.i. 16, Doc. E/4060 (1965).

52. GA Res.2462(XXIII) 1968, para. 2(a).

53. GA Res.3362(S-VII) 1975, para. V(12). See also Annual Report[s] of the Committee on Food Aid Policies and Programmes to the Economic and Social Council, the FAO Council and the World Food Council; and see Doc. A/38/202: E/1983/94, paras. 26 and 31. Cf. Art. IV of the Food Aid Convention, text and Final Act of the Washington Conference of 11 March - 30 April 1980 at HMSO Cmnd. 8009.

54. WHO Constitution, 14 UNTS, p. 185.

55. See e.g. 'Promotion of Prevention of Adverse Health Effects of Disasters and Emergencies through Preparedness', Res. WHA 34.26 (22 May 1981); WHO, Seventh General Programme of Work Covering a Specific Period (1984-1989 inclusive), Doc.A/35/4 (1982).

56. See Proceedings of the United Nations Conference on Trade and Development: Fourth Session, Nairobi, 5-31 May 1976, Doc.TD/218 (1977-1978).

57. See UNESCO, Doc.22 C/26 (5 August 1983). See also e.g. 'Select Bibliography of Unesco Publications, Reports and Documents Relating to Natural Hazards', (1961-1978 with Addendum); Intergovernmental Conference on the Assessment and Mitigation of Earthquake Risk, Paris, 10-19 February 1976, Final Report, pp. 20 and 22; and generally, UNESCO, Report[s] of the Director-General on the Activities of the Organization.

58. See generally, GA Res.2997(XXVII) 1972; UNEP, Report[s] of the Governing Council, GAOR, Supplements; UNEP, 'Review of the Priority Subject Area, Natural Disasters', Report of the Executive Director, UNEP Report No. 3 (1977); Bruha, T., 'Internationale Regelungen zur Schutz vor technisch-industriellen Umweltnotfällen', 44 ZaöRV 1984, p. 1.

59. Articles of Agreement of the International Bank for Reconstruction and Development, 2 UNTS, p. 134; 606 UNTS, p. 294. Proposed Second Amendment to the Articles of Agreement of the International Monetary Fund, 15 ILM 1976, p. 499.

60. IAEA, Guidelines adopted on 29 April 1983 by the Expert Group on Guidelines for Mutual Emergency Assistance Arrangements, Doc.N5-TC-478.2, 3 May 1983. See also IAEA, General Conference, GC(VIII)/RES/177; IAEA, GOV/INF/392 and GOV/1144 (1967); IAEA, TECDOC-237 (1980); and Memorandum of Understanding between IAEA and UNDRO, 25 April 1977.

61. See generally World Meteorological Convention, 1947, 77 UNTS, p. 143; Agreement relating

to the International Telecommunications Satellite Organization (INTELSAT), 1971, 10 ILM 1971, p. 909; ITU, International Telecommunications Convention, 1973 (1974); Convention on the International Maritime Satellite Organization (INMARSAT), 15 ILM 1976, p. 1051, e.g. Art. 3(1). Cf. Doc.A/AC.105/240 (1979), Annex 1; Doc.A/38/202: E/1983/94, pp. 9-12; Wallerstein, M.B., 'New Organizational Approaches for Speeding Food Relief in International Disasters: The Potential Contribution of Technology', 4 *The International Journal of Disaster Studies and Practice* 1980, p. 73. See also World Administrative Radio Conference, 1977, Res. 10 and Res. 640.

62. See chapter 7, note 19.

63. Cf. chapter 3, note 23; 8 *UN Chronicle*, No. 11, December 1971, pp. 116-117; Berkowitz, M., 'Bangladesh', 14 *HILJ* 1973, p. 565; Gottlieb, G.A.G., 'The UN and Emergency Humanitarian Assistance in India-Pakistan', 66 *AJIL* 1972, p. 362.

64. Cf. e.g. OSRO reports Nos. 1-13, 4 June 1973 - 28 February 1975, entitled 'On the Drought Situation in the Sahelian Zone and Relief Measures Undertaken by the UN System', issued at Rome, FAO; Doc.A/9733 and A/9737 (1974); Doc.A/10346 (1975); US Senate, Committee on the Judiciary, Hearing before the Subcommittee to investigate Problems connected with Refugees and Escapees, 93 Congress, 1st Session, 'World Hunger, Health and Refugee Problems', Part I, 'Crisis in West Africa', 25 July 1973 and Part IV, 'Famine in Africa', 21 March 1974; Glantz, M.H. (ed.), *The Politics of Natural Disaster, The Case of the Sahel Drought*, 1976; Brown, B.J., 'The UN and Disaster Relief in the Sahel, 1973-75', 1 *The International Journal of Disaster Studies and Practice* 1977, p. 145.

Chapter 7

1. Yaoundé Conventions, texts at 2 ILM 1963, p. 971; 9 ILM 1970, p. 484.

2. ACP-EEC Convention of Lomé, 28 February 1975, entered into force 1 April 1976, 128 ECTS 1975; 14 ILM 1975, p. 595. See e.g. Simmonds, K.R., 'The Lomé Convention and the New International Economic Order', 13 *CMLRev* 1976, p. 315.

3. Second ACP-EEC Convention of Lomé, 31 October 1979, Official Journal of the European Communities, 1980, L347, p. 2; 19 ILM 1980, p. 327. See Simmonds, K.R., 'The Second Lomé Convention: The Innovative Features", 17 *CMLRev* 1980, p. 415; Macalister-Smith, P., 'The EEC and International Humanitarian Assistance', *Legal Issues of European Integration* 1981/1, p. 89.

4. See European Parliament, Working Documents 1978-9, Doc.414/78 (31 October 1978), and Doc.669/78 (9 March 1979); Debates of the European Parliament, No. 1-255, 18 April 1980, pp. 281-283.

5. See respectively, Agreement between the EEC and Jordan on the Supply of Skimmed Milk Powder as Food Aid, Brussels, 12 November 1973, 14 ECTS 1974, Art. V; Agreement between the EEC and Mauritania on ... Food Aid, Brussels, 12 November 1973, 17 ECTS 1974, Art. V; Agreement between the EEC and Bangladesh on ... Food Aid, Brussels, 15 November 1973, 25 ECTS 1974, Art. V.

6. See e.g. Agreement between the EEC and the ICRC on ... Food Aid, Brussels, 3 February 1975, 120 ECTS 1975; Agreement between the EEC and Catholic Relief Services on ... Food Aid, Brussels, 28 May 1975, 129 ECTS 1975; Agreement between the EEC and UNHCR on the Supply of ... Emergency Food Aid, Brussels, 9 December 1975, 61 ECTS 1975; EEC Council Decision

Concluding the Convention between the EEC and UNRWA, COM (79) 762, 31 December 1979, 45 ECTS 1980. For statistics on allocations for emergency assistance, see current issues of *The Courier*, Commission of the European Communities publication, bi-monthly. For Community aid for refugees, see the report of R. Dury to the European Parliament, October 1983, and *The Courier*, No. 83, January-February 1984, pp. 50f.

7. See Council of Europe, Motion for a Recommendation on European Solidarity in the Face of Natural Disasters, Doc.2764 (22 April 1970), CECA Docs., 22nd Session, Vol. II; Motion for a Recommendation on the Establishment of an International Emergency Fund for Natural Disaster Relief Work, Doc.2867 (17 December 1970), CECA, Docs., 22nd Session, Vol. VIII; Report on European Solidarity in Disaster Relief, Doc.2997 (15 September 1971), CECA, Docs., 23rd Session, Vol. VII, part II; CECA, Recommendation 645 (4 October 1971), CECA, Official Report, 23rd Session, 8th Sitting, p. 264; 'On Precautions against Natural and Other Disasters and the Planning and Provision of Disaster Relief', CE, Committee of Ministers, Res. (72) 6 (18 February 1972). Cf. EEC Council Directive of 24 June 1982 on the major-accident hazards of certain industrial activities, Official Journal of the European Communities, L 230, Vol. 25, 82/501/EEC.

8. Conference of Local and Regional Authorities of Europe, 20-22 June 1978, Res.102 (1978). See also European Outline Convention on Transfrontier Co-operation between Territorial Communities or Authorities, Madrid, 21 May 1980, *European Treaty Series* No. 106.

9. Outline Model Agreement between local and regional authorities on the development of transfrontier co-operation in civil protection and mutual aid in the event of disasters occuring in frontier areas, adopted by the CE Committee of Ministers, 9 December 1982, see CE Doc. Transfront/Office (83) 4. See also, CE, 'Transfrontier Co-operation, International, Interregional and Local Agreements', Transfront/Office (83) 1 prov. (April 1983).

10. See e.g. 2 *The International Journal of Disaster Studies and Practice* 1978, p. 101; Hanning, H., *The Peaceful Uses of Military Forces*, 1967. See also chapter 9, note 5.

11. See generally, Thomas, A. van W. and Thomas, A.J., *The Organization of American States*, 1963; and see 1 *The International Journal of Disaster Studies and Practice* 1977, p. 173. For the statute of the inter-American fund for emergency assistance, OAS Council, 28 May 1968, see OAS Doc. Ser.G/VI, C-1974.

12. Convention Establishing a Permanent Inter-State Drought Control Committee for the Sahel, Ouagadougou, 12 September 1973, 13 *ILM* 1974, p. 537; see also Doc.A/9178 (5 October 1973).

13. See ASEAN Declaration for Mutual Assistance on Natural Disasters, Manila, 26 June 1976. Cf. Phillipines, Presidential Decree No. 1566.

14. International Convention on the simplification and harmonization of customs procedures, Kyoto Convention, 18 May 1973, (Cmnd. 5938 (TS 36/1975)), Annex F.5; relevant provisions are reproduced in UN Doc.A/32/64 (1977), Annex II.

15. See e.g. Morison; Bighinatti, E.V., 'Natural Disasters: The Voluntary Agency Role', 89 *ICVA News*, April 1981, p. 2. See generally, White, L.C., *International Non-Governmental Organizations*, 1951; Lador-Laderer, J.J., *International Non-Governmental Organizations*, 1963; Skjelsbaek, K., 'The Growth of International Non-Governmental Organizations in the Twentieth Century', 25 *International Organization* 1971, p. 420; Chiang, Pei-heng, *Non-Governmental Organizations at the United Nations*, 1981.

16. See e.g. Rodgers, R.S., 'Facilitation Problems of International Associations', Union of International Associations, Publication No. 171, 1960.

17. See ESC Res.288B(X) 1950; ESC Res.1296(XLIV) 1968.

18. Schachter, O., *et al., Towards Wider Acceptance of UN Treaties* 1971, p. 50.

19. See e.g. Forsythe, 1977, pp. 181f; Freymond, J., *Guerres, Révolutions, Croix-Rouge*, 1976, pp. 98-101; Mertens, P., 'Les modalités de l'intervention du Comité International de la Croix-Rouge dans le conflit du Nigéria', XV *AFDI* 1969, p. 183; Wiseberg; Carl, B.M., 'American Assistance to Victims of the Nigeria-Biafra War: Defects in the Prescriptions on Foreign Disaster Relief', 12 *HILJ* 1971, p. 191.

20. Morison, p. 96. See e.g. *Role of Voluntary Agencies in International Assistance* (1974), Advisory Committee on Voluntary Foreign Aid, US Agency for International Development.

21. Voluntary Agency Consultation on the Indo-Chinese Refugee Problem, ICVA, Statement of Consultation, 18-19 July 1979.

22. Gottlieb, 1971, pp. 422 and 424.

23. International Air Transport Association, Resolution 788 (previously Res.200), valid until 31 December 1983, see Passenger Services Conference Resolutions, Manual, 3rd ed., 1983.

24. See International Road Transport Union, Geneva, Handbook of International Road Transport, 1982; 'Report on the relief operation conducted by the International Road Transport Union (IRU) after the earthquake of 23.11.1980 in Italy'; cf. Baradei, p. 32.

25. Oppenheim, Vol. I, p. 254. See also Kunz, J.L., 'The Status of the Holy See in International Law', 46 *AJIL* 1952, p. 308; Vallier, I., 'The Roman Catholic Church: A Transnational Actor', 25 *International Organization* 1971, p. 479; Köck, H.F., *Die völkerrechtliche Stellung des Heiligen Stuhls*, 1975.

26. E.g. see Doc.CDDH/SR.52, CDDH, Vol. VII, pp. 135-137, paras. 79-83; *IRevRC* 1977, p. 368.

27. See generally, Breycha-Vauthier, A.C. and Potulicki, M., 'The Order of St. John in International Law', 48 *AJIL* 1954, p. 554; Breycha-Vauthier, A.C., 'L'Ordre S.M. Jeroselymitain de Malte: Evolutions Récentes', 16 *ZaöRV* 1955-6, p. 500; Farran, C.d'O., 'The Sovereign Order of Malta in International Law', 3 *ICLQ* 1954, p. 217; O'Connell, D.P., *International Law*, Vol. 1, 1965, p. 95 and cf. XLVIII *BYIL* 1976-77, pp. 433-434; Prantner, R., *Malteserorden und Völkergemeinschaft*, 1974.

28. Final Act, Geneva, 27 July 1929, Para. II, at Schindler and Toman, p. 244.

29. Following discussion of Draft Art. 5 of Protocol I, see Doc.CDDH/I/SR.27, CDDH, Vol. VIII, pp. 269-270, paras. 104-110; Doc.CDDH/SR.58, CDDH, Vol. VII, p. 317, para. 186. See also Ordre Souverain Militaire de Malte, *Annales*; and *Annuaire*.

30. Doc.CDDH/SR.58, CDDH, Vol. VII, p. 317, para. 186.

31. See also Hanning.

32. See also chapter 9, note 2.

33. Bundesverfassungsgesetz vom 30.Juni 1965 über die Entsendung österreichischer Einheiten

zur Hilfeleistung in das Ausland auf Ersuchen internationaler Organisationen, Bundesgesetzblatt für die Republik Österreich, 55, No. 173, p. 933 (1965), para. 8.

34. See e.g. Chen, p. 259; Clos, pp. 14 and 25-27; CECA, Docs., 23rd Session, Vol. VII, Doc. 2997, Part II, para. 9(e) and (f).

35. See e.g. Principles and Rules for Red Cross disaster relief, XXIst IConfRC 1969, Istanbul, Res.XXIV, Para. 12; 'Accord d'entraide et d'assistance mutuelle dans le cas de catastrophes naturelles et d'autres calamités', agreement between the Red Cross Societies of Italy and Yugoslavia, Belgrade, September 1971; Agreement for mutual assistance of 1972 between the Red Crescent Societies of Algeria, Morocco and Tunisia.

36. United Kingdom – United States, exchange of notes, 1 December 1948, 81 *UNTS*, p. 93. Cf. the Agreement between India and the United States of 9 July 1951 on duty-free entry of relief supplies, 147 *UNTS*, p. 43; United States – Afghanistan, exchange of notes dated 20 March 1954 concerning emergency wheat aid, 229 *UNTS*, p. 8.

37. Agreement dated 20 October 1964, New Delhi, 534 *UNTS*, p. 77. Cf. the Agreement between the United States and India for duty-free entry and defrayment of inland transportation charges of voluntary agency supplies and equipment, New Delhi, 5 December 1968, 713 *UNTS*, p. 352.

38. Czechoslovakia and the German Democratic Republic, Convention concerning assistance in the event of natural disasters, Prague, 6 October 1956, amended 28 May 1963, 501 *UNTS*, pp. 109 and 122.

39. E.g. Canada – United States, exchange of notes concerning civil emergency planning, 8 August 1967, *TIAS* 6325; Mexico – United States, 3 May 1968 amended 28 March 1972, *TIAS* 6481 and 7308, 698 *UNTS*, p. 219; Mexico – United States, 15 January 1980, *TIAS* 10013; France – Monaco, Agreement on mutual assistance between the French and Monegasque relief and civil defence services, Paris, 16 April 1970, 747 *UNTS*, p. 160; United States – Guatemala, 14 May 1976, *TIAS* 8692; United States – Italy, 9 June 1976, *TIAS* 8416; France – Federal Republique of Germany, Convention entre la République fédérale d'Allemagne et la République française sur l'assistance mutuelle en cas de catastrophes ou accidents graves, 3 February 1977, Bundesgesetzblatt, 1980, Teil II, 33; France – Belgium, Convention sur l'assistance mutuelle en cas de catastrophes ou d'accidents graves, 21 April 1981; see also Council of Europe, 'Transfrontier Co-operation, International Interregional and Local Agreements', CE Transfront/Office (83) 1 prov. (April 1983).

40. See e.g. Nordic Mutual Emergency Assistance Agreement in Connection with Radiation Accidents, Vienna, 17 October 1963, 525 *UNTS*, p. 75; Federal Republic of Germany – Switzerland, Agreement on radiation protection in case of emergency, 31 May 1978, Bundesgesetzblatt, 1980, Teil II, 563 (see also Agreement concerning radiological disaster relief, 31 May 1978); CE Doc. Transfront/Office (83) 1 prov. (April 1983), *supra* note 39; and see chapter 6, note 60.

41. See Bruha; and see chapter 6, note 58.

42. See e.g. Doc.E/C.6/52/Add 6 (25 May 1966), Appendix E; Krimgold; UNDRO, *Disaster Prevention and Mitigation*, Vol. 9, 'Legal Aspects' (1980).

Chapter 8

1. See e.g. Chen, pp. 259 and 271f; Clos, P., 'Projet pour servir à la création d'un Organisme International de Sauvetage', undated, UN Library, Palais des Nations, Geneva, Call No. 362 Al No. 32; Kennedy, E.M., 'International Humanitarian Assistance', 12 *VJIL* 1972, p. 299 and p. 307; cf. 'Principes énoncés par le Senateur Ciraolo', in Borgeaud, Annexe 1, p. 210.

2. See e.g. Ads (1974), pp. 343-350; Green, S., pp. 68-70; US General Accounting Office, Report to the Congress by the Comptroller General of the United States, 'Need for an International Disaster Relief Agency', ID-76-15, 15 May 1976; see also US General Accounting Office, Report to the Congress by the Comptroller General of the United States, 'Observations on the Guatemalan Earthquake Relief Effort', ID-76-71, 23 August 1976, pp. 37-38.

3. ESC Res.1049(XXXVII) 1964, para. 3; Doc.E/4036 (1965).

4. GA, 3rd Com., 1291 Mtg., Doc.A/C.3/SR 1291 (1965), paras. 6 and 17; Report of the ACABQ, 20 GAOR, Ann., a.i. 53, Doc.A/5883 (1965); GA Res.2034(XX) 1965; see also ESC Res. 1090C(XXXIX) 1965; Doc.E/4554 (1968); GA Res. 2435(XXIII) 1968, para. 4; ESC Res.1546 (XLIX) 1970; Doc.ST/SGB/131/Amend 24 (26 October 1970).

5. 'Assistance in Cases of Natural Disaster', Interim Report of the Secretary-General, Doc. E/ 4853 (12 May 1970), at p. 51.

6. GA Res.2717(XXV) 1970, para. 4(c); see also ESC Res.1546(XLIX) 1970.

7. Doc.E/4994 (13 May 1971).

8. See e.g. ESC Res.1518(XLIX) 1970; GA Res.2643(XXV) 1970.

9. See e.g. 'Development and Co-ordination of the Activities of the Organizations within the UN System', 37th Report of the ACC, Doc.E/5012 (1971), Part I, Ch. I, H, p. 12, paras. 41-43; discussion at 51 ESCOR Plenary, a.i. 14, e.g. Mtgs. 1773, 1786 and 1787; Mtg. 1790, paras. 1-51.

10. ESC Res.1612(LI) 23 July 1971, adopted by 24 votes to 0, 2 abstentions.

11. See 26 GAOR, 3rd Comm., a.i. 59, Mtg. 1888; 26 GAOR, Plenary, a.i. 59, Mtgs. 1961 and 2018.

12. GA Res.2816(XXVI) 14 December 1971, para. 3, adopted by 86 votes to 0, 10 abstentions.

13. GA Res.2959(XXVII) 1972. See 'Assistance in cases of natural disaster and other disaster situations', Doc.E/5151 (1972); 'Assistance in cases of natural disaster and other disaster situations', Doc.A/8854 (1972).

14. 'Assistance in cases of natural disaster and other disaster situations, Activities of the Office of the United Nations Disaster Relief Co-ordinator', Doc.A/9063 (1973), para. 27.

15. ESC Res.1803(LV) 1973; GA Res.3152(XXVIII) 1973. See also Doc.A/9398 (1973).

16. See ESC Res.1891(LVII) 1974. See also, in 1974, ESC Res.1833(LVI); ESC Res.1834(LVI); ESC Res.1874(LVII); ESC Res.1876(LVII); ESC Res.1878(LVII); GA Res.3242(XXIX); GA Res. 3244(XXIX); GA Res.3253(XXIX). And see 'Assistance in cases of natural disaster and other di-

saster situations, Activities of the Office of the United Nations Disaster Relief Co-ordinator', Doc. A/9637 (1974).

17. See GA Res.3440(XXX) 1975, para. 1(a); ESC Res. 1972(LIX) 1975. See also 'Office of the United Nations Disaster Relief Co-ordinator', Doc.A/10079 and /Add 1 (1975); Doc. E/AC.24/SR 574-576 and 580; Doc.E/5744 (1975).

18. GA Res.3532(XXX) 1975.

19. See Doc.E/AC.24/24/SR 590-594; Doc.A/C.2/31/15 (1976).

20. See A/RES/31/173 (1976); A/RES/32/56 (1977); A/RES/34/55 (1979). See also 'Office of the United Nations Disaster Relief Co-ordinator', Doc.A/31/88 (1976); Doc.A/32/64 (1977); Doc.A/33/82 (1978); Doc.A/34/190 (1979); 'Special Economic and Disaster Relief Assistance, Office of the United Nations Disaster Relief Co-ordinator', Doc.A/35/228 (1980).

21. Statement of the Norwegian delegate, see 27 GAOR 3rd Com. a.i. 61, Mtg. 1959, para. 24. Cf. Doc.E/4994, p. 9, para. 17; 26 GAOR, 3rd Com., a.i. 59, Mtg. 1890, e.g. paras. 38 and 66. See also *supra*, note 11.

22. Draft Additional Protocol I, Art. 62; see CDDH, Vol. III, p. 282. Draft Additional Protocol II, Art. 33; see CDDH, Vol. IV, p. 105.

23. Memorandum of Understanding between UNDRO and UNHCR, Geneva, 13 July 1978; reprinted at 3 *The International Journal of Disaster Studies and Practice* 1979, p. 355.

24. Cf. Doc.A/10079/Add 1 (1975), p. 6; Doc.A/33/82 (1978), p. 7; Doc.A/35/228 (1980), pp. 7-8; A/38/201 – E/1983/69 (1983), pp. 4-7 and 39.

25. See 'Assistance to Displaced Persons in Ethiopia', Doc.E/1980/104 (18 July 1980).

26. 'Evaluation of the Office of the United Nations Disaster Relief Co-ordinator', Joint Inspection Unit, October 1980, Doc.JIU/REP/80/11.

27. Doc.E/1981/16, and Annex, 9 March 1981; see ESC Res.1980/43 (22 July 1980).

28. Doc.A/36/73/Add 1; Doc.A/36/75/Add 8 (18 May 1981).

29. ACC Decision 1981/2; Doc.E/1981/37/Corr 1 (28 May 1981).

30. 'Strengthening the capacity of the United Nations system to respond to natural disasters and other disaster situations', A/RES/36/225 (17 December 1981).

31. 'Special Economic and Disaster Relief Assistance: Office of the United Nations Disaster Relief Co-ordinator', A/RES/37/144 (17 December 1982). See also 'Office of the United Nations Disaster Relief Co-ordinator', Doc.A/38/201 – E/1983/69 (1983) and 'Special Economic, Humanitarian and Disaster Relief Assistance', Doc.A/38/202 – E/1983/94 (1983).

Chapter 9

1. South West Africa, Second Phase, Judgment, ICJ Rep. 1966, p. 5 at p. 34.

2. Agreement of 29 July 1970, following the earthquake of 31 May 1970; 739 UNTS, p. 127. See also 2 *The International Journal of Disaster Studies and Practice* 1978, p. 32.

3. Doc.E/4994 (1971), Annex III; see also GA Res.2816(XXVI) 1971, para. 8(e). Cf. CE, Consultative Assembly, Docs., 23rd Session, Vol. VII, Doc. 2997 (1971), Part II, para. 9(3) and (f).

4. 13 February 1946, 1 UNTS, p. 15. See also Convention on the Privileges and Immunities of the Specialized Agencies, 21 November 1947, 33 UNTS, p. 261; Agreement on the Privileges and Immunities of the International Atomic Energy Agency, 1 July 1959, 374 UNTS 147. Cf. Nordic Mutual Emergency Assistance Agreement in Connection with Radiation Accidents, 17 October 1963, 525 UNTS, p. 75, Art. VI.

5. See also Ward, C.J., *Foreign Armed Forces in the Relief of Natural Disaster*, Dissertation for M.A., Department of War Studies, King's College, University of London, December 1975; Lazareff, S., *Status of Military Forces under Current International Law*, 1971; Genot, p. 355; Baradei, pp. 37-41. Cf. chapter 7, notes 10, 31, 32 and 33.

6. See 59 *ILA* 1980, pp. 521-527, and 5-7. See also 55 *ILA* 1972, pp. 317-327; 57 *ILA* 1976, pp. 309-320; 58 *ILA* 1978, pp. 461-472; and 'Le Secours Etranger d'Urgence en Cas de Catastrophe Naturelle devant l'International Law Association', 27 *ADIM* 1977, p. 34.

7. GA Res.2816(XXVI) 1971, para. 8(e).

8. For the text of the measures, see Doc.A/32/64 (1977), Annex II.

9. See ESC Res.2102(LXIII) 1977; XXIIIrd IConfRC 1977, Res. VI; A/RES/32/56 (1977), para. 3.

10. 'Office of the United Nations Disaster Relief Co-ordinator', Report of the Secretary-General, Doc.A/34/190 (1979), p. 11, para. 39. See also ESC Res.2102(LXIII) 1971).

11. 'Special Economic and Disaster Relief Assistance, Office of the United Nations Disaster Relief Co-ordinator', Report of the Secretary-General, Doc.A/35/228 (1980), p. 18, para. 68. Cf. Doc.E/1981/16 (1981), Annex, pp. 24-25, paras. 60-61.

12. Baradei, M. El, *et al, Model Rules for Disaster Relief Operations*, Policy and Efficacy Studies No. 8, UNITAR, 1982, p. 3.

13. Green, S., *International Disaster Relief*, 1977, pp. 66-67.

14. Cf. Borgeaud, pp. 211-212; Langeais, p. 13; Genot, p. 355; Perruchoud, pp. 249-251. See also Oliver, pp. 196-197.

15. UNA-USA, *Acts of Nature, Acts of Man: The Global Response to Natural Disasters*, United Nations Association of the United States, Policy Studies Panel on International Disaster Relief, July 1977, cf. pp. 6, 11 and 83.

16. Tansley, D., *Final Report: An Agenda for the Red Cross*, Joint Committee for the Reappraisal of the Red Cross, 1975, p. 80.

17. See 'The ICRC, the League and the Tansley Report', Considerations of the International Committee of the Red Cross and of the League of Red Cross Societies on the Final Report on the Re-

appraisal of the Role of the Red Cross, Geneva, August 1977, p. 14; XXIIIrd IConfRC 1977, Report of Commission I, Doc.p/7 a/1, para. 24; Meurant, J., 'Principles on the Protection of Disaster Victims', *Panorama*, LRCS, 1977/6, p. 3.

18. See XXIIIrd IConfRC 1977, Res.II; LRCS, General Assembly, First Session, Geneva, 4-6 October 1979, a.i. 12, Doc.AG/12/1, and Record, a.i. 13, pp. 129-130; LRCS, Disaster Relief Advisory Committee, 11th Session, Geneva, 2-3 May 1981, a.i. 12, Doc.CCS/12/1 and 2; XXIVth IConfRC 1981, Manila, 7-11 November 1981, Commission II, a.i. 6, Doc.CGO/6/1.

19. See 'Request for the inclusion of an additional item in the agenda of the thirty-sixth session, New International Humanitarian Order', Doc.A/36/245 (1981); A/RES/36/136 (1981); 'New International Humanitarian Order', Report of the Secretary-General, Doc.A/37/145 (1982); 'New International Humanitarian Order', Report of the Secretary-General, Doc.A/38/450 (1983); 'New International Humanitarian Order', Report of the Third Committee, Doc.A/38/691 (1983); A/RES/38/125 (1983).

20. The study and the draft "Convention concerning the expediting of emergency relief" were written by Dr. Jiri Toman. Following the meeting of experts in 1983, the Convention was redrafted and entitled "Convention on expediting the delivery of emergency assistance".

21. A summary of the introductory statement is at Doc.A/C.2/38/SR.34; see also A/RES/38/202 (1983).

22. See Office of the United Nations Disaster Relief Co-ordinator, Report of the Secretary-General, Addendum, Doc.A/39/267/Add. 2 – E/1984/96/Add. 2 (18 June 1984).

Annex 1

Geneva Convention of August 22, 1864, for the Amelioration of the Condition of the Wounded in Armies in the Field

ARTICLE 1

Ambulances and military hospitals shall be recognized as neutral and, as such, protected and respected by the belligerents as long as they accommodate wounded and sick.

Neutrality shall end if the said ambulances or hospitals should be held by a military force.

ARTICLE 2

Hospital and ambulance personnel, including the quarter-master's staff, the medical, administrative and transport services, and the chaplains, shall have the benefit of the same neutrality when on duty, and while there remain any wounded to be brought in or assisted.

ARTICLE 3

The persons designated in the preceding Article may, even after enemy occupation, continue to discharge their functions in the hospital or ambulance with which they serve, or may withdraw to rejoin the units to which they belong.

When in these circumstances they cease from their functions, such persons shall be delivered to the enemy outposts by the occupying forces.

ARTICLE 4

The material of military hospitals being subject to the laws of war, the persons attached to such hospitals may take with them, on withdrawing, only the articles which are their own personal property.

Ambulances, on the contrary, under similar circumstances, shall retain their equipment.

ARTICLE 5

Inhabitants of the country who bring help to the wounded shall be respected and shall remain free. Generals of the belligerent Powers shall make it their duty to notify the inhabitants of the appeal made to their humanity, and of the neutrality which humane conduct will confer.

The presence of any wounded combatant receiving shelter and care in a house shall ensure its protection. An inhabitant who has given shelter to the wounded shall be exempted from billeting and from a portion of such war contributions as may be levied.

ARTICLE 6

Wounded or sick combatants, to whatever nation they may belong, shall be collected and cared for.

Commanders-in-Chief may hand over immediately to the enemy outposts enemy combatants wounded during an engagement, when circumstances allow and subject to the agreement of both parties.

Those who, after their recovery, are recognized as being unfit for further service, shall be repatriated.

The others may likewise be sent back, on condition that they shall not again, for the duration of hostilities, take up arms.

Evacuation parties, and the personnel conducting them, shall be considered as being absolutely neutral.

ARTICLE 7

A distinctive and uniform flag shall be adopted for hospitals, ambulances and evacuation parties. It should in all circumstances be accompanied by the national flag.

An armlet may also be worn by personnel enjoying neutrality but its issue shall be left to the military authorities.

Both flag and armlet shall bear a red cross on a white ground.

ARTICLE 8

The implementing of the present Convention shall be arranged by the Commanders-in-Chief of the belligerent armies following the instructions of their respective Governments and in accordance with the general principles set forth in this Convention.

ARTICLE 9

The High Contracting Parties have agreed to communicate the present Convention with an invitation to accede thereto to Governments unable to appoint Plenipotentiaries to the International Conference at Geneva. The Protocol has accordingly been left open.

ARTICLE 10

The present Convention shall be ratified and the ratifications exchanged at Berne, within the next four months, or sooner if possible.

In faith whereof, the respective Plenipotentiaries have signed the Convention and thereto affixed their seals.

Done at Geneva, this twenty-second day of August, in the year one thousand eight hundred and sixty-four.

Source: *International Red Cross Handbook*, 11th ed., 1971, p. 7; original French text at *CTS*, Vol. 129, p. 361.

Annex 2

Convention Establishing an International Relief Union, Geneva, July 12, 1927[1]

The President of the Albanian Republic; the President of the German Reich; His Majesty the King of the Belgians; the President of the United States of Brazil; His Majesty the King of Great

---

[1] *Deposits of ratifications:*

Ecuador	July 30, 1928.
Italy (including Italian Colonies)	August 2, 1928.
Egypt	August 7, 1928.
Roumania	September 11, 1928.
India	April 2, 1929.
Finland	April 10, 1929.
Hungary	April 17, 1929.
Belgium	May 9, 1929.

Britain and Ireland and of the British Dominions beyond the Seas, Emperor of India; His Majesty the King of the Bulgarians; the President of the Colombian Republic; the President of the Cuban Republic; the President of the Polish Republic for the Free City of Danzig; His Majesty the King of Egypt; the President of the Republic of Ecuador; His Majesty the King of Spain; the President of the Republic of Finland; the President of the French Republic; the President of the Hellenic Republic; the President of the Republic of Guatemala; His Serene Highness the Governor of Hungary; His Majesty the King of Italy; the President of the Latvian Republic; His Serene Highness the Prince of Monaco; the President of the Republic of Nicaragua; the President of the Republic of Peru; the President of the Polish Republic; the President of the Portuguese Republic; His Majesty the King of Roumania; I Capitani Reggenti of the Republic of San Marino; the President of the Czechoslovak Republic; the President of the Turkish Republic; the President of the Republic of Uruguay, and the President of the United States of Venezuela:

In view of the Preamble of the Covenant of the League of Nations, which contemplates the promotion of "international co-operation... by the prescription of... just... relations between nations..."; and

In view of Article 23 (f) of the Covenant of the League of Nations, which states that the Members of the League of Nations "will endeavour to take steps in matters of international concern for the prevention and control of disease"; and

In view of Article 25 of the Covenant of the League of Nations, which states that "the Members of the League of Nations agree to encourage and promote the establishment and co-operation of duly authorised voluntary national Red Cross organisations having as purposes the improvement of health, the prevention of disease and the mitigation of suffering throughout the world"; and

Considering that such principles meet with the approval of all States;

Desiring to render aid to each other in disasters, to encourage international relief by a methodical co-ordination of available resources, and to further the progress of international law in this field, ... have agreed as follows:

Monaco	May 21, 1929.
Venezuela	June 19, 1929.
Germany	July 22, 1929.
San Marino	August 12, 1929.
Albania	August 31, 1929.
Poland and Free City of Danzig	July 11, 1930.
Greece	January 16, 1931.
Bulgaria	May 22, 1931.
Czechoslovakia	August 20, 1931.
Turkey	March 10, 1932.
France	April 27, 1932.

Accessions:

Sudan	May 11, 1928.
New Zealand	April 27, 1928,

On the understanding that no contribution to the initial fund of the Union will fall due by New Zealand before the commencement of the next financial year in that country, viz., April 1st, 1929.

Great Britain and Northern Ireland	January 9, 1929.

This accession does not include any of His Britannic Majesty's Colonies, Protectorates or territories under suzerainty or mandate.

Luxemburg	June 27, 1929.
Switzerland	January 2, 1930.
Yugoslavia	August 28, 1931.
Persia	September 28, 1932.

Entry into force: December 27, 1932.

ARTICLE 1

The High Contracting Parties agree to establish an International Relief Union in accordance with the provisions of the present Convention and the Statute hereto annexed.

The Members of the International Relief Union shall be such Members of the League of Nations and such States not Members of the League of Nations as are Parties to this Convention.

ARTICLE 2

The objects of the International Relief Union are:

(1) In the event of any disaster due to *force majeure*, the exceptional gravity of which exceeds the limits of the powers and resources of the stricken people, to furnish to the suffering population first aid and to assemble for this purpose funds, resources and assistance of all kinds;

(2) In the event of any public disaster, to co-ordinate as occasion offers the efforts made by relief organisations, and, in a general way, to encourage the study of preventive measures against disasters and to induce all peoples to render mutual international assistance.

ARTICLE 3

The International Relief Union shall operate for the benefit of all stricken peoples, whatever their nationality or their race, and irrespective of any social, political or religious distinction.

Nevertheless, the action of the International Relief Union is limited to disasters occurring in the territories of the High Contracting Parties to which the present Convention applies, and to such disasters occurring in other countries as in the opinion of the Executive Committee mentioned in Article 6 are likely to affect such territories of the High Contracting Parties.

ARTICLE 4

Action by the International Relief Union in any country is subject to the consent of the Government thereof.

ARTICLE 5

In the establishment and working of the International Relief Union, the free co-operation is envisaged:

(1) Of national Red Cross Societies, in conformity with Article 25 of the Covenant of the League of Nations, and of institutions or organisations constituting *de jure* or *de facto* unions of such societies;

(2) Of all other official or non-official organisations which may be able to undertake the same activities for the benefit of stricken populations, if possible in co-operation with Red Cross Societies and institutions or organisations above mentioned.

ARTICLE 6

The International Relief Union shall be directed by a General Council, which shall appoint an Executive Committee in accordance with the provisions of the present Convention and of the Statute hereto annexed.

The General Council of the International Relief Union shall consist of Delegates of all the Members of the International Relief Union, there being one Delegate for each Member.

Each Member of the International Relief Union may entrust its representation in the General Council to its national Red Cross Society or to one of the national organisations referred to in Article 5.

ARTICLE 7

The International Relief Union shall have its seat in the city in which the seat of the League of Nations is established.

It may have all or part of its administrative services in any place selected by the Executive Committee.

ARTICLE 8

Within the limits of its objects and in accordance with the prescriptions of the national legislation of the country concerned, the International Relief Union shall be able, either in its own name, or in the names of persons acting in its behalf, to sue or be sued, and to acquire, with or without consideration, and to possess property of any kind, subject to the provisions of Article 12.

ARTICLE 9

Each of the Members of the League of Nations and the States not Members which are Parties to the present Convention shall contribute to the establishment of an initial fund of the International Relief Union. This fund is divided into shares of 700 Swiss francs each. Each Member of the League of Nations will subscribe a number of shares equal to the number of the units of its contribution to the expenses of the League of Nations. The contribution of States not Members of the League of Nations will be fixed by the Executive Committee, according to the principles applied in determining the contributions of Members of the League of Nations.

ARTICLE 10

The High Contracting Parties will endeavour to accord to the International Relief Union and to the organisations acting in its behalf, in accordance with the provisions of Article 5 of the present Convention and of the Statute, in all of their territories to which the present Convention applies, and in so far as is possible under the local law, the most extensive immunities, facilities and exemptions for their establishments, for the movements of their staff and supplies, for relief operations and for the publicity of appeals.

ARTICLE 11

The resources of the International Relief Union shall consist, in addition to the initial fund provided for in Article 9:

(1) Of voluntary grants made by Governments;
(2) Of private contributions; and
(3) Of the donations and bequests referred to in Article 12.

ARTICLE 12

The International Relief Union may receive donations and bequests of all kinds. Donations and bequests may be made with or without special conditions or restrictions as to their use in a particular country, for a particular category of disasters, or for a particular disaster.

Donations and bequests may be accepted only if they are in conformity with the objects of the Union as defined in Article 2 and 3 of the present Convention and with the law of the particular country concerned.

ARTICLE 13

Nothing in the present Convention shall be interpreted as involving a restriction of any kind on the freedom of the societies, institutions or organisations mentioned in Article 5, when they are acting on their own account.

ARTICLE 14

The High Contracting Parties agree that all disputes between them relating to the interpretation or application of this Convention shall, if they cannot be settled by direct negotiation or by some other method of amicable settlement, be referred for decision to the Permanent Court of International Justice. The Court may be seized of the dispute, if necessary, by the application of either of the Parties. In case either or both of the Parties to such a dispute should not be Parties to the Protocol of December 16th, 1920, relating to the Permanent Court of International Justice, the dispute shall be referred, at the choice of the Parties and in accordance with the constitutional procedure of each of them, either to the Permanent Court of International Justice or to a tribunal constituted in accordance with the Hague Convention of October 18th, 1907, for the Pacific Settlement of International Disputes, or to some other tribunal of arbitration.

ARTICLE 15

The present Convention, of which the French and English texts are both authentic, shall bear this day's date and, until April 30th, 1928, it may be signed on behalf of any Member of the League of Nations or of any State not a Member, represented at the Conference at Geneva, or to which the Council of the League of Nations may have communicated a copy of the Convention for this purpose.

ARTICLE 16

The present Convention is subject to ratification. The instruments of ratification shall be deposited with the Secretary-General of the League of Nations, who shall notify their deposit to all signatory or acceding States.

ARTICLE 17

On and after May 1st, 1928, any Member of the League of Nations or any State mentioned in Article 15 may accede to the present Convention. This accession shall be effected by a notification made to the Secretary-General of the League of Nations, to be deposited in the archives of the Secretariat. The Secretary-General shall at once notify such deposit to all the signatory and acceding States.

ARTICLE 18

The present Convention shall not come into force until ratifications or accessions shall have been deposited in the name of at least twelve Members of the League of Nations or non-Member States of which the combined contributions amount to six hundred shares. The date of its entry into force will be the ninetieth day after the receipt by the Secretary-General of the League of Nations of the last of such ratifications or accessions. Thereafter, the present Convention will take effect as to each party ninety days after the receipt of the instrument of ratification or notification of its accession.

For the application of this Article, the Secretary-General of the League of Nations will make a provisional estimate of the contributions of States non-Members of the League of Nations.

In compliance with the provisions of Article 18 of the Covenant of the League of Nations, the Secretary-General will register the present Convention upon the day of its coming into force.

ARTICLE 19

Any Member of the International Relief Union may withdraw from the Union by giving one year's notice in writing to the Secretary-General of the League of Nations.

The provisions of the present Convention shall cease to be applicable to the territory of the withdrawing Member one year after the receipt of such notice by the Secretary-General of the League of Nations.

The Secretary-General of the League of Nations shall notify all Members of the Union of the receipt of any notice of withdrawal.

ARTICLE 20

Any High Contracting Party may, at the time of signature, ratification or accession, declare that, in accepting the present Convention, he does not assume any obligations in respect of all or any of his colonies, protectorates or territories under suzerainty or mandate; and the present Convention shall not apply to any territories named in such declaration.

Any High Contracting Party may give notice to the Secretary-General of the League of Nations at any time subsequently that he desires that the Convention shall apply to all or any of his territories which have been made the subject of a declaration under the preceding paragraph and the Convention shall apply to all the territories named in such notice ninety days after its receipt by the Secretary-General of the League of Nations.

Any High Contracting Party may at any time declare that he desires that the present Convention shall cease to apply to all or any of his colonies, protectorates or territories under suzerainty or mandate and the Convention shall cease to apply to the territories named in such declaration one year after its receipt by the Secretary-General of the League of Nations.

ARTICLE 21

The revision of the present Convention may be requested at any time by one-third of the Members of the International Relief Union.

The Statute annexed to the present Convention may be modified by the General Council. For that purpose, three-fourths of the Members of the General Council must be present at the meeting, and the modification must be approved by two-thirds of the Members present.

Statute of the International Relief Union

ARTICLE 1

Each delegate in the General Council may have a substitute who may attend the meetings of the Council, but who shall act in an advisory and deliberative capacity only in the absence of the delegate.

Representatives of international relief organisations or other qualified organisations or institutions may be invited to be present in a consultative capacity at the meetings of the General Council.

The Secretary-General of the League of Nations may attend or be represented at any meeting of the General Council.

ARTICLE 2

The General Council shall be convoked by the Executive Committee at the seat of the International Relief Union every two years. In the interval of the two years, it may meet at any place fixed by the Executive Committee. The Executive Committee shall call a meeting of the General Council on the request of one-fourth of the Members of the General Council.

The first meeting of the General Council shall be summoned by the Council of the League of Nations.

ARTICLE 3

The notice summoning a meeting of the General Council must be sent out at least three months in advance and must contain the agenda of the meeting.

A quorum of the General Council will require the presence of the delegates of one-half of the Members of the International Relief Union, subject to the provisions of Article 21 of the Convention; all decisions shall be taken by a majority of the votes cast, except in cases where a large number of votes is required by the present Statute.

ARTICLE 4

The General Council shall elect the Members of the Executive Committee and their substitutes by a majority of two-thirds of the votes cast. It shall establish by the same majority the necessary regulations for the execution of the present Statute.

The General Council shall determine, by majority vote, its own Rules of Procedure which may provide for the election of Members of the Executive Committee by absolute majority of the votes cast in case several ballots may have failed to result in an election.

The General Council shall be competent to deal with all the affairs of the International Relief Union.

ARTICLE 5

The Executive Committee shall consist of seven Members who, with their substitutes, shall be elected for a period of two years.

In cases of vacancy for any cause whatever, the Executive Committee shall fill such vacancy by designating one of the substitutes to hold office until the expiration of the unfinished term.

Two representatives of the international organisations of the Red Cross (the International Committee of the Red Cross and the League of Red Cross Societies) may participate in the work of the Committee in a consultative capacity.

The Secretary-General of the League of Nations may attend or be represented at any meeting of the Executive Committee.

The Executive Committee shall determine its own Rules of Procedure.

ARTICLE 6

The Executive Committee shall meet at least once each year at the seat of the International Relief Union, on the convocation of its President. The President shall fix the date and the place of other meetings.

ARTICLE 7

The Executive Committee shall be the agent of the International Relief Union, and it may be the trustee of funds subject to special conditions or restrictions. The Executive Committee shall have the most extensive powers for the execution of all instruments which are in conformity with the objects of the International Relief Union and in its behalf.

The Executive Committee shall represent the International Relief Union in dealing with the League of Nations, with Governments, with the organisations mentioned in Article 5 of the Convention and with all persons and corporate bodies. It shall have power to institute or to defend any action at law in the name of or on behalf of the International Relief Union. It shall have power to effect compromises.

The Executive Committee shall collect the funds, employ them, invest them, and administer them as trustee or fiduciary administrator; and, in the name of the International Relief Union, shall handle all banking and insurance operations.

The Executive Committee shall make and authorise contracts of all kinds and shall control all supplies.

The Executive Committee shall fix the regulations for the investment of the funds of the International Relief Union.

In case of disaster, the Executive Committee shall have power to act on behalf of the International Relief Union, to organise relief and to make appeals for funds.

ARTICLE 8

Subject to the provisions of Article 9, the Executive Committee may delegate all or any of its powers to one or more of its Members.

ARTICLE 9

Any instrument executed by the Executive Committee, acting as trustee or fiduciary administrator of any donation or bequest, made subject to special condition or restriction, must bear the signature of at least two Members.

The signatures of two Members shall be required also for any alienation of property.

ARTICLE 10

Without prejudice to the provisions of Article 18, the Executive Committee shall submit an annual report of its activities and operations to the Members of the International Relief Union. This report shall also be communicated to the Secretary-General of the League of Nations in order that it may be brought to the knowledge of the Council and Assembly of the League of Nations. The report shall also be brought to the knowledge of the public.

ARTICLE 11

The Executive Committee shall be assisted by experts who may be consulted either individually or collectively.

These experts shall be named by the Executive Committee, one or more experts being chosen for each country or each geographical zone comprising several countries, as may be determined by the Executive Committee in agreement with the interested countries.

The experts shall be named for a period of three years; they must reside in the zone for which they are named; the Executive Committee may in any case where it may be found to be necessary, in addition to the experts above mentioned, name deputy-experts who shall not be subject to the condition of residence.

The appointment of each expert or deputy-expert must be made in agreement with the Member or Members interested.

ARTICLE 12

The Executive Committee shall convoke the experts whose collaboration is deemed to be necessary, or shall seek their opinions by correspondence whenever the circumstances so require.

ARTICLE 13

The travelling and subsistence expenses and allowances of the delegates to the General Council shall be borne by the authorities by which they are appointed.

The travelling and subsistence expenses and allowances of the Members of the Executive Committee and of the experts shall be borne by the budget of the International Relief Union. Members of the Executive Committee and experts shall receive no salary.

ARTICLE 14

The international organisations of the Red Cross (International Committee of the Red Cross and the League of Red Cross Societies) shall be invited to provide at their expense and to the extent which they consider to be compatible with their resources, the permanent and central services of the International Relief Union. These services shall be under the direction of the Executive Committee.

ARTICLE 15

Relief work in each zone shall be effected on behalf of the International Relief Union by the organisations mentioned in Article 5 of the Convention and existing in that zone.

If any one zone comprises several States or if in one zone several such organisations participate in the work of relief, the Executive Committee shall take such steps as may be necessary to coordinate efforts made and the distribution of relief. In particular, it may set up for this purpose, with the consent of such organisations, regional committees, account being taken in the recruiting of their Members of technical capacity, experience and administrative convenience.

In the event of a disaster, the Executive Committee should as a general rule be informed by the expert or experts of the zone affected.

ARTICLE 16

The International Relief Union shall establish, apart from the initial fund and other funds which it may deem it necessary to constitute:

(1) A working capital fund, maintained:

(a) By the income from the initial fund and the reserve hereinafter provided for;

(b) By retaining a portion not exceeding one per cent of all sums placed at the disposal of the International Relief Union.

This working capital fund shall cover the costs of the ordinary and permanent services of the International Relief Union, in the exceptional case when such costs are not paid by the international organisations of the Red Cross (International Red Cross Committee and League of Red Cross Societies).

(2) A Reserve, maintained:

(a) By the surplus from any funds not wholly expended for their special purposes;

(b) By a deduction from all sums placed at the disposal of the International Relief Union without being dedicated to any special object. This deduction, together, if necessary, with the sum deducted for the working capital fund, shall not exceed a total of five per cent.

This reserve will be used primarily to reconstitute the initial fund provided for in Article 9 of the Convention, and secondarily to supply or supplement the relief given in case of disasters for which no special donations are available.

ARTICLE 17

The funds of the International Relief Union, with the exception of such sums as may be required for current expenses, shall be deposited either in the same banks as the funds of the League of Nations or in other banks approved by the General Council.

ARTICLE 18

The Executive Committee shall draw up an annual balance sheet of the International Relief Union.

The balance sheet shall show the assets and liabilities of the International Relief Union, as well as accounts of all financial operations connected with each disaster.

ARTICLE 19

The League of Nations is asked to provide, under such conditions as it may determine, for the auditing of the accounts of the International Relief Union, it being understood that the League of Nations assumes no responsibility thereby.

Source: *LNTS*, Vol. CXXXV (1932-1933), p. 247.

Annex 3

Red Cross Declaration of Principles for International Humanitarian Relief to the Civilian Population in Disaster Situations

The XXIst International Conference of the Red Cross,

noting that in the present century the international community has accepted increased responsibility for relief of human suffering in any form,

whereas human suffering in all its manifestations is of deep concern to the conscience of mankind and world opinion requires effective action for the relief of such suffering,

affirming that one of the major purposes of the community of nations as laid down in the Charter of the United Nations is to achieve international co-operation in solving international problems of an economic, social, cultural or humanitarian nature,

noting with satisfaction the improvements in the ability of the international community to provide various forms of humanitarian relief as a result of international agreements and through the International Red Cross and other impartial international humanitarian organisations,

recognising that further steps have to be taken by the international community to ensure prompt and effective relief action to civilian populations in natural or other disaster situations,

adopts the following Declaration of Principles:

1. The fundamental concern of mankind and of the international community in disaster situations is the protection and welfare of the individual and the safeguarding of basic human rights.
2. Relief by impartial international humanitarian organisations for civilian populations in natural or other disaster situations should as far as possible be treated as a humanitarian and non-political matter and should be so organised as to avoid prejudicing sovereign and other legal rights in order that the confidence of the parties to a conflict in the impartiality of such organisations may be preserved.
3. The activities of impartial international humanitarian organisations for the benefit of civilian populations should be co-ordinated in order to secure prompt action and effective allocation of resources and to avoid duplication of effort.
4. Disaster relief for the benefit of civilian populations is to be provided without discrimination and the offer of such relief by an impartial international humanitarian organisation ought not to be regarded as an unfriendly act.
5. All States are requested to exercise their sovereign and other legal rights so as to facilitate the transit, admission and distribution of relief supplies provided by impartial international humanitarian organisations for the benefit of civilian populations in disaster areas when disaster situations imperil the life and welfare of such populations.
6. All authorities in disaster areas should facilitate disaster relief activities by impartial international humanitarian organisations for the benefit of civilian populations.

(XXIst International Conference of the Red Cross, Istanbul, *Resolution XXVI*, September 1969)

Annex 4

Principles and Rules for Red Cross disaster relief

General provisions

Field of application	1. The present rules apply to disasters, that is to situations resulting from natural or other calamities.
Basic principles	2. The Red Cross in its endeavour to prevent and alleviate human suffering, considers it a fundamental duty to bring relief to all disaster victims.
Assistance and mutual aid	3. It is the duty of National Societies to prepare themselves to give assistance in the event of a disaster.

In view of the solidarity binding them together they shall help one another when faced with a situation exceeding their resources.

In assisting each other in this way, while respecting the independence of each of them and the sovereignty of the stricken country, National Societies contribute to the strengthening of friendship and peace among peoples.

Role of the Red Cross

4. Prevention of disasters, assistance to victims and reconstruction are first and foremost the responsibility of the public authorities. In principle Red Cross help is of an auxiliary and complementary nature and operates basically in the emergency phase. However, if circumstances require and provided the Red Cross is assured of the necessary resources and means, it may undertake longer-term assistance programmes.

Ways and means of assistance

5. Red Cross assistance to the victims is given free of charge and without any distinction as to nationality, race, religion, social condition or political opinion. It is made available on the basis of the relative importance of individual needs and in the order of their emergency.

Red Cross relief is administered with care and its utilisation is the subject of precise reports.

Co-ordination

6. Considering that assistance to disaster victims requires co-ordination both at the national and international levels, the Red Cross, whilst remaining true to its Principles, should, in the implementation of its programme, endeavour to take into account the help given by other national and international organisations.

Organisation and preparation at the national level

National relief plan

7. In order to cope with the effects of disasters, each country should have a national plan outlining an effective organisation of relief. If such a plan does not exist, the National Society should instigate its establishment.

The national plan shall assign to all sections of the community – public services, Red Cross, voluntary agencies, social welfare organisations and qualified persons – precise tasks in the fields of disaster prevention, relief and reconstruction.

Management of the plan

8. To ensure rapid mobilisation as well as complete and effective use of material and personnel resources, the national plan should envisage co-ordination through the establishment of a centralised direction. Such central direction should be able to provide precise and official information on the effects of a disaster, its evolution and the needs.

Participation of the Red Cross

9. The extent of the Red Cross relief programme depends on the responsibilities delegated to the National Society by its government or by the national relief plan. As a general rule, the Red Cross programme is limited to the provision of first aid, medical and nursing care, food supplies, clothing, shelter, services for the prevention of epidemics, including health education, social welfare, tracing services and other forms of emergency assistance.

Preparation

10. Each National Society must prepare itself to assume the responsibility devolving on it in case of disaster. It must establish its own plan of action, adapt its organisation accordingly, recruit, instruct

and train the necessary personnel, and ensure the availability of the reserves in cash and kind which it might need in the emergency phase of the relief operation.

League technical assistance

11. The League of Red Cross Societies will endeavour to assist National Societies with their organisation and preparedness for relief actions, in particular by offering them the services of technicians and contributing to the instruction and training of their personnel. It will encourage and facilitate exchanges of information between Societies so that the experience of some will be of benefit to others.

Agreements on mutual assistance

12. National Societies should endeavour to conclude agreements on mutual assistance in the event of disaster with the National Societies of neighbouring countries. The League shall be informed.

Exemptions and other facilities

13. National Societies should make every effort to obtain facilities from governmental or private transport services in their countries for the rapid transport, whenever possible free or at reduced rates, of relief supplies, including goods in transit, for disaster victims.

National Societies should also endeavour to obtain from their governments exemption from all taxes and customs duties concerning the entry into and the transit through the country of funds and relief supplies intended for the victims of disasters.

Furthermore, they should seek to obtain travel facilities and the quick granting of visas for Red Cross personnel taking part in relief operations.

International assistance

Role of the League

14. The League of Red Cross Societies is the information and co-ordination centre for all international assistance in the event of a disaster. Therefore, even if National Societies do not envisage asking for outside assistance, it is essential that they inform the League quickly of every large-scale disaster occurring within their countries, of the extent of the damage and the measures taken.

Requests for assistance and appeal

15. Any request from a National Society of a stricken country for international assistance shall be addressed to the League. Such a request must contain all available information on the general situation, the number of persons to be helped and the nature and quantities of relief supplies needed in order of priority by the National Society to carry out its specific responsibilities.

On receipt of such a request, the League will, when conditions call for it, launch an appeal to all National Societies – or, depending on the circumstances, to a certain number of them – containing all necessary information on the disaster and on the special conditions of the country. No appeal will be launched by the League without a request from the National Society of the stricken country or without its agreement.

The League can, however, take the initiative to offer special assistance, even though the National Society has not asked for it. The National Society will consider such offers with urgency and goodwill, bearing in mind the spirit in which they are made.

Regular communication of information

16. The National Society of the stricken country will keep the League informed on the development of the situation, the relief given and

the needs still to be met. This information will be communicated to the National Societies to which the appeal has been made.

Information on assistance

17. When, as a result of a League appeal or as a result of mutual agreement or other special circumstances, a National Society gives assistance to the Society of a stricken country it will immediately inform the League. Such information will contain the amount of gifts in kind, including quantity, value and means of transportation.

Collections abroad

18. Unless there is a previous agreement, the National Society of a stricken country will not try to obtain, either directly or indirectly, funds or any other form of assistance in the country of another Society and will not permit its name to be used for this purpose.

League liaison officer

19. When a National Society is in receipt of international assistance the League will assign to this National Society a liaison officer or a team of delegates, whose name or names will be communicated to it as rapidly as possible and whose number will depend on the magnitude of the disaster.

The chief delegate will be responsible for the judicious and effective utilisation of the team of experts with a view to helping the National Society with such activities as the reception, warehousing and distribution of relief supplies received from abroad, information, communication and with all other activities that will contribute to the effectiveness both of the relief operation itself, undertaken by the National Society involved, and of the assistance of sister Societies.

All staff assigned by the League will have the task of assisting the National Society and not of taking over its basic responsibilities.

The chief delegate should be given all facilities to send to the League by the most rapid means all the information likely to enable it to back up its appeals to National Societies and inform them as fully as possible on the needs resulting from the disaster and then on the use made of the relief received. He should advise the National Society concerned of the measures taken and foreseen both by the League and the National Societies which are giving it their support.

Use made of gifts

20. A National Society which benefits from the assistance of sister Societies will give the League liaison officer the opportunity to see on the spot the use made of the gifts received.

Accounting and auditing requirements

20A. A National Society which receives cash donations from sister Societies and the League shall submit to the latter half-yearly statements of the use of such funds, until such time as a final statement can be presented, showing in detail the origin of cash donations and their use over the whole period. These interim and final statements shall whenever possible be submitted within three months of the end of the period to which they relate.

The final statements shall be examined and reported on either by public accountants, or by auditors recognised by the government of the country concerned. In relief actions continuing for more than one year such examination and reporting shall also be carried out annually, until the relief action is completed.

For donations in kind, statements showing the origin and use of such contributions shall be submitted to the League each half year and also finally at the end of the relief action; no examination or reporting by auditors is required.

Representatives of donor Societies

21. Donor Societies which desire to send representatives to the spot, particularly to collect information material for the public supporting the relief action in their country, shall obtain the previous agreement of the central headquarters of the National Society of the stricken country. They should keep the League informed.

Execution entrusted to the League

22. When the administrative organisation of the Society in the stricken country does not enable it to meet the situation, the League may, at the request of that Society and with its co-operation, assume the local direction and execution of the relief action.

Foreign personnel

23. Personnel provided by donor Societies will be placed under the direction of the National Society of the stricken country or of the League, when the direction and execution of the relief operation have been entrusted to it.

Non-solicited or spontaneous relief

24. If a National Society wishes to send relief supplies which are not mentioned in the appeal launched by the League, it shall first obtain the agreement of the National Society of the stricken country or of the League. When there has been no appeal from the League, but a National Society nevertheless wishes to send relief supplies to the Society of a stricken country, the previous agreement of that Society is also required and the League shall be informed.

Donating supplies while receiving assistance

24A. A National Society in receipt of international assistance needed in its own country shall not contribute assistance of a similar nature to a sister Society without the prior authorisation of the League.

How to use gifts

25. Gifts sent to a National Society may only be used for the purpose designated and will serve in the first place to give direct assistance to the victims.

A beneficiary Society may in no event use cash gifts received to cover its administrative expenses included in its ordinary budget, nor may a beneficiary Society transfer cash gifts donated to it to another organisation or group for use by that organisation or group.

If in the course of a relief operation it is necessary to sell or exchange a part of the goods received, the donors – or the League which represents them – will be consulted. The funds or goods thus obtained may only be used for the relief action.

Relief surplus

26. Goods or funds remaining on hand after the termination of a relief action shall not be used or expended except pursuant to an agreement between the National Society of the stricken country and the League, after consultation by the League with the donor Societies concerned. Such an agreement might include the return of the goods or the funds to the donor Societies.

Transmission and forwarding of relief

27. Assistance donated by a national Society to a stricken country will always be sent through Red Cross channels, either direct to the National Society or through the intermediary of the League. Funds sent to the League will be specifically earmarked for the disaster for which they are contributed and will either be sent to the National Society of the stricken country or, with its concurrence, utilised by the League according to the needs of the relief operation.

National Societies and the League may agree to transmit to a stricken country relief from non-Red Cross sources. In such cases, however, the relief will be utilised by the National Society or, with its concurrence by the League in conformity with the present rules.

Final provision

Special cases

28. Every disaster relief operation carried out in a country where there is war, civil war, or internal disorders, shall be regulated by the provisions of the Agreement of April 25th 1969 between the ICRC and the League.

(*XXIst International Conference of the Red Cross, Istanbul, Resolution XXIV, September 1969, with revisions*)

Annex 5

General Assembly Resolution 2816 (XXVI), Assistance in cases of natural disaster and other disaster situations

The General Assembly,

Bearing in mind that throughout history natural disasters and emergency situations have inflicted heavy loss of life and property, affecting every people and every country,

Aware of and concerned about the suffering caused by natural disasters and the serious economic and social consequences for all, especially the developing countries,

Also aware of the varying needs of nations experiencing such disorders, which present new challenges for international co-operation,

Concerned about the ability of the international community to come to the aid of countries in a disaster situation,

Recalling its resolutions 2034 (XX) of 7 December 1965, 2435 (XXIII) of 19 December 1968, 2608 (XXIV) of 16 December 1969 and 2717 (XXV) of 15 December 1970, and Economic and Social Council resolutions 1533 (XLIX) of 23 July 1970 and 1546 (XLIX) of 30 July 1970 on assistance in cases of natural disaster,

Expressing appreciation of the Secretary-General's comprehensive report[1] and of its perceptive examination of all aspects of the question, and taking note of the relevant passage in his statement to the Economic and Social Council on 5 July 1971,[2]

Taking note of Economic and Social Council resolution 1612 (LI) of 23 July 1971 on assistance in cases of natural disaster and other emergency situations,

Noting the study, annexed to the Secretary-General's report, on the legal status of disaster relief units made available through the United Nations,[3]

Mindful of the need to strengthen and make more effective the collective efforts of the international community, and particularly the United Nations system, in the field of international disaster assistance,

---

1. E/4994.
2. See *Official Records of the Economic and Social Council, Fifty-first Session*, 1773rd meeting.
3. E/4994, annex III.

Bearing in mind that assistance provided at the request of the stricken countries, without prejudice to their individual country programmes under the United Nations Development Programme, can be an effective contribution to the rehabilitation and development of the stricken areas,

Bearing in mind also that the possible response of the International Bank for Reconstruction and Development and other credit organizations and development agencies to a request from the Governments concerned for complementary assistance to the stricken areas, without prejudice to the assistance provided by those organizations for the normal development programmes of the stricken countries, can be an important element in the reconstruction and development of those areas,

Noting the competence of the United Nations and its related agencies, the United Nations Children's Fund, the United Nations High Commissioner for Refugees and the World Food Programme to render assistance in cases of natural disaster and other disaster situations,

Nothing futher the key role which the resident representatives of the United Nations Development Programme could play at the country level,

Recognizing the vital role in international relief played by the International Red Cross and other voluntary societies,

Recognizing further the necessity to ensure prompt, effective and efficient response to a Government's need for assistance, at the time of a natural disaster or other disaster situation, that will bring to bear the resources of the United Nations system, prospective donor countries and voluntary agencies,

1. Calls upon the Secretary-General to appoint a Disaster Relief Co-ordinator,.who will report directly to him and who will be authorized, on his behalf:

(a) To establish and maintain the closest co-operation with all organizations concerned and to make all feasible advance arrangements with them for the purpose of ensuring the most effective assistance;

(b) To mobilize, direct and co-ordinate the relief activities of the various organizations of the United Nations system in response to a request for disaster assistance from a stricken State;

(c) To co-ordinate United Nations assistance with assistance given by intergovernmental and non-governmental organizations, in particular by the International Red Cross;

(d) To receive, on behalf of the Secretary-General, contributions offered to him for disaster relief assistance to be carried out by the United Nations, its agencies and programmes for particular emergency situations;

(e) To assist the Government of the stricken country to assess its relief and other needs and to evaluate the priority of those needs, to disseminate that information to prospective donors and others concerned, and to serve as a clearing-house for assistance extended or planned by all sources of external aid;

(f) To promote the study, prevention, control and prediction of natural disasters, including the collection and dissemination of information concerning technological developments;

(g) To assist in providing advice to Governments on pre-disaster planning in association with relevant voluntary organizations, particularly with the League of Red Cross Societies, and to draw upon United Nations resources available for such purposes;

(h) To acquire and disseminate information relevant to planning and co-ordinating disaster relief, including the improvement and establishment of stockpiles in disaster-prone areas, and to prepare suggestions to ensure the most effective use of available resources;

(i) To phase out relief operations under his aegis as the stricken country moves into the stage of rehabilitation and reconstruction, but to continue to interest himself, within the framework of his responsibilities for relief, in the activities of the United Nations agencies concerned with rehabilitation and reconstruction;

(j) To prepare an annual report for the Secretary-General, to be submitted to the Economic and Social Council and to the General Assembly;

2. Recommends that the Disaster Relief Co-ordinator should be appointed by the Secretary-General normally for a term of five years and at a level comparable to that of an Under-Secretary-General of the United Nations;

3. Endorses the Secretary-General's proposals for an adequate permanent office in the United Nations which shall be the focal point in the United Nations system for disaster relief matters;

4. Recommends that that office should be headed by the Disaster Relief Co-ordinator and located in Geneva, be a distinct element within the United Nations Secretariat and be augmented as necessary by short-term secondment of personnel for individual emergencies;

5. Requests the Secretary-General to prepare for the Economic and Social Council at its fifty-third session, taking into account any relevant suggestions and the experience gained by the Disaster Relief Co-ordinator, a report on any further steps which may be required to enable the Disaster Relief Co-ordinator adequately to perform the functions entrusted to him under the present resolution;

6. Further endorses the plan for a roster of volunteers, to be drawn from experienced staff members of the United Nations system and interested non-governmental organizations, who could be made available at very short notice;

7. Recommends that the Disaster Relief Co-ordinator should maintain contact with the Governments of States Members of the United Nations or members of specialized agencies or of the International Atomic Energy Agency concerning available aid in emergency situations, such as food supplies, medicines, personnel, transportation and communications, as well as advice to countries in pre-disaster planning and preparedness;

8. Invites potential recipient Governments:

(a) To establish disaster contingency plans with appropriate assistance from the Disaster Relief Co-ordinator;

(b) To appoint a single national disaster relief co-ordinator to facilitate the receipt of international aid in times of emergency;

(c) To establish stockpiles of emergency supplies, such as tents, blankets, medicines and non-perishable food-stuffs;

(d) To make necessary arrangements for the training of administrative and relief personnel;

(e) To consider appropriate legislative or other measures to facilitate the receipt of aid, including overflight and landing rights and necessary privileges and immunities for relief units;

(f) To improve national disaster warning systems;

9. Invites potential donor Governments:

(a) To respond promptly to any call by the Secretary-General or, on his behalf, by the Disaster Relief Co-ordinator;

(b) To consider and to continue offering on a wider basis emergency assistance in disaster situations;

(c) To inform the Disaster Relief Co-ordinator in advance about the facilities and services they might be in a position to provide immediately, including where possible relief units, logistical support and means of effective communication;

10. Decides to authorize the Secretary-General to draw on the Working Capital Fund in the amount of $200,000 for emergency assistance in any one year, with a normal ceiling of $20,000 per country in the case of any one disaster;

11. Further invites all organizations of the United Nations system and all other organizations involved to co-operate with the Disaster Relief Co-ordinator.

(Adopted by the *2018th plenary meeting*, voting 86-0-10, *December 4, 1971*)

Annex 6

General Assembly Resolution 36/225, Strengthening the capacity of the United Nations system to respond to natural disasters and other disaster situations

The General Assembly,

Recalling its resolutions 2816 (XXVI) of 14 December 1971, by which it established the Office of the United Nations Disaster Relief Co-ordinator, 3234 (XXIX) of 29 November 1974 on the strengthening of that Office, 3440 (XXX) of 9 December 1975, in which it provided, *inter alia*, for measures to be taken in support of the activities of the Office, and 3532 (XXX) of 17 December 1975 on the financing of emergency relief assistance and technical co-operation activities of the Office,

Recalling also its resolution 31/173 of 21 December 1976 on financial arrangements for the Office of the United Nations Disaster Relief Co-ordinator,

Recalling further the International Development Strategy for the Third United Nations Development Decade,[1]

Recalling the report of the United Nations Conference on the Least Developed Countries containing the Substantial New Programme of Action for the 1980s for the Least Developed Countries, in particular the section concerning disaster assistance for the least developed countries,[2]

Deeply concerned about the increasing number of natural disasters and other disaster situations, the economic burden borne by disaster-stricken and affected countries, particularly the developing countries, and the disruption thereby caused to their development process,

Also recalling its resolution 35/107 of 5 December 1980,

Further recalling Economic and Social Council resolution 1980/43 of 23 July 1980 regarding international efforts to meet humanitarian needs in natural disasters and other disaster situations,

Fully cognizant of the sovereign interests and rights of affected countries and of the primacy of their role in caring for the victims of natural disasters and other disaster situations,

Anxious that the international community should respond speedily and effectively to calls for emergency humanitarian assistance,

Recognizing that the quality and appropriateness of material and other assistance provided by the international community should meet the particular needs of the populations of disaster-affected areas,

Recognizing the contribution made by the United Nations system to the relief of suffering and provision of humanitarian relief in natural disasters and other disaster situations,

Recognizing that the primary responsibility of administration, relief operations and disaster preparedness lies with the affected countries and that the major part of the material assistance and human effort in disaster relief comes from the Governments of those countries,

Recognizing also the importance in international relief of the contribution of the International Committee of the Red Cross, the League of Red Cross and Red Crescent Societies and appropriate voluntary organizations,

Recognizing further that, in order to attain an effective co-ordination system of humanitarian and disaster relief assistance, it is essential to strengthen and improve the capacity and effectiveness of the Office of the United Nations Disaster Relief Co-ordinator and the United Nations system as a whole in order to enable the Office to respond to natural disasters and other disaster situations speedily, efficiently and effectively, and thereby ensure prompt delivery of concerted relief,

---

1. Resolution 36/56, annex.
2. *Report of the United Nations Conference on the Least Developed Countries, Paris, 1-14 September 1981* (United Nations publications, Sales No. E.82.I.8), part one, sect. A. para. 59.

Recognizing that a major constraint for the United Nations system to respond effectively to natural disasters and other disaster situations has been the shortage of resources,

1. *Takes note* of the reports of the Secretary-General and other reports on international efforts to meet humanitarian needs in emergency situations, as well as on measures for strengthening the capacity of the United Nations system to respond to natural disasters and other disaster situations[3] and of the statement made by the United Nations Disaster Relief Co-ordinator before the Second Committee on 5 November 1981;[4]

2. *Reaffirms* the sovereignty of individual Member States, recognizes the primary role of each State in caring for the victims of disasters occurring in its territory and stresses that all relief operations should be carried out and co-ordinated in a manner consistent with the priorities and needs of the countries concerned;

3. *Reaffirms* the mandate of the Office of the United Nations Disaster Relief Co-ordinator, established by the General Assembly in resolution 2816 (XXVI) as the focal point of the United Nations system for disaster relief co-ordination, and calls for strengthening and improvement of the capacity and effectiveness of the Office;

4. *Endorses* the approaches outlined by the Secretary-General in his comments on the report of the Joint Inspection Unit concerning the role of the Office of the United Nations Disaster Relief Co-ordinator in the various phases of disaster assistance;[5]

5. *Requests* the Secretary-General to continue to take the necessary steps to strengthen the management operations of the Office of the United Nations Disaster Relief Co-ordinator;

6. *Stresses* the need to take full advantage of information provided by existing early-warning monitoring systems that have been developed to strengthen the capacity of the United Nations system in responding to natural disasters and other disaster situations and to co-ordinate, as far as feasible and useful, all the relevant early-warning systems, and stresses that, to this effect, the capability of the Office of the United Nations Disaster Relief Co-ordinator in information collection and dissemination should be further strengthened and improved;

7. *Urges* the appropriate organs, organizations and bodies of the United Nations system, including the United Nations Children's Fund, the Food and Agriculture Organization of the United Nations, the World Health Organization, the Office of the United Nations High Commissioner for Refugees, the World Food Programme and other appropriate bodies, to co-operate closely, in their respective areas of competence, with the Office of the United Nations Disaster Relief Co-ordinator in disaster relief activities and other disaster situations, to respond effectively to the needs of the situation and to comply promptly with the requests of disaster-affected countries;

8. *Decides* that, in response to a request for disaster relief from a disaster-stricken State and, as necessary, in particular in disaster-prone countries, the United Nations resident co-ordinator shall, with the full concurrence, consent and participation of the Government, convene meetings of the concerned organs, organizations and bodies of the United Nations system to plan, monitor and take immediate action to provide assistance and the International Committee of the Red Cross, the League of Red Cross and Red Crescent Societies and appropriate voluntary organizations may be invited to participate in such meetings with the approval of the host country;

9. *Decides* that, following a request for disaster relief from a disaster-stricken State and whenever required to deal effectively with complex disasters and emergencies of exceptional magnitude, the Secretary-General or his representative, who would normally be the United Nations Disaster Relief Co-ordinator, shall convene meetings of the concerned organizations of the United Nations system in order to develop a concerted relief programme and conduct *ad hoc* consultations with

---

3. See A/36/73 and Add. 1, A/36/259 and E/1981/16 and Corr. 1, annex. See also decision 1981/2 of the Administrative Committee on Coordination (ACC/1981/DEC/1-10).
4. *Official Records of the General Assembly, Thirty-sixth Session, Second Committee*, 29th meeting, paras. 33-40.
5. A/36/73/Add. 1.

the heads or representatives of the agencies concerned with disaster-relief questions, with a view to ensuring speedy and efficient delivery of goods and services to the disaster-stricken areas, and decides that these *ad hoc* consultations should draw on information provided by the Government concerned, as well as on the assessments of the United Nations Disaster Relief Co-ordinator, the resident co-ordinator and representatives of other United Nations organizations in the countries concerned, and take into account advice offered by the International Committee of the Red Cross, the League of Red Cross and Red Crescent Societies and appropriate voluntary organizations in the field with the understanding that all agencies with responsibilities for natural disasters and other disaster situations should be involved at the appropriate level in such consultations;

10. Decides that, once it has been determined – on the basis of the above-mentioned information and consultations – that an exceptional or complex natural disaster or other disaster situation requiring system-wide actions exists, the Secretary-General shall designate, at the international level, a lead entity from among the United Nations organizations, agencies and bodies, including the Office of the United Nations Disaster Relief Co-ordinator, and, at the country level, the appropriate entity of the United Nations system to carry out relief operations, taking into account the specific requirements of the situation and in consultation with the host Government, and calls upon all organs, organizations and bodies of the United Nations system to co-operate closely with one another in their relief operations;

11. Invites the Administrative Committee on Co-ordination to examine urgently the role of the lead entity and participating organs, organizations and bodies of the United Nations system in complex disaster situations, taking into account decision 1981/2 of that Committee, and requests the Secretary-General to submit a report, through the Economic and Social Council at its second regular session of 1982, to the General Assembly at its thirty-seventh session, on the deliberations of the Committee;

12. Strongly calls upon all States to respond positively and expeditiously to the Secretary-General's appeals for contributions to meet natural disasters and other disaster situations;

13. Reiterates in particular, its appeal in resolution 35/107 for increased contributions to the Trust Fund of the Office of the United Nations Disaster Relief Co-ordinator, in particular to the subaccount for humanitarian emergency relief;

14. Stresses in this regard the need to strengthen the operational capacity and the human, material and financial resources available to individual agencies and organizations, in order to enable them to play their respective roles more promptly, efficiently and effectively in natural disaster and other disaster situations;

15. Requests all States to ensure a full flow of information to the Office of the United Nations Disaster Relief Co-ordinator, especially regarding relief actions, and also to provide the United Nations system with the necessary personnel and logistic support;

16. Urges Governments in disaster-prone countries to explore further, with the assistance of the donors, appropriate organs, organizations and bodies of the United Nations system, the possibility of improving storage, communication and transportation facilities, as well as measures to ensure disaster preparedness and prevention;

17. Also urges the international community to assist disaster-prone countries, upon their request, with the establishment of effective national early-warning systems, the development of contingency plans for disasters and the strengthening of assessment capacity for relief requirements and for distribution and monitoring of relief supplies;

18. Calls upon organs, organizations and bodies of the United Nations system involved in the provision of humanitarian assistance and disaster relief to establish emergency units or focal points if they are not already in existence;

19. Reaffirms the need for the international community to respond fully to requests for emergency and humanitarian assistance, in particular through increased financial contributions for affected developing countries, bearing in mind the relevant provisions of the International Development Strategy for the Third United Nations Development Decade and of the Substantial New Pro-

gramme of Action for the 1980s for the Least Developed Countries, as well as those of the Trust Fund of the Office of the United Nations Disaster Relief Co-ordinator;

20. Requests the Secretary-General to submit a preliminary progress report on the implementation of the present resolution to the General Assembly at its thirty-seventh session, through the Economic and Social Council at its second regular session of 1982, and a comprehensive report to the Assembly at its thirty-eighth session, through the Council at its second regular session of 1983.

(103rd plenary meeting, 17 December 1981)

Annex 7

General Assembly Resolution 37/144, Special Economic and Disaster Relief Assistance, Office of the United Nations Disaster Relief Co-ordinator

The General Assembly,

Recalling its resolution 36/225 of 17 December 1981, by which it reaffirmed the mandate of the Office of the United Nations Disaster Relief Co-ordinator and called for the strengthening and improvement of the capacity and effectiveness of the Office,

Recalling also its resolution 35/107 of 5 December 1980, by which it reaffirmed the necessity of ensuring a continued sound financial basis for the Office of the United Nations Disaster Relief Co-ordinator and extended until 31 December 1983 the term of the Trust Fund established pursuant to its resolution 3243 (XXIX) of 29 November 1974 and modified under its resolutions 3440 (XXX) of 9 December 1975 and 3532 (XXX) of 17 December 1975 and by its decision 33/429 of 19 December 1978,

Recalling further its resolution 34/55 of 29 November 1979, by which it requested an increase in emergency disaster assistance, with a normal ceiling of $30,000 per country in the case of any one disaster,

Deeply concerned about the additional economic burden placed upon the developing countries and by the increasing number of natural disasters and other disaster situations, as well as the disruption caused to their development process,

Recognizing the contribution made by the United Nations system to the relief of suffering and provision of humanitarian relief in natural disasters and other disaster situations,

Recognizing also that the primary responsibilities of administration, relief operations and disaster preparedness lie with the affected countries and that the major part of the material assistance and human effort in disaster relief comes from the Governments of those countries,

Recognizing further the importance of the contribution of the International Committee of the Red Cross, the League of Red Cross and Red Crescent Societies and appropriate voluntary organizations,

Recognizing that, in order to attain an effective co-ordination system of humanitarian and disaster relief assistance, it is essential to strengthen and improve the capacity and effectiveness of the Office of the United Nations Disaster Relief Co-ordinator and the United Nations system as a whole in order to enable the Office to respond to natural disasters and other disaster situations speedily, efficiently and effectively, thereby ensuring prompt delivery of concerned relief,

Recognizing that a major constraint on an effective response of the United Nations to natural disasters and other disaster situations has been the shortage of resources,

1. Takes note with appreciation of the report of the Secretary-General on the work of the Office of the United Nations Disaster Relief Co-ordinator[1] and of the statement made by the Co-ordinator before the Second Committee on 2 November 1982;[2]

1. A/37/235 and Corr. 1.
2. See A/C.2/37/SR.27, paras. 1-9.

2. Takes note of the progress made by the Secretary-General and the Administrative Committee on Co-ordination in initiating improvements in the management operations of the Office of the United Nations Disaster Relief Co-ordinator and in establishing modalities for the implementation of the procedures, outlined in General Assembly resolution 36/225 and decision 1982/1 of the Administrative Committee on Co-ordination, for dealing with requests for disaster relief from a disaster-stricken State and for dealing with complex disasters and emergencies of exceptional magnitude;

3. Takes note of the appreciation expressed by the Governments of Chad and Lebanon for the activities undertaken by the United Nations Disaster Relief Co-ordinator in those two countries, and requests him to continue his action in response to needs as they arise;

4. Requests the Secretary-General to facilitate, when necessary, rapid appointment of temporary staff and procurement of supplies by the United Nations Disaster Relief Co-ordinator in order to permit a timely response to requests for emergency assistance;

5. Requests the Secretary-General to raise the normal maximum of $30,000 to $50,000, the additional $20,000 to come from voluntary sources, to permit the United Nations Disaster Relief Co-ordinator to respond with grants to requests for emergency disaster assistance up to a total of $600,000 in any one year, with a normal ceiling of $50,000 per country in the case of any one disaster;

6. Authorizes the Secretary-General to permit the United Nations Disaster Relief Co-ordinator to mobilize additional voluntary resources to meet the needs presented by complex disasters and emergencies of exceptional magnitude;

7. Decides to maintain as from 1 January 1984 the Trust Fund of the Office of the United Nations Disaster Relief Co-ordinator and its sub-accounts;

8. Reiterates, in particular, the appeals made in its resolutions 35/107 and 36/225 for increased contributions to the Trust Fund established pursuant to its resolution 3234 (XXIX) and modified as indicated in the second preambular paragraph and in paragraph 7 above;

9. Endorses the measures taken by the Secretary-General and the Administrative Committee on Co-ordination to implement General Assembly resolution 36/225 and calls upon the Secretary-General, who will normally be represented by the United Nations Disaster Relief Co-ordinator, to consult with the concerned agencies of the United Nations system in order to develop concerted relief programmes as a basis for united appeals for funds to be launched by the Co-ordinator on behalf of the Secretary-General;

10. Reiterates its desire further to strengthen and improve the capability of the Office of the United Nations Disaster Relief Co-ordinator to take full advantage of information provided by existing early-warning systems and to co-ordinate, to the extent feasible and useful, all relevant early-warning systems, taking into account new technological developments in this field, including communications;

11. Urges all Governments and relevant organs and organizations to co-operate with the United Nations Disaster Relief Co-ordinator and to improve in particular their flow of information on relief assistance, action and plans;

12. Calls upon the specialized agencies and other consitutent organizations of the United Nations system, in order to eliminate wasteful duplication of resources, to co-ordinate, in accordance with the provisions of paragraph 3 of General Assembly resolution 36/225, their efforts at all stages of the response of the international community to natural disasters and other disaster situations;

13. Reaffirms its belief that the strengthening and reinforcing of the Office of the United Nations Disaster Relief Co-ordinator offers the most efficient and economic means of effectively co-ordinating the relief activities of the United Nations system as a whole in the interest of the survivors of disasters, and requests the Secretary-General to assign a higher priority to strengthening, preferably within the means at his disposal, the financial and manpower resources of the Office;

14. *Requests* the Secretary-General to submit a comprehensive report on the implementation of General Assembly resolution 36/225, including a report on the implementation of the present resolution, to the Assembly at its thirty-eighth session, through the Economic and Social Council at its second regular session of 1983.

(109th Plenary Meeting, 17 December 1982)

Annex 8

Draft Convention on Expediting the Delivery of Emergency Assistance

The Parties to this Convention,

Bearing in mind that throughout history, disasters and emergency situations have inflicted heavy loss of life and property affecting every people and every country,

Aware of and concerned about the suffering caused by disasters and the serious economic and social consequences for all, especially the developing countries, and bearing in mind also relevant provisions of the International Development Strategy,

Noting that the international community has willingly rendered assistance in individual cases of disaster and continues to do so whenever necessary,

Concerned to improve the ability of the international community to provide emergency humanitarian assistance speedily and effectively,

Recalling the principles of international law as expressed in the Declaration on Principles of International Law concerning Friendly Relations and Co-operation among States in accordance with the Charter of the United Nations, adopted on 24 October 1970 by the General Assembly of the United Nations, in particular the principle of the duty of States to co-operate with one another in accordance with the Charter and the principles of sovereign equality of States and non-intervention within the domestic jurisdiction of any State,

Welcoming the establishment by the General Assembly of the United Nations of the Office of the United Nations Disaster Relief Co-ordinator to mobilize, direct and co-ordinate the relief activities of the various organizations of the United Nations system and to co-ordinate United Nations assistance with assistance given by all sources of external aid,

Have agreed as follows:

Part I. General Provisions

ARTICLE 1

Definitions

In this Convention:

(a) "Emergency assistance", hereafter referred to as "assistance", means the relief consignments and services of an exclusively humanitarian and non-political character provided to meet the needs of those affected by disasters;

(b) "Disaster" means any natural, accidental or deliberate event (not being an ongoing situation of armed conflict) as a result of which assistance is needed from outside the State upon whose territory the event occurred or which has been affected by the consequences of the event;

(c) "Relief consignments" means goods such as vehicles, foodstuffs, seeds and agricultural equipment, medical supplies, blankets, shelter materials or other goods of prime necessity, forwarded as assistance to those affected by disasters;

(d) "Services" means the personnel, equipment, means of transport and action necessary to meet the needs;

(e) "Receiving State" means the State on whose territory assistance is needed [being given] [being provided] under this Convention;

(f) "Assisting State or organization" means the State or intergovernmental organization, or international or national non-governmental organization, providing or co-ordinating assistance under this Convention;

(g) "Transit State" means a State upon whose territory emergency assistance destined for a Receiving State is transhipped or through whose territory assistance must be transported to reach the Receiving State.

ARTICLE 2

Objective of the Convention

The objective of this Convention is to expedite the delivery of assistance following disasters.

ARTICLE 3

Principles

1. Assistance provided under this Convention shall be in accordance with the following Principles:

(a) Respect for the sovereignty of the Receiving State and non-intereference in its internal affairs;

(b) Co-operation with the appropriate authorities of the Receiving State and respect for and observance of its laws;

(c) Abstention from any activity which is inconsistent with the objective of this Convention and from any commercial or political activity on the territory of the Receiving State.

2. The Receiving State shall have, within its territory, responsibility for facilitating the co-ordination of operations to meet the situation created by the disaster.

ARTICLE 4

Scope of application

1. This Convention applies to all assistance provided by an Assisting State or organization to a Receiving State.

2. This Convention shall apply during the whole period of the disaster and shall cease to apply on the termination of all relief operations.

Part II. Assistance

ARTICLE 5

Assistance

1. The basic conditions for the delivery of assistance in case of disaster are:

(a) Assistance shall be free of charge unless otherwise specified in this Convention or agreed between the Assisting State or organization and the Receiving State;

(b) The Receiving State shall ensure the most effective use of the assistance provided and shall use it for the purpose for which it is intended, unless otherwise agreed by the Assisting State or organization;

(c) Assistance shall be distributed or provided without discrimination of any kind such as race, colour, sex, language, religion, political or other opinion, national and social origin, birth or other status;

(d) The Parties to this Convention shall give priority to the delivery of assistance, including its transport, provision of the necessary transit facilities and distribution;

2. A Receiving State and an Assisting State or organization may agree to terms other than those contained in this Convention without derogating from the basic conditions of this Convention.

ARTICLE 6

Exchange of information

1. Parties to this Convention which obtain information about events which may lead to a disaster and which would assist the provision of assistance under this Convention should immediately notify those States likely to be affected, as well as the Office of the United Nations Disaster Relief Co-ordinator and/or other appropriate organizations.

2. Parties to this Convention which obtain information that may be useful in helping States affected by a disaster shall make such information available to the States affected and, with their agreement, to the Office of the United Nations Disaster Relief Co-ordinator and/or other appropriate organizations.

3. When the United Nations Disaster Relief Co-ordinator is requested or required to exercise his co-ordinating functions, the Parties to this Convention shall inform him about the development of the situation, the assistance needed and provided, and the relief consignments which are being or could be made available.

4. Information provided in confidence in connection with the assistance should be protected from disclosure by the recipient of the information to the maximum extent possible and should not be misused.

ARTICLE 7

Protection and facilities

1. The Receiving State shall take all practicable measures to ensure the security (*sureté*) of relief personnel and the protection of all premises, facilities, means of transport, relief consignments and equipment used in connection with the assistance.

2. The Receiving State shall [without prejudice to existing instruments on privileges and immunities to which it is a Party] grant to the Assisting State or organization and its personnel the necessary [privileges, immunities] protection and facilities for the expeditious performance of their functions under this Convention. In particular, the Receiving State shall:

(a) Promptly issue, without cost, multiple transit, entry and exit visas for personnel representing Assisting States or organizations;

(b) Facilitate freedom of access to and freedom of movement in the disaster area for such personnel in the performance of their agreed functions;

(c) Permit the Assisting State or organization and its personnel access to the site or sites outside the disaster area where its relief consignments and equipment are stored prior to distribution;

(d) Recognize university degrees, professional certificates and other certificates of competency and licences held by relief personnel and necessary for the performance of their agreed function;

(e) Waive any work permits that may be required under its laws;

(f) Waive income tax on the salaries and emoluments of the personnel of the Assisting State or organization [if the imposition of such taxation would involve double taxation].

3. The Receiving State shall return, or authorize and facilitate the re-export of, any material and equipment provided by the Assisting State or organization and not used for assistance purposes or which, having been used, the Assisting State or organization wishes to retain.

ARTICLE 8

Communications

1. The Receiving State shall, to the extent compatible with national security, authorize and facilitate disaster relief telecommunications required by the Assisting State or organization and [if necessary] authorize the Assisting State or organization to operate its own means of internal and external communications.

2. The Receiving State shall, to the extent possible, provide communications over national telecommunications networks on a priority basis and free of charge.

ARTICLE 9

Notification

1. The Assisting State or organization shall notify the designated authority in the Receiving State in advance of the dispatch of assistance, giving appropriate details, including in particular the intended time and place of arrival of personnel, relief consignments and equipment.

2. The Receiving State shall acknowledge to the Assisting State or organization the receipt of relief consignments. In case of loss or damage, the Receiving State shall immediately inform the Assisting State or organization or organizations and shall decide in consultation with it the measure to be taken.

ARTICLE 10

Qualitative nature of assistance

1. An Assisting State or organization shall ensure that its assistance is appropriate to the assessed needs and that it conforms to the traditions and usages in the Receiving State.

2. An Assisting State or organization shall ensure that its assistance complies with the quality, health and other relevant standards or regulations of the Receiving State, except in so far as these standards or regulations are waived or modified for the duration of the relief operations.

ARTICLE 11

Packaging, labelling and marking

The Assisting State or organization shall, whenever practicable, use an appropriate internationally established system for packaging, labelling and marking relief consignments.

ARTICLE 12

Identification

1. Assisting States or organizations which use an internationally recognized distinctive sign should use that sign to identify their relief consignments, equipment, means of transport, personnel and their locations as necessary.

2. Assisting States or organizations which do not use such a sign should use the international distinctive sign of civil defence. This is an equilateral blue triangle on an orange background.

3. Receiving States and Assisting States or organizations shall take measures necessary to supervise the display of these signs and to prevent their misuse.

ARTICLE 13

Exportation

1. Assisting States shall ensure that domestic export documentation requirements do not delay the dispatch of relief consignments and equipment.

2. Assisting States should limit their requirements for export documentation to a single form based on the United Nations Layout Key for Trade Documents. A model for such a form is appended to the present Convention.

3. Relief consignments and equipment shall be cleared rapidly and as a matter of priority by Customs authorities, and any examination shall be limited to that deemed necessary to ensure compliance with the laws and regulations which the Customs are responsible for enforcing.

4. Clearance, examination and relase of relief consignments shall, if necessary, be arranged outside the business hours of the Customs authorities and/or at a place other than a Customs office.

ARTICLE 14

Importation

1. The Receiving State shall exempt relief consignments and equipment from all customs duties and charges of any kind imposed on or in connection with importation and from all internal taxes or other internal charges of any kind.
2. The Receiving State shall exempt relief consignments and equipment from any import prohibitions or restrictions.
3. The Receiving State shall, to the extent possible, exempt relief consignments and equipment from regulations concerning health, hygiene and animal protection, where such regulations would delay importation.
4. The Receiving State shall ensure that domestic import documentation requirements do not delay the delivery of relief consignments and equipment.
5. The Receiving State should limit its requirements for import documentation to a single form based on the United Nations Layout Key for Trade Documents. A model for such a form is appended to the present Convention.
6. Relief consignments and equipment shall be cleared rapidly and as a matter of priority by Customs authorities, and any examination shall be limited to that deemed necessary to ensure compliance with the laws and regulations which the Customs are responsible for enforcing.
7. Clearance, examination and release of relief consignments shall, if necessary, be arranged outside the business hours of the Customs authorities and/or at a place other than a Customs office.

ARTICLE 15

Financial provisions

Unless otherwise agreed between an Assisting State or organization and the Receiving State, the Receiving State shall assume the costs of:

(a) The unloading, storing, handling, insuring, forwarding and distributing of relief consignments and equipment;

(b) The local administrative, personnel and logistics support needed for the delivery of assistance.

ARTICLE 16

Accounting

The Receiving State shall maintain such accounting and statistical records with respect to relief consignments and their distribution as may be agreed to be necessary and shall furnish upon request such records and reports to the Assisting State or organization.

ARTICLE 17

Irregularities

1. The Parties to this Convention shall, within their respective jurisdictions, initiate appropriate proceedings with respect to acts involving unlawful diversion or misappropriation of relief consignments or equipment.

2. The Assisting State or organization and the Receiving State shall bring to each other's attention any difficulties arising in the practical implementation of this Convention.

ARTICLE 18

Termination of assistance

The Receiving State or an Assisting State or organization may give notice of termination of assistance and where necessary the Parties to this Convention which are affected by such notice shall then arrange to bring the assistance to an orderly conclusion under the terms of this Convention.

Part III. Transport

ARTICLE 19

Facilities

1. The Parties to this Convention, whether Receiving, Assisting or Transit States, shall provide on a priority basis adequate means of transport and related services for the speedy transport of relief consignments and movement of relief personnel.

2. The Parties to this Convention shall facilitate the transport of assistance. They shall, to the extent possible, make appropriate arrangements to ensure expeditious handling, clearance, transshipment, storage and onward movement of relief consignments and equipment on or through their territories.

3. Where transport and related services cannot be provided free of charge, the charges shall be limited to the extent possible and in any case shall not be higher than those applied by the State concerned in the transport of its own supplies.

4. The Receiving State shall, in case of need, authorize the Assisting State or organization to operate its own means of transport.

ARTICLE 20

Transit

1. The Parties to this Convention shall:

(a) Grant the right of transit across or over their territories to the relief consignments, equipment and personnel of the Assisting State or organization, and to their means of transport, proceeding to or returning from the Receiving State;

(b) Exempt relief consignments and equipment from any requirements for bonding and from all customs duties or other charges of any kind imposed in connection with the transit;

(c) Ensure the security of assistance in transit through their territories.

2. The Parties to this Convention should limit their requirements for transit documentation to a single form based on the United Nations Layout Key for Trade Documents. A model for such a form is appended to the present Convention.

3. Examination by Customs authorities of relief consignments and equipment in transit shall be limited to that deemed necessary to ensure compliance with the laws and regulations which the Customs are responsible for enforcing.

ARTICLE 21

Air transport

1. The Parties to this Convention shall grant without undue delay permission for the overflight, landing and departure of civil aircraft operated by or on behalf of an Assisting State or organization for the transport of assistance. Such aircraft shall also be authorized to operate within the territory of the Receiving State as required for the delivery of assistance.

2. The operation of aircraft other than civil aircraft shall be subject to the prior authorization of the Party to this Convention within or over whose territory the aircraft would operate.

Part IV. Liability

ARTICLE 22

Liability

1. The Receiving State shall bear all risks and claims resulting from, occurring in the course of, or otherwise connected with the assistance rendered on its territory. In particular, the Receiving State shall be responsible for dealing with claims which might be brought by third parties against the Assisting State or organization or its personnel. The Receiving State shall hold the Assisting State or organization or its personnel harmless in case of any claim or liabilities in connection with the assistance, except in respect of liability of individuals having caused damage intentionally or recklessly with the knowledge that damage may result.

2. The Receiving State shall compensate the Assisting State or organization for the death of, or temporary or permanent injury to its personnel, as well as for loss of or damage to non-perishable equipment or materials, caused within its territory in connection with the assistance.

3. An Assisting State shall bear all risks and claims in connection with damage or injury occurring in its own territory.

4. This Article shall not prejudice any recourse action under the applicable national law, except that recourse actions can be brought against the personnel of an Assisting State or organization only in respect of damage or injury which they have caused intentionally or recklessly with the knowledge that damage may result.

Part V. Final Provisions

ARTICLE 23

Depositary

The Secretary-General of the United Nations shall be the depositary of this Convention and of all related instruments, notifications, declarations etc.

ARTICLE 24

Signature, ratification, acceptance, approval and accession by States

1. This Convention shall be open for signature to all States until [[a]]
2. This Convention is subject to ratification, acceptance or approval by signatory States.
3. This Convention shall remain open for accession by all States from the date when it is opened for signature.

ARTICLE 25

Acceptance by intergovernmental organizations

This Convention shall be open for acceptance by intergovernmental organizations, to be effected in the form of a notification.

ARTICLE 26

Undertaking of application by non-governmental organizations

1. Non-governmental organizations that are called upon to provide emergency assistance may undertake to apply the provisions of this Convention for the purpose of those operations in which they participate.
2. The undertaking shall be in the form of a written declaration.

---

[a] Not more than one year after the date of opening for signature.

ARTICLE 27

Entry into force

1. This Convention shall come into force on the thirtieth day following the date of deposit of the second instrument of ratification, acceptance, approval or accession by a State.

2. For each State or intergovernmental organization that ratifies, accepts or approves this Convention or accedes thereto after the deposit of the second instrument of ratification, acceptance, approval or accession by a State, this Convention shall enter into force on the thirtieth day after the deposit of the corresponding instrument.

ARTICLE 28

Provisional application

Any Party may, at the time of signature, ratification, acceptance, approval or accession, declare that it will apply this Convention provisionally pending entry into force in accordance with article 29, from such date as it will determine.

ARTICLE 29

Application of other agreements on emergency assistance

1. This Convention is without prejudice to the applicability of other agreements concluded by a Party before its entry into force.

2. The entry into force of this Convention shall not prevent a Party from subsequently concluding other agreements on emergency assistance provided that the rights and obligations of the other States and organizations applying the provisions of this Convention are not affected.

ARTICLE 30

Reservations

[Alternative A]

No reservations may be made in respect of any provision of this Convention.

[Alternative B]

Reservations may be made in respect of any provision of this Convention except [...].

ARTICLE 31

Settlement of disputes

[Alternative A]

1. Any dispute relating to the interpretation or application of this Convention shall be settled by direct negotiations between the parties to the dispute or, failing this, shall be settled in accordance with such procedures as may be adopted by a [two-thirds] majority of the Parties to this Convention.

2. Where the dispute involves a non-governmental organization having undertaken to comply with the provisions of this Convention, the decision referred to in paragraph 1 of this article shall provide for equitable participation by that organization in the settlement procedures.

[Alternative B]

1. Any dispute relating to the interpretation or application of this Convention shall be settled by direct negotiations between the parties to the dispute or, failing this, shall be submitted to arbitration if a [two-thirds] majority of the Parties to this Convention so agrees.

2. For the purpose of arbitration:

(a) The parties to a bilateral dispute shall each designate one arbitrator, and the arbitrators so designated shall in turn elect a third arbitrator, who shall serve as the chairman of the arbitral commission.

(b) The parties to a multilateral dispute shall, by unanimous decision, designate a chairman and two other arbitrators.

(c) Should the parties to the dispute or their arbitrators fail to effect the required designations, any party to the dispute may request the President of the International Court of Justice to effect such designation.

ARTICLE 32

Amendments and revision

1. Any Party may propose amendments to this Convention. The text of the proposed amendment shall be communicated to the depositary for the purpose of circulation among the Parties. The proposed amendment shall be deemed to have been accepted if, within ninety days from the date of circulation, no objection has been notified to the depositary by any of the Parties.

2. Apart from the procedure in paragraph 1 above, any Party may, by a notification to the depositary, request the convening of a review conference to revise this Convention. The depositary shall make arrangements for the convening of such a conference if, within [three] months from the circulation of the request, a majority of the Parties have expressly agreed thereto.

ARTICLE 33

Denunciation

1. Any Party may at any time denounce this Convention by written notification to the despositary.

2. The denunciation shall take effect upon the expiry of a period of one year from the date of deposit of the notification.

Done at . . . . on . . . .
in one original in the Arabic, Chinese, English, French, Russian and Spanish texts, all being equally authentic.

(Source: Doc.A/39/267/Add. 2 – E/1984/96/Add. 2, 18 June 1984).

BIBLIOGRAPHY

Ads, O.H., *International Disaster and International Law*, Ph.D. Thesis No. 3592, University of Sheffield, 1974.
— *Prevention and Relief of International Disasters*, Munich, EVG Export Verlag, 1980.
Aga Khan, S., 'Legal Problems Relating to Refugees and Displaced Persons', 149 *RdC* 1976-I, p. 290.
— 'Disasters: myth and reality', *UNDRO News*, November/December 1983, pp. 6-10.
Alexandrowicz, C.H., *World Economic Agencies*, London, 1962.
— *The Law-Making Functions of the Specialised Agencies of the United Nations*, Angus & Robertson, 1973.
Alston, P., 'Human Rights and Basic Needs', 12 *RDH* 1979, p. 19.
— *Development and the Rule of Law*, International Commission of Jurists, Conference on Development and the Rule of Law, 27 April - 1 May 1981, Basic work paper, 1981.
Asher, R.E., *et al, The United Nations and Promotion of the General Welfare*, 3 vols., Brookings Institute, 1957.

Balogh, E., 'World Peace and the Refugee Problem', 75 *RdC* 1949-II, p. 363.
Baradei, M. El, *et al, Model Rules for Disaster Relief Operations*, Policy and Efficacy Studies No. 8, UNITAR, 1982.
Barton, J.L. *Near East Relief 1915-30*, Macmillan, New York, 1930.
Basdevant, J., 'Deux Conventions Peu Connues sur le Droit de la Guerre', XXI *RGDIP* 1914, p. 3.
Baxter, R.R., 'Humanitarian Law or Humanitarian Politics? The 1974 Diplomatic Conference on Humanitarian Law', 16 *HILJ* 1975, p. 1.
Bekele, M., *et al, Food and Population*, FAO, Rome, 1976.
Bello, E.G., *African Customary Humanitarian Law*, Oyez/ICRC Geneva, 1980.
Belshaw, H., 'The Food and Agriculture Organization of the United Nations', 1 *International Organization* 1947, p. 291.
Berkowitz, M., 'Bangladesh', 14 *HILJ* 1973, p. 565.
Bernhardt, R. (ed.), *Encyclopedia of Public International Law*, North-Holland, Amsterdam, 1981-.
Best, G., *Humanity in Warfare*, London, 1980.
Bighinatti, E.V., 'Natural Disasters: The Voluntary Agency Role', 89 *ICVA News* April 1981, p. 2.
Bindschedler-Robert, D., 'Red Cross', in Bernhardt, R. (ed.), *Encyclopedia of Public International Law.*
Black, C.E. and Falk, R.A. (eds.), *The Future of the International Legal Order*, 3 vols., Princeton UP, 1971.
Bleicher, S.A., 'The Legal Significance of Re-citation of General Assembly Resolutions', 63 *AJIL* 1969, p. 444.
Bloch, J., *Les Inscriptions d'Açoka*, Les Belles Lettres, Paris, 1950.
Borel, E., 'L'Organisation Internationale de la Croix-Rouge', 1 *RdC* 1923, p. 569.
Borgeaud, M.-A., *L'Union Internationale de Secours*, Recueil Sirey, Paris, 1932. (Also Thèse No. 371, Faculté de Droit, Université de Genève, 1931.)
Bothe, M., 'Rechtsprobleme humanitärer Hilfaktionen zugunsten der Zivilbevölkerung bei bewaffneten Konflikten', in *Beiträge zur Weiterentwicklung des humanitären Völkerrechts für bewaffnete Konflikte*, Hamburg, 1973, p. 24.
— 'Relief Actions', in Bernhardt, R. (ed.), *Encyclopedia of Public International Law.*
Bourquin, M., 'Pouvoir Scientifique et Droit International', 70 *RdC* 1947-I, p. 331.
Breycha-Vauthier, A.C., 'L'Ordre S.M. Jérosolymitain de Malte, Evolutions Récentes', 16 *ZaöRV* 1955/6, p. 500.

Breycha-Vauthier, A.C. and Potulicki, M., 'The Order of St. John in International Law', 48 *AJIL* 1954, p. 554.
Brown, B.J., 'The United Nations and Disaster Relief in the Sahel, 1973-75', 1 *The International Journal of Disaster Studies and Practice* 1977, p. 145.
— *Disaster Preparedness and the United Nations*, UNITAR, New York, 1979.
Brownlie, I., *International Law and the Use of Force by States*, OUP, 1963.
Bruha, T., 'Internationale Regelungen zum Schutz vor technisch-industriellen Umweltnotfällen', 44 *ZaöRV* 1984, p. 1.
Burley, L.A., 'Disaster Relief Administration in the Third World', XV *International Development Review* 1973, p. 8.
Burwell, D.G., 'Civilian Protection in Modern Warfare', 14 *VJIL* 1973-4, p. 123.
Byrne, M.D., 'The International Relief Union', 134 *The Contemporary Review* 1928, p. 365.

Carl, B.M., 'American Assistance to Victims of the Nigeria-Biafra War: Defects in the Prescriptions on Foreign Disaster Relief', 12 *HILJ* 1971, p. 191.
Cassin, R., 'Les Droits de l'Homme', 140 *RdC* 1974-IV, p. 321.
Chacko, C.J., 'International Law in India', 1 *IJIL* 1960-1, pp. 184-192, 589-598; 2 *IJIL* 1962, pp. 48-64.
Chen, L.C., *Disaster in Bangladesh*, Oxford UP, 1973.
Chiang, Pei-heng, *Non-Governmental Organizations at the United Nations*, Praeger, 1981.
Ciraolo, G., *L'Unione Internazionale di Soccorso*, Rome, 1934.
— 'Secours international aux populations', *Dictionnaire Diplomatique*, Académie Diplomatique Internationale, Paris, 1973, p. 693.
Clos, P., 'Projet pour servir à la création d'un Organisme International de Sauvetage', undated, UN Library, Palais des Nations, Geneva, Call No. 362 A1 No. 32.
Copans, J. (ed.), *Sécheresses et Famines du Sahel*, 2 vols., Paris, 1975.
Coursier, H., 'Définition du Droit Humanitaire', *AFDI* 1955, p. 223.
— 'L'Evolution du Droit International Humanitaire', 99 *RdC* 1960-I, p. 361.
— *The International Red Cross*, ICRC, Geneva, 1961.
— 'The Red Cross and Refugees', *IRevRC* 1966, p. 631.
Cuny, F.C., *Disasters and Development*, OUP, 1983.

Dacy, D.C. and Kunreuther, H., *The Economics of Natural Disasters*, Free Press, USA, 1969.
D'Amato, A.A., 'On Consensus', VIII *CYIL* 1970, p. 104.
— *The Concept of Custom in International Law*, Cornell UP, 1971.
Daniel, P., *Deep'n as It Come, The 1927 Mississippi River Flood*, Oxford UP, 1977.
Davis, I., *Shelter After Disaster*, Oxford Polytechnic Press, 1978.
Davis, M., 'Some Political Dimensions of International Relief: Two Cases', 28 *International Organization* 1974, p. 127.
Davis, M. (ed.), *Civil Wars and the Politics of International Relief*, Praeger, New York, 1975.
Davis, M. and Seitz, S.T., 'Disasters and Governments', 26 *Journal of Conflict Resolution* 1982, pp. 547-568.
De Schutter, B., 'De Rol van de Verenigde Naties in Humanitaire Interventies', in *Miscellanea, W.J. Ganshof van der Meersch*, 3 vols., 1972, Vol. 1, p. 435.
Des Gouttes, P., *Commentaire de la Convention de Genève du 27 juillet 1929*, Geneva, 1930.
Diallo, I.B.Y., *Les réfugiés en Afrique*, Vienna, Stuttgart, Braumüller, 1974.
Diallo, Y., 'Humanitarian Law and Traditional African Law', *IRevRC* 1976, p. 57 and 'African Tradition and Humanitarian Law', *IRevRC* 1976, p. 387.
Dimbleby, J., 'Acts of Man', 94 *New Statesman*, 29 July 1977, p. 141.
Dinstein, Y., 'The International Law of Civil Wars and Human Rights', 6 *IYHR* 1976, p. 62.
— 'The International Law of Inter-State Wars and Human Rights', 7 *IYHR* 1977, p. 139.
Draper, G.I.A.D., 'The Geneva Conventions of 1949', 114 *RdC* 1965-I, p. 59.
— 'The Law of Ransom during the Hundred Years War', 7 *RDPMDG* 1968, p. 263.

Drost, P.N., *Human Rights as Legal Rights*, Leiden, 1951.
Dunant, H., *Un Souvenir de Solférino*, Geneva, 1862. (Also as *A Memory of Solferino*, British Red Cross Society, London, 1947.)
— 'A Proposal for Introducing Uniformity into the Conditions of Prisoners of War', 2nd ed., London, 1872.
— 'Addresse aux Nations de l'Extrême-Orient', VIIIe Congrès Universel de la Paix, Hamburg, 14 August 1897.
Dynes, R.R., *Organized Behaviour in Disasters*, Heath Lexington, 1970.

Earthscan, *Natural Disasters: Acts of God or Acts of Man*, London, 1984.
El-Farhan, A.H., *The United Nations Relief and Works Agency for Palestine Refugees in the Near East*, Ph.D. Thesis, New York University, 1979.
El-Khawas, M., 'A Reassessment of International Relief Programs', in Glantz, M.H. (ed.), *The Politics of Natural Disaster, The Case of the Sahel Drought*, Praeger, 1976, p. 77.
Emden, A. van, 'The Special Position of the Red Cross', *IRevRC* 1966, p. 321.
Eze, O.C., 'Les Droits de l'Homme et le Sous-Développement', 12 *RDH* 1979, p. 5.

Fairley, H.S., 'State Actors, Humanitarian Intervention and International Law: Reopening Pandora's Box', 10 *Georgia Journal of International and Comparative Law* 1980, p. 29.
Falk, R.A., 'The US and the Doctrine of Nonintervention in the Internal Affairs of Independent States', 5 *Howard LJ* 1959, p. 163.
— 'On the Quasi-Legislative Competence of the General Assembly of the United Nations', 60 *AJIL* 1966, p. 782.
Falk, R.A. (ed.), *The Vietnam War and International Law*, 4 vols., Princeton UP, 1968-76.
Farer, T.J., 'Definition of International Armed Conflict', *RBDI* 1971, p. 20.
Farran, C. d'O., 'The Sovereign Order of Malta in International Law', 3 *ICLQ* 1954, p. 217.
Fischer, B. de, 'L'Ordre Souverain de Malte', 163 *RdC* 1969-II, p. 1.
Fisher, H.H., *The Famine in Soviet Russia, 1919-1923*, USA, 1927.
Fitzmaurice, G., 'The Future of Public International Law and of the International Legal System in the Circumstances of Today', Institut de Droit International, *Livre du Centenaire 1873-1973*, 1973, p. 196.
Forsythe, D.P., 'UNRWA, The Palestine Refugees, and World Politics: 1949-69', 25 *International Organization* 1971, p. 26.
— 'The Present Role of the Red Cross in Protection', Joint Committee for the Reappraisal of the Red Cross, Background Paper No. 1, 1975.
— 'Who Guards the Guardians: Third Parties and the Law of Armed Conflict', 70 *AJIL* 1976, p. 41.
— 'Political Prisoners: The Law and Politics of Protection', *VJTL* 1976, p. 295.
— 'The Red Cross as Transnational Movement', 30 *International Organization* 1976, p. 607.
— *Humanitarian Politics*, JHUP, 1977.
Fowler, D.B., 'The Developing Jurisdiction of the UN High Commissioner for Refugees', 7 *RDH* 1974, p. 119.
Franck, T.M. and Rodley, N.S., 'After Bangladesh: The Law of Humanitarian Intervention by Military Force', 67 *AJIL* 1973, p. 275.
Freymond, J., 'The ICRC within the International System', *IRevRC* 1972, p. 245.
— 'Confronting Total War: A 'Global' Humanitarian Policy', 67 *AJIL* 1973, p. 672.
— *Guerres, Révolutions, Croix-Rouge*, Institut Universitaire de Hautes Etudes Internationales, Geneva, 1976.
Friedman, L. (ed.), *The Law of War, A Documentary History*, Vol. 1, New York, 1972.
Friedmann, W., 'The Uses of 'General Principles' in the Development of International Law', 57 *AJIL* 1963, p. 279.
— *The Changing Structure of International Law*, London, 1964.

— 'The Relevance of International Law to the Process of Economic and Social Development', 60 *ASIL* 1966, p. 8.
— 'General Course', 127 *RdC* 1969-II, p. 47.
— 'Human Welfare and International Law', in *Transnational Law in a Changing Society* (ed.), Colombia UP, 1972, p. 113.
Fry, A.R., *A Quaker Adventure*, London, 1926.

Ganji, M., *International Protection of Human Rights*, Geneva, 1962.
Gay, G.I., *The Commission for Relief in Belgium, Statistical Review of Relief Operations*, Stanford UP, 1925.
Gay, G.I. and Fisher H.H., *Public Relations of the Commission for Relief in Belgium, Documents*, 2 vols., Stanford UP, 1929.
Genot, G., 'L'Aide Internationale d'Urgence en Cas de Catastrophe', XXIX *Studia Diplomatica* 1976, p. 313.
Ginsburgs, G., 'The Soviet Union and the Problem of Refugees and Displaced Persons, 1917-1956', 51 *AJIL* 1957, p. 325.
Glahn, G. von, 'The Protection of Human Rights in Time of Armed Conflict', 1 *IYHR* 1971, p. 208.
Glantz, M.H. (ed.), *The Politics of Natural Disaster, The Case of the Sahel Drought*, Praeger, New York, 1976.
Goodrich, L.M. and Hambro, E., *Charter of the United Nations, Commentary and Documents*, 3rd. ed., London, 1969.
Goodwin-Gill, G.S., *The Refugees in International Law*, Clarendon, Oxford, 1983.
Gorgé, C., *The International Relief Union*, IRU, Geneva, 1938.
Gottlieb, G.A.G., 'International Assistance to Civilian Populations in Armed Conflicts', 4 *NYUJILP* 1971, p. 403.
— 'The United Nations and Emergency Humanitarian Assistance in India-Pakistan', 66 *AJIL* 1972, p. 362.
Graham, M.W., 'Humanitarian Intervention', XXII *Michigan LR* 1923-4, p. 312.
Grahl-Madsen, A., *The Status of Refugees in International Law*, 2 vols., Sijthoff, Vol. 1, 1966; Vol. 2, 1972.
— *Territorial Asylum*, Oceana, 1980.
— 'The League of Nations and the Refugees', *AWR Bulletin*, No. 2, 1982, pp. 86-97.
— 'International Refugee Law Today and Tomorrow', *Archiv des Völkerrechts*, 1982, pp. 411-467.
— 'Identifying the World's Refugees', 467 *Annals of the American Academy of Political and Social Science* 1983, pp. 11-23.
Grahl-Madsen, A. and Toman, J. (eds.), *The Spirit of Uppsala*, Proceedings of the Joint UNITAR-Uppsala University Seminar on International Law and Organization for a New World Order, Uppsala 9-18 June 1981, Walter de Gruyter, 1984.
Green, L.C., 'The Individual and his Status in International Law', 1 *IJIL* 1960-1, p. 415.
— *Law and Society*, Sijthoff, 1975.
Green, S., *International Disaster Relief*, McGraw-Hill, 1977.
Green, S. and Stephens, L.H. (eds.), *Disaster Assistance*, New York UP, 1979.
Griffith, S.B., *Sun Tzu, The Art of War*, Oxford UP, 1963.
Gross, L., 'United Nations and the Role of Law', 19 *International Organization* 1965, p. 537.
Gurlt, E., *Zur Geschichte der internationalen und freiwilligen Krankenpflege im Krieg*, Leipzig, 1873.
Gutteridge, J.A.C., *The UN in a Changing World*, Manchester UP, 1969.

Hagman, G., et al, *Prevention Better than Cure, Report on human and environmental disasters in the Third World*, Swedish Red Cross, Stockholm and Geneva, 1984.
Hambidge, G., *The Story of FAO*, New York, 1955.

Hambro, E., *Fridtjof Nansen*, Oslo, 1976.
Hammarskjold, D., 'Liberty and Law in International Life', in *International Law in a Changing World* (ed.), Oceana, New York, 1963, p. 22.
Hanning, H., *The Peaceful Uses of Military Forces*, Praeger, 1967.
Henkin, L., 'The UN and Human Rights', 19 *International Organization* 1965, p. 504.
Herczegh, G., 'Recent Problems of International Humanitarian Law', in Haraszti, G. (ed.), *Questions of International Law*, Sijthoff-Akademiai Kiado, 1977, p. 77.
Heuven Goedhart, G.J. van, 'The Problem of Refugees', 82 *RdC* 1953-I, p. 265.
Higgins, R., *The Development of International Law Through the Political Organs of the United Nations*, Oxford UP, 1963.
Hill, M., *Towards Greater Order, Coherence and Co-ordination in the UN System*, UNITAR Research Report No. 20, 1974.
Hocké, J.-P., 'Action humanitaire: protection et assistance', *RevICR* 1984, p. 11.
Holborn, L.W., *The International Refugee Organization*, Oxford UP, 1956.
— *Refugees: A Problem of Our Times*, 2 vols., New Jersey, 1975.
Holdsworth, D., 'The Present Role of the Red Cross in Assistance', Joint Committee for the Reappraisal of the Red Cross, Background Paper No. 3, 1975.
Hoover, H., *Years of Adventure: 1874-1920*, Macmillan, New York, 1961.
Huber, M., 'Principes d'Action et Fondements de l'Oeuvre du CICR 1939-46', *RevICR* 1947, p. 45.
— *L'Idée de la Croix-Rouge*, Geneva, 1953.
— *La Pensée et l'Action de la Croix-Rouge*, Geneva, 1954.

Jacobson, H.K., *The USSR and the UN's Economic and Social Activities*, Notre Dame UP, 1963.
Jenks, C.W., *The Common Law of Mankind*, Stevens, London, 1958.
— 'Law, Freedom and Welfare in Action for Peace', in *International Law in a Changing World* (ed.), Oceana, New York, 1963, p. 1.
— *A New World of Law*, Longmans, London, 1969.
Jennings, R.Y., 'Some International Law Aspects of the Refugee Question', XX *BYIL* 1939, p. 98.
— 'The Progress of International Law', XXXIV *BYIL* 1958, p. 334.
— 'International Law', In Bernhardt, R. (ed.), *Encyclopedia of Public International Law*.
Jessup, P.C., 'International Law in the Post-War Period', 36 *AJIL* 1942, p. 49.
— 'Political and Humanitarian Approaches to Limitation of Warfare', 51 *AJIL* 1957, p. 757.
— 'A Half-Century of Efforts to Substitute Law for War', 99 *RdC* 1960-I, p. 1.

Kalshoven, R., *The Law of Warfare, A Summary of its Recent History and Trends in Development*, Sijthoff, Henry Dunant Institute, 1973.
— 'Reaffirmation and Development of International Humanitarian Law Applicable in Armed Conflicts, The Diplomatic Conference, Geneva 1974-1977', 8 *NYIL* 1977, pp. 107-135; 9 *NYIL* 1978, pp. 107-171.
Kaplan, M.A. and Katzenbach, N. de B., *The Political Foundations of International Law*, New York, 1961.
Kelsen, H., *The Law of the United Nations*, Praeger, 1950.
Kennedy, E.M., 'International Humanitarian Assistance', 12 *VJIL* 1972, p. 299.
Kimminich, O., *Humanitäres Völkerrecht – Humanitäre Aktion*, Kaiser-Grünewald, Munich, 1972.
— 'History of the Law of Nations, Since World War II', in Bernhardt, R. (ed.), *Encyclopedia of Public International Law*.
Knitel, H.G., 'Les Délégations du Comité International de la Croix-Rouge', XVI *ÖZöRV* 1966, p. 304.
— 'Le Rôle de la Croix-Rouge dans la Protection Internationale des Droits de l'Homme', XIX *ÖZöRV* 1969, p. 1.
Köck, H.F., *Die völkerrechtliche Stellung des Heiligen Stuhls*, Duncker & Humblot, Berlin, 1975.
Krimgold, F., *The Role of International Aid for Pre-Disaster Planning in Developing Countries*, Avdelningen För Arkitektur, Stockholm, 1974.

Kröger, E., *International Assistance in Natural Disasters*, Dissertation for the Academic Diploma in Tropical Public Health, University of London, London School of Hygiene and Tropical Medicine, No. 150, June 1971.
Kunz, J.L., 'Plus de Lois de la Guerre?', XLI *RGDIP* 1934, p. 22.
— 'The Status of the Holy See in International Law', 46 *AJIL* 1952, p. 308.
— 'The Laws of War', 50 *AJIL* 1956, p. 313.
— 'The New US Army Field Manual on the Law of Land Warfare', 51 *AJIL* 1957, p. 388.

Lachs, M., 'The Law in and of the United Nations', 1 *IJIL* 1960-61, p. 429.
Lador-Lederer, J.J., *International Non-Governmental Organizations*, Sijthoff, 1963.
— *International Group Protection*, Sijthoff, 1968.
Langeais, G., *Les Nations Unies face aux catastrophes naturelles*, Librairie générale de droit et de jurisprudence, Paris, 1977.
La Pradelle, P. de G. de, 'L'Organisation des Secours Aériens en Cas de Désastre Naturel', XXXV *Revue Générale de l'Air et de l'Espace* 1972, p. 129.
— 'Réflexions sur la Troisième Session de la Conférence Diplomatique de Genève sur le Droit International Humanitaire', 27 *ADIM* 1977, p. 7.
La Pradelle, P. de G. de and Voncken, J., 'Le Secours International et les Calamités Publiques', *La Revue des Deux Mondes* 15 February 1960, p. 680.
Lauterpacht, E. (ed.), *H. Lauterpacht, International Law: Collected Papers*, 4 vols., Vol. 2, Cambridge UP, 1975.
Lauterpacht, H., 'The Law of Nations, the Law of Nature and the Rights of Man', XXIX *TGS* 1943, p. 1.
— 'The Grotian Tradition in International Law', XXIII *BYIL* 1946, p. 1.
— 'The Universal Declaration of Human Rights', XXV *BYIL* 1948, p. 354.
— *International Law and Human Rights*, London, Stevens, 1950.
Lazareff, S., *Status of Military Forces under Current International Law*, Sijthoff, 1971.
Ledermann, L., 'The International Organization of the Red Cross and the League of Red Cross Societies', 42 *AJIL* 1948, p. 635.
Lendorf, A., 'Quelques aspects logistiques des activités d'assistance du CICR', *RevICR* 1983, pp. 71-81.
Levie, H.S., *Prisoners of War in International Armed Conflict, Documents on Prisoners of War*, 2 vols., 1978-1979.
Liang, Y.-L., 'Access to UN Headquarters of Representatives of Non-Governmental Organizations in Consultative Status', 48 *AJIL* 1954, p. 434.
Lillich, R.B., 'Forcible Self-Help by States to Protect Human Rights', 53 *Iowa LR* 1967, p. 325
— 'Intervention to Protect Human Rights', 15 *McGill LJ* 1969, p. 205.
— 'Humanitarian Intervention: A Reply to Ian Brownlie and a Plea for Constructive Alternatives', in Moore, J.N. (ed.), *Law and Civil War in the Modern World*, Johns Hopkins, 1974, p. 229.
Lillich, R.B. (ed.), *Humanitarian Intervention and the United Nations*, Virginia UP, 1973.
Long, F., 'The Impact of Natural Disasters on Third World Agriculture', 37 *American Journal of Economics and Sociology* 1978, p. 149.
Luard, E., *International Agencies: The Emerging Framework of Interdependence*, Macmillan, 1977.

Macalister-Smith, P., 'International Disaster Relief: Recent Developments in the United Nations', 2 *The International Journal of Disaster Studies and Practice* 1978, p. 201.
— 'Human Rights and Disaster Relief', 5 *Holdsworth Law Review* 1980, p.173.
— 'The International Relief Union', 5 *The International Journal of Disaster Studies and Practice* 1981, p. 147.
— 'The EEC and International Humanitarian Assistance', *Legal Issues of European Integration* 1981/1, p. 89.

— 'Comity', in Bernhardt, R. (ed.), *Encyclopedia of Public International Law.*
— 'United Nations Relief and Works Agency for Palestine Refugees in the Near East', in Bernhardt, R. (ed.), *Encyclopedia of Public International Law.*
Macdonald, R.St.J., *et al* (eds.), *The International Law and Policy of Human Welfare*, Sijthoff, 1978.
Mangone, G.J. (ed.), *United Nations Administration of Economic and Social Programs*, Columbia UP, 1966.
Manning, D.H., *Disaster Technology: An Annotated Bibliography*, Oxford, 1976.
Marks, S.P., 'Principles and Norms of Human Rights Applicable in Emergency Situations: Underdevelopment, Catastrophes and Armed Conflicts', in Vasak, K. (ed.), *The International Dimensions of Human Rights*, UNESCO, 1982, Vol. 1, p. 175.
Meredith, B., 'Forbodings of Disaster', 26 *International Organization* 1972, p. 699.
Mertens, P., 'Les Modalités de l'Intervention du Comité International de la Croix-Rouge dans le Conflit du Nigéria', XV *AFDI* 1969, p. 183.
Meurant, J., 'Principles on the Protection of Disaster Victims', *Panorama*, LRCS, 1977/6, p. 3.
— 'Apropos the New Constitution of the League of Red Cross Societies', *IRevRC* 1978, pp. 192 and 250.
Meyer, M.A., 'Development in Disaster Relief Laws and Organization: The Emergency Phase', 86 *ICVA News*, July 1980, p. 24.
Mitrany, D., 'The Functional Approach to World Organization', XXIV *International Affairs* 1948, p. 350.
Montandon, R., 'Pour une Coordination de l'Effort Scientifique dans la Lutte contre les Calamités', Société de Géographie, Genève, 1927.
Moore, J.N., 'The Control of Foreign Intervention in Internal Conflict', 9 *VJIL* 1969, p. 205.
Moore, J.N. (ed.), *Law and Civil War in the Modern World*, Johns Hopkins UP, 1974.
Moreillon, J., *Le Comité international de la Croix-Rouge et la Protection des détenus politiques*, Institut Henry Dunant, 1973.
Morison, R.F., 'International Disaster Action: advancing slowly, but how surely?', 4 *The International Journal of Disaster Studies and Practice* 1980, p. 93.
Morse, B., 'Practice, Norms and Reform of International Humanitarian Rescue Operations', 157 *RdC* 1977-IV, pp. 125-189.
Mudge, G.A., 'Starvation as a Means of Warfare', 4 *The International Lawyer* 1970, p. 228.
Münch, F., 'Die Martens'sche Klausel und die Grundlagen des Völkerrechts', 36 *ZaöRV* 1976, pp. 347-373.

Nanda, V.P., 'The US Action in the 1965 Dominican Crisis', 43 *Denver LJ* 1966, p. 439.
— 'A Critique of UN Inaction in the Bangaldesh Crisis', 49 *Denver LJ* 1972, p. 53.
— 'Humanitarian Intervention and the UN', 14 *VJIL* 1974, p. 791.
Nikam, N.A. and McKeon, R. (eds.), *The Edicts of Asoka*, Phoenix, USA, 1966.

O'Connell, D.P., *International Law*, 2 vols., Vol. 1, 1965.
Oliver, T.W., *The UN in Bangladesh*, Princeton UP, 1978.
Oppenheim, L., *International Law*, Lauterpacht, H. (ed.), 2 vols., Vol. 1, 8th ed., 1955; Vol. 2, 7th ed., 1952.

Parry, C., *The Sources and Evidences of International Law*, Manchester UP, 1965.
Patrnogic, J., 'International Institute of Humanitarian Law: Some Reflections on the Protection of Human Beings', 10 *The International Lawyer* 1976, p. 551.
— 'Protection de la Personne Humaine au Cours des Catastrophes Naturelles', 27 *ADIM* 1977, p. 16.
— 'Protection from Disasters – A Human Right', *UNDRO News*, March 1980, p. 5.
Paxman, J.M. and Boggs, G.T. (eds.), *The United Nations: A Reassessment, Sanctions, Peacekeeping and Humanitarian Assistance*, Virginia, 1973.

Perruchoud, R., *Les Résolutions des Conférences Internationales de la Croix-Rouge*, Institut Henry-Dunant, 1979.
— *International Responsibilities of National Red Cross and Red Crescent Societies*, Henry Dunant Institute, Geneva, 1982.
Pictet, J. *et al*, *Commentary, The Geneva Conventions of August 12 1949*, 4 vols., ICRC, Geneva, 1952-1960.
— 'Le Signe de la Croix–Rouge', *RevICR* 1949, p. 167.
— 'La Croix-Rouge et les Conventions de Genève', 76 *RdC* 1950-I, p. 1.
— *Red Cross Principles*, ICRC, Geneva, 1956.
— 'The Development of International Humanitarian Law', in *International Law in a Changing World*, (ed.), Oceana, New York, 1963, p. 114.
— 'The Principles of International Humanitarian Law', *IRevRC* 1966, p. 455.
— *Humanitarian Law and the Protection of War Victims*, Sijthoff-Henry Dunant Institute, 1975.
— 'The Fundamental Principles of the Red Cross', *IRevRC* 1979, pp. 130f.
— *Les principes fondamentaux de la Croix-Rouge. Commentaire*, Geneva, Institut Henry Dunant, 1979.
Plender, R., *International Migration Law*, Sijthoff, 1972.
— 'Admission of Refugees: Draft Convention on Territorial Asylum', 15 *San Diego LR* 1977, p. 45.
Prantner, R., *Malteserorden und Völkergemeinschaft*, Berlin, Munich, 1974.
Proudfoot, M.J., *European Refugees: 1939-52*, London, Faber and Faber, 1956.

Quarantelli, E.L. (ed.), *Disasters, Theory and Research*, Sage, 1978.

Ramcharan, B.G., *Humanitarian Good Offices in International Law*, Martinus Nijhoff, 198^.
Rechid, A., 'L'Islam et le Droit des Gens', 60 *RdC* 1937-II, p. 371.
Reid, I., 'The Evolution of the Red Cross', Joint Committee for the Reappraisal of the Red Cross, Background Paper No. 2, 1975.
Reut-Nicolussi, E., 'Displaced Persons and International Law', 73 *RdC* 1948-II, p. 1.
Rich, R.A., 'The Right to Development as an Emerging Human Right', 23 *VJIL* 1983, pp. 287-328.
Rodgers, R.S., *Facilitation Problems of International Associations*, Union of International Associations, Publ. No. 171, Brussels, 1960.
Rosas, A., *The Legal Status of Prisoners of War*, Helsinki, 1976.
Rosenau, J.N. (ed.), *International Aspects of Civil Strife*, Princeton UP, 1964.
Rougier, A., 'La Théorie de l'Intervention d'Humanité', 17 *RGDIP* 1910, p. 468.
Ruegger, P., 'The Juridical Aspects of the Organization of the International Red Cross', 82 *RdC* 1953-I, p. 483.

Salzberg, J., 'UN Prevention of Human Rights Violations: The Bangladesh Case', 27 *International Organization* 1973, p. 115.
Samuels, J.W., 'Human Rights in Man-Made Disasters: International Law, Government Policy and the Nigerian Experience", X *CYIL* 1972, p. 3.
— 'Commentary', in Paxman, J.M. and Boggs, G.T., *The United Nations: A Reassessment, Sanctions, Peacekeeping, and Humanitarian Assistance*, 1973, p. 135.
— 'Organized Responses to Natural Disasters', in Macdonald, R.St.J. *et al*, *The International Law and Policy of Human Welfare*, 1978, pp. 675-690.
— 'The Relevance of International Law to the Prevention and Mitigation of Natural Disasters', in Green, S. and Stephens, L. (eds.), *Disaster Assistance*, 1979, p. 245.
Sandoz, Y., 'The Application of Humanitarian Law by the Armed Forces of the United Nations Organization', *IRevRC* 1978, p. 274.
— 'La Place des Protocoles additionels aux Conventions de Genève du 12 août 1949 dans le droit humanitaire', 12 *RDH* 1979, p. 135.
Sastry, K.R.R., 'Hinduism and International Law', 117 *RdC* 1966-I, p. 503.

Saunders, H.St.G., 'The Red Cross and the White', London, 1949.
Schachter, O., 'The Evolving Law of International Development', 15 *CJTL* 1976, p. 1.
— *Sharing the World's Resources*, Columbia UP, 1977.
Schachter, O., *et al, Toward Wider Acceptance of UN Treaties*, UNITAR, New York, 1971.
Schindler, D. and Toman, J. (eds.), *The Law of Armed Conflicts, A Collection of Conventions, Resolutions and Other Documents*, Sijthoff-Leiden, 1973.
Schnyder, R., 'Les Aspects Juridiques Actuels du Problème des Réfugiés', 114 *RdC* 1965-I, p. 339.
Schwarzenberger, G., *International Law and Order*, Stevens, 1971.
Sharp, W.R., 'Field Administration in the UN System', Stevens, 1961.
Sheets, H. and Morris, R., *Disaster in the Desert, Failures of International Relief in the West African Drought*, Humanitarian Policy Studies, Carnegie Endowment for International Peace, 1974.
Simmonds, K.R., 'The Lomé Convention and the New International Economic Order', 13 *CMLRev* 1976, pp. 315-334.
— 'The Second Lomé Convention: The Innovative Features', 17 *CMLRev* 1980, pp. 415-435.
Simpson, J. Hope, *The Refugee Problem*, Oxford UP, 1939.
Singh, N., 'International Law in India', 2 *IJIL* 1962, pp. 65-82, 143-163, 318-355; 3 *IJIL* 1963, pp. 44-62.
Skeet, M., *Manual for Disaster Relief Work*, Churchill Livingstone, 1977.
Skjelsbaek, K., 'The Growth of International Non-Governmental Organisations in the Twentieth Century', 25 *International Organization* 1971, p. 420.
Smith, D.C. (ed.), 'Disasters and Disaster Relief', 309 *Annals of the American Academy of Political and Social Science*, January 1957.
Socini Leyendecker, R., *Le Azioni di Soccorso nel Diritto Internazionale Umanitario*, Milan, 1979.
Sohn, L.B. and Buergenthal, T., *International Protection of Human Rights*, Bobbs-Merrill, 1973.
Sørensen, M. (ed.), *Manual of Public International Law*, Macmillan, 1968.
Steiner, H.J., 'International Law, Doctrine and Schools of Thought in the Twentieth Century', in Bernhardt, R. (ed.), *Encyclopedia of Public International Law*.
Stephens, T., *The United Nations Disaster Relief Office*, Thèse No. 303, University of Geneva, 1978; University Press of America, 1978.
Stevens, C., *Food Aid and the Developing World*, London, 1979.
Stoessinger, J.G., *The Refugee and the World Community*, University of Minnesota Press, 1956.
Stone, J., *Legal Controls of International Conflict*, New York, 1954.
Stowell, E.C., *Intervention in International Law*, Washington, 1921.
— 'La Théorie et la Pratique de l'Intervention', 40 *RdC* 1932-II, p. 91.
— 'Humanitarian Intervention', 33 *AJIL* 1939, p. 733.
Sybesma-Knol, R.G., *The Status of Observers in the United Nations*, Kluwer, 1981.

Takemoto, M., 'The Scrutiny System under International Humanitarian Law', 19 *JAIL* 1975, p. 1.
Tansley, D., *Final Report: An Agenda for the Red Cross*, Joint Committee for the Reappraisal of the Red Cross, 1975.
Thirlway, H.W.A., *Customary International Law and Codification*, Sijthoff, 1972.
Thomas, A. van W. and Thomas, A.J., *The Organization of American States*, 1963.
Toman, J., *Index of the Geneva Conventions for the Protection of War Victims of 12 August 1949*, Sijthoff-Henry Dunant Institute, 1973.
Turner, B.A., *Man-Made Disasters*, Wykeham, London, 1978.

UNA-USA, *Acts of Nature, Acts of Man: The Global Response to Natural Disasters*, United Nations Association of the USA, Policy Studies Panel on International Disaster Relief, July 1977.
Urhobo, E., *Disaster Relief Administration* Ibadan Daystar Press, 1978.

Vallier, I., 'The Roman Catholic Church, A Transnational Actor', 25 *International Organization* 1971, p. 479.

Vasak, K. (ed.), *The International Dimensions of Human Rights*, 2 vols., Paris, UNESCO, 1982.
Veuthey, M., 'The Red Cross and Non-International Conflicts', *IRevRC* 1970, p. 411.
— *Guérilla et Droit Humanitaire*, Institut Henry Dunant, 1976. Also ICRC, 1983.
Virally, M., 'The Sources of International Law', in Sørensen, M. (ed.), *Manual of Public International Law*, 1968, p. 116.
Visscher, C. de, *Théories et Réalités en Droit International Public*, 4th ed., Paris, 1970; also *Theory and Reality in Public International Law*, Princeton UP, 1968.
Vitta, C., 'La Coopération Internationale en Matière d'Agriculture', 56 *RdC* 1936-II, p. 300.

Wallerstein, M.B., 'New Organizational Approaches for Speeding Food Relief in International Disasters: The Potential Contribution of Technology', 4 *The International Journal of Disaster Studies and Practice* 1980, p. 73.
Ward, C.J., *Foreign Armed Forces in the Relief of Natural Disaster*, Dissertation for MA, Department of War Studies, University of London King's College, December 1975.
Weis, P., 'The International Protection of Refugees', 48 *AJIL* 1954, p. 193.
— 'The 1967 Protocol Relating to the Status of Refugees', XLII *BYIL* 1967, p. 39.
Weisberg, H.L. 'The Congo Crisis 1964: A Case Study in Humanitarian Intervention', 12 *VJIL* 1971-2, p. 261.
Weiss, T.G. and Jordan, R.S., *The World Food Conference and Global Problem Solving*, Praeger, 1976.
Weissman, B.M., *Herbert Hoover and Famine Relief to Soviet Russia: 1921-23*, Hoover Institution, Stanford, 1974.
Western, K.A., *The Epidemiology of Natural and Man-Made Disasters*, Dissertation for the Academic Diploma in Tropical Public Health, No. 189, London School of Hygiene and Tropical Medicine, University of London, June 1972.
Westgate, K.N. and O'Keefe, P., *Some Definitions of Disaster*, Occasional Paper No. 4, Disaster Research Unit, University of Bradford, 1976.
White, G.F. (ed.), *Natural Hazards: Local, National, Global*, Oxford UP, 1974.
White, G.F., Haas, J.E. *et al*, *Assessment of Research on Natural Hazards*, MIT, Massachusetts, 1975.
White, L.C., *International Non-Governmental Organizations*, Rutgers UP, 1951.
Wilhelm, R.-J., 'Problèmes relatifs à la Protection de la Personne Humaine par le Droit International dans les Conflits Armés ne présantant pas un Caractère International', 137 *RdC* 1972-III, p. 311.
Wiseberg, L.S., 'Humanitarian Intervention: Lessons from the Nigerian Civil War', 7 *RDH* 1974, p. 61.
Woodbridge, G., *UNRRA, The History of the United Nations Relief and Rehabilitation Adminstration*, 3 vols., Columbia UP, 1950.
Wright, Q., *A Study of War*, 2nd ed., Chicago UP, 1965.

Zayas, A.-M. de, *Nemesis at Potsdam*, Routledge & Kegan Paul, (1979).
— 'United Nations Relief and Rehabilitation Activities', in Bernhardt, R. (ed.), *Encyclopedia of Public International Law*.

Index

GPSR Compliance

The European Union's (EU) General Product Safety Regulation (GPSR) is a set of rules that requires consumer products to be safe and our obligations to ensure this.

If you have any concerns about our products, you can contact us on ProductSafety@springernature.com

In case Publisher is established outside the EU, the EU authorized representative is:

Springer Nature Customer Service Center GmbH
Europaplatz 3
69115 Heidelberg, Germany

Batch number: 10830943

Printed by Printforce, the Netherlands